MISSION ON THE RHINE

James F. Tent

MISSION
ON THE
RHINE

Reeducation and Denazification in American-Occupied Germany

The University of Chicago Press
Chicago and London

JAMES F. TENT is an associate professor of history at the University of Alabama in Birmingham.

The University of Chicago Press, Chicago 60637
The University of Chicago Press, Ltd., London

©1982 by the University of Chicago
All rights reserved. Published 1982
Printed in the United States of America
86 85 84 83 82   9 8 7 6 5 4 3 2 1

Publication of this volume was
made possible by a grant from
the Exxon Corporation.

Library of Congress Cataloging in Publication Data

Tent, James F.
  Mission on the Rhine.

  Bibliography: p.
  Includes index.
  1. Education and state—Germany (West)—History.
  2. Germany—History—Allied occupation—1945– .
  3. Denazification. I. Title.
  LC93.G4T46   379.43   82-4896
  ISBN 0-226-79357-5   AACR2
  ISBN 0-226-79358-3   (pbk.)

To the Wymans and the Koeppels
whose friendship epitomizes the worth of the exchange programs

Contents

Preface

The author learned early in this study that archival sources and published works alone could not provide a complete picture of America's education-reform efforts in occupied Germany. Its completion is therefore due in large part to the willingness of veterans of the Occupation to offer their time and resources in filling in the gaps, thus allowing him to read the evidence more carefully. As one of them remarked, "The telephones were always busy in Military Government," and, as a result, written records were not always available. Dr. John Taylor and Dr. Herman Wells provided useful insights into events that took place at the top of the education organization. Dr. Martin Mayes, Vaughn DeLong, Dr. Lawrence Derthick, Paul Bodenman, and Dr. Kenneth Bateman provided a close view of operations within the various Länder. Dr. Mayes and Dr. Martin Ackerman kindly provided source materials unavailable elsewhere as did James L. Sundquist, the former Control Officer at OMGUS. Colonel William Swarm patiently explained the intricacies of civil-affairs doctrine, Edwin Costrell offered insights into the demanding role of a university officer, and State Department veterans Elwood Williams III and James Donovan supplied valuable information and materials.

Thanks are also due to James Hastings, Dr. Brewster Chamberlin, Dr. Michael Fichter, and Edward McCarter for invaluable aid with OMGUS documents. Dr. Henry Kellermann, Professor Diethelm Prowe, Professor John Gimbel, and Professor Jurgen Herbst read the manuscript and improved the author's perspective on the Occupation and on the two educational systems. Thanks are due also to Professor Eul-Soo Pang and Mr. Henry F. Inman for advice and support. The list of German contributors is also great. Professor Walther Peter Fuchs and Dr. Klaus J. Bade of the University of Erlangen, Dr. Rainer Hambrecht of the Staatsarchiv München, Frau Professor Laetitia Boehm and Dr. Müller of the Munich University Archives, Professor Heinrich Scholler of the Munich University law faculty, Herr Hans Ruppel of the Stadtarchiv Offenbach, Professor Harold Hurwitz of the Free University, Dr. Wolfgang Kalischer of the Westdeutschen Rektorenkonferenz in Bonn, Professor Manfred Heinemann of the University of Hannover, Herr Hermann Graml and Dr. Chrisoph Weisz of the Institut für Zeitgeschichte, and Dr. Volker Dotterweich of Augsburg University helped too. Affie. Martin and Barbara Stedl performed superbly in finishing the manuscript. My thanks to all of them and to my family, who sacrificed much to the completion of this project. I wish to thank my university's Faculty Research Council for grants-in-aid that enabled me to gather source materials. Sincere thanks are also due to Ms. Dorah H. Sterne, Dr. A. H. Russakoff, Ms. Elizabeth O'Neal Shannon, and the Birmingham Progress Club for making the publication of *Mission on the Rhine* possible. The University of Chicago Press deserves special thanks for encouraging and supporting this book at all stages of publication.

The endnotes are, of necessity, replete with rather cumbersome citations of government documents. The reader will find assistance for interpreting these both in the notes themselves and in "A Note on Sources" (pages 319–22). All interviews cited in the notes were conducted by me. Quotations from government documents have been lightly edited to bring them into harmony with the adjacent text, to spare the reader from the unpleasantness of constant shifts of style in such matters as hyphenation and punctuation.

Birmingham, Alabama
September 30, 1981

Glossary

ACA   Allied Control Authority
ACC   Allied Control Council
ADO   Area Division for Occupied Areas, Department of State
AG   Adjutant General
AKEC   Allied Kommandatura Education Committee
ASTA   Allgemeiner Studenten-Ausschuss (German student government)
BDM   Bund deutscher Mädel (League of German Maidens)
CAB   Civil Administration Branch, Military Government
CAD   Civil Affairs Division of the War Department, later the Department
   of the Army
CCS   Combined Chiefs of Staff
CDU   Christian Democratic Union
CIC   Counterintelligence Corps
COA   Commission on Occupied Areas
CRALOG   Council of Relief Agencies Licensed to Operate in Occupied
   Germany
CSU   Christian Social Union, sister party to the CDU in Bavaria
DANA   Deutsche Allgemeine Nachrichten Agentur (German news agency)
DMG   Deputy Military Governor (General Lucius D. Clay)
DP   Displaced Person
EAC   European Advisory Commission
E&CR   Education and Cultural Relations Divison
E&RA   Education and Religious Affairs Branch
EIL   Experiment in International Living
ETO   European Theater of Operations
FIAT   Field Information Agency, Technical
FU   Free University
Fragebogen   Questionnaire to determine the National Socialist or mili-
   taristic activities of Germans; distributed by Military Government.
G-5   Civil affairs–military government section

HICOG Office of the High Commissioner (U.S.), Germany
HJ Hitler Jugend (Hitler Youth)
IA&C Internal Affairs and Communications Division
ICD Information Control Division
IIE Institute of International Education
IPCOG Inter-Agency Policy Committee on Germany
JCS Joint Chiefs of Staff
KWG Kaiser Wilhelm Gesellschaft
Land German political subdivision, roughly corresponding to an American State.
Länderrat Council of German Minister Presidents
Landkreis or Kreis County
Meldebogen Questionnaire to determine the National Socialist or militaristic activities of Germans, distributed under German Law no. 104 for the Liberation from National Socialism and Militarism
MG Military Government
NEA National Education Association
NS/NSDAP National Socialist German Workers' Party (Nazi)
OMGB Office of Military Government for Bavaria
OMGBS Office of Military Government for Berlin Sector (usually written as OMG Berlin Sector)
OMGBE Office of Military Government for Bremen Enclave (usually written as OMG Bremen)
OMGGH or OMGH Office of Military Government for Greater Hesse (or Hesse)
OMGUS Office of Military Government (U.S.) for Germany
OMGWB Office of Military Government for Württemberg-Baden
OSS Office of Strategic Services
OWI Office of War Information
PEB Policy Enforcement Branch
PH&W Public Health and Welfare Division
RGCO Regional Government Coordinating Office
R/O Reorientation Branch, CAD
SA Sturmabteilung (Brownshirts; Storm Troopers)
SED Sozialistische Einheitspartei Deutschlands (Socialist Unity Party)
SHAEF Supreme Headquarters, Allied Expeditionary Force
SMA Soviet Military Administration
SS Schutzstaffel (Nazi Blackshirts who controlled police and concentration camps and served in special military units)
SWNCC State-War-Navy Coordinating Committee
T/O Table of Organization

UNESCO   United Nations Educational, Scientific, and Cultural Organization

UNRRA   United Nations Relief and Rehabilitation Agency

UPC   University Planning Committee

USFET   United States Forces, European Theater

US Group CC   United States Group Control Council

WSC   Working Security Committee

Chronology

1942

June 19   The State Department's General Advisory Committee meets for the first time to discuss education reconstruction in occupied territories.

1944

January 1   SHAEF, activated for cross-Channel invasion, includes German Country Unit to advise Supreme Commander on occupied Germany.

July   State Department's Interdivisional Committee on Germany completes first paper on subject of German reeducation.

August   E&RA section at SHAEF submits first education directive. American and British policy-planning staffs separate into U.S. Group Control Council (US Group CC) and Control Commission (British Element) respectively.

September   Morgenthau Plan reaches height of influence.

1945

January   Archibald MacLeish is appointed Assistant Secretary of State for Cultural Affairs.

May–June   Advisory Committee on German Reeducation convenes at State Department and approves SWNCC 269/5, later known as "Long-Range Policy Statement on German Reeducation."

May 8   VE Day—victory in Europe; all German forces surrender.

June   JCS 1067 is adopted as official U.S. policy for occupied Germany. It is punitive in spirit but contains important loopholes to control disease and unrest.

June 4   First German schools reopen in Aachen.

July   Potsdam Conference. Four-power Potsdam Declaration calls, among other things, for the denazification, demilitarization, and democratization of German education.

August 15   First German medical school reopens at Heidelberg University.

October 1   German elementary schools reopen in American Zone. OMGUS replaces US Group CC.

Military Government Law No. 8, instituting rigorous denazification, goes into effect.

November–December   German secondary schools and institutions of higher education begin reopening in American Zone.

1946

January   E&RA becomes a branch of Internal Affairs and Communications Division.

March   General Clay rejects offer of new education chief or cultural adviser.

German Law Number 104 for Liberation from National Socialism and Militarism goes into effect.

April   American journalists file stories alleging U.S. failure to denazify German schools and universities.

June 25   General Clay orders investigation of German universities.

July–December   Purge of German universities.

August 21   Long-Range Policy Statement for German Reeducation released as SWNCC 269/5.

August–September   U.S. Education Mission tours U.S. Zone and issues its Mission Report.

September   Secretary of State Byrnes calls for German economic recovery in a speech at Stuttgart.

October 24   SWNCC Directive 269/8 is adopted, allowing the exchange of persons between the United States and Germany. It is released on March 31, 1947.

1947

January   General Clay refuses to increase reorientation funds. He also issues January 10 directives ordering submission of school-reform plans by the Länder.

Dr. Alois Hundhammer becomes education minister in Bavaria.

February   First American visiting experts begin arriving in the U.S. Zone.

February 28   Exchange of cultural and educational materials is implemented by the adoption of SWNCC Directive 269/10. It is released on October 7, 1947.

President Truman announces the Truman Doctrine.

March 14   The MGR 8s are adopted.

April 1   First German school-law proposals are due at OMGUS.

April 23   John W. Taylor leaves E&RA; R. T. Alexander becomes acting chief.

May–August   Bureau of the Budget Task Force examines Military Government.

June 25   ACA Directive 54 goes into effect.

July 11   JCS 1779 replaces JCS 1067. It is reconstructionist in tone and places greater emphasis on reorientation programs.

August 12   SWNCC 269/11 amends SWNCC 269/8 to allow visits of Germans to countries other than the United States and of persons from countries other than the United States to Germany.

November   Herman B. Wells arrives in Germany as Clay's cultural adviser.

December   E&RA in Bavaria orders Hundhammer to submit a school-reform proposal to the Bavarian Landtag.

1948

March   General Clay informs Washington of growing Soviet belligerence. Education and Cultural Affairs Division is created.

April   The expulsion of three students from Humboldt University sets in motion the call for a Free University.

June   The Soviet blockade of West Berlin begins.

June 1   The Berlin school law is approved.

June 19   Conversion day to the Deutschmark in the three Western zones. Wells returns to the United States.

August   Clay and Ehard produce a compromise on Bavarian school reform, by agreeing on a law for free tuition and free textbooks.

September   R. T. Alexander departs from Military Government.

November   The Free University comes into existence in Berlin.

1949

February   The Hessian school law passes.

April   The Bremen school law passes.

May   The Occupation Statute for the three Western zones is adopted; it omits controls on education.

September   Military Government ceases operations and is replaced by the Office of the High Commissioner.

Introduction

Following total defeat in 1945, German society underwent greater change as the result of four years of military occupation than it had experienced during twelve years of National Socialist rule. When the United States joined with its wartime allies in administering German territory, most of southern Germany became the U.S. Zone of Occupation. Victory over an evil ideology was bound to inspire a sense of mission in the conquerors, and all four occupying powers proposed to transform the defeated people into a peace-loving, or at least less dangerous, society. Assistant Secretary of State Archibald MacLeish suggested to Secretary of State Byrnes in July, 1945, that U.S. policy for Germany must "encourage the self-government of people on the grounds that tyrannies have been demonstrated to be dangerous to the security of the world and that nations in which the people govern themselves are more likely to keep peace and to promote the common interests of mankind."[1] MacLeish and others wished to avoid the revival of a totalitarian Germany in which the state would wield absolute power over the individual. To institute a democracy in Germany required establishing more than the outward forms of popular governance. Free elections, democratic constitutions, independent political parties, and local self-government were simply institutional features; they required an inner spirit to give them meaning. "Reeducation" became the conquerors' catchword to describe their efforts to democratize Germany.

The concept of reeducation achieved common usage in World War II at a time when propaganda, psychological warfare, and mind control were the stock-in-trade of all combatant nations. The term, which had been borrowed from the jargon of psychiatrists, became a pet phrase of politicians and journalists during the war. Marshall Knappen, a Rhodes Scholar and early participant in America's education-reform effort, ob-

1

served with apprehension the naive and extravagant expectations the public entertained about reeducation: "With touching faith in the effectiveness of professional educators, they felt that, once the Germans were defeated, the proper formula applied to their school system would eliminate the danger of their starting future wars."[2] As victory in Europe materialized, the American occupation machinery evolved two branches that were expected to deal most directly with the reeducation effort. The wartime psychological-warfare division was transformed into the peacetime Information Control Division (ICD), responsible for control of the media. Formal education became the responsibility of a much smaller branch of the American bureaucracy in Germany: the Education and Religious Affairs Branch (E&RA). It is this component of the Occupation machinery, dedicated to democratizing Germany through reeducation, that forms the subject of this study.

The issue of reeducation lay at the heart of the German Occupation. Even though the results were not immediately apparent, education reform rivaled even economic recovery as the most vital experience for victor and vanquished after 1945. Several factors were of major importance in determining the outcome of the American experiment in influencing another society through altering its educational system. First, the educational systems of the two nations were radically different because of different social needs and different traditions. Second, education policies and education reform had to be conducted through military government, a form of bureaucracy that was not only somewhat alien to Americans but was not particularly compatible with reeducation toward democracy. Third, U.S. policymakers and policy implementers in both Washington and Germany displayed ambivalence about their general goals for Germany and for education reform in particular. Finally, because of the unexpected complexity of the operation of reeducation in Germany, such phenomena as regional differences, administrative structures, and influential personalities made varying impacts on policy in the several parts of German territory under American control.

This study is not a comprehensive survey of all American educational programs in Germany. Instead, it focuses on events and issues selected to represent the major thrust of education reform. Some programs, interesting in themselves but not central to the success or failure of the policy of reeducation, have been excluded; adult education, German prisoner-of-war reeducation, youth activities, and religious affairs fall into this category. It is the issues that were central to the education debate—denazification, elementary- and secondary-school structure, teacher training, university reform, and cultural exchange—that serve as the focus of this narrative.

Americans and Germans approached education from two utterly different perspectives. The German educational edifice, dating back to the early nineteenth century, had long trained different social groups for different tasks. In a clearly class-stratified society, it imparted starkly contrasting economic and social skills to separate social groups at an early age. The American tradition, dating from roughly the same time, strove to impart common values and goals to a heterogeneous population. Commonality—not exclusivity—dominated the American educational tradition. The Americans viewed education as proceeding not simply from the school but from the family, the community, the church, and the social group as well. German conceptions of *Erziehung* were hardly so broad-based. They restricted education to the formal learning obtained in a school environment. The stark contrasts between the two nations' educational systems played a commanding role in what transpired under the banner of reeducation in American-occupied Germany after 1945.

The Americans never viewed education solely in terms of a system for imparting knowledge. Given their broadly defined concept of education, they tended to see it as a panacea for all of the perceived weaknesses in society. This conception profoundly influenced the evolution of American educational philosophy and structure from the earliest days of the republic. Thomas Jefferson, drawing on the tenets of the Enlightenment, asserted that an ignorant people could not long remain free; the fledgling democracy needed an informed citizenry to survive. Later, Governor William Sewell of New York offered a corollary for arriving immigrants: America granted asylum to the oppressed and in return expected to receive the newcomer's allegiance, which was to be demonstrated by his learning American ways. In the 1840s, leading figures, Horace Mann among them, perceived a threat to the nation's moral fiber and called for common nondenominational schools—a move that backfired and provided impetus for parochial, especially Catholic, education. At about the same time, pressure from skilled and unskilled working-class groups created free education and equality of educational opportunity; now schools would serve social needs as well as moral and republican ones. The result was the growth of the common-school movement, sometimes referred to as the public-school or universal-education or popular-education movement, led by Horace Mann and a host of other dedicated advocates. The schools they envisaged were to be not only free but of high quality, suitable for all members of the community. They were determined that the common school would not be synonymous with the paupers' school. The movement was successful. By the time of the Civil War, the common school was a singular characteristic of American public education. It was free, publicly controlled, and publicly supported. It offered moral, civic, and intellectual lessons, fostered republican sentiments, Americanized immigrants, and acted as a social leveler.

The secondary public high school grew out of the common school in the last half of the nineteenth century. It supplanted the diverse privately supported academies, the survivors of which evolved as replicas of the British public schools. At first the American public high schools were a middle-class phenomenon and primarily served parents in the cities who did not want to board their children out. But by the 1880s, as the result of widespread urbanization and industrialization, the public high school became the normal secondary school in the United States, and, as its numbers grew, its purpose changed. High schools as public institutions were more prone to standardization than the private academies. They were better suited to inculcating the widening stream of immigrants with American values, and they fitted into the urban environment better than the private academies did. Moreover, they promised to be efficient in an age that prized efficiency, a promise used to good effect by the new generation of professional educational administrators, who were rapidly replacing the politics-infested school boards as the real power in public school administration. From its origins down to the eve of World War II, the public high school served as a structural complement to the common school, and it was based on the same unifying goals.

The public high school evolved rapidly from a college preparatory school to a "people's college" concept, with widely varying curricula under the same roof for all pupils. In 1893 the National Education Association's Report of the Committee of Ten on Secondary School Structure specifically stated that the secondary school did not exist only to prepare pupils for college. Its primary function was to prepare them for life. The curricula the Report proposed were still heavily weighted toward classical and foreign languages, but the Committee admitted an English curriculum for the nonuniversity-oriented pupils. In 1918 another NEA-appointed group, the Commission on the Reorganization of Secondary Schools, made the shift more forcefully toward the "people's college" approach by issuing its "Seven Cardinal Principles." Only one principle, "command of fundamental processes," dealt with academic goals. The others stressed those broader educational concerns characteristic of the American system, such as citizenship, worthy use of leisure (arts, literature, etc.), ethical character, health, and vocational efficiency. The public high school was no longer a predominantly college-preparatory school. Now a logical extension of the common school, it became the capstone of a comprehensive, unified educational system. By 1940 the secondary schools' enrollment had expanded dramatically to include half of all school-age youngsters, and it was still rapidly expanding when the war came.

The influence of America's best-known educational philosopher, John Dewey, was considerable, perhaps in spite of rather than because of the progressive-school movement frequently associated with his name. (American educators in Military Government would translate and distribute Dewey's statements on democracy and education throughout the U.S. Zone.) From the turn of the century until the 1930s, Dewey succeeded, through his writings and his influential teaching posts, first at the University of Chicago and then at Columbia Teachers College, in spreading his ideas far beyond the confines of any one movement. Dewey stressed the direct functional relationship between classroom learning activities and real-life experiences. His philosophy of education, crudely put, was that learning comes from problem-solving. The child confronts a problem, grapples with it, and, by a process of gathering information, posing hypotheses, and experimenting, manages, with help from teachers, learning materials, and other pupils, to acquire understanding as well as knowledge; the learning comes from the reasoning process involved in solving the problem. This contrasted with the orthodox practice of providing facts for the child to digest. Learning theories aside, Dewey's proposals for public education were far-reaching. He advocated using everyday experiences in the classroom to promote easier learning through understanding. That formed only a starting point for Dewey, who maintained that the child could then advance from the familiar to the unfamiliar, a message he repeated to the more militant progressives, who had oversimplified him. Thus, educational theorists and administrators took a hard look at classical and foreign languages, which were to experience rapid decline in the public high-school curriculum after World War I.

Just as important as his views on learning was Dewey's perception of education in democracy. Schools had the responsibility to teach democracy by teaching democratic living. In a heterogeneous society like that of the United States, it was vital, Dewey felt, for citizens of one social group to intermingle at an early age with others of varying economic, racial, and religious backgrounds. By gathering them into one educational system, the schools could advance a common set of values, interests, and goals. At the same time, they would teach democracy by practicing it. They would encourage pupils to determine and to advance their common purposes in learning, and in the process the various social groups would acquire mutual respect. Schools, Dewey affirmed, build democratic living and produce social progress. While not all of his ideas entered the mainstream of American education theory and practice, his perceptions of the close connection between education and democracy struck a responsive chord. His was a modification and updating of the rationale for the common-school movement of the nineteenth century. Thus, on the eve of World War II, American educational philosophy and practice had evolved a comprehensive elementary–secondary school system, forming a single educational ladder for all social groups under one school roof. Its curriculum offerings had abandoned all pretense at classical training, and the school system was viewed as a vehicle of social improvement for a heterogeneous, often turbulent, nation. By 1940 American educators, especially administrators, subscribed to a "one best system" mentality—to borrow David Tyack's phrase. As the American armies poured over the Rhine in 1945, their education officers confronted an educational system based on radically different premises.

Germany's traditional elementary and secondary schools formed two separate and distinct types of education, with little or no provision for transfer between them. One provided a minimum education for the masses. The second was for an elite, largely middle-class, minority. Throughout the nineteenth century the separate tracks served to categorize children when they first entered school at the age of six, so that no overlapping occurred. After 1918 one of the few egalitarian advances in the Weimar educational edifice was the creation of the *gemeinsame Grundschule*, or common foundation school, offering a four-year undifferentiated curriculum for all children. At the age of ten a sharp separation took place when a 10 percent minority—still largely but not exclusively middle class— entered the secondary schools, never to mingle again with pupils of the *Volksschule*, or elementary school. For the majority, public education lasted for eight years and was then followed by a period of vocational training. Those who survived the demanding secondary curriculum (attrition was on the order of 80 percent) completed an additional nine years of schooling on top of the four received in the *Grundschule*. The survivors earned the badge of a cultivated German: the *Abitur*. They then trained at the universities for professional careers.

The original purpose of the most prominent secondary school, the *humanistisches Gymnasium*, had been to create a harmonious personality capable of reaching its highest intellectual potential. The most prominent advocate of this neohumanism in education was Wilhelm von Humboldt, Prussia's education minister at the time of the Napoleonic occupation of Prussia. Humboldt drew inspiration from Greek antiquity, which was much in vogue following the literary revival led by Goethe and Schiller. Greek norms were tantamount to perfection. Therefore, Humboldt's movement stressed Greek studies above Latin, which had a French and Roman Catholic taint. But Humboldt also widened the narrow grammar-school curriculum to include history, geography, music, and the arts as aids to developing the stated ideal, the harmonious personality. The Humboldt reforms affected secondary schools and universities most because they were obviously suited only to the gifted minority whose parents could afford to underwrite an education that lasted for thirteen years. As the nineteenth century advanced, the spirit of the *Gymnasia* gradually changed. Hints of nationalism had been present at their inception, which is not surprising, given the reaction to the French hegemony that lasted in Central Europe until 1814; after 1871, however, nationalism permeated the spirit of the *Gymnasia*. Another hallmark was a growing stress on formal discipline. Defeat in World War I did not alter these trends, and the secondary schools and universities became centers of nationalistic opposition to the Weimar Republic. The Nazis, no respecters of humanism, reinforced the trend toward discipline and nationalism, thus perverting, almost beyond recognition, the original spirit of the *Gymnasium*.

Modernization imposed significant changes in secondary-school organization. Starting in the 1880s the humanistic Gymnasium began to give ground to the *Realgymnasium*, which taught Latin but not Greek, and to the *Oberrealschule*, which stressed modern languages, science, and mathematics. After 1918, reformers called for a more flexible and more unified educational system. Thus the *Aufbauschule*, or accelerated-learning school, offered an intensified six-year curriculum for pupils coming from rural areas and for the late bloomers. A new type of secondary school, the *deutsche Oberschule*, offered a core curriculum of German grammar, literature, and history plus fluency in one foreign language. Some outsiders feared a nationalistic motive in forming the *deutsche Oberschule* so soon after the 1918 defeat.

Despite these innovations and numerous experimental curricula and programs, little progress toward a unified or comprehensive school emerged in the Weimar Republic; this was due in part to periodic economic crises, stout opposition from educational traditionalists, and polarization of the political parties over education reform. No one in the Weimar Republic thought it possible to divorce education from politics. Yet there were signs of change, as the creation of the *Grundschule* and the *Aufbauschule* attested. Discussions over an *Einheitsschule*, or comprehensive school, were a prominent feature of the Weimar Republic and formed an undeniable part of the tradition in German educational theory dating back as far as J. W. Süvern's 1817 draft of a school law for Prussia.

The Nazis were slow to attack the structure if not the spirit of the German educational system. Finally, in 1938, they imposed a "reform" that shortened secondary schooling from the traditional nine years to eight in order to draft youths for compulsory labor service and the military. The *deutsche Oberschule* became the normal secondary school, with some distinction made between modern languages and scientific curricula. The Allies discovered to their surprise in 1945 that the *Gymnasia*, despite their humanistic tradition, had survived in roughly the same numbers to the end of the war, indicating the Nazis' success in perverting their spirit. In fact, the Nazis prized the *Gymnasia*'s continuing emphasis on discipline and opened five National Political Institutes (Napolas) in 1942 as *Gymnasia*. Another secondary school, the *Adolf Hitler Schule*, emerged as an *Aufbauschule* for children of party officials. The capstone of the Nazis' educational edifice was supplied by the sinister SS-run *Ordensburgen*. The creation of a unified ministry of education in Berlin caused considerable resentment in the provincial districts, but this new body did not attempt any ambitious reorganization of the educational system.

By 1945, as the twelve-year Reich drew to an end, the structural organization of the German schools had changed little since the reforms of the Weimar Republic. The secondary schools had remained substantially middle class. The Nazis had made no attempt at integrating elementary and secondary schooling into a common educational ladder, despite much noise about creating a new egalitarian society. Thus, the German educational system of 1945 clearly displayed its nineteenth-century antecedents to victor and vanquished alike.

Most of the education officers who accompanied the American armies into Germany and later formed the core of the education branch of military government in the Occupation were educational administrators, the majority of whom tended to be suspicious of educational practices that varied from their own. The most prominent comparative educator and theorist in their midst, Richard Thomas Alexander of Columbia Teachers College, was more intimately acquainted with trends in German education than any other American.

R. T. Alexander, who had been dean of the experimental New College at Columbia in the interwar years, held pronounced views on German education. These he imparted with varying degrees of success to the key education officers in the Occupation, men like John Taylor, who headed the education effort for two years, and other key E&RA officers in the various Länder. Alexander had observed German education at first hand in the pre-1914 Kaiserreich and, especially, in the Weimar Republic. He recognized the changes and the debates then raging in Germany but worried about certain currents in the fledgling republic: he decried the partisan political approach to school problems on the part of the numerous parties, criticized church-state tensions—which, he implied, were the fault of the Catholic hierarchy—and castigated the *deutsche Oberschule* as being too inward-directed and too self-consciously German. But he reserved his sharpest criticism for the Germans' unwillingness to open secondary schools to groups other than the gifted. "Certainly it is in sharp contrast to the practice in America," he wrote in 1929, "where we believe in the open educational road for everybody almost regardless of intellectual ability." He likened the current academic leadership to the failed social and political aristocracy in Germany: "The group which claims for itself the privilege of excluding others from its ranks tends to become arrogant and in the end always suffers the humiliation of forced capitulation." Alexander predicted that the German secondary schools would have to modify their curricula and standards, as the Americans had done, to accommodate more heterogeneous groups, and he also predicted that the present practice in the universities of accepting all secondary-school graduates would eventually cease. In 1929 he had felt unable to predict what course German education would take, torn as it was by political extremism from without and by partisan prejudices from within.[3] In 1945, when he joined Military Government in Berlin, Alexander was no longer merely an observer of German education but an influential participant in its revival.

The concept of administering the civil affairs of an occupied territory through military government was not entirely new to the U.S. War Department, but it was not a responsibility with which the Army felt comfortable. The Army had conducted military government in the Mexican War after 1846, once again on a larger scale in the defeated Confederacy after 1865, and following smaller campaigns in the Caribbean, especially in Puerto Rico and Cuba at the end of the nineteenth century. The Philippine experience was longer-lasting and served to discredit imperialism in the United States. Later, after World War I, the Americans controlled a million Rhinelanders for several years. However, despite these sporadic experiences with military government, the Army had not developed a lasting tradition in civil affairs and by all accounts had given a mediocre performance at best. In fact, weaknesses in past operations spurred the Army to prepare more adequately for military government operations in World War II, which it performed on a far greater scale and, generally, with greater success than before.

Some civil-affairs functions were straightforward and were accepted as an Army responsibility without demur. "Civil affairs" included control of the enemy's legal, political, and economic apparatus and supervision of public health and safety. It also required control of public information. There were perhaps twelve major civil-affairs functions that the Army identified. Education was not among them.

From the first, control of education was a responsibility that fitted only imperfectly into military-government operations. It attracted little attention and had the lowest of priorities. The neglect first became apparent in the North African and Italian campaigns in 1942 and 1943, where reports of grossly inadequate edcation staffing surfaced. The same problem materialized again in 1944, during preparations for the invasion of Europe, when SHAEF planning staffs and G-5 civil-affairs detachments were minuscule and unable to obtain adequate information for either short- or long-term planning. The War Department itself was responsible for the insularity of its military-government planning staffs, since it had adopted a taciturn policy toward civilian government agencies because of conflicts with the State Department and Treasury concerning North African operations. The War Department's actions compounded an already serious planning vacuum in high government that resulted from President Roosevelt's reluctance to prepare concrete plans for postwar Germany. Once disputes arose between the State Department and Treasury over postwar plans, the War Department, loath to enter Germany with no plan at all, hastily accepted the Joint Chiefs of Staff (JCS) Directive 1067, which embodied large portions of the punitive Morgenthau Plan. JCS 1067 scarcely addressed itself to the issue of education or reeducation, but the Army's problems with that function had barely begun. The Army was reluctantly entering an occupation of long duration, and no other agency was prepared to handle the responsibility for education.

Despite warnings from high State Department officials, such as Archibald MacLeish and Robert Murphy, and complaints from Military Government education officers, the Army failed to upgrade its priorities for education within Military Government. The result was that it provided inadequate staff and support for accomplishing even the minimum educational goals of the Occupation, such as denazification. The status of reeducation also remained low, so that press criticism and rumors of inadequate support for education staffs gave E&RA an unenviable reputation within Military Government, among the Germans, and at home among the informed public and potentially helpful circles of influential educators.

No early or dramatic reversal of the situation occurred. Military Government failed to obtain an influential education chief in 1945. In 1946 General Lucius Clay, the Military Governor, refused to reopen the search, claiming that present staff was adequate. In January, 1947, he declined a threefold increase in reorientation funds for cultural aid and exchange programs, in part because of the necessarily higher priorities for food and other basics for the Germans. Alexander, as interim education chief, initiated forceful policies, designed to restructure German education at almost the same time that Clay allowed the return of Land (state) political systems to German control. Despite earlier warnings to coordinate Military Government policies, the reverse occurred. The denazification wave of 1946 ignored the educators' advice and discredited any progress to date. In 1948 a similar lack of coordination surfaced when demands for certain school reforms collided head-on with financial stringencies imposed by currency reform. In the meantime a new JCS directive, No. 1779 of July, 1947, reflecting State Department reconstructionist attitudes, gave greater priority to education and tied it more closely to the broader political and economic policies associated with recovery. Clay eventually obtained a cultural adviser and, faced with the fast-developing Cold War, steadily shifted his priorities. Funds to end a chronic paper shortage suddenly materialized. Imaginative faculty exchanges between German and American universities, which Clay had rejected earlier, received his support. The founding of the Free University in Berlin enlisted his enthusiastic endorsement, and at the Berchtesgaden Conference in October, 1948, he assigned the highest priority to education programs. In the end, education emerged as a major Military Government responsibility after all, although no one claimed that education programs had proceeded smoothly under its aegis. Recognition of the vast effort needed and the urgency required came very late in Military Government operations.

The Washington bureaucratic maze in World War II was not conducive to developing consistent or logical plans for the Occupation, and all facets of national policy, including the notion of reeducation, suffered accordingly. The best and most sustained effort came from the State Department, which remained consistently reconstructionist in its overall goals for Germany. Yet there, too, the specifics of a policy of cultural reorientation remained elusive, in part because of War Department failure to cooperate in planning; in part because of Treasury influence with President Roosevelt to impose a punitive occupation policy, which largely negated reeducation concepts; in part because of dissension at the State Department; and in part, finally, because of a general lack of recognition, on the part of the highest government leaders, of the combined importance and difficulty of the reeducation programs. This disarray among official government agencies caused a policy gap at the end of the war, since JCS 1067 offered no specific guidance. Some concerned planners, like Archibald MacLeish at the State Department, tried to emphasize the need for more American commitment to Secretary of State Byrnes before the Potsdam Conference. The director of the Office of War Information, Elmer Davis, had warned President Truman of this, but to no avail. The Potsdam Declaration gave even less attention to the subject than JCS 1067 had; it left the four victor nations each to go its own way with respect to cultural policies in its zone, a fact that later had great significance for the Americans. State Department concern about American educational programs grew as the educators' troubles mounted. It endorsed a War Department plan for a U.S. Mission to Germany in 1946, then questioned the conclusion the Mission drew. It saw its aid and exchange programs stalled in 1947 because of Military Government noncooperation. However, the resulting stalemate began to dissipate when the State Department regained its prewar status in the Washington power structure. JCS 1779 embodied many of the State Department's reconstructionist precepts in a host of political and economic programs. After 1947 State Department involvement in the education program grew steadily, as did cooperation with the Army and with Military Government. State Department-inspired programs of aid and cultural exchange expanded in importance in the last two years of Military Government operations, and the stage was set for the transition to even vaster cultural programs in the years of the High Commission in Germany. Some State Department officials worried about the loss of an overt control function in education, but experience proved that the shift to advice and assistance was the wiser course.

If all major agencies had underestimated the complexity of the reorientation programs, they also underestimated the cultural diversity and importance of local conditions in Germany. From Land to Land, different political and economic realities, different traditions, and different educational needs prevailed. A central control function, unless sensitive to these differences, could easily provoke local antagonisms, as happened most dramatically in Bavaria. Belatedly, this too was recognized, by the issuance of JCS 1779, but not before the seeds of confrontation had been planted by the prior issuance of Military Government directives to conform to a given set of principles, embodied in the U.S. Education Mission's report. The impact of the personalities involved in the reeducation effort also influenced events at times, along with a myriad of other factors peculiar to each locality.

The combination of all these factors affected the American attempt to "reeducate" the Germans. Marked differences in educational traditions, the imperfect meshing of education functions with the military bureaucracy, a general lack of recognition, at the highest levels of our government, of the complexity, subtlety, and commitment that reorientation programs would require, and an underestimation of the diversity of needs and expectations within Germany all combined to hinder American efforts at "reeducating" the Germans toward democracy—which was, after all, the central goal of the Occupation.

1

Planning for Reeducation

Interested Parties

In the aftermath of the Allied victory in World War II the concept of reeducation was inextricably bound to the notion that the Allied nations could democratize Germany and the other Axis powers. Although stemming from the jargon of psychiatry, the term "reeducation" never received a precise definition. It was to be a rehabilitative process based on the assumptions of the Enlightenment that human nature is essentially rational and "good." Private academic organizations, writers and journalists, refugee groups, and psychiatric circles helped to popularize the idea, although the influence of the private sector on the government agencies concerned with the problem was not clear-cut. One result of the popularization of reeducation was a general tendency for the layman to see the problem as straightforward and independent of other policies being made for occupied Germany. The official agencies charged with responsibility for policy-making quickly discovered that, despite its outward simplicity, the creation of a workable reeducation program was complex and fraught with uncertainty. The process was also dependent on progress toward an overall policy with respect to Germany, and it was precisely in the realm of postwar planning that the Roosevelt Administration displayed confusion and uncertainty.

Scholarship in recent years has pointed to a general muddle on the part of U.S. agencies involved in planning the German occupation.[1] The problem started at the highest level with President Roosevelt's reluctance to prepare for an occupation during wartime, a reluctance that increased as his health declined. Lacking presidential leadership, several government agencies adopted widely differing positions, ranging from an openly reconstructionist policy at the State Department to a punitive, destabilizing scheme at Henry Morgenthau's Treasury Department. Given the failure to reconcile these differences, America's forces entered Germany without a coherent national policy, a situation that reduced the chances for cooperation among the victor nations.

Franklin D. Roosevelt was unique among American presidents in receiving part of his childhood education in Germany. His experiences as a schoolboy in the pre-1914 Kaiserreich were not entirely convivial, and he claimed ever afterward a prejudice against German militarism and high-handedness.[2] During World War II his public comments on Germany reflected an ambivalent attitude. In August, 1941, he joined Winston Churchill in issuing the Atlantic Charter, which labeled Germany the destroyer of world peace but also envisaged Germany as participating in an economically interdependent family of nations in the coming peace. Similarly, the President called for Germany's unconditional surrender at Casablanca in 1943 but added that American and Allied intentions were to destroy only National Socialism, not the German people. A desire to cooperate with Josef Stalin explains at least part of Roosevelt's harsh rhetoric, but unconditional surrender—a plausible demand during U. S. Civil War sieges, where it was born—eliminated any bargaining room for the Axis powers and insured a military occupation of Germany. The President continued his erratic course, at first opposing any plans, then supporting Henry Morgenthau's pastoralization scheme in 1944, until public opinion forced him away from that uncompromising course. Thereafter, until his death, the President, tugged first one way by State Department reconstructionists and then another by hard-line Treasury officials, failed to establish clear guidelines for his policymakers. The War Department supported neither side consistently, seeking above all to minimize its role in the future occupation. When, in the spring of 1945, the Joint Chiefs of Staff (JCS) issued their declaration, JCS 1067, it proved ambiguous. Secretary Morgenthau was convinced that it embodied his approach. State and War Department officials had inserted certain loopholes, which they expected would allow a positive approach. Thus VE Day—May 8, 1945— found Americans still lacking a consensus on postwar plans for Germany. Attitudes toward reeducation faithfully mirrored the continuing uncertainties of American postwar policy.

Responsibility for planning reeducation policies was not vested in any one agency prior to the end of the war. Above all, the Department of State and the War Department produced plans on the subject but for the most part failed to cooperate with each other. As a civilian agency, the State Department was a logical center for planning, and it showed more sustained concern for developing an education policy than any other agency. In 1942 and 1943 a General Advisory Committee on Postwar Foreign

Policy, composed of State Department officials and expert civilian consultants, conducted a series of preliminary studies on peacetime needs. Educational reconstruction figured prominently on their agenda. In mid-1943 they were succeeded by several "country" committees (committees responsible for policy in individual Axis states), including an Interdivisional Committee on Germany, which, in September, 1943, produced America's first official policy paper on postwar Germany. Then in May, 1944, the same experts forged a position paper on education reform at the War Department's request. Later still, in May, 1945, Assistant Secretary of State Archibald MacLeish formed an Advisory Committee on German Re-Education, which, with civilian assistance, proposed the first long-term plans on education reform. A State-War-Navy Coordinating Committee (SWNCC) finally cleared the policy as SWNCC Directive 269/5 in the summer of 1946, although key education personnel serving with Military Government had known of its features from the outset of the Occupation. Responsibility for implementation of reeducation programs remained a sore point between the two departments. The War Department viewed long-range programs as a State Department responsibility; the latter contended that, as a policymaking body, it was not suited to administer large-scale programs.[3]

During the period of hostilities, the War Department repeatedly expressed its desire that civilian agencies take responsibility for long-range occupation policy, yet it was equally determined that these agencies should not interfere in War Department operations in the war zones. It announced that a new arm of the Army would assume responsibility for controlling civilian populations in occupied territory. Aware that in the aftermath of previous wars the Army had been caught ill-prepared to govern civilian populations, the War Department determined at the outset of World War II to devise a military-government capability. Inspired by reports of deficiencies in the post-1918 Rhineland Occupation, the Army in 1940 issued a field manual on the subject, FM 27–5, *Military Government*, and in 1942 it inaugurated a practical organization by opening a School for Military Government at the University of Virginia in Charlottesville. During the war over two thousand civilian experts, including two hundred educational administrators, received commissions for military-government service. At about the same time, the War Department created a Civil Affairs Division (CAD) to plan and coordinate military-government operations around the world. The CAD was formed in part because overlapping responsibilities among government agencies in North Africa had caused General Eisenhower to complain of civilian interference in the war zone. That experience hardened War Department resolve to prevent civilian agencies (notably the State Department) from interfering with War Department operations during hostilities. The Army's military-government officers would plan and execute short-term policies for the period of the fighting and then relinquish control to civilians shortly after the armistice. Or so it was hoped.[4]

The arm of the War Department most intimately involved in planning for the occupation was a subdivision of General Eisenhower's Supreme Headquarters, Allied Expeditionary Force (SHAEF). Responsible for planning the invasion of Europe, the Anglo-American command contained several "country units" to organize military-government field detachments for operations in liberated Europe. The German Country Unit (GCU) contained a very small subsection for education and religious affairs (E&RA), which contributed plans for education policy to an overall field manual intended for the Supreme Commander and his troops. Fearful of provoking Soviet suspicions over Anglo-American collusion on any but military operations, SHAEF separated the two national components of the GCU into a U.S. Group Control Council (US Group CC) and a Control Commission (British Element). The US Group CC and its complement of education officers operated through the summer of 1945, when it was replaced by an Office of Military Government (U.S.) for Germany (OMGUS).[5]

At the end of 1943, in an effort to increase the tempo of postwar planning, the British succeeded in organizing with the Soviet Union and the United States a tripartite European Advisory Commission (EAC). The Roosevelt Administration reacted unenthusiastically, giving minimal support to America's representative to the EAC, Ambassador to Britain John G. Winant. Nevertheless, Winant, with the aid of civilian experts, offered some measure of support to the GCU planners on education policies. To coordinate EAC operations with Washington, the President created a Working Security Committee (WSC), composed of representatives from the State, War, and Navy departments, but this elaborate bureaucratic apparatus functioned poorly, and the GCU therefore had to plan for the occupation of Germany in what amounted to a policy vacuum.[6] Its members' major accomplishment was a reconstructionist-inclined draft, the *Handbook for Military Government in Germany Prior to Defeat or Surrender*, which put them squarely at odds with the third influential agency in postwar German planning: the Treasury Department.

Josef Goebbels had singled out Henry Morgenthau for vicious propaganda attacks during the war. In doing so, he made an enemy of a powerful figure, who, along with Britain's Lord Vansittart, became the leading advocate of a harsh peace. Through unofficial channels Morgenthau obtained a copy of the SHAEF *Handbook* and delivered it to the President, who immediately condemned any reconstructionist approach.[7] Thus began the saga of the Morgenthau Plan, which continued to cause controversy to the end of the war. The Treasury Deparment never formally entered the discussions on education, confining itself instead to matters of economic recovery—or, rather, chastisement. Morgenthau's thoughts on German reeducation were rudimentary. His suggestion to Secretary of War Henry Stimson and his assistant, John J. McCloy, to flood German classrooms with Allied officers was scarcely taken seriously by anyone, including himself,[8] and his influence in the realm of reeducation is detectable only in the emphasis he placed on the three negative "D's" for the Occupation: denazification, demilitarization, and decartelization. The fourth "D," namely democratization, was the one positive goal. Neither it nor reeducation, which was indelibly tied to democratization, fitted convincingly into the punitive Morgenthau scheme. However, one of the cardinal principles to emerge independently among the various planning groups was the interdependence of all occupation policies, whether they were concerned with politics, economics, or social change. The sum of their interaction was what would determine the success or failure of reeducation and therefore of the democratic rebirth of Germany.

Initial Discussions

The concept of reeducation as a conscious policy did not emerge suddenly, from one individual or group, but gradually and with growing intensity as the war hardened national resolves. Public interest was quickened by growing coverage of the subject by groups of academics, social and behavioral scientists, and vocal refugee groups. Yet the complexities of the reeducation process largely eluded public consciousness; the idea itself was taken on faith, as a kind of curative magic. It was within official government agencies that actual reeducation policymaking took place, and it was, above all, the State Department's initial policy studies that had a measurable influence on the course that the reeducation programs eventually took.

In 1942 and 1943 the State Department's General Advisory Committee for Post-War Foreign Policy (GAC) grappled with the issue before recommending that a planning body for reeducation be established within the State Department. The group usually met at the fashionable Cosmos Club in Washington, D.C.; it included distinguished education leaders as well as State Department officers and occasional War Department observers. One of the earliest speakers to address them was Walter Kotschnig, a professor of education from Smith College, who urged that the government provide trained personnel for "relief and reconstruction" in all the war-damaged European states, including the defeated enemy nations. However, Kotschnig foresaw a critical shortage of personnel for these vital tasks, including education, and he accordingly recommended new curricula at American universities in languages and other skills so that the graduates could aid in postwar reconstruction. He reported that the Nazis were making a systematic effort to annihilate intellectuals and educators in German-occupied eastern Europe and disclosed that "in Poland, Czechoslovakia, and Yugoslavia every secondary school and university had been closed." For Germany he saw a special case emerging. There, he said, "most of the work will have to be done by the nationals"; an ideological reorientation of German teachers would therefore be necessary. Kotschnig speculated that selected older teachers could receive new training, while "large numbers of the younger group, those under thirty, could be brought to live in the United States and given a chance to understand life in a democracy and free country." Such an undertaking was feasible only through the provision of large-scale governmental funding.[9]

The participants then attacked the problem of appropriate control agencies for reeducation or cultural reconstruction. Kotschnig opted for an international education organization patterned on prewar League of Nations offices. He also suggested taking some practical measures immediately: "Steps might be taken now to plan textbooks which might replace the textbooks in use in Nazi Germany." These ideas were provocative, but they also evoked pessimistic responses. John W. Studebaker, at that time U.S. Commissioner of Education, opposed the large-scale training programs Kotschnig proposed because they contained no "definite goals as to what type of training would best fit the needs" and because Kotschnig failed to indicate "in what fields people would be assured an opportunity to serve." Therefore, talk about "war minors" for university students and a new kind of Civil Conservation Corps for the postwar period never progressed beyond the the realm of speculation.[10]

By February, 1943, Archibald MacLeish, at that time Librarian of Congress and soon to become an assistant secretary of state, also attended the meetings of the GAC. MacLeish had concluded that the United Nations was the most promising organization for conducting what he called the "deintoxication" of the Axis populations. He considered such activities entirely feasible "unless we are prepared to ignore the experience of the past few years in demonstrating the power of psychological weapons," and he quoted the President's and Winston Churchill's joint statement at Casablanca that it was the Allies' intention to destroy the philosophy, not the peoples, of enemy nations. At present he could identify no agency that was working on the "reeducation of public opinion" in the enemy nations.[11] A representative from the CAD candidly agreed but reminded MacLeish and the committee that the War Department "was concerned chiefly with practical preparations for military government." The CAD's expectation was that overall postwar policy was subject to decision "by higher officials of the War and State departments." Military-government officers presently being trained were administrators who would handle the practical needs of the occupation and would be dependent on others for overall policy. The discussants recognized that military-government activities as then conceived for the period of hostilities would be largely negative but observed that deintoxication was a "delicate psychological problem necessitating the attention of the best education minds available." Therefore, following the initial phase of negative tasks, such as denazification, the victors would initiate a "secondary period, in which relief and rehabilitation measures would become effective." The consensus of the GAC was that the State Department must assume responsibility for the task, since the CAD, the Office of Strategic Services (OSS), the Office of War Information (OWI), and various relief agencies would not, or could not, do so.[12]

It was Archibald MacLeish who suggested that the State Department assemble a committee of competent educators to help form policy. Grayson N. Kefauver, at that time dean of Stanford University's school of education, applauded this idea, as did the rest of the group. Kefauver reminded the assembled persons that several private groups were also studying the problem, and he hoped a future planning agency could coordinate their activities and make their collective knowledge available to the government.[13]

The participants were generally optimistic that a program of reeducation could succeed, and one of their early conclusions was that it would be wise to take into account the cultural attainments of the enemy nations. Kefauver maintained that a guiding principle for future planners should be that "the readjustment of education in those countries is [to be] worked out by the peoples themselves with the assistance of a group we and the other United Nations might select to formulate the operating policy." While the thrust of the committee's thinking was positive, pessimism was also voiced. One speaker cited a lack of American experts on German education, a "profound difference of educational philosophy between groups in the United States," the probable disintegration of central government in Germany, and German resistance to overt programs of reeducation. However, the majority resisted the "laissez-faire" implications of such objections. In any case they were not inclined to confine reeducation to the educational sphere. "A whole process of reconstruction—psychological, economic, military and political—will be needed for the shaping of a new Germany," they reasoned. "The education program is not to be considered independently of the other aspects of the problem."[14]

The committee's discussions attracted attention from higher echelons. Vice President Henry Wallace spoke to the group briefly. He confined his remarks largely to the warning not to attempt to write new textbooks for the Germans. Possibly refugee groups in America could perform that task, but Wallace claimed that he found some of them espousing "a curiously totalitarian ideology." Kefauver was not deterred by Wallace's reservations. He reminded the committee that several private groups were also studying reeducation. The refugees, for example, with their "scholarly background, knowledge of the country and its culture, are trying to single out the healthy elements which German culture might contribute to a peaceful world." However, Wallace was not alone in his reservations about mixing refugees and reeducation. When, two years later, a committee was formed along the lines MacLeish had suggested, State Department officials openly stated their reluctance to include refugees.[15]

By June, 1943, the General Advisory Committee expanded the number of participants for its final discussions on reeducation. Included, among others, were Laurence Duggan of the Institute of International Education, William G. Carr of the National Education Association, and George Zook from the American Council on Education. Vice President Wallace spoke first on an issue that figured prominently in this final meeting: the integration of reeducation programs with other aspects of occupation policy. Wallace reminded the committee that economic chaos in the Weimar Republic had poisoned many Germans' opinions against democracy and "made it possible," he added, "for teachers gradually to direct political thought along Nazi lines." George Shuster pursued the same theme, reminding his listeners that, in the interwar period, private American firms had issued fifteen large loans for German, Austrian, and Polish educational reconstruction. The coming peace would see financial need on so vast a scale that only government support would be adequate to the task.[16] At this stage in the war there was still no clear conception of what agency should direct education reconstruction in Europe as a whole or in Germany in particular. Stringfellow Barr, president of St. John's College, opposed preparing reeducation programs on a national rather than international basis. He claimed that by giving aid through a United Nations organization there would be a "considerable gain in not making us appear in our habitual and unpopular role of missionary to the world; instead it will be a question of the world's rehabilitating itself rather than the United States bringing the world to order." Barr saw the future reeducation program as confronting the United States with a paradox: "There is an embarrassment," he stated, "about trying to force people to have freedom." William G. Carr agreed that the danger existed. "Nevertheless," he countered, "despite the psychological dilemma in trying to force freedom on people, unless the liberal movement in the Axis countries is strong enough to bring about a freeing of the minds of the people of those countries, the United States, as a member of the United Nations, should exercise whatever control may be necessary to do so."[17]

One of the final matters the discussants considered was the transition between the inevitable military occupation of Germany and the creation of a longer-lasting period of "readjustment." Controls were to be expected in the first period for schools, churches, and the press and radio. The problem was to determine which controls must be eliminated in the second period. A State Department representative, Dr. Shotwell, gave evidence of past mistakes. He stated "that after the last war the Germans accepted the regulations set forth under martial law but objected strenuously when restrictions were maintained under civilian controls." Shotwell expected that the American military government would make use of German advisers, who would indicate necessary changes in personnel and procedure. But the period following military government must not, he warned, "be tainted with military controls." The participants accepted that idea and once again pressed for the concept that successful programs of cultural reconstruction not only required international cooperation but were closely dependent on developments in the political and economic spheres.[18]

These studies made by the General Advisory Committee included in embryonic form most of the important issues that would confront policymaking groups in the future. In the summer of 1943, within days of the committee's last meeting, the State Department formed an Interdivisional Committee for Germany headed by David Harris of the department's research staff. This new committee of German experts, drawn from throughout the department, completed its first paper on the political reorganization of Germany in September, 1943. It was the first official plan for postwar Germany. Reflecting the thinking of the GAC, Harris's circle called for a settlement that would entail "a minimum of bitterness" among the Germans by encouraging economic recovery and reducing controls to a level compatible with security. They also felt that the United States and its allies should coordinate their policies so as to ease the difficulties of governance and to prevent any room for maneuver by revanchist Germans bent on playing one Allied power against another. The paper did not recommend dismemberment, and it conceded reparations only for the repair of war-damaged economies, especially that of the Soviets.[19] However, while the State Department might have been first with a postwar policy, it had to reckon with more influential rivals in the Roosevelt Administration. Secretary of State Cordell Hull did not appear to enjoy the President's confidence to the same degree as Treasury Secretary Morgenthau and the War Department's Henry Stimson. David Harris's Interdivisional Committee continued to function, and, at the CAD's request, it produced a policy paper on reeducation in the spring of 1944, ostensibly to aid General Eisenhower's military-government planning staff at SHAEF. The principles outlined in that paper deserve attention elsewhere (see below, pp. 29–30), but they clearly showed the influence of the State Department's GAC discussions of 1942 and 1943. The paper's practical effect at the time was nonexistent, since its issuance coincided with the unveiling of the Morgenthau Plan and the consequent confusion that disrupted planning efforts among the government agencies in the summer of 1944.

In this same mid-war period various private groups interested in the concept of reeducation became active. Other scholars have pointed to influential articles and opinions offered from 1943 to the end of the war by psychiatrists, notably Richard Brickner and Kurt Lewin. Among the public it became fashionable to refer to the neurotic mental state of the German people and to advocate reeducation as a rehabilitative process for the postwar years. Evidence for the influence of psychiatry is also to be found in the recurring claim by various planning groups that the Germans must participate actively in their own reeducation—a cardinal principle of group therapy. Such assumptions, which surfaced in the early discussions of the GAC in 1942 and 1943, suggest that even in mid-war the impact of psychiatry was significant.[20] Less certain was the influence of private citizens' groups, such as an umbrella academic organization known as the Universities Committee on Post-War International Problems, which represented fifty leading universities. Trained talent for the Occupation ultimately came from Military Government training programs rather than from any "war minors" scheme, as earlier propounded by Walter Kotschnig. A second group, consisting of representatives from various professions and the civil service, formed in New York an Institute on Reeducation of the Axis Countries; in 1944 it became part of a U.S. Committee on Educational Reconstruction.

Probably the least influential participants in the reeducation debate were the German émigrés. Refugees figured prominently in the Council for a Democratic Germany, led by Paul Tillich and officially sponsored by the American Association for a Democratic Germany. The latter included, as its vice-chairmen, Reinhold Niebuhr and Dorothy Thompson. The reeducation program promoted by this group circulated in the State Department in 1945, as did an OSS report on the opinions of five celebrated writers: Thomas Mann, Lion Feuchtwanger, Emil Ludwig, Alfred Döblin, and Bruno Frank.

Tillich's group offered a "Program for the Reconstruction of the Schools and the Educational System in Germany," which was perceptibly tougher in tone than any policy devised at the State Department. For example, it recommended blanket dismissals of all German teachers immediately, with the possibility of probationary reinstatement later. It advocated the use of émigré-conceived textbooks and claimed that "a school system built on the equality of all classes will be the best means of reawakening in the German people the desire for education and knowledge, which is the prerequisite for further democratic advancement." It criticized Germany's previous educational system as preserving class privileges, and it proposed a radical restructuring of the schools in the Occupation. It charged that universities posed even greater problems and should remain closed until completely democratic faculties were available—a lengthy process—and it warned that some of the German youth, having been conquered by the Nazi spirit, "must be subjected to temporary or permanent supervision."[21]

The five famous writers featured in the OSS report were even more adamant. Lion Feuchtwanger asserted that "Three million Nazis must be arrested, killed, or exiled to forced labor." Bruno Frank called for an army of occupation for a generation as the only guarantor of peace. "German youth will understand only power," he claimed. Alfred Döblin was even less sanguine: "Educating the Germans is almost hopeless because the majority of the professional classes are Nazis." The schools and universities were in the hands of reactionaries, he claimed; reform was therefore hopeless. A notable feature of the OSS report was the drastic inconsistency of the authors' remarks. Thus Döblin, despite his pessimism, felt that the Allies should hold only a supervisory function in education and should place it in the hands of anti-Nazis. Lion Feuchtwanger proposed a Goebbels-style propaganda campaign in favor of democracy; others discussed the possibility of deliberately fostering a religious revival. Feuchtwanger even proposed sending large numbers of German youth abroad as labor battalions and as student groups. The OSS reporter finally gleaned some central ideas from the discussions: "All of the distinguished novelists . . . warned against attempting to impose an educational pattern on Germany from the outside." Moreover, none of them had any use for the Morgenthau Plan, which they felt would wreck Germany. The report faithfully recorded the musings of five intellectuals. However, it cannot have impressed many as a sober, coherent document, and the State Department's David Harris refused to consider employing German refugees on an advisory committee for German reeducation at the end of the war.[22]

The SHAEF Handbooks

That the State Department was in advance of other agencies in planning for the postwar period is hardly surprising. Yet, it was under the aegis of the vastly larger War Department that concrete planning for the occupation of Germany began. The first control to be imposed on the Germans would be a military government, to be deployed behind the front-line troops in conquered territory. Anticipating that responsibility, the Army commissioned nearly two thousand civilian administrators during the war to provide the civil-affairs skills needed to make a military government function. John W. Taylor was typical of the civilian officers selected by the Army for a military-government role. He was an educational administrator; his doctoral dissertation at Columbia Teachers College was on Weimar youth groups; and he had had practical teaching experience in Berlin schools. As such, he personified the type of expert the Army was seeking. He volunteered for military service in 1942 and was one of the first products of the School for Military Government in Charlottesville. (Dorothy Thompson, by castigating this as a "school for Gauleiters," later hardened the Army's resolve to avoid training personnel for long-term political control.) Hastily transferred to North Africa, Taylor nearly suffered the fate of most of the other two hundred educators selected by the Army for military-government assignments, namely, diversion to more immediate wartime duties. He received orders in 1943 to help with Italian educational reconstruction, but a chance meeting with Professor Thomas Vernon Smith saved him for the German Occupation. Smith wanted the Italian slot but had been ordered to join SHAEF at London for planning the invasion of Germany. He convinced General Eisenhower of the wisdom of a switch in assignments. Thus it was Taylor who arrived in London in early 1944.[23]

Considerable dissension had developed in the War Department on how to organize civil affairs and military government in the field, and the problems had by no means been solved when Taylor reported to SHAEF. The bulk of the civil-affairs officers arriving that spring were to form mobile "G-5" civil-affairs detachments, which, deployed at intervals behind the fighting forces, would form a continuous military government across liberated and occupied territory. A smaller number of officers were to form planning staffs to provide field manuals for the G-5 teams and practical advice for the theater commander. They were also to begin the work that would ultimately result in a postwar "static" military government in enemy territory. The largest of these "country units" was the German Country Unit (GCU), to which Taylor was assigned. The problem the GCU faced was that the War Department remained uneasy about its role as a civil-affairs planning agency, even for short-term policies, during hostilities. Logically, the GCU should have had intimate contact with American civilian agencies, such as the State Department, but at precisely that point the CAD proved most determined to prevent civilian meddling in the war zone. The GCU was therefore in an unenviable position. The hundred-odd officers on the staff all faced great difficulties in overcoming the planning vacuum, and for Taylor and the minuscule education staff the frustrations were even greater.[24]

The British participants in the GCU were favored by their proximity to their own government's agencies and resources. For example, their education leader on the GCU, Lieutenant Colonel G. R. Gayre, and his successor, Donald Riddy, readily received information and advice from the British Board of Education and from Sir Alfred Zimmern in the Foreign Office. Theoretically, the Americans under Taylor should have had comparable support from Ambassador Winant at the EAC and the EAC's coordinating agency in Washington, the Working Security Committee (WSC). In reality nothing of the sort occurred. The War Department representatives on the WSC were suspicious of the EAC and refused to cooperate with State or Navy representatives in sending instructions on to Winant. George F. Kennan aptly described the situation as one in which official Washington was fearful that the EAC might "by some mischance actually do something." Grayson N. Kefauver, who had participated in the GAC discussions a year earlier, was with Winant in the spring of 1944 and stayed on in London until the following October. However, neither he nor the ambassador was able to provide up-to-date information on Washington's position with respect to postwar Germany. Despite these considerable handicaps, Taylor and his fellow officers on the GCU continued to labor on their chief undertaking: the "Handbook on Germany Prior to Defeat or Surrender." In the six months of the GCU's existence, from March to August, 1944, the "Handbook" was its one tangible achievement. Yet, a lack of adequate knowledge about the Roosevelt Administration's intentions toward Germany caused the GCU to land in the midst of a major government dispute over plans for the defeated nation.[25]

The "Handbook" was supposed to offer practical guidance only for the short term, but the staff quickly learned that such strictures were artificial. The first steps taken on German soil by the Americans would set the stage for the rest of the occupation. The GCU planners gamely improvised, despite the continuing blackout of policy information in the spring and summer of 1944. They took the Anglo-American Atlantic Charter as a logical statement of intent. Since it pertained to Germany, the Charter led the planners to assume the resurrection of a Weimar-style Germany with a responsible central government. Like the State Department officials on the GAC and on the Interdivisional Committee on Germany, the planners of the GCU proposed a reconstructionist course for military government. They were also using the Army's "bible" on civil affairs, the Field Manual (FM) 27–5, which had prescribed a military government that was "just, humane, and as mild as practicable." The general goal was to create a stable peace and to convert a hostile nation into an ally. Thus, in its practical way, FM 27–5 mirrored the intentions of the highest echelons of American leadership, both in and out of government—or so the SHAEF planners thought. Accordingly, the tone of the GCU's first handbook was positive and reconstructionist.[26]

In their initial version of the "Handbook," the first attempt at practical policymaking for the occupation, Taylor's staff sought to minimize controls and negative actions. To be sure, they were prepared to remove National Socialist influence from the teaching staffs and learning materials. However, their program called for a rapid reopening of the school system and left the existing school types and structure largely unchanged. They presumed that the American staff on hand would be small and that the great bulk of the tasks would be handled by anti-Nazi Germans. The manual proposed that "Military Government should limit its interference in educational matters to the minimum which general conditions require. Foreign interference in education will surely alienate the feelings of the population, including even most of the anti-Nazis." The staff also warned against assuming direct control over reform of the education system and regarded the employment of foreign-born teachers as "highly inadvisable." Other practical recommendations included the rapid reopening of schools wherever the battle zone receded. The schools could also serve as feeding centers and health-care clinics and thus attract high attendance. Textbooks were a problem, but the education section predicted that adequate numbers of older works from the Weimar period had survived and could replace the Nazi-tainted works, especially in sensitive areas such as history and biological sciences. Teachers might also orally dictate portions of texts to children on an emergency basis. They further recommended that German authorities handle the vetting of textbooks, with military-government support. The staff proposed that libraries leave Nazi-influenced materials on the shelves, where new learning materials would expose their deceit. They condemned book-burning as too reminiscent of the practices of the Third Reich. Finally, they suggested that the Germans write their own new textbooks. Forced use of imported or refugee-produced works would cause strong resistance. "The decision should be left to the Germans," was their stock comment on this and many of the other problems associated with educational reconstruction. Thus, the GCU's "Handbook" was positive in tone; it gave maximum initiative to the Germans in all phases of reform, including denazification and, at a later date, the activities associated with structural and curricular reform.[27]

President Roosevelt did not care for the "Handbook" and banned its distribution. He and Henry Morgenthau were more irked by the reconstructionist political and economic provisions than by anything contained in the education proposals. Nevertheless, Taylor's work became the subject of some "differences of opinion among the interested Washington agencies on proposed modifications of the directive and . . . consequently no decision on it was ever reached." The trouble did not lie with the EAC's Washington link, the Working Security Committee, because its State-War-Navy representatives had developed a position similar to that outlined in the "Handbook." At the height of the Morgenthau controversy at the end of August, 1944, the WSC had itself appealed for a program of positive educational reconstruction, which could best be accomplished, it felt, through "competent and politically trustworthy German leadership." There were no Treasury representatives on the WSC.[28]

The proposals and intentions that surfaced at this time demonstrated that communication across the Atlantic was haphazard. Ambassador Winant forwarded a series of draft directives on the occupation to the State Department in September, one of which was titled "Control of German Education." It simply disappeared. At the same time, the British Government dispatched thirty-six of its own occupation directives to America, including one on reeducation, but these, too, had little effect in Washington. Another symptom of the communication gap was the fate of the State Department's first policy paper on education in Germany. The Interdivisional Committee on Germany prepared it at the request of the CAD in May, 1944, to aid Taylor's staff, but the draft disappeared after being reviewed in July, 1944, and did not resurface until 1945, when Archibald MacLeish examined it while preparing his own views on the subject.[29]

By September, 1944, Allied troops were entering German territory for the first time, so that a replacement "Handbook" was urgently needed. With the breakup of the GCU, Taylor's tiny staff now formed part of the US Group CC, which, in cooperation with the Control Commission (British Element), began to forge new directives in great haste. Obedient to the President's call for a tougher stand, the education officers hardened the tone, if not the substance, of their new directives. They stated at the outset that "the aim is to take control of the German educational system and thoroughly to de-Nazify and demilitarize it." But a corollary was that assumption of control must be "by indirect means, employing personnel of the existing German educational system as far as possible, as purged or freed from Nazi and militaristic influence." Unlike the previous directives, the new set proposed to close all schools until the Supreme Commander was satisfied that evil influences had been purged from teaching staffs and learning materials and that there was an adequate supply of new teachers and textbooks. This SHAEF *Handbook* referred specifically for the first time to the need for emergency SHAEF textbooks to replace tainted ones. There was also a new requirement: all Nazi books were to be impounded.[30]

It was possible to interpret the new directives as embodying a harsher "Morgenthau" approach to reeducation, but that interpretation ignored several more immediate factors, which emerged in the late summer and autumn of 1944. First, the SHAEF staff discovered that their expectations about the availability of old but usable Weimar texts were too optimistic and that, in all likelihood, they would have to remove virtually every textbook in order to eliminate National Socialist influence from learning materials. One of the major undertakings of the education staff that summer was the selection of appropriate Weimar texts from the ones Taylor and his mentor, R. T. Alexander, had assembled at Columbia Teachers College before the war. Experience gleaned in the Mediterranean Theater indicated that it was "impossible for the schools of Italy to function without textbooks," a fact corroborated by veterans like George Geyer, who had inspected the schools of Naples. Italian schools had opened at intervals rather than uniformly on a specific date set by the theater commander. The Army had urged rapid reopenings as a way to keep children off the streets, and the minuscule education staff was willing to comply, since it could oversee only limited areas at any given time. Reports indicated that the elimination of fascist elements in the Italian school system was haphazard and slow, a shortcoming that resulted, at least in part, from the staggered reopenings.[31] Thus, partly as a matter of experience and partly because of the realization that textbooks were a potential bottleneck, the SHAEF staff incorporated new procedures in its *Handbook*. Taylor later claimed that he and his staff had had to convince a reluctant Army to agree to the uniform-closing procedure because the Army still preferred to see the children in the schools rather than on the streets. On the other hand, the earlier proposal to use schools as feeding centers and health clinics disappeared from the revised edition.[32]

The tougher tone of the new *Handbook* placed the education officers in the uncomfortable position of having to seek democratization through reeducation by negative means, namely, controls and purges. The paradox was not lost on Marshall Knappen. He stated that the very nature of military government would prevent German authorities from being free agents with respect to education, but he added that the Americans hoped to give them the maximum of freedom and keep the iron hand hidden in the velvet glove as much as possible. Since the six education officers at the US Group CC had been conducting a training program for field education officers in Manchester, prior to the D-Day invasions, the spirit in which they set about their new tasks was more closely identified with the first "Handbook" than with the second. Maximum German initiative and the reopening of most existing schools predominated. The revised *Handbook* simply enlarged on the negative chores tied to denazification. For example, it established categories of "black, gray, and white" education officials, depending on their degree of involvement in, or opposition to, National Socialism. Special technical manuals that were to accompany the field education officers would supply further details. Five thousand names appeared on the lists of desirables and undesirables.[33] The education provision in the *Handbook* simply offered more detail and was couched in language that made it compatible with the rest of the political, economic, and social directives. However, no one confused the *Handbook* with long-range occupation policy. That sticky issue was still to be resolved as the last year of the war slowly ebbed.

Long-Range Planning

Despite the fact that the War Department was determined to prevent civilian interference in military-government operations during hostilities, it was a War Department request that provided the initiative for David Harris's Interdivisional Committee on Germany to prepare a position paper on education. In March, 1944, John H. Hilldring, director of the War Department's Civil Affairs Division, received an urgent cable from his British counterpart, Sir Frederick Bovenschen, requesting policy guidance for the occupation period for Taylor and his staff.[34] Lacking any contact with the SHAEF planners, Harris's group produced a paper reflecting the State Department's reconstructionist attitude. The influence of the earlier studies, prepared by the GAC, was also apparent. Education remained a means of democratizing the Germans: "In the interest of effecting a fundamental change in the German attitude toward war and ultranationalism, this Government should encourage and foster the cultivation of democratic principles and practices in the German schools." The writers were aware, they claimed, that the task was difficult and complex but saw "no constructive alternative" to creating an education system "in which a humanitarian and international point of view supersedes the current ultranationalism." They specifically rejected foreign control over the schools or the imposition of curricula from the outside. "Effective reform of German education must come from the Germans themselves, drawing upon the finer aspects of their own cultural tradition." The task, as they saw it, was to foster a positive program and to assist the Germans in making fundamental changes. Echoing the conclusions of the GAC, the Interdivisional Committee repeated the warning that reeducation must not proceed in a vacuum: "It [the Committee] foresees that the German reaction to the whole body of measures taken by the victors will be the major influence in determining future German attitudes, and it believes that on that German reaction will depend the success or failure of any attempt at scholastic reform."[35]

While the Interdivisional Committee had strong views on the goals and general spirit with which Americans should conduct education reconstruction, it was not able at this stage to come to grips with the actual machinery needed for success. Its members presumed that local school administrations could be employed following denazification: "Civil-affairs administration should invite local communities, as a first step in the revival of self-government, to assume the initiative in reopening and reforming the schools." They theorized that groups of "reputable citizens" might form advisory committees to aid the Occupation forces, especially in the earliest phases of control. For the longer term, these State Department officers envisaged a "special agency of the central tripartite authority in Berlin." They recognized that at present the administrative machinery was simply conjectural. They considered forming a body of "reliable German educators" to assist the central Berlin authority but refused to elaborate on its powers or discretion. Nevertheless, they, like the members of previous State Department committees and the education officers at SHAEF, presumed that active German participation was indispensable.[36] As noted above, this first long-range document on the reform of German education, although completed and reviewed by the State Department's Committee on Post-War Programs in July, 1944, never crossed the Atlantic because of the flare-up over the Morgenthau Plan. It did not resurface until 1945.

Following the rise and fall of the Morgenthau Plan in the autumn of 1944, no clear decision on policy was possible. President Roosevelt remarked at that time to Secretary of State Hull: "Speed on these matters is not essential at the present moment. I dislike making detailed plans for a country which we do not yet occupy."[37] However, with the President inclining first toward one agency's views and then another's, frustrations surfaced as the final victory approached. In January, 1945, Archibald MacLeish was appointed Assistant Secretary of State for Cultural Affairs. One of his first tasks was to answer an angry memorandum from Lieutenant Colonel Mark Dewitt Howe of the CAD, who complained about lack of progress in educational planning to date. Howe had seen State Department and EAC proposals that tended to expand the number of Allied and German advisory groups in the educational sphere. The EAC suggested that "reliable German administrators" be made responsible for the preparation of a statement of detailed educational objectives. State Department officials then added a second German agency, a Planning Commission nominated by "satisfactory" German educational authorities and approved by Allied Supreme Command. "Such a complete delegation to the Germans of responsibility," Howe complained, "for the reformation of the system and such an elaborate procedure for the postponement of reform would appear to guarantee the frustration of our objectives." He stated that, now that the occupation was imminent, the State Department, which had shown no desire to engage in vigorous planning, must now accept major responsibility for it. "Neither Ambassador Winant nor the four officers working with the Control Council in London can be expected to solve specific issues without far more guidance from the U.S. Government than they have yet received," wrote Howe. A failure to produce specific plans now would see the Americans "forced to adopt the British, Russian, or French plan, and it is doubtful if, in the long run, such plans will meet the standard which informed opinion in this country will come to demand of us in Germany." What was needed was "a program which will give definite answers to the difficult questions and will not be satisfied with the reiteration of good intentions and high aspirations."[38]

Thus prodded, MacLeish went into action. He reviewed the Interdivisional Committee's report, which had finally reappeared, and then forwarded his thoughts to a fellow cultural-affairs officer, Bryn Hovde. MacLeish found the original report intelligent and sensible until it tried to solve the administrative tangle. Then he observed a tendency to give responsibility to "friendly or liberal or civilized or, in any case, anti-Nazi Germans, who will be able to take over the job which—as we very well say—we cannot do for ourselves." MacLeish hoped such indigenous personnel would be available but could offer no assurances. "What this all means to me is that the basic question of the reeducation of Germany probably cannot be approached intelligently until we have occupied Germany and have learned whether or not the civilian personnel we need for our assistance actually exists." MacLeish was convinced that the moment for intensive planning was not yet at hand. In a third draft of a paper entitled "German Education under Military Government" he persisted in retaining the Planning Commission of German advisers to the Allied authorities, despite Howe's earlier objection. German responsibility was to remain a primary concern for the State Department.[39]

In a later note to MacLeish, Howe suggested that the State Department cease preparing directives for the immediate situation because the War Department's revised *Handbook* was adequate for immediate and short-range guidance for the G-5 civil-affairs teams. "Our own private concern," Howe added, "has been that the U.S. side of the Control Council may not be adequately organized or prepared for the long-range treatment of the German educational problem, and it has been our suggestion that the State Department might assemble outstanding and qualified educational authorities to formulate a U.S. position and then collaborate with the other Allied representatives in carrying it out." MacLeish was happy to accommodate Howe. He had already made the same suggestion in 1943 during the discussions of the GAC.[40]

Seizing on the War Department's suggestion to assemble a committee of "outstanding and qualified educational authorities to formulate a U.S. position," Bryn Hovde issued a call, later that spring, for "persons of overall judgment about German education in relation to the life of the nation and Europe." He also recognized the need to include "persons with some specialized knowledge of different aspects of German education."[41] During two meetings in May and early June, 1945, the civilian education leaders conferred with five State Department officials, with Mark Howe from CAD, and with John Taylor, who had flown in from Europe to recruit new staff and to attend the conferences. This new Advisory Committee on German Reeducation began by examining America's official occupation-

policy document. The Joint Chiefs of Staff had just given their assent to
JCS Directive 1067 on Germany, which showed the repressive hand of
Henry Morgenthau but also included certain loopholes, at War Department insistence. A liberal interpretation of the so-called "disease and
unrest" formula, which enabled the Occupation powers to supply food
and other emergency relief in order to maintain better control over the
population, might become the vehicle for a more humane policy. In any
case, Secretary Morgenthau's political influence had been on the wane
since the previous autumn. President Roosevelt excluded him from the
Yalta proceedings, and Harry Truman was to drop him altogether from
his administration in July, 1945. JCS 1067 was not particularly concerned
with the issue of education reform. Howe opened the meeting with a call
for policy guidance on education because the "CAD regards the present
directive in 1067 as very meager and requiring immediate amplification."
Howe was correct that Section 14 of JCS 1067 was essentially only a brief
summary of the salient features of the wartime *Handbook*. Taylor offered
a description of the organization and guiding principles of the SHAEF
and US Group CC staffs and then spoke of the problems they were en-
countering in Germany. Thus briefed, the civilian education experts prepared to grapple with the task of formulating long-range policy—the policy
that, so far, had proved so elusive.[42]

The civilians brought a considerable expertise to the discussions. Reinhold Niebuhr had arrived from Union Theological Seminary to offer advice, especially with regard to denominational education. Eduard C.
Lindemann of the New York School of Social Work was an expert on adult
education. Dean Martin McGuire, of Catholic University, and John Milton
Potter, president of Hobart College, rounded out the original group. David
Harris and Leon Fuller represented the State Department's Central European Division. Bryn Hovde, Gordon Bowles, and Haldore Hanson spoke
for State's Division of Cultural Cooperation. MacLeish and Eugene N.
Anderson also attended most of the sessions.

One of the nagging questions that had plagued previous policy groups
was now in the process of being answered: there would be no central
German authority through which to work. Howe informed the group that
decentralization had become an objective of Military Government, and,
in the absence of a central German government, initiative on many policy
issues, including education, would fall to the four zonal commanders.
Since the Allied Control Council, presently taking shape, was expected
to act only by unanimous decision, Howe predicted that decisions would
have to be made independently on the lower level. The Americans would
be controlling several Länder (states); U.S. Military Government would
therefore have to issue uniform directives, since, unlike the British, the
American staff had chosen to ban any zone-wide educational administra-

tion. The present advisory group would, Howe hoped, provide the necessary policy guidance. John Taylor agreed, stating that his education officers had entered Germany with no long-range policy directives, "since it was believed that all educational activities could be deferred until victory was won."[43]

What was to become America's "Long-Range Policy Statement for German Reeducation," SWNCC 269/5, began as a draft statement prepared by Gordon Bowles, Leon Fuller, and Eugene Anderson for the civilian group to respond to. They proposed a period of controls designed to eliminate National Socialist influence in education. This would pave the way for "the initiation of a program for the reconstitution of a German cultural life." Simultaneously, the Germans must learn to accept again such ideals as the dignity of the individual, ethnic and religious toleration, the impartial rule of law, individual freedoms, civic responsibility, and the equality of nations and races. The civilians on the new Advisory Committee warned of the limits to Allied influence: "In the exercise of their functions, the occupational authorities should bear in mind that permanent changes can be effected only as they are developed and maintained by the Germans themselves. The occupational authorities should seek to effect the progressive transfer of authority in education to responsible Germans as rapidly as conditions permit. As authority is transferred, Allied control should become increasingly unobtrusive." The civilian participants agreed, adding that it was important to utilize to the fullest "those native German cultural resources which reflect the universal aspects of civilization." The committee identified anti-Nazis with strong religious, political, and intellectual convictions as likely coworkers in the effort at cultural resurgence. A fourth group might emerge "from the family's (particularly the women's) resistance to the totalitarian state." There followed a list of measures that might aid such a program, including a recommendation that America "restore as soon as feasible the cultural relations between Germany and other nations."[44]

A follow-up meeting in early June allowed the Advisory Committee to add to the document the advice of presidents Edmund Day of Cornell University, George Shuster of Hunter College, and Frank Graham of the University of North Carolina. The crucial policy of the document remained the same: maximum use of German resources. "The reconstruction of the cultural life of Germany must be in large measure the work of the Germans themselves" was the guiding principle. The members then proposed that the government establish a permanent commission to handle German educational problems as they arose. It might advise the President directly or work through the State Department. Representatives from the Office of War Information (OWI) judged that the problems involved were too large for one agency and recommended coordinating the current scattered efforts of several groups. They pointed out that SHAEF's Psychological Warfare Division (later the Information Control Division, or ICD, in Military Government) and Education and Religious Affairs Section were running separate programs and that the Provost Marshal General (PMG) was administering reeducation programs for German prisoners of war. Each agency was handling one aspect of the problem, but a presidential commission with OWI support could coordinate all efforts. MacLeish sidestepped this suggestion, stating that the present Advisory Committee was essentially fulfilling the coordination function. Mark Howe was perceptibly cooler; he claimed that the War Department already had too many commissions with which to deal. Despite an appeal by OWI's director, Elmer Davis, to President Truman, the commission idea was effectively halted, and, as events proved, the Advisory Committee had also concluded its work. Its second meeting proved to be its last. At the time, however, it appeared to have an active future, and the State Department officials gave special attention to its composition. They wanted a small group of about ten individuals, including women. Members were to be chosen for a number of qualifications, only one of which was knowledge of German education. David Harris expressed the opinion that the advisory body would need "illuminated horse sense, not technical knowledge." There was one group the officials specifically wanted to avoid as potential members: "Department representatives expressed official reluctance to utilize the services of German refugees on this committee." Not all committee members agreed with that opinion. Reinhold Niebuhr later proposed to MacLeish that "a German scholar, now an American citizen"—a man like Robert Uhlich of Harvard—would be useful for postwar planning.[45] In any event, the Advisory Committee, which completed its long-range policy document in June, 1945, was destined to serve no longer.

Perhaps the most significant development following the Advisory Committee's dissolution was the fact that neither the State Department nor the War Department was able to locate a suitable educational administrator to lead the education programs in Germany. They attempted to recruit Edmund Day and then Frank Graham, but even telegraphed appeals from President Truman were unavailing. In each instance the nominee claimed he had already taken war-related leaves of absence and that his board of trustees demanded his presence to handle the avalanche of soldiers-turned students following demobilization. MacLeish and other State Department officials continued to canvass the country in search of a nationally recognized administrator, but without result. In early July, Anderson received an ominous report from Howe at CAD to the effect "that quite probably the Army would exercise only police power so far as German education is concerned, and would depend upon the Department of State or some other civilian agency to supply the necessary personnel for supervision

and control." Thoroughly alarmed, Bryn Hovde immediately contacted
Howe, but after further discussions he was able to report to MacLeish:
"The Army will itself do this work under the leadership of some very
competent person whom it is hoped the Department of State will supply."[46]
The Army was assuming responsibility for reeducation only reluctantly.

John Taylor combined his duties on the Advisory Committee with recruiting new personnel for the task ahead. His most successful effort was
to secure the services of his former graduate adviser, Professor Richard
Thomas Alexander, dean of Columbia Teachers' experimental New College
in the 1920s and '30s and, by common consent, the most knowledgeable
American with respect to German education. Civilian recruitment was
now necessary because the Army was refusing to accept new commissions
in the midst of redeployment and demobilization. Howe had told the
Advisory Committee that "there will be considerable use of United States
civilians . . . since there are not sufficient qualified persons in uniform."[47]
The scattering of most of the two hundred education officers originally
commissioned during the war took on new significance as the Occupation
got under way. The fact that John Taylor, who had just received promotion
to major, had to return to Europe to take charge of the American education
programs was equally significant. Unable to name a prestigious educational
leader to become E&RA Chief of Military Government, the State Department refused to release the results of its intense labors.[48] SWNCC 269/
5 remained under wraps and did not become official policy until its public
release in the summer of 1946. Unofficially it exerted influence through
Taylor, who continued to head the education undertaking until April,
1947.

During Taylor's absence in the spring of 1945, the ten-man education
section of US Group CC moved into temporary headquarters at Höchst,
near Frankfurt. This skeleton staff had experienced considerable upheaval
since its original days at Shrivenham Hall; it had moved first to London
in time for the V-1 attacks, then to Versailles, and finally to Höchst at
war's end. Eventually it found more permanent accommodations in Berlin,
where it remained through most of the Occupation. As a mere section of
a branch within a division, it was far removed from the center of power,
unlike such groups as the economic and legal advisers or even information
control. E&RA did not achieve division status until March, 1948, when
it altered its name, slightly, to Education and Cultural Relations Division
(E&CR).

In mid-May, 1945, the staff took time off from its immediate duties to
hold policy discussions at the same time as Taylor and the Advisory Committee were meeting in Washington. It produced a study to deal with
"those education policies . . . in which it is anticipated that there will be
the most interest and probable criticism when information concerning

these policies is released for consideration by journalists and professional critics," and it identified these policy areas as denazification, the degree of American controls, and the problem of finding leadership for the programs.[49]

The E&RA officers were inclined to treat denazification pragmatically. Their original plan was that party members or members of affiliates like the National Socialist *Lehrerbund* (Teachers League) should "not necessarily be prevented from holding teaching positions if their party affiliations prove to have been, for the most part, passive." The staff knew that such a policy might incur criticism. However, early field reports indicated that all male—and most female—teachers had been required to join the party; blanket dismissals now would therefore paralyze the educational system. They reasoned that "the average teacher is willing to adapt himself or herself to whatever political change may come. Consequently, it is believed that, by eliminating a comparatively small minority of confessed Nazis, it will be possible to secure liberal teaching in the schools provided that the general effect of Allied occupation is to foster liberal influences in Germany as a whole."

The second principle espoused by the E&RA staff was one of indirect American control, "using available German civilian administrators and teachers as far as possible." U.S. Army field manuals upheld the principle of "indirect control and maximum use of indigenous civilian resources," so the staff was prepared to ignore all proposals to use teachers imported from outside. "If a genuine German democracy is to be developed, it must come from the German people themselves." Echoing Marshall Knappen's recommendation that Military Government cloak the iron fist, they concluded that "the most effective way of imposing a democratic program on the German people is to have it at least seem to come from them and, insofar as possible, really originate with them as far as the details are concerned."

Finally, the members of the staff registered their desire to secure a permanent education chief immediately. Taylor had functioned well as head of the SHAEF planning group, but the consensus was that the position required a celebrity, someone who would carry greater influence in Military Government and at home: "It is the policy of the Education and Religious Affairs Branch," the report continued, "to secure a chief whose name and previous educational record will command public respect." The staff preferred a chief "with an outstanding civilian background in the field of educational administration." Among its top candidates were Frank Graham and George Shuster. They also considered military administrators, among them General Troy Middleton. Significantly, they considered and rejected R. T. Alexander for the job, first describing him as the "greatest living American authority in the field of

German education," then objecting that he was "unfortunately not con- sidered a good administrator."[50] The staff's desires were not entirely re- alistic. As a mere section of the nascent Military Government, its influence was slight. The lesson was made perfectly clear when John Taylor, still a junior officer, rejoined them a few days later with the news that his personnel recruitment had netted the services of Richard Thomas Alex- ander.

A Final Appeal

The gap that opened up between aims and realities in America's reedu- cation programs at the end of hostilities was troublesome not only to the E&RA Staff but to other observers as well. Archibald MacLeish recognized that, despite the plans being forged in the State Department, existing official policy in the form of JCS 1067 paid scant attention to the issue of reeducation. Even the Advisory Committee's "Long-Range Policy" state- ment (SWNCC 269/5) had required some tough preliminary paragraphs in order to secure Henry Morgenthau's approval—an approval that was necessary, since Morgenthau continued to wield influence through his participation in the decisions of the Inter-Agency Policy Committee on Germany (IPCOG), which exercised final approval on *all* policy. For ex- ample, MacLeish and the Advisory Committee prefaced their statement on denazification by describing it as a means of offering "the German people present and tangible evidence that Germany lost the war, that Germans individually and through national organizations were responsible for brutalities and inhumanities in the prosecution of the war for which punishment is due, and that the constraint of the German people during the period of the Occupation is a direct and necessary consequence of Germany's fanatical conduct of the war." A second statement, inserted to mollify the Treasury Secretary, left an uncertain impression: Germany's imminent economic reorganization, "while impressing upon the German people the consequences of their responsibility for the war, will permit them to survive as a nation and to participate creatively in the economic life of their time." When, a full year later, SWNCC 269/5 was finally released to the public, these tough preliminary paragraphs had disap- peared.[51]

MacLeish saw an opportunity almost immediately to alert new leader- ship to the neglect of reeducation when incoming Secretary of State Byrnes was preparing to attend the Potsdam Conference. In two draft memoranda, dated July 12 and July 18, 1945, of which only the latter was actually sent, MacLeish appealed forcefully for greater attention at the highest levels to programs of reeducation. He warned bluntly that "common agreement as to the American purpose in the occupation of Germany does not exist."

No concrete definition of purpose existed in official documents to date. Yet logic dictated that Americans must accept the responsibility. They had chosen not to eliminate the German people or to garrison the country permanently—actions that would have been morally and practically impossible. It followed, therefore, that the United States must seek to change "the mentality of the German people to the end that Germany . . . [may] eventually be permitted to live without surveillance and control." Now that the world had terrible new weapons of destruction, it was imperative that Americans do their best to change German attitudes toward war. Reeducation was the only answer, since annihilation and permanent subjugation were unthinkable. Having decided to replace an old set of values and ideas with another, the Americans were necessarily entering a contest with another nation, for the Soviets clearly had an alternative ideology in view. The Americans presumably were seeking to reawaken German respect "for the worth and dignity of human beings and a belief in basic principles of justice and in the right of men to govern themselves." As a positive goal, reeducation formed the core of American occupation aims and stood out from the negative aims of denazification and demilitarization.[52]

In a redraft, prepared in cooperation with the Secretary's staff on July 18, MacLeish used the analogy of criminal justice to make his appeal for greater urgency with respect to reeducation programs. Noting that public demands for harsh sentences usually subside in a short time, allowing many criminals under life sentence to receive paroles, MacLeish claimed to see a similar trend emerging with respect to the defeated enemy; "it is highly improbable," he said, "that Allied occupation of Germany—at least American occupation—can be continued beyond the period of a few years." The real war-making potential in Central Europe lay not in Germany's industrial plant. Rather, it existed in the minds of a talented, technologically sophisticated people. Reeducation remained the best safeguard for the future. Despite the advice set forth in earlier planning statements, MacLeish detected a strong tendency among the American public and many political figures "to make a distinction between political, economic, and military measures for Germany on the one hand, and measures for what is called the 'reeducation' of the German people on the other." Holding that all aspects of occupation policy must work together if they were to have the necessary impact, he proposed that the occupying powers judge their actions "not by their immediate consequences alone but by their ultimate effect upon the social and political structure of Germany." It was the long-range political consequences that would determine the success or failure of the Occupation. MacLeish's greatest fear was that the highest echelons of authority were paying only lip service to reeducation: "[Its] purpose," he stated, "must be warmly approved and not shamefacedly admitted." It was his hope, too, that Secretary Byrnes would propose at Potsdam "a common Allied position as to the question of the kind of Germany we wish to see established and the means we propose to bring it about."[53]

The Potsdam Declaration offered only this terse statement with respect to the problem: "German education shall be so controlled as completely to eliminate Nazi and militarist doctrines and to make possible the successful development of democratic ideas."[54] Since the pertinent American directive, JCS 1067, was also "very meager," as Mark Howe of the CAD readily admitted, MacLeish had just cause to express concern that the highest political authorities were underestimating the central importance of reeducation to the success of the Occupation. The Potsdam Declaration on education controls was sufficiently broad that the four occupying powers had freedom to effect any changes they desired without regard to the consequences in the other zones. Eventually, in June, 1947, the four-power Allied Control Council issued its ACA Directive 54, which theoretically committed each member to produce common reforms. By most estimates the directive arrived two years too late. For the time being, the State Department's "Long-Range Policy Statement on German Reeducation," SWNCC 269/5, remained in limbo, awaiting the moment when the government would announce a new director for education programs in Military Government. The reality was that in May, 1945, the US Group CC counted ten education officers among its ranks to help with the vital first operations of denazifying and reviving a zonal educational system for nearly twenty million people. Much depended on the success of their efforts. If the American public perceived the initial negative tasks as having failed of accomplishment, the entire concept of reeducation might fall into discredit.

First Operations in Germany

In their first year of operations, education and religious-affairs officers of Military Government grappled with two overriding problems: denazification and the revival of the existing educational system. In attempting these enormous tasks, E&RA encountered formidable obstacles, which threatened to jeopardize future efforts to reconstruct the educational system in such a way as to encourage democratic trends in the new society. The E&RA organization discovered quickly that it was inadequately staffed to oversee its major responsibilities. It lacked both essential resources and authority to function efficiently within the framework of its parent, Military Government. Unknown in the United States, the E&RA organization had difficulty in attracting or retaining quality personnel even though policy-planning groups had, since 1942, recognized that the mission it was supposed to perform demanded talent, resourcefulness, and sophistication with regard to German conditions. The fears registered by well-placed observers like Archibald MacLeish and Elmer Davis were realized in the first emergency phase of the Occupation. Reeducation remained isolated from other major occupation policies. Preoccupied with ending the chaos in Germany, the highest echelons of Military Government honored reeducation mostly in the breach. In essence, E&RA, which handled the formal aspects of reeducation, undertook grave responsibilities but had neither the resources nor the influence to fulfill them. The results of these shortfalls would later come back to haunt Military Government.

The Germans immediately began referring to the postsurrender period as their nation's "zero hour." The phrase was entirely appropriate as far as education was concerned. As World War II drew to a close, the entire educational system ground slowly to a halt, a victim of the paralysis that spread through all sectors of the stricken society. Section 14 of Directive

JCS 1067 to General Eisenhower was unequivocal: "All educational institutions within your zone, except those previously reestablished by Allied authority, will be closed." Section 14 also envisaged a progressive reopening of the system by stages, starting with the elementary schools and then extending, as rapidly as conditions permitted, to the secondary and higher educational institutions. "After Nazi features and personnel have been eliminated," the directive continued, "you may formulate and put into effect an interim program within your zone and in any case may permit the reopening of such institutions and departments which offer training which you consider immediately essential or useful in the administration of military government and the purpose of the occupation."[1] As far as education reform was concerned, JCS 1067 posed relatively modest objectives and confined itself to purging the old system and then readying it sufficiently to reopen the school doors. There was no directive for any ambitious scheme of restructuring the educational system.

Aachen

As early as autumn, 1944, education officers began to acquire practical experience in Germany's schools. Aachen became the first German town of note to be occupied by Allied troops. Most of the population, obeying an S.S. evacuation order, had retreated with German forces to the east. However, as the front stabilized and a harsh winter descended, some of the former inhabitants began to drift back to their homes. Eighty-five per cent of the city was now rubble, and the peacetime population of 160,000 had fallen to 14,000 by year's end. A Military Government detachment had promptly moved into the city and began for the first time the job of erecting the machinery of occupational authority. By February, 1945, one detachment officer, Major Hugh M. Jones, was able to offer a preliminary report on educational needs in the ancient city of Charlemagne. He had already received numerous requests from concerned parents to reopen the schools promptly. He soon learned why: "Though there are not many children in Aachen at this time," he reported, "most of them have not had any formalized schooling for almost one year. . . . Parents of those that are here are most anxious that schools be opened as soon as possible, for they fear that the loss of a year's education is very serious." Accordingly, Jones ordered the appointment of a committee of five politically untainted Aachen citizens to plan for the reopening of the schools; they were to serve without pay. Aachen's Oberbürgermeister, Franz Oppenhoff, who was later murdered by Nazi assassins, appointed (with American approval) a certain Dr. Breuer as Bürgermeister of Schools and Culture to work with the five-member committee, and they began to survey the situation. It was bleak.[2]

In normal times Aachen had had over fifty educational institutions, ranging from elementary schools up to a technical institute. In 1945 nearly all of them were destroyed. Concerned at first only with elementary schools, the German committee expected to use the twelve surviving buildings for elementary education. Teaching staffs had suffered grievously; 80 percent of the male teachers had departed for military duty. Now only forty-seven teachers remained to fill out the Allied *Fragebogen*, or questionnaire, on their political activities under the Third Reich. Of the twenty-six nonparty members, most were housewives, who, because of their non-professional status, had not been forced to join the movement. Thus the pool of politically acceptable teaching talent in Aachen was made up, for the most part, of forty-to-fifty-year-old women—a situation that would repeatedly occur throughout the U.S. Zone.[3]

One of Jones's most persistent problems was the critical shortage of adequate schoolbooks. The ubiquitous SHAEF *Handbook* warned that "many textbooks will be found to be thoroughly adulterated with Nazi ideology." The warning was accurate. Of the books formerly in use, Jones could locate only one suitable primer, and even it required removal of the last four pages. There were two newly composed manuscripts, consisting of fairytales, poetry, stories, and legends of Aachen. The concept of using local material was sound, but there was no plant for producing the necessary printing plates in Aachen. Finally a shipment of emergency textbook plates arrived at Aachen's one surviving newspaper plant, and in April, 1945, Germany's first "postwar" school texts began rolling off the press. This feat was the result of a concerted effort by Taylor's education staff, starting in the spring of 1944, to find replacement texts for the emergency period.[4]

The more the staff members studied the problem, the more they realized how difficult it was to solve. Swiss texts were unacceptable because of linguistic and cultural differences. Works by German refugees were politically acceptable, but the authors' status as exiles might easily arouse nationalistic antagonisms. Taylor's staff therefore chose to use unexpurgated Weimar-era textbooks, to circumvent charges of foreign authorship or propaganda. But to locate Weimar schoolbooks was anything but easy in wartime Europe. The British had no collection of German texts, and any hope of acquiring Swedish collections faded because of the tenuous wartime links to that neutral country. Then John Taylor had an inspiration. In the 1920s one of his duties as a graduate student under Professor Richard Thomas Alexander had been to collect textbooks during trips to Germany. Between them Taylor and Alexander had amassed a considerable collection for the library of the International Institute at Columbia Teachers College. "Knowing that all those books were still there," he recalled, "I requested that they microfilm about 250 textbooks." The microfilms arrived in due course in London for evaluation, and, after consulting with their British colleagues, E&RA selected several works that they felt to be least objectionable. No one suggested that they were ideal.[5]

Evidence of excessive nationalism and militarism abounded even in pre-Hitler books. For example, a history survey for seventh- and eighth-graders recounted the glorious exploits in war of Frederick the Great and Prussia, a topic entirely unsuited to the present time. The education staff therefore inserted a disclaimer of sorts in each emergency textbook:

> This textbook is one of a series which is being published by order of the Supreme Commander of the Allied Expeditionary Force for emergency use in German schools in the area occupied by his forces. It has been selected after a thorough examination of many of the books in use in Germany before the Nazi accession to power. It is a textbook of German authorship and has been reprinted without textual alteration. Its issue does not imply that it is entirely suitable from an educational point of view or otherwise. It is merely the best book which could be found in the circumstances and must serve until Germany produces better textbooks of its own.[6]

With selections and procedures established, the E&RA staff had plates made in London and shipped the precious set to Aachen, but they were lost en route. A second shipment of plates finally arrived in early 1945, and the books were assembled in Aachen's newspaper plant. Working under highly adverse conditions, the Americans succeeded in printing 40,000 textbooks in time for the June 4 elementary-school openings. Yet, despite the prodigies performed in securing these reprints, the education officers experienced considerable criticism by parents that the SHAEF textbook program was ineffective. An E&RA member, Oscar Reinmuth, who had labored so long on text selections, inspected the results in Aachen. He issued a blunt verdict to his superiors a few weeks after VE Day: "The textbook problem is not solved . . . by the reprinting of SHAEF emergency textbooks. I am convinced that the complaint made at Aachen will be repeated all over: 'These textbooks are not adapted to our area.' "[7] The solution was, of course, to have German authors produce their own new works, but that was impossible in the chaotic conditions of 1945.

On June 4 ten of Aachen's schools reopened, the first to do so in the three Western zones. Twenty-two teachers began instructing 1,300 children in the first four elementary grades, using SHAEF texts and, especially, blackboards and verbal instruction. A disconcerting discovery was made that the pupils of the families that had fled eastward with the Nazis were more advanced than those who had remained behind. Long absence from school had weakened discipline, but the war had also influenced the pupils' career goals. Dumont Kenny, from US Group CC, listened to the children's plans to become "farmers, architects, and everything but soldiers," and he remarked in his report: "They never want to be soldiers." The mixed Protestant-Catholic school board was pleased that religious instruction had returned to the schools, and 4,000 Catholic parents were petitioning Military Government to reopen denominational schools.

School Superintendent Heinrich Beckers offered a brief inaugural speech in which he announced that, after twelve years, "we are allowed to open our schools according to our plans and our teaching system." By that he meant a system free of National Socialism. Because of strong church influence, local resentments had lingered after the Nazis ended denominational education in 1937. Now, Beckers and other spokesmen called for a renewed alliance of home, church, and school. Dumont Kenny also interviewed Bishop Van de Velder of Aachen, who announced that he was "pleased with the present temporary school setup, which he considers similar to the pre-Nazi system." The revival of Germany's educational system had begun, and, if the Aachen experience was any indication, it would revive along pre-1933 lines.[8]

Growing Pains

Aachen was a relatively small city in the German scheme of things, and, having been captured for nearly eight months by the time of the surrender, it was not typical of the way the Occupation began, either for Military Government or for the Germans. Only in May, 1945, did the vastness of the educators' mission reveal itself. Following E&RA's staff meeting of May 14 at Höchst, many of the senior officers scattered to the various districts of the U.S. Zone to observe civil-affairs field detachments and to advise them on educational procedures. Their findings were mixed at best and indicated that education reconstruction had made a difficult start. It was obvious from the beginning that any program that had a chance of succeeding needed massive assistance, not only from the G-5 detachments but also from specialized Military Government units, such as Special Branch, which was responsible for denazification, and from the Counterintelligence Corps (CIC) and the Information Control Division (ICD). Most important of all was the degree to which the Germans themselves were willing to cooperate in reforming their own educational system, even when that meant purges and disruptions. E&RA in May, 1945, faced enormous responsibilities in a potentially poisonous environment.

One of the first to report on his activities in the field was the peripatetic Oscar Reinmuth, who had just completed an inspection tour of the Third Army area in Bavaria. He observed that little had yet been accomplished in the way of educational change, in part because of "the legitimate demand of more immediate problems of higher priority." Restoring the minimum life-supporting services in Germany's ruined population centers took precedence. But Reinmuth predicted that the G-5 detachments, if left to their own devices, would not accomplish even the crucial first tasks of educational reform. Of the thirty-five field detachments he had visited, only one had assigned an officer to full-time education duties. The rest, regarding education as a third or fourth priority, had given the job to inexperienced junior officers, and this meant, in effect, that nothing was being accomplished. Reinmuth was able through force of personality to persuade the other detachments to tackle their education responsibilities, and though he was gratified at the energy and enthusiasm the young officers displayed, he was dismayed by their lack of other qualifications. He stated: "Owing to the peculiar situation in the educational and religious world in Germany, an officer . . . charged with the supervision of these fields of activity, should be a man not only with a graduate degree but with a full background of educational experience." A few officers did possess those qualifications, but detachment leaders were reluctant to assign them to education duties.[9]

Just as discouraging was the nearly total ignorance on the part of U.S. Military Government field officers as to what initial education policy was supposed to be. In 1944 the US Group CC had produced a technical manual for education officers, to provide solutions for field problems. To his dismay Reinmuth discovered that the months of intensive effort that had been spent in developing the 130-page SHAEF *Technical Manual of Education and Religious Affairs* were seemingly in vain: the manual was nowhere to be found. He finally located some copies at Third Army Headquarters and distributed them to half of the field detachments. Advising the adoption of its five-point program, he remarked:

> Fundamentally, our work is one of supervision, not actual administration; hence the vetting and appointment of a *Schulrat* in each Kreis is the first step in a five-point program. The second step is to have this person gather the factual information regarding the schools, teachers, and equipment. . . . Third, is the vetting by CIC of prospective school officials and teachers on the basis of the *Fragebogen* passed out by the *Schulrat*. Fourth is a formal request for permission to reopen the first four years of the elementary school . . . and fifth is a requisition of the necessary number of emergency textbooks to be provided by SHAEF.[10]

Reinmuth's practical advice produced some results, for the detachments increased their efforts in the educational program. "There is strong unanimity of feeling," he reported, "on the part of all commanding officers of the detachments visited that the educational program is of the greatest importance, and they heartily welcome the program outlined." The Army had reasons of its own to cooperate: the sooner the schools opened their doors, the sooner would potentially mischievous children be off the streets. In Bavaria the detachments were keenly aware of the problem. In Coburg and Bad Kissingen, Military Government teams reported considerable juvenile delinquency, and in Bamberg two youths had set an ammunition train on fire—with spectacular results.[11]

Loss of physical plant posed another major problem. Reinmuth reported that in Bavaria virtually all the school buildings that had escaped destruction were now in use as billets, military hospitals, or displaced-persons camps. He estimated, however, that by autumn enough educational plant would be vacated to allow opening the first four years of elementary school. Shortages of politically cleared teaching staffs were widespread. Once again, as at Aachen, the Americans were counting on using women who had not been coerced into joining the party and older, unencumbered men. In Bavaria, at least, the detachments' preliminary findings were that over 50 percent of all elementary-school teachers had been party members. "Opinion of the Military Government officers is that reliable teachers can be found in sufficient numbers, but not always in strict conformity with the letter of the [denazification] directive." At that early stage the detachments were prepared to use common sense when a teacher's credentials were open to interpretation. (Within a few months, however, that flexibility would disappear.) Reinmuth also recorded that in Bavaria the local reaction to the SHAEF emergency textbooks was mixed, just as it had been in Aachen.[12]

Military Government's own organizational structure added to the general confusion because of the two chains of command: one for US Group CC and its replacement, Military Government, and one for SHAEF and its successor, United States Forces, European Theater (USFET). Eventually the tangled lines were sorted out, but for the moment the field detachments resisted taking bold initiatives without orders from higher authority. Despite such bureaucratic snarls, Reinmuth expressed confidence that Bavaria's elementary schools could be reopened as early as September; the longer-range problems of secondary and higher education could be tackled later. He reported that Military Government had established cordial relations with the Catholic hierarchy but urged caution in handling confessional schools: "every attempt should be made not to alienate the Church's connection with the school program."[13]

Other senior E&RA officers were less optimistic than Reinmuth. Marshall Knappen was less concerned with initial start-up procedures than he was in developing a long-term field organization for E&RA. What chiefly worried him was the fact that available education professionals were not being used effectively in the Military Government detachments. After visiting Bavaria and Württemberg-Baden, he forwarded a report to the highest echelons of Military Government. Robert Murphy, who was now General Lucius Clay's political adviser, was horrified by it. Knappen, a former Rhodes Scholar and one of the three most experienced personnel in E&RA, predicted nothing less than a disaster for America's education programs:

> The status of the Education and Religious Affairs field organization leaves much to be desired. While a very few additional officers are reported as assigned to this work, qualified Education and Religious Affairs men are still being diverted to noneducational activities, such as general administration or intelligence work. It is estimated that as yet there are not more than fifteen (15) officers working in the Education and Religious Affairs field in the entire ETO. Furthermore, liaison between field officers and higher headquarters is very poor. . . .
>
> Without exception all the Education and Religious Affairs officers consulted were most discontented with their status and most discouraged about the prospect for effective future service in this field. . . . They feel themselves faced with a stupendous task in which the higher authorities have so far shown very little interest. Most of the men, including several former college presidents and others of similar caliber, came in as Captains or even Lieutenants, and, after nearly two years of active duty, only one of them has received promotion, and that was while on a noneducational assignment. . . . NEARLY ALL THE EDUCATION AND RELIGIOUS AFFAIRS OFFICERS ARE ANXIOUS TO LEAVE THE SERVICE AS SOON AS POSSIBLE, AND, UNLESS DEFINITE AND DRASTIC ACTION IS TAKEN TO REMEDY THIS SITUATION WITHOUT DELAY, THERE CAN BE NO PROSPECT OF AN EFFECTIVE SUPERVISION OF THE ADMINISTRATION OF THE GERMAN EDUCATIONAL SYSTEM.[14]

Knappen urged an immediate shift in priorities and proposed as a first step a vast printing program, to produce at least four million textbooks rather than the few thousand produced in Aachen. He also urged Military Government to make available the two hundred qualified E&RA officers originally recruited by the Army "so that a dozen men are not asked to reorganize, from the ground up, the schools systems for a population roughly equivalent to that of the United States west of the Mississippi."[15]

Robert Murphy promptly sent a synopsis of Knappen's report to General Clay, warning him of a disaster in the making. "I am seriously disturbed by the picture which the report draws," he wrote. "It is apparent that our whole program for the reestablishment of a sane and democratic system of education in Germany is in jeopardy, primarily at the present stage because of a lack of emphasis on personnel needs. It would appear that men to complement and oversee a vigorous educational program are not being used for the purpose for which they were originally earmarked."

Murphy recommended that Military Government allocate the necessary education officers immediately. One of Clay's aides read Murphy's communications and replied only that the general "has the problem very much in mind."[16] Emergency textbook production rose sharply, but the personnel situation remained unchanged. For example, in August, 1945, Edward Y. Hartshorne, a higher-education officer, investigated conditions in the university towns of the U.S. Zone. They were bad enough, but he also reported the disappearance of a number of education officers from the G-5 detachments, "who left word that they had departed for the United States."[17]

Given the massive redeployments and manpower reductions in Europe at war's end, it was perhaps inevitable that E&RA should experience acute personnel woes. A kind of "demobilization fever" set in, to use one historian's phrase, and its spirit infected all Military Government officers. Many field Military Government personnel who had been respected professionals in civilian life had experienced frustration in uniform by being kept waiting in the wings for so long. Military Government's dual-command muddle proved to be the last straw for many, who redeployed for home and for renewed civilian careers. By the end of 1945 the dual-command issue was settled when OMGUS became the sole headquarters in Berlin, issuing policy and coordinating implementation procedures.[18]

The new, simplified, command structure helped E&RA overcome some of its problems in the field, but it still remained a minor force in the Occupation machinery. Certain civil-affairs functions, such as Legal, Economic, Public Safety, and Manpower, achieved division status, and SHAEF's Psychological Warfare Division, now known as Information Control Division (ICD), continued to enjoy unusual independence and recognition. E&RA, however, remained a mere section until January, 1946; it then rose to branch level. Not until March, 1948, did it become a full division. Its highest-ranking officers were Taylor and Knappen, who served as captains in the war, were raised to majors in the summer of 1945, and finally became lieutenant colonels that winter. Unfortunately, on the chessboard of Military Government, the central figures wore generals' stars. However, inconspicuousness also carried occasional advantages. Because of their low status, the E&RA staff did not suffer the fate of other expert but junior-grade officers, who saw their posts taken over by senior military officers in the mad scramble for secure positions at the outset of the Occupation. Had E&RA achieved division status in 1945, John Taylor would not have been its director.[19]

E&RA sections or branches were established for each Land Military Government in the U.S. Zone. Bavaria, Greater Hesse, Württemberg-Baden, Bremen Enclave, and Berlin Sector formed the five Länder, each with an organization patterned after OMGUS in Berlin. Theoretically, each branch chief received directives from E&RA, OMGUS, and dispensed them to the Land E&RA staff and to each German education ministry. However, in practice the branch E&RA chiefs could exercise considerable independence, and much depended on their working relationship with the senior Military Government officer, the Land director. In Bavaria, for example, the Land director sometimes played as strong a role in E&RA affairs as Taylor or his successor. Land directors also had the final decision on selecting senior education personnel. Typically, each branch had specialists for religious affairs, for elementary, secondary, and higher education, for youth activities, for adult education, and for library and textbooks. Depending on the needs of the Land, there might be several staff members assigned to a given field. Then too, depending on demand, a staff section might be increased or decreased in size to meet specific program demands. Textbook analysts were sorely needed in the first year of the Occupation, but that demand began to taper off as German educational staffs took on greater responsibility. There were zone-wide freezes on all Military Government personnel hirings, followed by increases or, in January, 1947, a 10 percent reduction in staff. Sometimes theater personnel moved into E&RA from specialist organizations after their particular mission had been completed. Some officers transferred from the G-5 civil-affairs detachments. Others came to E&RA from the Strategic Bombing Survey, Field Information Agency, Technical (FIAT), and United Nations Relief and Rehabilitation Agency (UNRRA), among others. However, the addition of new staff from the theater and from E&RA recruitment in the United States amounted to only a trickle. Until 1947 E&RA consisted of forty officers, and it did not grow appreciably until 1948. Sharp limits on personnel had a direct bearing on E&RA's methods of operation and on its goals.[20]

In July, 1945, Taylor established his E&RA headquarters in Berlin with a staff of about six officers, most of whom were frequently on inspection trips in the Zone during the first hectic summer of the Occupation. E&RA's parent organization at that stage was the Public Health and Welfare Branch (PH&W), led by a former U.S. surgeon general, Morrison C. Stayer. Then, in 1946, E&RA came under the direction of the Internal Affairs and Communications Division (IA&C), where it remained for most of the Occupation. With a regular Army commission as major general, Stayer outranked all other officers in the theater. Since he sympathized with the educators' plight in being so far down on the Military Government ladder, he would sometimes bypass the many echelons of the bureaucracy and place education reports directly on Lucius Clay's desk. Taylor, like so many other junior officers, had high praise for Clay's administrative abilities, and he utilized his weekly staff meetings to air problems directly before the Military Governor.[21] Direct access to the highest office was helpful, but it did little to relieve the shortcomings that Knappen, Reinmuth, and other E&RA officers had observed at the outset of the Occupation. Thus, when high-ranking War Department officers visited Berlin that summer, the E&RA staff in Berlin made a point of discussing the situation directly.

The problem E&RA faced was hardly unknown to Washington. When Assistant Secretary of War John J. McCloy and the CAD's General John Hilldring accompanied President Truman to the Potsdam Conference, they paid a call on the E&RA offices. Taylor's staff recounted all the obstacles they had encountered, ranging from a lack of basic transportation for education specialists to morale problems engendered by two years of military service without recognition or promotion. Most important of all, the staff urged McCloy and Hilldring to redouble their efforts to find a well-known educational figure as chief of E&RA. "Mr. McCloy," the staff minutes read, "indicated that these matters would be taken back to Washington and an effort would be made to get speedy action."[22]

Denazification: General

The most perplexing problem confronting Military Government was denazification. A central requirement of JCS 1067, the SHAEF *Handbook*, and the Potsdam Declaration, it was considered a crucial goal of the Occupation; yet, as policy, it proved maddeningly difficult to execute. In all areas of public life it affected Germans and Military Government alike in their efforts to rebuild, and education proved in no way immune to the vicissitudes of this basic policy. Between March and October, 1945, definitions of who was a Nazi changed at least three times. Eventually, articles in the American press critical of denazification efforts to date hardened Military Government's resolve to impose stricter standards and definitions. The problem was that, no matter what criteria were established for deciding who had been genuine party members, glaring injustices were bound to occur. For example, in its March, 1945, directive, SHAEF G-5 decided that persons who had joined the party after January, 1933, could retain their positions if they had not held any rank or leadership position or had not contributed to the furtherance of National Socialism in some significant way. Later, when accusations appeared in the American press that military authorities had been too soft on the Nazis in Aachen, Military Government showed itself to be surprisingly sensitive, especially when these accusations appeared in prestigious newspapers.[23] Thus, by June it became mandatory to remove anyone who had ever joined the party at any time or had held public office after 1933. The G-5 detachments then began to complain that such drastic standards made their task impossible, since no qualified Germans were left for creating a civil administration. Thus, when the press became quiescent, for the moment, the draconian interpretations of Nazism began to soften. On June 29 a Military Government directive appeared that established a cutoff date of May 1, 1937, for party membership on the grounds that, after that time, German professionals had had to join up or else lose their jobs. The G-5 detachments worked under these new guidelines through the rest of the summer.

Then articles once again appeared in the *New York Times*, the *New Republic*, and elsewhere, attacking Military Government's willingness to work with conservative German officials, such as Bavaria's newly appointed minister president, Fritz Schaeffer. Although an anti-Nazi, with concentration-camp credentials to prove it, Schaeffer was not averse to retaining questionable German assistants in high public office. The Americans were unprepared to deal with an enigma like him. Then Raymond Daniell of the *New York Times* launched an exposé of Nazis retaining important posts in private business and industry. Following Schaeffer's forced resignation, a climax finally came in September when Clay's deputy, General Clarence L. Adcock, and his civilian aide, Walter L. Dorn, traveled to Munich to investigate the matter and were followed by a team of curious reporters. It was then that General George Patton made his supremely inept observation that "The Nazi thing is just like a Democrat-Republican election fight."[24]

All hope of an orderly denazification effort vanished. Even as Patton was being stripped of his Army command, Clay hurriedly promulgated Military Government Law No. 8, prohibiting employment of Nazis either in private or in the public sector in any capacity other than common labor. After Patton's fall, the lesser commanding officers of Military Government took no chances. An enormous new wave of denazification rolled through the American Zone in October.[25] This, then, was the unsettling backdrop against which America's education staff began denazifying the teaching ranks in Germany's educational system.

After the G-5 civil-affairs detachments had restored basic services in the U.S. Zone, they were able to turn their attention to longer-term problems, such as reviving local government, the local economy, and social services, such as the school systems. Progress in reviving education depended heavily on the denazification initiatives of individual detachment commanders. A chronicler for the Third Army in Bavaria recorded that in one *Landkreis* an inspecting officer discovered "a detachment at the beginning of July which had given no thought to the matter of education." Another claimed that it was too understaffed to make the attempt.[26] Fortunately, these were exceptions. The majority were busily appointing a *Schulrat* (superintendent) in each school district and conducting surveys of teaching staffs and learning materials. In midsummer, when the teams were working under the milder June 29 denazification directive, one historical report indicates that the detachments were trying conscientiously to abide by it: "In the choice of a *Schulrat* the spirit and letter of the prescriptions for denazification had to be loyally observed, and there is every indication that the price of their observance in inconvenience, apparent loss of efficiency, and even injustice was loyally paid by every detachment in the field."[27]

It was perplexing to discover that so many former party members were not disagreeable, boorish tyrants. When politically acceptable Germans interceded for colleagues who had been party members, the task became even less pleasant, but the Americans stuck grimly to the job. Thus, when Detachment H6D3 in Regensburg received a plea by five reliable nonparty teachers that their able superintendent be retained, the request was denied.[28] He had joined the party in 1935. Many detachments found it difficult to apply even the milder 1937 cutoff date categorically. Even so, they recognized that they must adhere to uniform standards. "Yet," one report concluded, "it must be admitted that many influential members of the community regarded the dismissals of some nominal Nazis as an injustice." Detachment I14D3 at Waldmünchen in Bavaria uncovered instances where Catholics had joined the party in order to hinder its influence in the schools as well as to save their jobs. "Many appeals on their behalf were made, and had to be diplomatically answered," the report continued. The detachment was embarrassed when the local priest also tried to intercede. They were able to "sidetrack" him into "an engagement to survey the textbooks in the local schools."[29]

Many detachments were pleasantly surprised to find German civilians cooperating in the selection of acceptable administrative personnel. The Regensburg detachment reported that "most decisions about the office of *Schulrat* were made with the advice of the civilians best entitled to be consulted, and . . . in several instances the *Schulräte* who were temporarily appointed took the initiative in finding their own better-qualified successors and consented to serve with or under them on *Kreis* school boards."[30]

Denazification of teaching staffs varied in severity, depending in part on the urgency Military Government assigned to it at a given time but chiefly on the degree of power that National Socialism had enjoyed in a given community. In May, Oscar Reinmuth had already indicated that the stringent denazification measures emanating from SHAEF in March were not likely to be strictly enforced.[31] The June 29 directive appeared more realistic, but it, too, sprang some surprises. Investigations in the larger cities showed that a very high percentage of teaching staffs had been party members. However, much had depended on the political inclinations of the individual *Schulrat* as to whether a school district was heavily indoctrinated or not. At Kitzingen and Mainburg in Bavaria, the ardent Nazi *Schulräte* had been highly successful. All teachers on their staffs had joined.

In Garmisch-Partenkirchen, on the other hand, only about 20 percent of the staff had to be dismissed as former Nazis. More typical were towns like Donauwörth, where 40 of a staff of 129 teachers were dismissed, or Bamberg, where 162 out of 362 were removed. For large regions, like that occupied by the Third Army in Bavaria, the best estimates that summer were that the denazification purge affected between 35 and 40 percent of the teachers.[32] The figure reached 50 percent by 1946.

Originally, the SHAEF *Handbook* had established its "black, gray, and white lists" of German educational personnel based on German guides and directories. Those on the black list faced instant dismissal because they had been war criminals, high administrative officials, or responsible officers in party-affiliated professional organizations like the N.S. *Lehrerbund* (Teachers League), N.S. *Dozentenbund* (University Instructors League), or the N.S.D. *Studentenbund* (Students League). The list also included anyone who had held office in the party itself, in the SS, the SA, *Gestapo*, or *Sicherheitsdienst*, all of whom were in automatic-arrest categories anyway. Nazi-appointed rectors of universities and all staff of the avowedly Nazi *Adolf Hitler Schulen*, *Napolas* (National Political Institutes), and the SS *Ordensburgen* (universities), plus adult leaders of the Hitler Youth (HJ) and League of German Maidens (BDM) also figured prominently on the black list.

The gray list included individuals of lower rank as subject to discretionary removal: *Schulräte*, regional administrators, professors, minor officers in party-affiliated professional organizations of lawyers, civil servants, and medical doctors, plus nominal members of the party or SA. The gray list concluded with individuals "who in their public speeches or writings have actively and voluntarily propagated National Socialism, militarism, or racialism."

The white list was composed of persons "whose character, professional standing, experience, and political reliability render them especially suitable to be placed in positions of responsibility." All together, five thousand names appeared on E&RA's three lists before the Occupation actually began, but the staff acknowledged that the lists were spotty.[33] Moreover, it was a dismaying fact that a majority of the Military Government detachments never received a copy of the SHAEF *Technical Manual*. Instead, the *Fragebogen* became the basic device for judging a German educator's political background. All adult Germans answered its 131 questions under oath and with witnesses' signatures. The local Special Branch, a subordinate office of the Public Safety Division, evaluated it. Special Branch investigators then placed the respondent in one of five categories: anti-Nazi, non-Nazi, discretionary removal (no adverse recommendation), discretionary removal (adverse recommendation), and mandatory removal. If falsification was suspected, Special Branch, Policy Enforcement Branch, and the CIC could investigate. The entire party-membership files, plus large numbers of affiliated-organization membership lists, had fallen into Allied hands, so that, presumably, the education officers and other specialist staffs could verify the *Fragebogen*. But Military Government lacked adequate means for distributing the lists to the field organization, where they would be of real use, and the bad situation was made worse by inadequate investigative or clerical staff, little or no copying equipment, and, above all, no time in which to weigh properly the records of thousands of individuals awaiting clearance in any given district. Only in the late spring of 1946 could education officers and others verify the accuracy of a *Fragebogen*, and by that time it was too late to save E&RA from public embarrassment over denazification in the institutions of higher learning.[34]

Denazification proved irksome for all branches of Military Government, especially those, like E&RA, that were attempting a reconstruction program requiring skilled personnel. The alternately harsh and lenient attitudes adopted by Military Government affected the classrooms as surely as they did industry or the civil service, and the near hysteria following the Patton affair came at precisely the moment the elementary schools in the American Zone were beginning to reopen their doors.

By mid-October, about 80 percent of eligible schoolchildren were again receiving instruction, although teacher-pupil ratios stood at 1:80 and sometimes 1:120. Replacement teachers often had little or no training. Theodor Heuss, historian, man of letters, and an anti-Nazi, had agreed to become the minister of culture in Württemberg-Baden when the Occupation began. Through the summer he and the Land school officials struggled valiantly with the problem of teacher shortages. The Americans helped establish emergency teacher-training courses for the mass of raw replacements. Then Heuss established competitive examinations for the teacher aspirants and created curricula for the emergency courses, which were to run for three to six months. Somehow he found physical facilities for the program. Throughout the zone similar efforts by Germans were under way to make good the loss of skilled teachers.[35] In Landsberg, Bavaria, Detachment IlF3 was highly encouraged by the enthusiasm exhibited by "a conference of 120 enthusiastic former teachers, new applicants, and administrative officials." A neighboring detachment, I1F2 at Schwabmünchen, reported similar results.[36]

By autumn the new wave of denazification threatened to overwhelm even the boldest feats of innovation. In Württemberg over half of all teachers had, by this time, fallen into the mandatory-removal category when local commanders began interpreting the two discretionary-removal categories as mandatory removals. In some places dismissals topped 80 percent. In desperation Heuss wrote to Military Government: "Owing to the extremely large number of removals, all [of our] schemes and the trouble taken are in vain." The emergency had deepened to the point that completely untrained individuals were about to take charge of the Land classrooms. School curricula were not arriving for the newcomers because of administrative failures and chaos in the mails. "The consequence," Heuss continued, "is that not only do our schools . . . sink to a very low standard, but the education of our children, too, which is of urgent necessity, is impossible along the lines wished by Military Government as well as by the Department of Culture."

Heuss felt that, of all the persons hastily dismissed, only about 10 or 15 percent had been convinced Nazis. The rest had joined under compulsion. He reminded Military Government that a priority target for the Nazis had been the Land ministries of culture and education. The new Nazi education ministers had rapidly fastened on superintendents, principals, and, gradually, the teachers, especially the males. Since teachers in rural villages were among the most articulate and competent community members, they became a natural target too. The coercion had been remorseless. "But only he who has lived twelve years under the Nazi terror can judge how enormous this pressure was and how much heroism and political insight were required to resist it," Heuss wrote. Having himself suffered humiliation and muzzling under the Nazis, he made it clear that he favored denazification but not the mechanical kind now being introduced. "Active Nazis must be recognized and eliminated," he stated. Heuss even proposed punishing those who had not resisted Hitler by imposing fines, demotions, temporary suspensions, and the like. He also warned against too great a dependence on youthful teacher replacements. Despite betrayals of their heritage, the older generation had at least been raised at a time before the Nazis could stifle truth, humanity, and religion. By contrast, the youth had been reared in a national cult of violence, intense nationalism, and hatred in the schools, in the Hitler youth organizations, in compulsory labor service, and then, most chillingly, in the armed forces. "They do not know peace," Heuss stated. "Many of them have grown up in a mental atmosphere that glorified force, ignoring, nay, violently denying, education in a religious and Christian spirit." Family life had gone to ruin with fathers at the front, mothers in the factory, and children concentrated in the evacuation camps, where education was replaced by National Socialist propaganda. The thought of turning these politically "unencumbered" young adults loose in the classroom was daunting. Heuss preferred the older generation. "It would not be difficult to scrape away their brown veneer and reawaken their powers of good, for which I am ready to answer and to be fully responsible. Give [us] your confidence and authority. We promise to deliver the teachers from Nazism and to make them agents of new and better ideas, enabling them to educate youth in the right spirit."[37]

The plea was as earnest as it was eloquent, and under different circumstances Heuss's opinion might have carried more weight. But, as one Land detachment in Württemberg-Baden observed, a "great fear" now swept through Military Government. MG Law No. 8 on denazification had appeared so hastily that many detachments first learned of it over Armed Forces radio. It contained ambiguities, and, with a witchhunt developing, most responsible officials wished to appear too zealous rather than too slack. By November Heuss's deputy, Theodor Bäuerle, reported that, as a result of the new denazification drive, 70 to 90 percent of all teachers had been dismissed. In *Kreis* Vaihingen/Enz, where nearly 150 teachers had been employed, only 20 now remained, supplemented by 40 emergency replacements. To compound the difficult situation, many replacements were North Germans, whom the Württemberg children understood only with great difficulty. Notwithstanding the presence of youthful teaching aides, the average age of teachers exceeded fifty. Bäuerle painted a picture of disconsolate teacher-outcasts watching the schools degenerate, manned by the aged or, worse, by the potentially dangerous youth auxiliaries.[38]

Such reports caused mounting concern in Berlin. By December, Taylor and others found gross inconsistencies in the application of denazification procedures from district to district or within the branches of Military Government. CIC had issued an "Arrest Handbook" that autumn, calling for the blanket arrest of all members of the *Höherendienst*, or middle to upper echelons of the German civil service. The result of this was that secondary-school teachers who carried the rank of *Studienrat* fell into the automatic-arrest category. "This has come to light due to our efforts to get secondary schools open," one E&RA staffer wrote in early December. Taylor contacted the CIC branch chief in Frankfurt, and, after several conferences, CIC agreed to call on all detention camps to establish review boards for imprisoned teachers. CIC was already aware that its automatic arrest of higher civil servants had netted many innocents, and as early as November 4 it instructed its personnel "that members of the *Höherendienst* falling into the automatic-arrest category do not have to be held but can be taken into custody and then released to continue their work if there is nothing else against them." More sensible than the blanket-arrest orders in the "Arrest Handbook," the November 4 instructions were an improvement, but they received only partial distribution. Not even the most optimistic Military Government officer claimed that denazification had gone smoothly. "I am sure many people were thrown out who should not have been thrown out and vice versa," Taylor later admitted. The gaffe of automatically arresting secondary-school teachers reinforced that assessment.[39]

Secondary education posed special problems for the E&RA staff, and not only with respect to arrest categories. Because opening the elementary schools had first priority, the higher grades had to wait their turn. It was not until October, when the lower schools were functioning again, that attention could turn to Germany's elite secondary schools. At Taylor's request, General Stayer sent a memorandum to General Clarence L. Adcock, Clay's chief of staff, calling attention to the need to reopen secondary schools. There were compelling reasons: "While the proportion of secondary schools to elementary schools is much smaller in Germany than in the United States, and the number of students comparatively smaller, the resumption of the work of these schools is of great importance in realizing the objectives of Military Government." Stayer noted that the students in attendance came mostly from "influential homes" and that within a few years they would "normally proceed to positions of influence and importance in the life of Germany." Of more immediate concern was the fact that they formed an age group potentially dangerous to the Occupation forces. After securing the concurrence of all other concerned agencies of Military Government, preparations for reopening the secondary schools began in October. The first institutions opened their doors in December. To be sure, they, like the elementary schools, suffered from a shortage in every conceivable category of physical plant, and their teaching staffs had also been decimated. Stayer observed that "the almost total lack of acceptable textbooks" could be bridged by the teachers' superior preparation and by their ability to improvise with syllabi and other materials at hand. There were problems, to be sure, but, as Stayer concluded: "The advantages of getting the work of these schools under way at this moment far outweigh this and other difficulties which may be encountered." Denazification of teachers and the vetting of learning materials in secondary schools took place in much the same way as with the elementary schools.[40]

Denazification: The Universities

Denazification of the institutions of higher education did not proceed in the same way as in the elementary- and secondary-school systems. One major difference was that the initial process of screening and the preparation for reopening reverted to the Germans; there was no intense involvement of G-5 detachments, Special Branch, PEB, CIC, or other Military Government agencies. A second factor was the rapidity with which the universities reopened their doors in the American Zone, a phenomenon that Military Government had not anticipated and that came about in an unexpected way. There were seven universities in the U.S. Zone, plus four polytechnic institutes, various professional schools, teacher-training

institutions, agricultural colleges, and the like. On orders from SHAEF
all of them had ceased operations in May, 1945. Originally no timetable
had been set for the higher institutions to resume instruction, but during
the summer of 1945 the fact that millions of Germans were sick, under-
nourished, or disabled provided heavy pressure to reopen at least the
medical faculties of some of the universities. Once they began functioning,
support faculties in the sciences, administrative offices, and then the faculties of philosophy clamored to reopen. By December, 1945, months
earlier than planned, most of the universities began functioning again.
The haste with which the reopenings took place, plus the unique fashion
in which denazification occurred, laid the basis for future criticism of
higher-education reform in the American press. It also handed E&RA a
major setback in its independence of operation within Military Government and in the image it projected to the public.

Major General Morrison C. Stayer was not a conventional military man.
One of the few officers in Military Government to experience at first hand
America's previous occupation of Germany, in the Rhineland from 1919
to 1923, Stayer returned to Central Europe in 1945 as chief surgeon at
USFET. He expressed grave concern about the state of public health and
warned that the Germans' official daily ration of 1,150 calories per day
was not enough to prevent disease caused by malnutrition. Military Government nutritional survey teams confirmed that 60 percent of all Germans
were on a diet leading to starvation, and Stayer promptly raised the specter
of "disease and unrest," a loophole in JCS 1067 that could be used to
justify humanitarian relief. With a worldwide food shortage in the offing,
neither Stayer nor General Clay could do much at first for the German
people's nutritional well-being, but medical care was another story. In
July, at an E&RA staff conference in Berlin, Stayer painted "an overall
picture of the present state of disorganization, desolation, starvation, and
sickness in Germany, [and an] increasing number of suicides."[41]

A week before, in the company of Edward Y. Hartshorne, Stayer had
embarked on a lengthy trip through the zone to inspect potential medical
facilities. On one trip they were joined by John J. Muccio, an assistant
to Robert Murphy, who shared their interest in Germany's renowned
universities. Muccio recalled that, "en route to Heidelberg, General Stayer
talked about opening the medical school there and several other medical
schools to meet the crying need for doctors. He stated that the idea was
to get from the German Army those medical students whose period of
instruction had been interrupted by the war." Muccio respected Stayer's
concern for public health. Nevertheless, he was concerned by what he saw
at Heidelberg and reported his impressions to Robert Murphy: "Neither
the General nor Dr. Hartshorne knew whether the faculty at Heidelberg
had been vetted and screened, and Dr. Hartshorne stated that no definite

system of control had yet been established at Heidelberg." Upon arrival, they parted for the day. "However," Muccio recounted,

> when we met again at the Europa Hotel, the Captain of MG appeared, and the three talked about affairs at the University. Apparently, the faculty had met and had decided to go back to the organizational setup obtaining at the University prior to the Nazis. Also, the faculty was having a meeting the following day to elect a new rector. Some of the medical faculty members have indicated to General Stayer that they have already "obtained permission of Military Government." The MG Captain said he knew nothing about such authorization. In the course of the conversation, reference was made to a Dr. Krehl, formerly head of the medical school, allegedly an outstanding Nazi, who would not be reinstated as head of the school but who would be allowed to take the chair in pathology.

Muccio was not slow to draw the consequences of so haphazard a revival at Heidelberg:

> On the return trip I expressed my concern at taking steps to reopen an institution not only of such national but international importance without first completely assuring that all active Nazis had been removed. I pointed out that reopening of such a school would immediately have a great deal of publicity, and it was all-important, therefore, that the institution be completely denazified, not only on account of its importance at the institution itself, but on account of the great psychological effect it would have on the Germans generally as an indication of whether we really mean business or not in eradicating Nazism.[42]

Despite Muccio's concern, Heidelberg University reopened its medical facilities on August 15, 1945. Publicity surrounding the event was as heavy as predicted, not least because the university's famed physician-turned-philosopher, Karl Jaspers, offered the opening address. Then, on September 3, Marburg University revived its medical faculty, followed by Munich a few months later. Hartshorne returned to E&RA headquarters in Berlin immediately following the first reopenings. He pointed to great progress in some details but warned that the vetting of faculties was incomplete. Later that month, at another E&RA conference, Hartshorne finally obtained agreement from Taylor and General Stayer on uniform denazification procedures for the universities. The timing was not auspicious, and events were to prove that neither E&RA nor the public had heard the last of Germany's medical faculties and their parent universities.[43]

For the moment, however, public reaction was receptive to Heidelberg's new beginning and to Karl Jaspers' opening address. With his training as a physician, his international fame as a philosopher, and his well-known disdain for the Nazis, Jaspers' was the proper voice to be heard on that occasion. "This is a great day for our university," he began. "It is a new beginning after the ruin which had overtaken the university for twelve years." Despite the devastation, there was much to be thankful for, because Germany's conquerors were not barbarians, intent on liquidating universities, as the Nazis had done in eastern Europe. He reminded his young veterans-turned-students that the German medical profession, takers of the Hippocratic Oath, had condoned euthanasia, murder of the mentally handicapped, pseudo-scientific "race hygiene" institutes, and similar horrors. Jaspers then identified a dangerous trend: overspecialization had robbed whole faculties of any sense of shared knowledge or of the interdependence of ideas, thus allowing the Nazis to seduce the naive specialists, who best suited their purposes. "These problems can be solved only when the whole of our world is alive in the individual scholar," he concluded. It was inappropriate to speak of a bright new future, and the best that the aged Jaspers, a witness to new beginnings in 1918 and 1933, could offer was "hard work toward remote ends and with very little hope for immediate happiness." For now, the mastering of the sciences, a struggle for truth, and the building of a new soul would be the students' only rewards.[44]

Acclaimed abroad, Jaspers' speech provoked controversy and outrage among many who heard it at first hand. Military Government representatives reported that a majority of the students reacted angrily when he asserted that scholarly and intellectual activity had returned to Germany only through outside force. By using the Socratic method of questioning, the aged philosopher tried to deflect one young critic's emotionalism during a subsequent discussion of the "truth" of what he had said, but the mood of his listeners remained sullen and unconvinced. August, 1945, lay too close to the war for many observers to view events dispassionately.[45]

Strong overtones of moral philosophy and religion were present in Jaspers' address, so that a question hung palpably in the air: If the medical faculty now had the right to open its doors, then why should the other academic disciplines remain in limbo? As Hartshorne later described it: "The cat was now out of the bag, and everyone else came forward with plans, proposals, and arguments to prove that his field as well should get under way. Doctors without the natural sciences would be 'inadequately trained'; without philosophy and the humanities they would be 'cultural boors.' "[46] Combining shrewdly, as it did, elements of idealism, practicality, and hope for the future, Jaspers' speech and the event it inaugurated acted as a clarion call to reopen the German universities. Soon a Military Government directive on the revival of institutions of higher learning appeared: "Recent experience has shown that the operation of a part of an institution of higher learning, for example the medical or theological faculty of a university, can continue effectively only when the machinery of the whole university is functioning."[47] General Stayer's practical innovations, based on humanitarian motives, had evoked a vigorous response in the German academic communities.

In September, 1945, a Military Government directive provided for one Military Government university officer for each institution of higher learning, a ratio the British were able to achieve but that came nowhere near fulfillment in the American Zone. In practice, American E&RA university officers had to oversee two, three, or even more institutions in addition to shouldering other duties. German initiative was therefore vital for the rebuilding of academia. The most prominent American officer for university affairs was Edward Y. Hartshorne, who arrived in undamaged Marburg in May, 1945. He contacted Professor Julius Ebbinghaus, who had prepared a radio address on the subject of German responsibility for the actions of the Nazi regime.

With Marburg still intact, Ebbinghaus expressed hope that the SHAEF directive closing all of the universities would soon be lifted, and he was dismayed to learn that no timetable yet existed for reopening them. Marburg might remain inoperative for two years. Ebbinghaus enjoyed a favorable reputation among the Allies, and in their early talks he and Hartshorne explored the possibility of forming a committee to act as liaison with Military Government. The initial goal would be to denazify the university. Then would come the broader questions of restructuring and reforming higher education. Hartshorne informed Ebbinghaus about reform committees in American universities and provided him with reports from his alma mater, Harvard, on "Tenure and Personnel" plus "General Education in a Free Society." He then appointed Ebbinghaus acting rector, and with Hartshorne's advice Ebbinghaus soon organized the first University Planning Committee (UPC) in the U.S. Zone. Such planning committees later became a feature at all of the universities. Hartshorne at first chose to keep his distance: "Although Professor Ebbinghaus invited the MG Education Officer to meet with the committee," he recounted, "it was felt advisable to let it develop a bit on its own initiative." Through the summer of 1945, Marburg's UPC considered what changes were now necessary. Military Government could supply general guidelines and objectives, but, according to Hartshorne, it would be much better if each university "put forward a 'citizens' committee' of this sort, capable of taking charge and not merely working under MG directives but of doing the job—our job—to all intents and purposes for us, and better than we could have done it ourselves."[48]

Marburg's committee comprised a dozen members, all of whom had either suffered under the Nazis or clearly had had nothing to do with them. Through the summer they began to turn out memoranda, such as their "Principles of Personnel Policy," which was more sophisticated than American denazification directives to date. Instead of depending on crude indices of involvement, such as the date an individual might have joined the party, the UPC examined the previous writings and pronouncements of faculty members. Another product of their work was a tract entitled "The Position of the University Teacher as a Civil Servant," which attempted to delineate the conception of academic freedom available to and incumbent upon Germany's civil servant–scholars.[49]

After twelve years of *Gleichschaltung*, or social coercion, the UPC's task was Herculean, and, given the early revival of the medical faculties and the pressure for full-scale operations, no UPC had an opportunity to evaluate the many-faceted problems of higher education at leisure. Yet Marburg's innovation was so successful that American directives on university reopenings, which appeared in November, incorporated the UPC and other features of the Marburg experience wholesale. Each E&RA university officer was ordered "to appoint, after investigation and approval, an outstanding faculty member to act as chairman of its Planning Committee. The Planning Committee will have a membership of five (5) to ten (10) politically acceptable persons from among the university's present and former faculty." In reality, the November directive merely confirmed what was already happening at the universities throughout the zone. On September 21 General Stayer announced that he was satisfied that UPCs could be formed at all universities scheduled for reopening. The November directive simply elaborated on the goals and operations of those committees. They were to provide an ongoing administration and begin framing new constitutions, which were expected within six months. The UPCs also received permission to delegate responsibilities to specialized subcommittees, which would attack isolated problems, including the actual drafting of a constitution, setting forth admission requirements, and planning housing and relief.[50]

An important feature of the UPC was the requirement that it organize an electoral body composed of politically unencumbered professors plus representatives from the *Dozenten*, or junior faculty, to nominate an acting rector. In turn, each faculty would propose an acting dean or director. However, the American university officer made the actual appointment and could "in exceptional instances appoint others." Later, when the new constitution had come into effect, elected officials would replace the appointees. A second vital function of the UPC was its prominent role in denazification. "In the investigation of persons proposed by the UPC for teaching or administrative positions at universities, use will be made of all possible sources of information, including *Fragebogen*, CIC records, university records, German Ministry of Education records, and personal interviews. In all discretionary or petitionable cases weight will be given to the overall estimate of an individual by the UPC." However, the university officer could request "specialist screening personnel" from higher authorities of Military Government. The same standards of denazification would obtain at the universities as for society as a whole. Reflecting the stricter measures in effect after the Schaeffer and Patton affairs, Military Government policy demanded that university personnel found to be compromised were to sever all affiliations with the university. "For example," the directive continued, "unacceptable members of medical faculties will be removed both from their teaching positions and their positions in university clinics and institutes."[51]

In addition to overseeing the activities of the UPC and its subcommittees, appointing temporary officers, and monitoring elections, each Military Government university officer was to analyze all curricular offerings. The university administration would submit a master list of academic courses before each semester "with a brief description of their contents and the names of the instructors." The November directive approved the organizing of preparatory courses for deficiently trained student-veterans, but it insisted that one course be obligatory for all returning students: "There will be included in every preparatory program a reorientation course . . . which will give factual presentations of world thought and of history within the last ten (10) years and will stress particularly Germany's relations to the world politically and economically." Reflecting American concern about Germany's war potential, the directive included a proviso that university rectors report to university officers on research conducted in their institutions. "In general, research or scholarly activity in the humanities will be considered part of the curriculum." However, scientific research that might contribute to Germany's war potential was banned, and the university officer was to insure that the directive was enforced.[52]

Since the universities were to establish standards of admission for students, the American university officers were supposed to insist that the responsible German authorities exclude anyone "seriously compromised with the Nazi party or otherwise unsuitable for university studies." Here the directive was vague in its meaning, and it left standards unclear. Since Nazis and "militarists" were the primary targets, strict interpretations could exclude former military officers, especially career officers. Given the changeability of denazification standards early in the Occupation, this ambiguity portended future trouble.

All students had to complete the ubiquitous *Fragebogen*, and a student committee named by the rector would screen every applicant. They would then forward the results to the American university officer. The directive banned student organizations—the *Verbindungen*, *Burschenschaften*, *Korporationen*, and their alumni organizations, known as *Altherrenbünde*. Religious and self-help organizations could organize with the assent of the rector and the university officer. In theory, student enrollments were limited by the university and its surrounding community's capacity to absorb them; in practice, all universities experienced serious overcrowding.[53]

It was readily apparent that each UPC would carry a trying workload, as would the hard-pressed rector. However, the heaviest burden of responsibility fell on the hapless E&RA university officer. Using his own experience as an example, Hartshorne reported that "Greater Hesse's officer found himself with four institutions to look after, with many responsibilities outside the Land (for example, problems at Heidelberg), and with periodic zonal responsibilities which took him to Berlin once a month, on the average, for consultation."[54] Nor was Hartshorne's situation unique. For a time only two officers oversaw Bavaria's elaborate higher-education system. Hartshorne was unusual in Military Government in that he was eminently qualified for his position, having published extensively about German universities. More typical was Edwin S. Costrell, who, as a young veteran with an M.A. in history from the University of Maine, was responsible for Würzburg and Erlangen universities, many smaller institutions of higher learning, and numerous administrative duties at E&RA headquarters in Munich.[55] Unfortunately, such heavy responsibilities for young, inexperienced staff were more the rule than the exception.

Hartshorne put the best face on a bad situation when he summarized the results of university reopenings a year after the first medical faculties had begun operations. The absence of a central German authority and the inability of Military Government to exert any intensive supervision was not altogether a disadvantage for the university, as he saw it. "On the contrary, this interim period, during which the institutions were thrown so largely on their own resources, forced the university administrations to assume a degree of autonomy and responsibility which took them back and even beyond their well-treasured traditions of academic self-government and forced them to think through many problems for themselves which they might otherwise never have been required to face."[56]

Self-governance did not make the universities' task any easier, and they, too, suffered from the erratic swings in the denazification policy. At first E&RA officers hoped that the purge would be light, but by August, 1945, their optimism had faded. "The results so far show a larger percentage of Nazis than expected, approximately four out of ten falling into the mandatory-removal category," stated one E&RA staffer.[57] There was fear that only enough faculty would survive in the zone to enable three universities to revive. Captain Samuel Shulits visited several technical institutes for E&RA, among them the Stuttgart Technische Hochschule and Hohenheim's agricultural college. In many cases physical destruction was not the major obstacle. "The vetting of teachers and students is the biggest problem in the schools at the present time," he wrote. In one institution

Shulits found a congenial and "very capable" director, who, to his regret, proved to be subject to mandatory removal because he had held high office in Nazi-occupied France.[58]

At Marburg the zone's first "university screening committee," a UPC subcommittee, began removing politically compromised faculty that summer. The screening committee used the 1937 membership date but also examined each individual's "political activity, character, and importance as a teacher and scientist." Marburg's screening committee moved forcefully. The law faculty saw half of its dozen professors dismissed. The sizable medical faculty suffered a 44 percent attrition; philosophy was reduced by 30 percent.[59] The intensity of the purges varied from institution to institution for the same reason that they had fluctuated in the lower schools. Under Hitler, a coercive administrative apparatus in the regional government or in the university often determined how heavily the faculties had turned toward the party. With few exceptions, the law and medicine faculties showed the highest removal rates at the universities. At Heidelberg—a Nazi "showcase" university—the percentages of mandatory removals were greater than elsewhere. Karl Jaspers was the central figure in a "Committee of 13," an unofficial grouping of professors who had an untarnished record of noncooperation with the Nazis. They were disturbed by developments in Heidelberg's leading administrative posts and were able, eventually, to end what they felt was a rearguard action by some to dilute the purge. Heidelberg's Nazi rector, Dr. Schmitthenner, who had also been the minister of education for Baden, appointed an interim rector and then fled before the American armies in April, 1945. Acting Rector Hoops was eighty, English-speaking, and personally unobjectionable, having traveled extensively in England and America before the war. However, Jaspers and others, suspecting that Hoops was not inclined to denazify vigorously, informed Military Government of his questionable elevation. The result was an immediate election, from which former party members and staff with a dubious record were excluded. Jaspers' unofficial "Committee of 13" became the heart of Heidelberg's UPC. Denazification began again, more vigorously. Removals amounted to 64 percent for medicine; 63 percent for political science; 60 percent for the natural sciences; 35 percent for law; and 29 percent for theology.[60]

Universities that, like Munich and Würzburg, had suffered extensive war damage postponed denazification, but, when they accomplished it, their figures proved to be somewhat lower. The reasons for the difference were often subtle and involved such factors as the personalities of the acting rectors, the composition of the UPCs and screening committees, the experience and assertiveness of the American university officer, the degree of cooperation of Land education ministries, and, sometimes, the sheer timing of the denazification effort. At Heidelberg, for example, denazification occurred in the autumn of 1945, at the height of the militant mood following the Patton affair and the issuance of MG Law No. 8. Ardor had cooled a few months later, when the damaged institutions took action.

Denazification of the universities was intense in the American Zone, but Hartshorne noted that it was milder than what he had observed in Berlin. He visited E&RA, OMGUS, periodically to report progress in the universities to Taylor and his staff, and on one occasion he paid a call at Berlin University. There the Soviets had adopted a similar policy of letting the faculty vet itself. "Their purge is more extreme than in our Zone," he informed the E&RA staff. "Any party member is out, and the result is that only about 200 teachers and professors are left out of approximately 700." The Russians had prepared no *Fragebogen*, Hartshorne added. Their methods were rough and ready; they were also effective.[61]

Denazification of student bodies did not proceed with any marked consistency at the universities, in part because no directives had appeared before approval was granted for the hasty reopening of the medical facilities. Each institution therefore grappled with the problem individually. In October Heidelberg's newly arrived university officer, Major Earl L. Crum, a historian and classicist from Lehigh University, was confronted with the imminent reopening of the theology and law faculties in addition to medicine. He was loath to postpone the scheduled reopenings and permitted vetting of students "at leisure, i.e., *after* the University opens, as otherwise too much time will be lost before opening the courses."[62] There was heavy pressure on the university officers not to impede reopenings. How they were to digest the myriad reports from the rector and from the UPC and its various subcommittees was not readily apparent. At Marburg, too, Hartshorne felt uneasy about the lack of specific denazification standards for students. Independently, he established his own requirements: no one subject to mandatory removal could be admitted, nor could SS veterans, *Reifevermerkler* (*Abitur* candidates awaiting their examination), or students who had passed the *Abitur* in 1945.[63]

Of the 1,661 male students who were cleared for admission to Marburg University, fully 96.7 percent were war veterans. Marburg also admitted 641 women, a marked contrast to the Nazis' 10 percent limitation rule.[64] The percentages varied slightly within each institution, but they all pointed to the same obvious fact: Germany's higher-education system must now make good twelve years of deferred training for a generation of young adults. Although the high proportion of veterans among students was universal among all combatant nations following World War II, its manifestation in Germany could easily be cast in a sinister light by unsympathetic or superficial observers. The presence of so many ex-soldiers at universities in the U.S. Zone posed a potential publicity hazard for E&RA.

Denazification figures for students were unreliable, and remained so, because of the deterrent effect that screenings had on potential applicants. If screening became rigorous in one institution, word quickly spread that doubtful applicants should defer their studies or try elsewhere. Figures for politically unacceptable students are therefore not as firm as for faculties, which were officially a part of each institution and could be monitored more closely. Nevertheless, denazification pressures directly affected students who had already been admitted, and the pressures experienced by Military Government sometimes hit students with great severity. Following the toughening of procedures under MG Law No. 8, many Land Military Government officials lumped the two discretionary-removal categories together with mandatory removals. E&RA officers in Bavaria protested against such arbitrary standards.[65] Nor were they alone. In December, 1945, a German denazification committee in Württemberg-Baden petitioned Military Government for greater flexibility in judging students who had held minor ranks in the *Hitler Jugend* or *Bund deutscher Mädel*. As evidence for its case, the German screening committee produced copies of N.S. wartime orders that decreed that all students attending teacher-training colleges were to become members of those institutions' Nazi youth groups. Once admitted, they were deemed to have held minor ranks and so passed into the party as a matter of course. In the denazification hysteria of autumn, 1945, such fine distinctions counted for little. The German committee noted that "most of the students who in the years 1943, 1944, and 1945 were received as members into the party on account of the above decrees were dismissed after screening by the local Military Government."[66]

Thus, reviving Germany's renowned institutions of higher learning proved to be as complex as it was frustrating for E&RA Branch. The challenges to all officers were daunting, and in the first months of the Occupation only Hartshorne emerged as a forceful leader. Starting with Marburg, he evolved a coherent program of denazification and reconstruction that utilized German resources to their fullest without letting events drift. Marburg was at the forefront of institutional development, and it was no coincidence that the first interzonal conference on higher education convened there in June, 1946. Rectors and distinguished scholars from the three Western zones considered reform procedures that were of common concern. Thus began the Marburg *Hochschulgespräche*, or university conferences, out of which, together with parallel British initiatives, emerged the Northwest German Rectors' Conference, which became the foundation for a central office of higher education when the Federal Republic emerged in 1949.[67] Hartshorne openly admired the British method of tackling higher-education problems at an early date. Their rectors' conference, for example, had already organized at Göttingen in September,

1945. While the rectors at Göttingen were impressing British Education Branch with their spirit of cooperation and reforming zeal, the atmosphere was utterly different to the south, in Württemberg-Baden. When the acting rector at Heidelberg, backed by the university senate, petitioned Military Government to permit a zonal rectors' conference to coordinate reconstruction policies, the request was denied.[68] Hartshorne's June, 1946, initiative in organizing the universities of the U.S. Zone by assembling rectors and other prominent academic leaders at the Marburg *Hochschulgespräche*—the first higher-education conference under American control—had not had uniform endorsement from Military Government. "It is a deplorable fact," an intelligence officer for ICD in Marburg wrote, "that . . . the organization of this conference was carried through almost exclusively by the personal efforts of . . . Dr. Hartshorne. All the delegates to the Conference were cognizant of the fact and extremely grateful."[69]

Hartshorne informed his superiors, in a year-end report, that the British had taken a more humane attitude toward denazifying students by granting a youth amnesty many months earlier than it had been granted in the U.S. Zone. Germans born in 1919 and after were exempt from the purges, which had caused such severe dislocations in Länder like Württemberg-Baden.[70] He noted that British university officers had helped establish student organizations and programs, such as university newspapers, and were giving them continued support. "The American Zone is fortunate in being able to watch and to learn from the developments in the British Zone, which, in this respect, have advanced faster." For that matter, the Americans had been tardy in imposing a *numerus clausus* (enrollment limitation) in certain overcrowded fields, such as theology, natural sciences, and—after the immediate postwar need had ebbed—medicine. "It is worth noting," he stated, "that the British educational Military Government authorities have, in this respect as in so many others, undertaken a more active and direct administration of German affairs than has been the case in the American Zone." The best that could be said for the American effort to date was that its ongoing "shortage of staff . . . contributed indirectly to a further development of local German enterprise."[71]

By December, 1945, most of the universities were functioning again or were on the verge of doing so. Unique in the educational structure of the U.S. Zone, they had carried almost complete responsibility for denazification and for reviving their institutions. E&RA's personnel shortages were so severe that the UPC formula, tested at Marburg and adopted elsewhere, had been merely realistic. It was also a promising experiment in democratic living, but much depended on how the highest echelons of Military Government viewed the results as the Occupation advanced. General Stayer's humanitarian actions in July, 1945, had started an unexpected chain of events, the consequences of which were still unseen at the end of the year.

Taking Stock

December, 1945, also found John Taylor and his E&RA staff gathered in Frankfurt to review what had been accomplished in the six months since peace had come. By then E&RA had risen to a paper strength of forty-one officers for the zone. Taylor offered the opinion that their accomplishments to date, while considerable, had been largely negative in nature and that this painful situation would continue for another six to eight months. "With personnel at hand in the field," he judged, "relatively little can be done in a positive way, since most of our time has been consumed by taking negative steps and getting the 'ox out of the ditch' as far as the schools are concerned." There was little doubt that personnel shortages were continuing to hamper operations, especially since many of the field staff were still being used by Military Government field commanders for "additional functions." Taylor continued: "Unless these officers can be unburdened as far as other functions are concerned, and unless additional personnel can be got into the field, we cannot expect the results which we should obtain in connection with a positive program to be realized."[72]

Taylor had praise for their accomplishments. By December 1, approximately 1.65 million German schoolchildren, or 86 percent of those eligible, were again receiving instruction, albeit under highly unfavorable conditions. The number of elementary-school teachers had risen to 21,000—all of them carrying onerous teaching loads. Emergency teacher-training courses were operating in all U.S.-occupied areas. The staff had processed 29,000 *Fragebogen*, representing 60 percent of the total expected, and had encountered a mandatory-removal rate of half the teachers on a zone-wide basis. Slightly more than half of the zone's 549 secondary schools were open. Three of the six universities were functioning, and the remaining three were preparing to start operations shortly. Such figures meant little, Taylor observed, to those who had not witnessed the devastation and social dislocation in Germany during the previous spring.[73]

Taylor felt it was time to turn the attention of his staff to the future. Increasingly, reconstruction must take on more positive tones, so that the intent would be seen as "influencing the reorientation of German educational institutions along democratic lines." His advice to his branch chiefs and their staffs was therefore "to direct German officials to draw up statements of general aims and objectives of German education to be presented to the U.S. education officials for approval." The Americans would then review the proposals and thus "exert their influence in the most effective manner." Taylor predicted that they could overcome resistance from German educational authorities. "Approval can be withheld until such documents have been set up in a manner consistent with our policies." He also suggested that they require the Germans to establish commissions to prepare the longer-range programs for the various fields of education. Once again he emphasized that "in the process of discussion and subsequent approval . . . the influence of the U.S. occupation authorities [can] be most effectively brought to bear." Now that the Occupation had been in operation for half a year, it was important that the Germans establish their long-term goals for education "in as reasonable a time as possible."[74] Taylor's expectations seemed reasonable, given his small staff. In fact, the preparation of long-range programs and investigative commissions did not come about until a year or more after the Frankfurt Conference of December, 1945.

Nevertheless, this E&RA conference of December 10 signaled the end of the first phase of America's effort to reconstruct German education. The painful negative measures of purging and vetting were, if not complete, at least moving toward completion. There was also a general recognition that the German authorities had in most cases been vital to the successes thus far attained. These facts prompted Major John Steiner, E&RA Branch Chief for Württemberg-Baden, to remind his countrymen that "there is a necessity for giving more dignity and authority to the top Germans chosen to run the education system of the three Länder in the U.S. Zone."[75] Certainly there were ample grounds to be pleased with the initiative of persons like Jaspers, Heuss, and Ebbinghaus, to name only a few. Despite its thin ranks and low status, the E&RA organization had performed creditably. But there were danger signs, too. The American public was largely unaware of what the educators from both sides were accomplishing; interest in Germany had ebbed sharply, and progress in educational matters was not what most journalists considered to be newsworthy. This indifference did not catch all parties by surprise; E&RA officers, as well as State and War department officials, had all sought to recruit a well-known education chief in order to attract favorable publicity, but in December, 1945, the prospects of finding the right person seemed as remote as ever.

John Taylor was well aware that the curtain of silence was potentially dangerous, and at the end of 1945 he was trying manfully to remove it. In late November he had consulted generals Stayer and McClure of PW&H and ICD, respectively, as well as Assistant Secretary of State William Benton about increasing the number of civilians serving in Military Government. Their expectation was that the State Department would take control of the Occupation in June, 1946. At the same conference, Taylor secured from Military Government's Manpower Board a planning directive, assuring E&RA of a personnel increase "relatively and absolutely" within the structure of Military Government.[76]

A few days later, on December 1, Taylor flew to London for two days of conferences with an old friend of E&RA, Grayson Kefauver. Recently elevated to the rank of minister within the State Department, Kefauver had just become America's chief representative to UNESCO and was preparing to return to the United States on a speaking tour. He had been well placed to help Taylor and the education section of the wartime GCU. However, the link was "completely unofficial," according to State Department officials, and when Archibald MacLeish took control of long-range planning in January, 1945, he reacted coolly to Kefauver's participation. "When Dr. Kefauver returned to London in April of this year," a State Department memo announced, "his instructions were to have nothing to do with the problem of reeducation. These instructions were issued at the insistence of Mr. MacLeish." However, Taylor was eager to have Kefauver's advice. Accordingly, General Eisenhower issued an invitation to the new minister to attend the December E&RA staff meeting in Frankfurt, "for information and for informal professional reactions to issues and problems dealt with in . . . the conference." Now that MacLeish was no longer involved with the program, Kefauver cabled William Benton and Eugene Anderson, seeking their approval. "In addition to any help I will give on problems concerned, I could give a report to [the State] Department on impressions of personnel and program," he wrote. This suggestion did not sit well with the officials at State's Division of Cultural Cooperation. They decided that Kefauver's presence in Frankfurt might drag the issue of German participation into UNESCO at a time when the new organization desired to steer clear of controversy. They also observed that "Dr. Kefauver has only an amateur's knowledge of Germany and of the problems of German reeducation. He does not know German and is unacquainted with the complexity of the issues involved." The message was unmistakable. Secretary of State Byrnes denied Kefauver permission to go to Frankfurt.[77]

John Taylor had different opinions about the matter, and, with Kefauver "barred" from Germany, he flew to London to see him there. E&RA still had no "big name" to aid its cause. Kefauver had been dean of education at Stanford. He was a minister in the State Department, a UNESCO representative, was willing to listen to E&RA's problems, and, better still, was about to tour the United States. Therefore, Kefauver was the next best thing to the celebrity everyone had been seeking. The idea was sound, but fate dictated a different outcome. During a speaking engagement in Los Angeles on January 5, 1946, Kefauver suddenly collapsed and died. E&RA was once again without an effective voice in the United States.[78]

Even before his meeting with Kefauver, Taylor had held a conference with Military Government leaders about the advisability of seeking an evaluation of the reeducation program. The proposal received consideration in time for Taylor to entrust it to Kefauver, who would then transmit it to Benton in Washington. Taylor suggested that a small committee, of three to five members, be drawn from State Department's Advisory Committee for German Reeducation to conduct an inspection tour of the zone the following spring. They would evaluate E&RA's program to date on the basis of the State Department's "Long-Range Policy Statement for German Reeducation," with which the E&RA staff members were already familiar.

Thus, the first initiative for proposing an evaluation committee came from Taylor, who reasoned that State would assume responsibility for governing Germany in 1946 and would want to be informed on the status of America's reeducation programs. Taylor's suggestion evoked no immediate response at State, and nothing more was heard about an evaluation committee until the next year.[79]

The first phase of E&RA's work in Germany had provided some surprises, some victories, and some hints of trouble ahead. The American field staff was able to answer unequivocally Archibald MacLeish's original question, whether or not there were Germans prepared to help in education reform. Massive German participation was indispensable in the first phase of the operation. Despite Marshall Knappen's gloomy prognosis, the educational system had revived, however shakily, in the autumn of 1945. Yet, despite these successes, there were storm warnings. By any measure, E&RA was understaffed, a chronic concern attested to by the repeated visits of key State and War department officials to discuss the problem at the E&RA offices in Berlin. McCloy, Hilldring, and Benton, to name only three, were justifiably concerned, and within Military Government there was growing recognition of the problem, as is demonstrated by the November directive to raise E&RA personnel "relatively and absolutely." Yet, in the end, nothing changed. E&RA still did not have its well-known educational administrator. Neither did it get the personnel increases promised by the Manpower Board. Whereas at one point nearly eighty officers were projected for education work for the spring of 1946, the actual number funded amounted to forty-three, almost identical to what it had been the previous autumn. Because of a budget squeeze, General Clay had had to accept a reduced field force of five hundred Military Government officers in the Länder, and E&RA had therefore also felt the pinch.[80]

The manpower crisis put E&RA in an embarrassing position. Oscar Reinmuth had been busy recruiting personnel in the United States to fill the projected slots. With E&RA's "relative and absolute" increase already in jeopardy, several of Reinmuth's hard-won recruits started "slipping off the hooks." Some educators felt that E&RA had to bear a disproportionate share of the burden. As one E&RA representative put it: "Apparently we are still paying the price for being in the lowest echelon."[81]

Finally, the lack of a well-known leader, while injurious to E&RA's performance in the initial operations, promised to be even more debilitating in the next stage, when the positive programs Taylor contemplated would require greater material resources and support from America. Without an effective spokesman in the corridors of Washington or addressing the informed public, E&RA had to depend on whatever support Military Government was willing and able to give—a support that, up to that point, had been meager.

A Second Purge

On a chilly day in January, 1946, Martin Niemoeller addressed a congregation of students in Erlangen. Following the war, his Evangelical Church had closely considered the problem of collective guilt—or collective responsibility—and Niemoeller had been one of the prominent spokesmen. He now offered the opinion that both the churches and the people must accept their share of it. They had not resisted Nazism in the early years of Hitler's power. Therefore, the evil events that had occurred at an increasing tempo after 1933 resulted from the people's passivity and moral indifference, despite clear danger signals. For many listeners, these were not congenial thoughts, coming so soon after the war, and, in the tradition of German students, part of the congregation "shuffled their feet to show disapproval."[1]

U.S. Army officers also heard him speak, as did representatives of the press. Unfortunately, the situation was not helped when, later that evening, unknown persons scribbled crude messages on the walls of several buildings to the effect that Niemoeller was a "tool of the Allies."[2]

At this time other unhappy events were taking place in the university town of Marburg. The university and its planning committee (UPC) had been a model for the reorganizing and reopening of all the other universities. Unfortunately, Marburg was also the headquarters for nearly 14,000 bored U.S. military personnel. Housing was tight, and military requisitions made it even tighter. The prewar Marburg population of 28,000 had swollen to 44,000 by 1945, while housing had been reduced by 40 percent. The Oberbürgermeister estimated that, on the average, nearly three Germans were crowded into each available room in the city.[3]

Marburg's citizenry, who had always been conservative, were unlikely to welcome even the best-behaved foreign troops, but the troops stationed at Marburg were not on their best behavior. By December, incidents between troops and students had increased to such an extent that Marburg's American university officer, Edward Y. Hartshorne, claimed that they were effectively undermining U.S. education-reform efforts in the Marburg area.

One evening a theology student, Wilhelm Brünger, who had been blinded in the war, was beaten up without provocation by some drunken American soldiers. When he learned that other theology students had suffered similar mistreatment, he reported the affair to Rector Julius Ebbinghaus, who related it to Hartshorne.[4]

American prestige was damaged further by the armed forces' inclination to requisition German housing without regard to political or humanitarian consequences. Professor Ernst von Drigalski and his wife had been longtime friends of intelligence officer Major Shepard Stone. At war's end they provided housing and valuable contacts for Stone and First Army's G-2 intelligence staff, and a few weeks later the professor became Greater Hesse's new minister of public health at the request of Military Government. Yet this did not prevent a quartermaster unit from ordering the Drigalskis and four other professors and their families to evacuate their homes on short notice in December, 1945. Similar requisitions had already turned into the street a sightless professor in Marburg's Institute for the Blind and a Nobel Prize laureate.

The effect on German public opinion was disastrous. Hartshorne decided he must act quickly, and he filed an extensive report to higher headquarters:

> During nine months of occupation of Marburg, the U.S. forces have done little to overcome the political opposition among the intellectual leaders, while through negligence and errors they have lost prestige among the active minority that has supported them. Looting, violence, and sudden unselective requisitioning of houses have occurred far beyond the combat period and do not appear to be on the decline.[5]

Hartshorne's report engendered concern at E&RA headquarters, and, at the end of January, John Taylor, who personally inspected the situation, convinced his division chief of the negative effects on civilian morale. They contacted General Clay's chief of staff, requesting the withdrawal of Army installations from Marburg and other university towns.[6]

Finally, at the end of February, generals Morrison Stayer of Public Health and F. C. Meade of Internal Affairs and Communications proposed to relocate transient soldiers away from Marburg. This time they were even more blunt: "Educational and political objectives of the first order are being jeopardized by the present situation in the Marburg area."[7] Still, no immediate action was taken, although responsible officers spoke of providing "increased discipline and troop education." Gradually, zone-wide troop redeployments reduced troop levels in Marburg in any case, but no dramatic change of climate took place there or elsewhere.

In the zone's other university towns the atmosphere was also negative. In Munich a student artist painted a watercolor of a student construction gang *(Bautrupp)* toiling away at the rubble of the university's demolished buildings while, in the foreground, a G.I. and his girlfriend strolled nonchalantly by.[8] On Christmas Eve, 1945, the *Göttingen Universitäts-Zeitung* reported the double suicide in Munich of a prominent physicist, Otto Hönigschmid, and his wife after they had been evicted from their apartment for the second time.[9] The students of Erlangen University were so terrorized by a sergeant of Military Police, later on in the Occupation, that it was many months before one of them had the courage to complain to university authorities and to Military Government.[10]

These incidents rarely found their way into the American press, but the Niemoeller incident received prominent attention. Marshall Knappen noted that press coverage of the Occupation left much to be desired. Inexperienced reporters, with little knowledge of Central Europe, had replaced seasoned veterans, and many of them were being pressured by their home offices to compile stories that fitted the domestic stereotypes of the Germans as sullen recalcitrants who learned nothing and forgot nothing. Moreover, the unspectacular progress in rebuilding an educational system did not make for exciting news copy.[11] But the hint of scandal at a university was irresistible. The Niemoeller incident caused military commanders throughout the zone to glance nervously at their universities. Following the Erlangen incident, Colonel William Dawson reacted strongly to rumors of incomplete denazification in Heidelberg. At the same time, the Counterintelligence Corps (CIC) reported continuing hostility to occupational authorities in the university towns, causing growing concern in the highest circles of Military Government. "It was agreed," the E&RA minutes for March 18, 1946, read, "that, as events developed, General Clay was to be kept informed personally."[12] A possible confrontation in the university towns loomed on the horizon.

Right in the midst of these ominous trends, the outlook faded for any increase in E&RA's personnel. Taylor, who finally raised the issue again with General Clay, reported that "the matter of delay in shipping individuals procured in the States to the Theater was discussed, and it was agreed that, if there was anything which could be done by the Commanding General, he would be glad to do it."[13]

Clay might be sympathetic to E&RA's problem, but there was little he could do to help. Dr. Mildred English, a specialist in elementary education, and Dr. Fritz Karsen, formerly a prominent education leader in the Weimar Republic and now an American citizen, waited for their travel permits,

passports, and military priorities for months before they could finally
board ship at the end of April, 1946. A lieutenant in the army would
almost certainly have boarded an airplane immediately if his German-based
units indicated they needed him quickly, but for E&RA it was a different
story. As one chronicler put it: "Air priorities were declined for these
much-needed individuals."[14]

However, in Washington the State Department and War Department
had not forgotten about E&RA's chronic personnel woes. In January,
1946, General John H. Hilldring, who was about to become an assistant
secretary of state, and Assistant Secretary of War John J. McCloy agreed
to renew the search for the elusive educational leader who was thought
to be essential for an effective program. On January 23 Hilldring wrote
to Assistant Secretary of State William Benton: "I believe one of the most
urgent problems connected with the cultural reconstruction and reorientation of the German people is that of selecting a top-notch American
educator who will go to Germany and direct the U.S. Government policies
for education."[15] Hilldring asked Benton to "arrange a meeting at an early
date between you and representatives of the War Department with a view
of completing this project." Two weeks later an equally frustrated Benton
assented but reminded Hilldring that the State Department had been
"trying for some time to find a person who would meet the unusual
requirements for this position and who would be able to accept." Calling
the education program a "delicate and crucial task," he stated, "I can
assure you that the matter will be pushed vigorously from this end."[16]

The meeting took place in early February, and, with Benton's concur-
rence, Hilldring wrote to Clay about filling the long-vacant position. "The
Secretary of War likewise feels that we need such a person," he added.
Hilldring also disclosed that, in a recent meeting with Eugene Anderson,
State Department officials had appeared confident for the first time since
1945 that they could finally secure his services. If Clay answered yes,
Hilldring promised to "push the selection of an appropriate person or
persons to an early conclusion."[17]

On March 6 General Clay's detailed reply surprised War and State
department officials. "Last July," he wrote, "I tried desperately to get an
educator of repute from the United States without success; the field was
too muddy. Hence we used the means on hand and found leadership from
the ranks. To supplant this leadership now would be a blow to present
personnel and to military government as a whole, as our people have
learned that ability brings them from the ranks." Clay was as concerned
for General Robert McClure's Information Control Division as he was for
John Taylor's E&RA. ICD had performed well in freeing the German
information media from the stranglehold of the Goebbels era. "I think
Bob McClure has done an excellent job," Clay concluded. His evaluation

of E&RA's performance was more complex. He admitted that the education staff had been forced to concentrate almost exclusively on denazification, restoring physical plant and facilities, and publishing emergency textbooks. "It has done this job well, even though in doing so it has had little opportunity to implant our own teaching philosophies," he wrote. He perceived that the latter job required "breaking up the traditional disciplined relationship between pupil and teacher," but he felt that, at last, the largely negative phase was drawing to a close. "Now that mechanical problems have been improved so greatly, this group is prepared to devote its maximum effort to the longer-range problem of reorienting the German educational system."[18]

With solid accomplishments behind it, Clay felt that E&RA was not in need of new leadership or of an elevated position within Military Government. The Deputy Military Governor had confidence in his education head:

> While Taylor has no national prestige to maintain him, he is a college professor with a fine educational background who has steeped himself in the German problem during the past year. He has agreed to civilianize [return to civilian status], to remain on the job, to see it through. To supplant him now would likewise discredit the results of his group and, in addition, would make it difficult to persuade other key personnel to remain with us. He has my confidence, and I am sure the respect and confidence of the three German Ministers of Education in our three Länder.

In the past, State and War department officials, as well as E&RA specialists, had considered establishing a new position of "cultural adviser" to Clay, leaving an E&RA chief in place to carry out administrative duties. In July, 1945, one State Department memorandum had even visualized the hiring of two or three experts on German education to aid the prominent cultural adviser, who was unlikely to be intimately acquainted with Germany's educational problems. However, because such an adviser might appear to have no real power, E&RA officers had feared that Military Government might not be able to attract the celebrated administrator they desired.[19] In 1946 Clay had another reason—based on experience—for opposing the creation of such a position. "Of course it would be possible to bring in an educator as a consultant or adviser to me. However, I have found through experience that this expedient usually does more harm than good, as the job here must be done by an organization working under established organizational procedures." Clay had recently experienced difficulties with a scientific adviser who had "blamed Public Safety Branch severely for treating *scientists* as Nazis, even though the record is clear."

Fearful of further "friction and misunderstanding," Clay preferred not to take on yet another adviser.[20]

General Clay in fact felt that the reeducation of Germans would occur only as the result of a wide spectrum of developments outside of education. "A cold and hungry people are not interested in the philosophy of life," he stated. "They are confronted with the realities of existence. Now we can only lay the foundation for the reeducation of Germany so that it will proceed apace when internal conditions give us a people eager to become informed of affairs beyond the daily struggle to survive." Clay wanted Hilldring to understand that the present catastrophe was clearly of the Germans' own making: "Please do not misunderstand my views as an expression of sympathy for the German people. They have earned the returns they are now receiving and must suffer in order that they may learn the bitter lessons of defeat. Nevertheless, we must recognize that their path must start upward again before they will apply these lessons to their future." Clay was reiterating in a carefully circumscribed fashion the tenets of State Department planning groups since 1942: reconstruction and German involvement in their own rehabilitation once the initial purgative actions were complete. "Our job, as I see it, is to see that only the right type of Germans are permitted to take leadership until democratic processes become a habit." Such changes would come slowly, and Clay made it clear that Military Government did not need Hilldring's "top-notch educator" now. "This is somewhat like sending a new general in to win the battle after the campaign has been planned and executed so that the battle may be won."[21] State and War department officials accepted Clay's opinion as final and agreed to discontinue the search "until such time as General Clay expresses the definite need for such an individual."[22]

At almost the same moment that Clay was declining Hilldring's offer, an article appeared in the *New Republic* entitled "The AMG Mess in Germany." Its author, Irving Wolfson, had served with American combat troops in 1945 and then, until the autumn of 1945, had served with a Military Government detachment in Dachau. Wolfson labeled Military Government's education program the most deficient element in a generally inept bureaucracy. Its personnel were incompetent, Wolfson wrote, and often "guilty of criminal stupidity and maladministration." He called for a maximum denazification effort, one that would "ruthlessly weed out all teachers with Nazi backgrounds, including those non-Nazis who received their training under the Third Reich." He intimated that teaching staffs and textbooks were still rife with National Socialism and urged that teacher training programs be established immediately and that Military Government "recruit qualified Americans and German exiles as teachers and supervisors."[23]

Wolfson was not alone in demanding direct intervention in the German educational system. As late as September, 1945, Arthur L. H. Rubin, who directed the War Department's Office of Military Training, had advocated a scheme by which American universities would "adopt" German institutions and send cadres to staff and organize them. However, Anderson at the State Department and McCloy and Hilldring at the War Department were unalterably opposed to schemes of direct control. As Hilldring mentioned to McCloy: "I have talked to a dozen prominent American educators on this subject. All of them decry the proposal that U.S. teachers be used. I agree with them most emphatically."[24] Yet Wolfson's article, a few months later, demonstrated that many Americans regarded such a course as imperative.

Wolfson's pessimistic message indicated that he, like many other independent observers of the German Occupation, was not well informed on America's current policy and past accomplishments. Nevertheless, his views were widely read. In contrast, Harvard historian Sidney B. Fay's balanced and accurate—if not sensational—account of progress and problems in the German universities aroused no special interest or comment, despite his impeccable source: his son-in-law Edward Y. Hartshorne. On March 13 the *New York Times* reported Military Government's dismissal of Rector Albert Rehm of Munich University, allegedly because he had not denazified his institution thoroughly.[25] Further isolated reports appeared in early April about defects in the U.S. educational program. Then two reporters, Raymond Daniell and Tania Long, unloaded a double-barreled blast at education reform in the Bavarian universities. Daniell's reportage on the Schaeffer and Patton affairs in 1945 and his revelations about ex-Nazis surviving as business leaders had expedited release of Military Government Law No. 8, contributing directly to yet another wave of denazification. Now his 1946 revelations were casting doubt on the educational program. Under such provocative headlines as "Nazi Virus Thrives in U.S. Zone," Daniell's disturbing account was the first and often the only image many Americans got of what the educational program had accomplished—or, rather, had not accomplished. Daniell wrote on April 22: "Not only is the University of Munich, three-quarters of whose students are discharged Wehrmacht officers, a hotbed of violent nationalism, but also in the rural schools any critical reference to Hitler or the Nazis is apt to be greeted by catcalls, boos, and other signs of displeasure. Boys and girls are openly debating whether to join one or another underground organization." He reported that a "Nazi" professor at Munich University was still teaching a course on "theories of race and heredity." Students openly referred to American occupational authorities as the "enemy," he claimed.[26] Daniell elaborated on his charges three days later.

Meanwhile Tania Long, also of the *Times* staff, reported similarly distressing trends at Munich University. She claimed that the university's personnel officer, Professor Reinhard Demoll, "makes no secret of his opinion that any German who assisted 'the enemy' is not acceptable on the faculties." Long reported that professors took "sly digs" at every opportunity at American authorities during lectures because these elicited enthusiastic student response. The few students who dared to deal sympathetically with Americans were tarred as "Quislings" or "collaborators." Long also claimed that many students were angry at projected prohibitions against admitting former officers to further study. Finally, she reported that, at a meeting of an officially sanctioned "Academic-Political Discussion Club," several German veterans talked about using brass knuckles and other violent weapons to disable unpopular figures, such as the new minister president of Bavaria, Social Democrat Wilhelm Hoegner.[27]

Such reports enraged the reading public, drowning out Drew Middleton's less dramatic account of the successes as well as the shortcomings of America's education-reform efforts.[28] Long's and Daniell's portrayals of the frustration, despair, and resentment among students and faculty at Munich could have applied equally to the total population, given the drastic decline in living standards. However, the charge that courses were being offered on race theories by former National Socialist professors or that right-wing terrorist groups were coalescing to repeat the "Fehm" political murders of the 1920s was as false as the assertion that non-Nazis were being systematically excluded, as "collaborators," from teaching positions.

A few days after these sensational articles appeared in the *Times*, Lieutenant Colonel Robert McRae, chief of the CAD's Reorientation Branch at the Pentagon, cabled John Taylor in Berlin asking for comments on Long's and Daniell's accusations.[29] Taylor forwarded the request to E&RA's branch chief in Bavaria for a reply. Alfred Pundt cabled back a stinging reply to Taylor for transmission to the War Department: "It is difficult to understand on what basis of fact the article was drafted. . . . Publication of the above-cited article would be a great disservice to the cause of Military Government's functional control in Bavaria."[30] Pundt then offered a systematic refutation of the specific charges.

The "Nazi" professor of Daniell's report, Prinz Wilhelm Karl von Isenburg, was not offering any course on race theories at Munich University. In fact, Isenburg was at the moment not teaching at all. "It must be well known to correspondents," Pundt added, "that courses on race and race theories are banned from German schools . . . and that application for lecturing on such courses would be disapproved as a matter of course." Denazification authorities determined that Isenburg had not engaged in any Nazi activities and "that very few professors at any German university enjoyed such a clean bill of health." Reinhard Demoll, who reportedly was blocking the appointments of any scholar who had "collaborated" with the "enemy," had been given an identically clean bill of health by Military Government's hard-nosed Special Branch. Pundt conceded that education officers had had little contact with student groups, "owing to the pressure of official business and acute personnel shortages," and therefore could not gauge student opinion precisely. But Munich University had opened its doors later than most other universities, amid scenes of great devastation. "It is only natural that the circumstances as well as the existing physical and moral devastation of Germany have been very painful for the younger generation of Germany to bear and that their reaction should take the form of resentment and protest." Daniell and Long should have known that Military Government was trying desperately to reinstate academic personnel whom the Nazis had persecuted and that Germans and Americans alike were making great exertions to repair the physical damage caused by the war. "It is hard to imagine," Pundt concluded, "how even the most incorrigible Nazi could have served the cause of National Socialism better than to publish an article so manifestly mendacious and misleading as the above one."[31] Within a month of his rebuttal, Alfred Pundt was replaced by Walter G. Bergman as the new chief of E&RA in Bavaria.

Bavaria's Land director, General Walter J. Muller, also found "glaring and demonstrable inaccuracies [giving] a very distorted picture of conditions in the University of Munich." Muller agreed that student dissatisfaction was manifest, but he assured higher headquarters that "rescreening of students to purge obnoxious elements is under way."[32]

Whether the reporting was accurate or not, it was effective. Military Government's gathering response to the Long and Daniell articles showed how sensitive the War Department and its field organization were to press criticism. In the fall of 1945, President Truman dispatched Byron Price, America's wartime director of censorship, to investigate press accusations of Military Government fumbling. Price reported that, despite noisy criticisms from some of the press corps, the United States had achieved notable progress in its zone, especially when compared to progress elsewhere. Making one of the earliest public demands for a reconstructionist policy, he warned against complacency and stated that a competent job in the future would require more tools, determination, and funding. Lacking these, he said, the United States should withdraw from the Occupation. Despite such reassurances, the press was able to cause as much consternation after the Price report as before.[33] Though Taylor transmitted them to McRae at the CAD, Pundt's and Muller's rebuttals never reached the American public. In Germany the unwelcome attention focused on the universities was beginning to force Clay's hand.

To understand the discrepancies between the press attacks and the Military Government reports, it is necessary to understand the nature and results of denazification at the universities. For Military Government, denazification in general had proved to be a colossal and persistent headache. In the summer and fall of 1945, policies kept changing, depending on which pressure Military Government felt most keenly at the moment: the desire to preserve trained personnel and programs or the fear of criticism by the American public. In addition, Military Government regulations on denazification were supplanted by new German directives, which became law on March 5, 1946, as well as a youth amnesty, which insulated young Germans from the worst effects of the purge. With the return of local German self-government in January, 1946, the Germans logically assumed responsibility for denazification. Under pressure from Military Government, the German Law Number 104, entitled "Liberation from National Socialism and Militarism," was signed by the three German Land ministers in March, 1946, but it took months to sort out German responsibilities and procedures. For a time Law Number 104 merely added a German presence to the denazification process. It did not eliminate the American presence. In fact, the Military Government agencies on denazification, such as Special Branch and investigative branches like CIC and Intelligence Branch of ICD, remained active in the field.

Military Government had had to make two contradictory assumptions about former party members. The first was that all Nazis were incorrigible and therefore beyond redemption. The second recognized that many Nazis were victims of circumstance and, as valued members of their communities, were worthy of rehabilitation. This contradiction, which helped to explain the vagaries of denazification under direct Military Government control, was also evident in Law Number 104.

Legal Council Karl Lowenstein, a professor of law from Amherst College, and historian Walter L. Dorn, from Ohio State University, made certain that the law provided for a scale of punishments for guilty persons: "Class I Major Offenders, Class II Offenders, Class III Lesser Offenders, Class IV Followers, and Class V Exonerated." Punishments for the guilty ranged from lengthy prison sentences to mere monetary fines. The new law established *Spruchkammern*, or denazification tribunals, staffed by politically cleared local citizens. All adult Germans submitted *Meldebogen*, shortened versions of Military Government's *Fragebogen*, so that they could be classified into one of the five categories. The new German law included an assumption that denazification meant a process of rehabilitation rather than a purge, as MG Law No. 8 had indicated.[34] Investigations were to continue in cases where falsifications were suspected. The *Spruchkammern*, like the earlier local policy-enforcement branches, elicited literally millions of *Meldebogen* to be examined.

Military Government detachments were apprehensive, and Land Military Government in Bavaria frankly predicted failure for denazification now that it was in German hands. In other words, most of the damaging accusations made by American reporters were untimely, given the already strained relations between Military Government and the new German involvement in denazification.

It is significant that the universities, in spite of apprehension among some Military Government detachments, had been charged with denazifying themselves a full six months before the passage of Law Number 104. Even Heidelberg University, which witnessed an extensive purge under Karl Jaspers' uncompromising leadership, had nearly closed its doors at the end of February, 1946, when Colonel William Dawson detected what he felt were irregularities in denazification there. In contrast, Munich University had had no forceful or uncompromising leadership comparable to Karl Jaspers', and it had had to cope with physical damage and confusion on a far greater scale than Heidelberg when it reopened. In a preliminary report submitted to Military Government on January 15, 1946, the University Screening Committee at Munich complained that it was being hampered in its work by competing duties. "The investigation of cases submitted by the Military Government coincided in time with the preparations of the University," they claimed. "This took up much of the time of the Planning Committee, many members of which were also members of the Screening Committee." The same committee claimed that many dismissals of administrative staff and a lack of trained replacements were causing numerous errors and delays in getting the necessary information about the cases in question.

But most perplexing for the Munich Screening Committee were the denazification standards, particularly with regard to applicants who had never been directly connected with the Nazi movement. "None of the cases investigated was a member of the party," they stated. Membership in affiliated organizations—the professional, social, civil-defense, and charitable organizations, which the Nazis had "coordinated" for twelve years—was also problematic. "In practically all of the cases examined here, the Committee came to the conclusion that dismissal from service was not called for. We think it right to let the decisive question be whether the man investigated can be trusted to put himself absolutely, and without denying the political past, at the service of reconstruction and take part as an academic teacher in the training of youth in the new spirit."[35]

With the exclusion of all nominal party members and many members of party-affiliated organizations, Munich University got a strong dose of denazification prior to its reopening in the winter and spring of 1946. Despite strenuous efforts, reconstruction of Munich was slow, with the result that it was one of the last universities in the U.S. Zone to resume operations. Its students organized their hardworking *Bautrupp* for building reconstruction in the autumn of 1945, and all students performed half a year of heavy labor before beginning studies. The faculty resumed teaching on a small scale in February, 1946, with twenty-six students in theology. The philosophy faculty began operating on March 3, followed by political science and economics at the end of that month and law only on April 9. The school of medicine reopened its doors at Munich in late June, nearly a year after the first medical school in the zone opened at Heidelberg. By early summer, 1946, Munich claimed to have 6,200 students receiving instruction from a faculty of only 140 instructors of various ranks.[36] Alfred Pundt, as E&RA branch chief, worked desperately to recruit individuals from other zones and other countries to supplement the sadly reduced staff. In early January he had urged Rudolf Pfeiffer, a famed philologist of Corpus Christi College, Oxford, to return to his native Bavaria. "Our denazification efforts have reduced the faculty and staff of the University of Munich to a point where many vital academic chairs will have to be filled," he wrote.[37] But his recruiting efforts rarely bore fruit. Most émigrés were understandably bitter against the Nazis and disillusioned by the silence their own colleagues had maintained during Hitler's purges. Even the few who considered returning realized that they faced a drastic lowering of living standards by returning to Germany at a time when civilian rations were perhaps 1,200 calories per day. Edward Y. Hartshorne was similarly disappointed in his bid for personnel from Swiss universities.

Pundt also had trouble with the rectorship at Munich University. Albert Rehm, the first American-appointed rector, protested the wholesale dismissals of faculty members. His replacement, Professor Karl Vossler, was seventy-three and in fragile health, a fact noted in the American press. As a liberal and a democrat, he seemed to show the proper academic and social credentials for the job: "The Nazis did not like him and he didn't like them, and though he was never arrested or in any serious trouble, he was retired because of age in 1938, and at the same time forbidden to give any more lectures at the University." However it became obvious almost immediately that Vossler was too old for the job. He was replaced by Georg Hohmann, a medical researcher, on June 21, 1946.[38] This succession of rectors demonstrated chronic leadership problems at Munich, especially marked when compared to the successes at Marburg and Heidelberg.

To add to Pundt's woes, Munich's recently reopened law school came under fire from an influential source: Karl Lowenstein. A law professor at Munich before the Nazis came to power, Lowenstein had emigrated to the United States and a post at Amherst College, from which he then took a leave of absence in order to advise Legal Division at OMGUS. With his work on Law Number 104 complete, he made a brief side trip to his old alma mater in Munich, where he became cognizant of the many rumors of irregularities. On the very day Tania Long's article appeared in the *Times*, Pundt was reading Lowenstein's report, which claimed that Munich's law faculty was full of Nazis. Although Lowenstein's information came in great part from only one source—Bavarian State Commissioner for Universities Otto Graf—he told Taylor of the situation and sent a copy of his report to Legal Division at OMGUS. Graf, a Social Democrat appointed by Minister President Hoegner, knew that he was mistrusted by the rest of the faculty. However, Lowenstein contended that "the real stumbling block for any democratic reform of the law school and of Bavarian higher education in general was Dr. Reinhard Demoll acting as chief of section for the Bavarian universities in the Ministry of Education." Demoll was guilty of "cronyism" and saw to it that a chair of racial sciences continued to be held by Professor Wilhelm Karl von Isenburg. Lowenstein also learned that a newly formed "political-academic discussion club" of students was imbued with extreme nationalism and militarism.[39] The similarities between Lowenstein's report and Tania Long's article indicated that the source for both was probably the same: Otto Graf.

Several weeks after Lowenstein had filed his report in Berlin, Private Erich Ortenau was on leave from a unit in the British Army to reclaim some personal property. A Bavarian by birth and formerly a medical student at Munich, Ortenau tried to contact his old mentor at the university clinic, Oswald Bumke, and was distressed to learn that Bumke had been dismissed. In his search, he discovered a conspiracy in the medical faculty and in the university in general. The web of intrigue centered around Professor Theodor Suess, a university referee at the Ministry of Education with alleged ties to prominent members of the other faculties and to other high officials in the Ministry of Education, including its Social Democratic director, Franz Fendt. According to Ortenau, there was even an *éminence grise*, one Albert Emmert, who, moving from office to ministry to institute, passed along information and warnings. Furthermore, the threads led to such groups as the Munich Rotary Club and to "anthroposophical circles." Ortenau concluded his report with the admonition that he had been in the Bavarian capital too short a time to uncover the entire conspiracy: "Where this trail is leading is, of course, a matter of conjecture," he wrote, "but, having been to Berchtesgaden and as a native of those parts [being] a bit more susceptible to what is going on there, I wonder if the trail doesn't lead right into the mountains . . . and to a couple of missing people as well."[40]

However, another source contradicted Ortenau. A report from Intelligence Branch of ICD confirmed the fact of the conspiracy but indicated that the "power behind the throne" lay elsewhere. "According to a German ICD agent who has access to inside information, the University of Munich is controlled now as in the past by a clique of extremely reactionary elements operating under the auspices of State Secretary Hans Meinzolt, who is in turn the confidence man of the Bishop for Bavaria, Hans Meiser. This clique, through Meinzolt, prevents professors or visiting lecturers who are not agreeable to them from gaining admission to the University."[41]

Given these circumstances, it was not surprising that Munich University had disposed of two rectors in rapid succession or that Alfred Pundt was replaced as branch chief in June, 1946. E&RA's responsible university officer, Isidore A. Barnett, tried gamely to keep abreast of events and to sort out the mass of conflicting information, but without success. At the same time, large quantities of denunciation reports, correspondence, and intelligence briefings of all kinds descended on the E&RA offices. By the end of the summer another university officer wrote: "There is so much chicanery, so many cross-purposes, that every piece of evidence must be weighed. It is a sad state of affairs, but we can actually not trust anybody . . . here to give a completely unbiased judgment."[42]

Beginning in March, General Clay received daily reports on the situation at the universities; prompted by these, the investigative branches of Military Government concluded that institutions of higher learning throughout the zone warranted a closer look. An intelligence race of sorts began, with Counterintelligence Corps, Policy Enforcement Branch, Special Branch, and Intelligence Branch of ICD all "helping" Education and Religious Affairs Branch. The result was a dramatic increase in the volume of reports circulating within Military Government. In one intelligence report, entitled "Female Students Report on Reaction at Munich University," the two who were questioned confided that whenever Frederick the Great's name was mentioned in lectures students pounded their desktops in approval.[43] Another report, with the intriguing title "Inscriptions in the WC of the University of Munich," described such mild graffiti as "Lord, send us the 5th Reich. The 4th is just like the 3rd."[44]

As a result of this flood of information and investigators, no one seemed to be in charge or capable of evaluating all the evidence. This heightened the atmosphere of suspicion and uncertainty.

Edward Y. Hartshorne, arriving from Marburg, began digesting the many intelligence reports, including Erich Ortenau's contribution. Then, on August 22, the mysterious Herr Emmert appeared at the E&RA offices, together with the dean of Munich University's medical school, to speak to I. A. Barnett about opening a medical school extension in Bamberg. Hartshorne acted promptly. "As Dr. Barnett could not identify him, I asked for his identity and official position." Albert Emmert claimed the need for secrecy as a CIC operative, and Hartshorne ordered him into an adjoining office to question him in the presence of Lieutenant Colonel Robert A. Reese, chief of Internal Affairs and Communications Division. Emmert admitted that he was a private citizen and an "author" who had never published anything because of Nazi persecution. When asked why he had not submitted his manuscripts to ICD, Emmert stated he was unaware of that organization's existence but said that he was well acquainted with all of the "cases" at the university. It then developed that no one had ever really demanded his *bona fides*. Hartshorne spoke to Rector Georg Hohmann about Emmert, and the newly installed rector replied that Emmert was, of course, the CIC operative. Hartshorne asked how he knew that, and Hohmann replied: "He told me." Hartshorne ended his report sharply. "It is requested that energetic steps be taken to ascertain from CIC whether or not Herr Emmert is known to them and is operating in their behalf, and, in the negative instance, that proceedings be instigated against him for falsely representing himself as a Military Government agent."[45]

Unfortunately, Hartshorne's forceful direction was only temporary, and his successors drifted with events. By September, Peter Vacca, chief of Special Branch in Bavaria, reported to the Intelligence director at OMGUS that "too many people are investigating." Walter Bergman at E&RA heartily agreed. In fact, Vacca revealed that Special Branch, which presumably oversaw all denazification efforts, had been unaware of ICD's Intelligence Branch investigation at Munich University, even though it had been under way since the previous April. He felt that in this instance ICD was exceeding its authority.[46]

A problem that all investigators faced and that played a role in the inaccurate journalistic coverage at Munich was the highly contradictory evidence that could be assembled on any given individual. Throughout the spring of 1946 the German *Spruchkammern* were expected to take progressively greater responsibility for denazification, yet they were staffed by local citizens who had had no legal or investigative training. They had to handle huge caseloads and assign each individual to one of the five often arbitrary categories. Like the Americans, the Germans found themselves penalizing some individuals who obviously had been Nazis in name only while letting other more guilty individuals escape too lightly.

Typical of the dilemmas the *Spruchkammern* faced was the case of a physician at the University of Munich who had acquired his medical training at the universities of Erfurt, Leipzig, and Berlin in the 1930s. Unprepossessing in personality or appearance, he was a competent medical scientist who seemed to live for his work, a fact that may have led to his receiving a year of research on tissue cultures in New York in 1937. On his return to Germany, the young researcher discovered that his lack of party affiliation had begun to hinder his professional advancement. He was assigned as an assistant to the Anatomical Institute at Munich, although his qualifications merited a higher position. By this time a dossier, which was following him relentlessly, contained the observation that he was professionally talented, "but a National Socialist he certainly is not. Politically, he has never taken a position at all. Instead, he, like so many other people, is not really against National Socialism, but neither has he ever been inwardly imbued with it either."[47] The director of his institute began to apply increasing pressure on him to join the party. Written communications greeted him, one after the other; then the follow-up phone calls began. Finally, in May, 1939, the young researcher broke and quietly joined the party, without any fanfare. He then received notification in August to begin paying small monthly dues to the SS and to attend meetings of the local SS medical auxiliary. He paid his dues but ignored the meetings and for the next six years immersed himself in research and teaching. Disgusted with his inactivity, the SS dropped him from its rolls in the spring of 1944. He never appeared in uniform, never used the fascist salute, and never discussed politics. After the war, when his case came up for consideration, the evidence was confusing and contradictory. Three subordinate workers in the Institute swore in writing that he had never been a party member and was certainly not in the SS. Other colleagues, including the new director of the Institute, claimed otherwise, stating that his whole medical career had been built around influence gained from membership in the SS. It was even hinted that his work in America may have been part of an SS effort to gather intelligence there. Nevertheless, the basic evidence was unequivocal: he had joined the party in 1939 and had been a "furthering member of the SS." This medical scientist, who had lived for his work, lost his job at the university on January 3, 1946.[48] His strategy of minimum obeisance proved to be his undoing.

Another case involved a professor of jurisprudence from Jena who had joined the Munich law faculty in 1938. He had had to struggle to attain the transfer because Gauleiter Sauckel in Saxony had tried desperately to keep him in Jena as an indispensable legal supporter of the party's interests there. He possessed an able legal mind and was in heavy demand by the party because his special interest was in the Nazi-inspired *Deutsches Bauernrecht* (German Peasant Law), which sharply limited inheritance and sales rights for small farmers in the Third Reich. Such laws were at variance with the rest of the German Civil Code and were not popular with many of the established law faculties, but the new arrival attacked his pet subject with gusto and for the next six years presented himself as the epitome of the National Socialist professional man. When passing acquaintances on the street, he parried conventional greetings with a stiff-armed salute and a loud "Heil Hitler!" He collected avidly for the Winter Relief and other charitable or war-related fund-raisings for the party and did not shrink from embarrassing reluctant donors with boisterous calls for everyone to do his share. Many acquaintances and neighbors did their best to avoid this unpleasant man, but they also feared his position, which all presumed to be that of a party judge in addition to his professorial duties. He and his aloof wife associated almost exclusively with other high Nazi officials and entertained them in their elegant eight-room apartment in a fashionable district of the Bavarian capital. When the fortunes of war soured and housing grew scarce, they did not have to share their dwelling with anyone and still possessed a motorcar, which they used to escape from Munich ahead of Patton's army in 1945. However, a month after the collapse, the law professor recovered his nerve and returned with his wife to reclaim their property. They were outraged to learn that fifteen Russian displaced persons had been assigned to their bomb-damaged dwelling. A convincing advocate, he marshaled an official from the city housing bureau, a German policeman, and an American MP and launched a "dawn attack" on the unsuspecting Russians. They were arrested for vandalism and theft. In the aftermath of the raid, however, a number of neighbors and acquaintances came forward to expose the law professor's unsavory past. They assured Special Branch that he was one of the oldest members of the party and a dreaded party judge to boot. In August, 1945, Captain George Bonfield of Military Government Detachment F213 in Munich reviewed the case and grew so angry at what he read that he immediately recommended to Special Branch that the man be removed from office, that his property be sequestered, and that he be reduced to the status of a day laborer. Furthermore, he should stand trial for causing the false arrest of the Russian DPs. But a year later the law professor was still teaching on the law faculty at Munich. He had never joined the party.[49]

A third type of professional was rarer: the person who was patently guilty. Even so, many months could pass before a final decision was rendered. One such case involved a medical researcher who had specialized in hereditary diseases. The institute he directed was prominent in the field, and before the war the professor had acquired an international reputation in this legitimate area of medical inquiry. Max Planck congratulated him on behalf of the *Kaiser Wilhelm Gesellschaft*, Germany's prestigious science foundation, for his elevation to the presidency of the International Federation of Eugenics Organizations in 1932. However, after the Nazis' seizure of power, his career took a more sinister turn, and evidence collected by Military Government at the end of the war indicated that he had approved enforced sterilizations and had overstepped the boundary between legitimate medical research and such National Socialist perversions as euthanasia and the maintenance of the pseudo-scientific "race hygiene" clinics. The medical celebrity felt himself sufficiently compromised that at war's end he tried to escape to his native Switzerland one step ahead of the American troops. The embarrassed Swiss refused him entry, and he wound up in jail. Despite impressive evidence, which included his successful application to the Gestapo for a gun permit, his party-membership file, correspondence with others about enforced sterilization, and various high decorations bestowed by Hitler himself, the trial dragged on interminably over distinctions between hereditary diseases and race hygiene.[50] However, in his case at least, the evidence was sufficiently damaging that no thought was given to his return to teaching after the war.

One central fact emerged from the proceedings of Special Branch and, later, of the *Spruchkammern*: truth was elusive. After a few months of experience, most investigators and Military Government personnel grew wary of accusations and statements by individuals. After twelve years of political repression, followed by defeat, there were too many old scores to settle. University Officer Edwin Costrell put the matter succinctly: "I *never* took denunciation reports at face value."[51] In this light, inaccurate press coverage of the type that appeared in the *Times* became more understandable. After all, even experienced Military Government officers were capable of judging situations incorrectly. Nevertheless, public exposure on this sensitive issue virtually required a crackdown of some kind at the universities. By May, General Joseph T. McNarney, commanding officer at USFET, was enraged by reports that students were allegedly referring to American forces as "the enemy," and he let his displeasure be known to Taylor and the E&RA staff. "The Theater Commander has instructed that prompt and vigorous action with reference to such students be taken," the E&RA minutes for May 25 read. "He specifically disapproves of the practice of not permitting such students to reregister in the succeeding term, as such action is not sufficiently vigorous."[52] In other words, student offenders should face instantaneous dismissal. Clay agreed with McNarney, and by mid-June his chief-of-staff had issued a communiqué to all university officers of the U.S. Zone:

> In order that we may assure General Clay and General McNarney as to the status of university students who have been found undesirable for being militarists or for other reasons, it is desired that you obtain through the Land Directors information showing for each of the major universities by name the number of students who have been dismissed after admission and the reasons other than academic disqualification.[53]

By the end of the month, Bavarian E&RA's division chief could report that in Bavarian universities 158 students had been expelled from Erlangen, 97 from Würzburg, and 20 from Munich. It was a hint of what would follow.

Lucius Clay had more than students in mind when on June 25, 1946, he sent a memo to Taylor's division chief, Governor Sumner Sewell of IA&C. "These reports re Munich University keep recurring," he wrote. "If even partly correct, something must be done. Will you get your people in touch with General Muller in Bavaria, find out the facts, and clean house if necessary? Dr. Dorn can help greatly. I would appreciate an early report."[54] The following morning John Taylor and Governor Sewell agreed that the situation in Munich required prompt examination by competent educational leadership. Two days later John Taylor was in Munich for talks with Land Director Muller, E&RA Branch Chief Walter Bergman, and E&RA's Chief of Higher Education Section Barnett.[55] In the discussions that followed, the local education officers contended that the situation was not out of control, although it merited close observation and supervision. Later, Bergman and Barnett, in their annual report, said that, "as the status of individual members of the several faculties were subjected to closer scrutiny, it became apparent that serious irregularities existed in a considerable number of cases. These irregularities were in the process of being dealt with individually, and in the course of time would doubtless have been properly disposed of." But it became apparent that Clay and McNarney expected more dramatic measures. The July 14 report continued: "However, pressure on higher echelons of Military Government resulted in the ordering of a formal comprehensive investigation under the direction of Policy Enforcement Branch, OMGUS."[56]

Taylor returned optimistically to Berlin. However, another round of unfavorable press coverage revealed nationalistic tendencies among students at Erlangen. Not long after his return to Berlin, Taylor received word from ICD that a DANA reporter had been covering events in Erlangen and, with ICD's permission, was about to break a story on the hostile political climate there. Taylor requested a delay until the facts could be substantiated; memories of the Daniell and Long articles were still keen. But on July 18, ICD replied: "We have again checked with Nuremberg on the Erlangen student story and have agreed with the author of the story, our Nuremberg correspondent, that it should go out. It has been rewritten, and an attempt has been made to include as much recent material as we were able to get."[57] DANA lost no time. The story broke in Berlin on the very day Taylor received ICD's final decision. General Muller in Bavaria had tried to kill the release but was too late. The DANA banner headline read: "Nazi and Militaristic Activity of Students of the Erlangen University Continues Today." The article claimed to have exposed a systematic effort by students, faculty, and administration to undermine democratic values at the university. Faculty members were reportedly contemptuous of Occupation authorities, law students were critical of the Nuremberg Trials, and there was talk of forming veterans' associations to repel attacks on officers "by word and deed." Some students were blatantly anti-Semitic, the article claimed, and harrassed the few Jewish students at the university. One former officer was reported as saying publicly: "Although I have got to keep my trap shut now, the day will come when I can take these jokers under my control, and then Auschwitz might be called a paradise." The same report claimed that leftist political meetings were being systematically disrupted and that Erlangen's personnel-review committee was recommending reinstatement of doubtful faculty, such as a professor who destroyed extensive membership records of the N.S. *Dozentenbund* at war's end or another who in 1933 had called for the burning of books written by Jews and Communists. The article listed numerous other hostile incidents and criticized the responsible authorities. "Nothing has been done by the directors of the University to stop or punish these demonstrations. This has been interpreted as a weakness of democratic reeducation and as a strength of the student groups who continue their Nazi propaganda." The readership was reminded of the January Niemoeller incident which had never been investigated either.[58] The implication was clear: Military Government had been remiss in allowing such bold challenges to its authority to continue unchecked.

John Taylor, aware of the consequences of this latest round of press criticism, wrote to Clay immediately, trying to forestall an overreaction by Military Government. He informed the Deputy Military Governor that he had already dispatched an education officer to Franconia for an investigation. "A new rector is due to be elected this next week at Erlangen," he added. "He will be instructed to clean house." Despite the ominous reportage, Taylor reminded Clay:

It must be expected that university student bodies will from time to time reflect student opinion on many questions. . . . In the opinion of the undersigned, a *completely quiet* and *apparently docile* student body would be more cause for alarm than one in which there were organized discussions and even occasional violent outbursts, since the former situation would probably indicate the existence of unofficial groups acting as outlets for differences of opinion.[59]

The Erlangen crisis demonstrated that concern about the universities was not confined to Munich. It appeared to be mushrooming throughout the centers of higher learning and gave many observers the impression that Military Government was no longer in control of the situation. In his memo to Clay, Taylor brought the problem back to events at Munich and tried to explain the underlying problem as "symptomatic of the Bavarian educational situation in general, namely, that of a nationalistic state with a conservative and, in many respects, reactionary tradition in higher education." Such being the case, Taylor recognized that supervision of Bavarian education required "vigorous and unceasing work by the highest caliber of control personnel if a lasting change in educational outlook is to be effected." Yet, the awkward fact remained that neither requirement was being met at present. Bavarian E&RA had only one formally assigned university officer, although in practice the teacher-training officer was

performing similar duties, especially since the onset of the crisis. It was
also clear that the expertise of the staff had to be raised as well. "Attempts
over the past three months to secure a highly qualified head of this section
from the States have been fruitless," Taylor explained. He informed Clay
that a well-qualified sociologist was about to be hired by OMGUS.

> He will be sent to Marburg for briefing by the most experienced
> Higher Education officer in Military Government, Dr. Hartshorne,
> and thence to assume the temporary leadership of the Bavarian Section
> for Higher Education until a suitable man can be procured from the
> United States. He will be instructed to give full time to the Munich
> and Erlangen universities with a view toward effecting a satisfactory
> solution to the recurring problems and difficulties in those two in-
> stitutions.[60]

By mid-July, with Clay's encouragement, Walter L. Dorn, who had
figured prominently in the Patton affair and then had helped draft the
German law for denazification, joined John Taylor in analyzing the situation. He concluded that there was a grain of truth in the rumors of
conspiracies and subterfuges at the chief Bavarian university. "The various
faculties of the University of Munich have been denazified in such a way
that the remaining professors are resorting to what amounts to a sit-down
strike [against] calling [in] new professors, who, I am quite certain, are
available," Dorn wrote. "No new appointments to professorial chairs are
made so long as there is the slightest chance that one or the other Nazi
professor might still be cleared." A clique that was controlling admissions
at the university seemed to have coalesced. Dorn continued:

> I know that anti-Nazi professors from Breslau, Berlin, Königsberg,
> and Vienna have applied at Munich. The invariable reply was that
> it was necessary to wait to see whether certain professors would be
> "cleared," a reply that is contrary to the spirit of Article 58 of the
> Law for Liberation, which speaks of "removal and exclusion," not
> suspension of ousted officials. The various faculties should be in-
> structed to make replacements at once, like any other agency of the
> Land Government. If, as reported, the wrong kind of appointments
> are being made, the source of this should be investigated and cor-
> rected.[61]

Dorn recognized that the situation demanded more talent and resources
than Military Government had been willing to expend. He agreed with
Taylor on one essential: "I can only subscribe to Dr. Taylor's remark that
E&RA Branch needs people of the highest caliber, if a lasting change in
the universities is to be effected. Otherwise we are merely playing marbles
with the tightest clique in German society . . . the 'guild' of German
university professors."[62] Dorn forwarded his evaluation to Clay's assistant

deputy, Charles K. Gailey, for comment. Gailey considered the proposals and pointed out, after a further discussion with Walter Dorn, that two divergent reactions to the crisis were forthcoming. "There seems to be some difference of opinion between Dr. Dorn and Dr. Taylor," he wrote to Adcock for Clay. "In talking with Dr. Dorn, he feels that some direct positive action should be taken at the present time." Dorn had come to the conclusion that only E. Y. Hartshorne was capable now of mastering the situation. Hartshorne "has demonstrated his ability to handle these professors and knows how to get things done," Gailey observed; "I am rather inclined to agree with Dr. Dorn and do not believe we will gain anything by adopting the policies suggested by Dr. Taylor."[63] Within a week Edward Y. Hartshorne was in Munich as the new chief of higher education for Bavarian E&RA. A major purge was about to begin.

Faced with the inevitable, E&RA branches in each Land went through the formality of requesting further investigations from Military Government's various intelligence and investigative agencies. Within a week, denazification teams, consisting of agents from Policy Enforcement Branch, Special Branch, and E&RA Branch began to form. ICD's Intelligence Branch, CIC, and other agencies supplied them with abundant information, and, amid continuing reports of irregularities, the denazification teams promptly went into action. Preliminary inspections at institutions of higher learning seemed to indicate that there was widespread evasion of Law 104.[64] The highest echelons of Military Government released a directive on September 21 entitled "Removal of Important German Officials." It demanded that all German officials exhibit "political and moral qualities capable of assisting in developing genuine democratic institutions in Germany." One of its provisions applied the same formula specifically to "all teaching and administrative personnel."[65] Inspections of each institution of higher learning took place in October and November. Each team received detailed instructions to inspect all persons employed at the universities, including faculty, administrative staff, technical support personnel, and even menial workers. "This directive will be construed in its broadest sense; it particularly covers those cases where faculty or staff members have been demoted and retained in any capacity . . . and all cases in which temporary employment authorization has been issued by any U.S. or German agency." In the past, when highly trained medical personnel had been dismissed from leadership positions, they had also received temporary licenses from Land governments to practice in university clinics as "ordinary labor."[66] On the basis of preliminary evidence, especially at Würzburg, the new directive was intended to plug that loophole.

For a start, each investigative team received from the rector "a true and complete list of all personnel associated with, part of the contributing

services of, and employed by, at, or for the institution, including volunteers
and those paid from private or other funds." After checking the university
rosters against Military Government records, they recorded the former
party affiliation of each employee, including membership in all the auxiliary organizations maintained by the Nazis, to which the literally thousands of university personnel in each institution had belonged. Agents
then sorted all cases into groups for discharge, closer examination, or
retention, and the lists compiled were to be inspected by several echelons
of authority. "The ADMG [General Adcock] has directed that the roster
be carefully reviewed personally by the Land Directors concerned, their
action indicated thereon, and the original returned to the field agent." The
implementing instructions were obviously designed to minimize personal
judgments and to remind each agent that his work was being observed
carefully by senior officers. Field agents were directed to "include recommendations for the prosecution of any and all U.S. and German personnel who appear to you to have acted contrary to the Law or regulations
(or spirit thereof) for denazification." Since the U.S. personnel who were
likeliest to have been involved in earlier purges were university officers
from E&RA, the clause served as an embarrassment and a potential threat
to E&RA personnel. This time Military Government meant business.[67]

Despite all the detailed instructions, agents had to use their own judgment in deciding an individual's degree of involvement with National
Socialism. Vaughn R. DeLong, as acting chief of E&RA in Greater Hesse,
urged Land Director James Newman to consider several factors in judging
an individual's guilt: "What were the circumstances under which membership in an organization was acquired?" DeLong asked. "What activities
did the individual carry out as a member?" Furthermore, he felt that the
attitude and actions of an individual in the past year of the Occupation
should also count for something.[68] Other denazification personnel were
not inclined to be so generous. Infantry Colonel James H. Howe, temporarily attached to another denazification team, maintained a more militant approach, even to the point of disagreeing with Land Director
Newman. Howe recommended dismissals for twenty-one staff in Darmstadt whom Newman considered to be politically harmless. Howe announced that he had "taken the position that in the field of education all
party members of several years, regardless of whether their membership
was passive . . . , fall under the provisions of paragraph 8, Memorandum
to Field Agents." Howe also refused to consider any claims that individuals
might have joined the party to combat its aims from within.[69] Unlike
DeLong, Howe had had no previous involvement with education or any
other program of reconstruction. As in the days of denazification following
the Patton affair, Howe adopted the safe formula that anyone who fell into

the equivalent of the discretionary categories of old MG Law No. 8 was subject to mandatory removal.

Everyone knew that this latest round of denazification must be severe. Even DeLong, who disagreed with the current harsh spirit, understood that the universities had caused so much embarrassing publicity that another scandal would shut them down entirely. It was better to act decisively now. In the company of Rector Walter Hallstein of Frankfurt University, he feverishly examined the status reports and rosters at that institution and weeded out staff who were questionable according to the latest, more rigorous standards. He did it with a heavy heart, but Frankfurt and the other universities remained open.[70]

Munich University, which had played a central role in causing the unwelcome purge, received particularly close scrutiny. In mid-November General Muller announced the results: Thirty-three of its faculty, or 14.3 percent, received dismissal notices effective immediately, as did ninety-five administrative and support personnel.[71] As it turned out, Munich fared no worse than the other institutions, which averaged an attrition of about 15 percent on a zone-wide basis. There was, however, a certain rough justice at Munich because some, but by no means all, individuals who had been at the center of the rumors, intelligence reports, and press attacks were among those who were removed. The National Socialist law professor who had never quite joined the party was one of them. So too were some of the more nationalistic teaching staff. However, Reinhard Demoll, who had been reported to be at the center of a dangerous reactionary clique, survived the draconian screening.[72]

There was yet another casualty of the purge: Edward Y. Hartshorne. After his move to Munich in early August, "Ted" Hartshorne, as his friends knew him, showed every indication of taking effective control of higher-education developments, not only in Munich but throughout Bavaria. On August 30 he and a driver raced north in their jeep to Würzburg to examine a crisis in that university's sole remaining hospital. En route along the Autobahn, another Army jeep pulled alongside, and its two uniformed occupants eyed E&RA's senior university officer briefly. They dropped behind for a moment but then pulled abreast once again. This time a shot rang out, and Hartshorne slumped over while his murderers sped out of sight. Later, criminal investigators found the mysterious jeep abandoned along the Autobahn, with two American Army uniforms inside it. Despite an intensive investigation, no suspects ever turned up, nor could anyone establish a motive. Hartshorne's death was as pointless as the fate of so many who had fallen in the recent war. Certainly he had had his failings and had shown his German and American coworkers that at times he could be overbearing and gruff. However, no one doubted his intelligence and effectiveness. All mourned his death, and there was universal recognition of his accomplishments in the realm of German higher education.[73] At Marburg, Julius Ebbinghaus offered a moving public eulogy, and highly placed German educational leaders expressed their regret in private communications as well. Robert Sallet, secretary of the University Rectors' Conference, wrote to Walter Hallstein at Frankfurt: "The sudden death of Hartshorne saddens me greatly. I valued him highly and rated him as one of the most knowledgeable Americans with respect to the German universities. Is anything known about his successor?"[74]

Hartshorne's successor was Major Nils J. Van Steenberg, whose checkered career had included engineering, a stint as a psychology instructor, administrator in the U.S. National Youth Administration, and war service with a G-5 detachment. Now he moved over from youth activities in Bavarian E&RA to become chief of the higher-education section. Although conscientious and enthusiastic, Van Steenberg impressed all observers as in no way comparable to Hartshorne in understanding the problems and needs of German higher education.[75] With troubles besetting it on all sides, E&RA could ill afford to lose a distinguished leader like Hartshorne or influential allies like Grayson Kefauver.

The tide of denazification advanced relentlessly. Heidelberg emerged with seventy-two fewer instructors, Frankfurt lost thirty-three, and Erlangen, although among the smallest universities in the zone, also lost thirty faculty, or 27 percent of its teaching staff. Nor did the axe swing evenly. Erlangen's law faculty dropped to one professor and one junior instructor by the beginning of 1947. One E&RA report indicated that two faculties were especially vulnerable: "The medical faculties were hit especially hard, since the Nazis appear to have campaigned for membership and support among the medical faculties with particular zeal. The same was the case with the faculties of jurisprudence. In some instances the operation of the university clinics was seriously affected, which meant that the results of the investigation were felt not only in the field of education but in that of public health as well."[76]

The purge put pressure on everyone. General Muller, who had to review and approve all the dismissals in his Land, was as responsible as his agents for a thorough cleaning. He, in turn, began to exert pressure on the Bavarian authorities. On October 2 he informed Minister President Hoegner that, "if any Tribunal improperly exonerates or classifies an individual, the matter will be reported to the Director of Military Government for Bavaria, who may direct a retrial by the Tribunal."[77] There was nothing to retard or soften the effects of denazification this time. Reports and complaints about severe dislocations and injustices now replaced the earlier charges of laxness, and the students, far from worrying about irregularities among the teaching staffs, faced increasing scrutiny from Military Government. Although a youth amnesty, permitting university studies for young party members born in 1919 or after, had become law at the same time as Law 104, it also contained a proviso that no more than 10 percent of any student body could be composed of such individuals. Throughout the purge and into 1947, a running game of hide-and-seek developed with the students. The Berlin Documents Center, which had finally begun to function with relative efficiency, could send back confirmation of whether any given student had or had not been a party member. Fritz Karsen, who was chief of higher education at E&RA, OMGUS, wrote to all the branches in April, 1947, reminding them of the 10 percent rule and requesting that "a careful investigation be immediately carried out at all the institutions of higher learning." They were to report negligence by the rector or admissions committee immediately to higher headquarters. Karsen displayed some ambivalence about the proposed removals. His final advice was that "the investigation and, if necessary, the removal of a considerable number of students be carried out with energy but also with the necessary tact and consideration of the individual cases, in order to avoid undesirable excitement."[78] He did not elaborate on just how this feat was to be accomplished. E&RA staffs around the zone complied by sending in lists of hundreds of students to the Berlin Records Center, a deluge it could not handle. When in August, 1947, research by a denazification officer in Greater Hesse indicated that as many as 30 percent of the students might have been party members, the potential for another purge loomed. However, by this time no one in Military Government had any enthusiasm for the fight. With General Clay's approval, the standard was relaxed. A memo of September 13, 1947, noted that "it is generally agreed that the present situation with respect to this problem calls for a modification of U.S. policy." E&RA officials had learned that even though the 10 percent limitation was based on a quadripartite document (CORC/P[46]18), not one of the other three zones was currently paying it the slightest heed. Therefore, the 10 percent rule was to apply only to students who fell outside the youth-amnesty provision. In effect, the loosening of the denazification standards allowed students in the U.S. Zone to breathe easier for the first time since the Occupation had begun.[79]

Unlike the students, the university rectors experienced ever greater tensions. Josef Martin at Würzburg had succeeded from the first in gaining the confidence of the faculties and of Military Government authorities. This conservative rector carried out orders and directives from Military Government promptly and conscientiously and established an effective working relationship with his E&RA university officer, Edwin Costrell. One E&RA observer noted that the promptness with which Würzburg fulfilled requests by Military Government was in happy contrast to what had happened at Erlangen. "Such requests are promptly fulfilled at Würzburg," he noted, "but only after long and continuous prodding at

Erlangen."[80] When rumors of yet another denazification drive surfaced in July, 1946, Martin double-checked personnel rosters in advance of the newly formed denazification teams. The teaching staffs looked clean, but on August 1 he dismissed, by his own account, "a large number of physicians, officials, and employees of the University-Luitpold Hospital" in cooperation with Military Government officers. No sooner was the task accomplished than the hospital's ability to function was jeopardized, "causing unrest among the population." After consulting with the Bavarian State Ministry for Special Tasks and with a Special Branch officer in Würzburg, Martin ascertained that some of the recently dismissed physicians could volunteer to work again without pay at the hospital as "ordinary labor." The same Special Branch officer, according to Martin, checked on the matter a second time with his superior officers, and, with their approval, the hospital rehired sixty-five workers in the same capacity as ordinary labor. Martin reasoned that, for each of them, "a leading position was hereby out of the question."[81]

In the meantime, Würzburg received its first visit from a denazification team headed by a formidable figure, Lieutenant Colonel Gordon Browning of Policy Enforcement Branch. Browning had already visited I. A. Barnett in Munich and informed him "of rumors or reports that Würzburg University was not fully denazified and asked for his opinion on it." According to Browning, Barnett did not deny that politically compromised faculty were at Würzburg but added that, as soon as American Military Government fired such staff, "they were hired at once by the French or the British, so it was a problem to know just what to do." Browning announced that he must dismiss such arguments. He proceeded on to Würzburg for his first look at a German university. Browning found the situation intolerable. "Not only was the clinic Nazi," he reported, "but every member of the Library force, two-thirds of the Administrative staff, and two members of the division of Liberal Arts were shown to be Nazis." All attempts to explain the retention of medical personnel as ordinary labor failed to impress Gordon Browning. He demanded the dismissal of "Nazi Doctors"—by which he meant Class IV followers—and noted with satisfaction that "within a matter of days they supplied a politically acceptable medical staff when required to, which could have been done much sooner if definite action had been taken." But Browning's "straightforward solution" brought chaos to the city's only functioning hospital, and, despite the risks involved, Martin and the German public-health authorities once more resorted to the desperate remedy of acquiring "ordinary labor." There was a one-dimensional quality to Browning's concluding statement on Würzburg: "From the standpoint of denazification this institution is in a satisfactory condition for the first time since VE Day."[82]

General Clarence Adcock read Browning's report and immediately conveyed to General Muller I. A. Barnett's observation about the tendency of dismissed university staff to migrate to other zones. Adcock condemned such reasoning.

I assume that the University of Würzburg is now denazified in fact. I would like to be able to inform General Clay that the same is true with respect to all other higher educational institutions in the U.S. Zone. In order that there may be no delay in this, I would like reports by October 15, 1946. The officers who make this investigation should be given copies of Col. Browning's report . . . in order that they will understand fully that at Würzburg Nazi personnel were not dismissed because they would be hired by one of our allies or because of the difficulty of obtaining suitable replacements by the German head of the university. Wherever failure to denazify at this late date is found to exist, I wish the inspecting officer in each case to report it personally to the Land Director, using this letter as his authority to see him, and then report the case to me through the usual channels.[83]

The time for debating about denazification had come to an end.

Subsequently, denazification teams visited each institution of higher learning, and another officer, Charles M. Emerick, examined evidence at Würzburg once more. While it was true that the nonmedical staff of instructors emerged nearly intact—there was only one dismissal—Emerick was as unhappy as Browning about Rector Martin's explanation for retaining physicians as ordinary labor. "The commission is not entirely satisfied with this statement, although it does indicate what were the pretexts for this illegal employment," he wrote. Mindful of General Adcock's wrath, Emerick recommended Josef Martin's dismissal, plus a sharp reprimand to the Bavarian Ministry for Special Tasks, which had approved of the technical loophole. Nothing was mentioned about the Policy Enforcement officers who purportedly had agreed to the rector's reinstatements.[84]

In the end, Martin did not lose his position, in great part because he could point out that the rest of the university faculties showed little evidence of any political associations with the National Socialist past. No one could accuse him of systematic evasion of the denazification directives. Moreover, he had established such a good working relationship with the university officer at Würzburg that Martin's faculties, recognizing this as a factor in his favor, reelected him to a second term. A later historical report for E&RA noted that "Würzburg also enjoyed the benefits of having a rector who has remained in office for two years."[85] All rectors faced formidable pressures in the Occupation. It was to Josef Martin's credit that he retained the confidence of Military Government and his own faculty during two years of intensive denazification.

Isolated triumphs aside, there was little doubt that the latest denazification wave set the educational program back. As one E&RA officer wrote, "The effect of the removals upon the operations of the universities was severe. . . . In some cases the work of a department had to be suspended, and in one or two cases the program of an entire faculty was all but brought to a standstill." Despite the wholesale removals, education officers admitted that the university administrations had carried out Military Government orders "promptly and completely." They noted that the German and American authorities tried to find replacements but were almost uniformly unsuccessful. "Institutional morale," the report continued, "sank to unprecedentedly low levels." Most students and faculty failed to discern any adequate basis for most of the dismissals, which had come with dramatic suddenness. Education officers discovered that potential replacements at Munich held back in fear of future purges.[86] Many of those who were removed had been nominal wartime party members who had held no rank and were members of the N.S. professional organizations. Typically, they fitted into Law 104's Class IV "follower" category, which, before the purge, had not been viewed as grounds for automatic dismissal. Würzburg's denazification lists showed that some of those who were purged had become disillusioned with National Socialism long before the war and had resigned from the party, but in 1946 such perceptiveness counted for little.[87] The drop in morale was also due to the drab atmosphere of instruction in overcrowded, often damaged classrooms, where a crush of students jammed around their sole surviving professor, taking notes on scraps of newspaper with a prized pencil stub. Those who experienced it never forgot the decaying odor of damp plaster that pervaded the cheerless, unheated halls of all the universities. One E&RA officer summed it up: "Objectively considered, one cannot be surprised that the reaction was what it was, and one might even be grateful that it was not more violent."[88]

With time, the disturbing effects of the unprecedented purge caused growing concern far outside the university communities of the zone. E&RA offices received letters of protest from scholars around the world, urging reconsideration for those politically least compromised under Hitler. Sometimes the victims' advocates came from unlikely circles. In December, 1946, three Oxford scholars, R. Pfeiffer, P. Maas, and E. J. Wellesz, wrote to E&RA in Munich protesting the abrupt dismissal of Professor Franz Dölger from his chair in Byzantine studies at Munich University. They stated that, from their personal experience up to 1938, they could testify that "Professor Dölger as an honest scholar and as a liberal Catholic was strongly opposed to all principles of Nazism." All three had been dismissed from their universities in the Third Reich and now wanted Military Government to know that even as victims of fascism they felt denazification had gone too far.[89]

In the State Department, reaction to the consequences of radical denazification turned from willing acceptance to serious concern. In February, 1947, State's Hans Speier, Herbert Marcuse, and Henry Kellermann of the Division of Cultural Relations reaffirmed "the primacy of political security over educational traditions and qualifications, even if such policy should result in slowing down, temporarily, the progress of educational reconstruction." They contemplated changing the composition of the current German screening committees to include known anti-Nazis to ensure an uncompromising stance on readmissions. Obviously this would work hardship on the surviving faculties, and they suggested that search committees recruit new educational talent from free professions, the civil service, civic organizations, and even from gifted students, who might infuse youthful vigor into the aging faculties. Kellerman recommended the termination of permanent teaching appointments in favor of short-term probationary appointments. Such an approach might have averted the present crisis, he felt, which was due in part to the difficulties of securing definitive evidence on any faculty member's political background.[90] Eventually, Kellermann would have second thoughts about denazification.

Back in the zone, such thoughtful schemes were beyond the reach of the harried E&RA officers. They were trying merely to hold their own as the net of denazification spread. Matters reached a climax of sorts when in April, 1947, Special Branch and Policy Enforcement Branch announced that Hans Meinzolt in the Bavarian Education Ministry would have to leave. The matter turned into a tug-of-war between the denazification branches and E&RA, with Meinzolt caught in between. Special Branch produced evidence to show that Meinzolt was too conservative, nationalistic, and militaristic to hold high administrative office. E&RA officers conceded that he was conservative, but not unusually so. Moreover, he was their most effective link with the Bavarian education ministry and had performed valuable service for Military Government.[91] By now such disputes were familiar, but this time the education officers decided to stand and fight. When ICD began to publish a series of articles in their weekly intelligence digest, known as *Trend*, E&RA's branch chief in Munich, Walter Bergman, protested so vigorously about the inaccuracy of ICD's claims that a concluding article on Meinzolt was quashed before it could appear. The American consul general in Munich, James R. Wilkinson, watched the confrontation closely. After listening to both sides, he offered a synopsis of why the confrontation had been inevitable:

It appears that the affair of Dr. Meinzolt typifies the possibly unavoidable divergence of Military Government thought which arises whenever questions of political reliability of German governmental officials are considered. Special Branch is that part of Military Government

responsible for making recommendations to other branches on the
reliability of such officials. When it finds evidence of Nazi tendencies
or of a militaristic or nationalistic background in the past records of
responsible German officials, it recommends that the man in question
be removed. The section of Military Government which is responsible
for supervision of any one of various ministries often objects to recommendations for removal from Special Branch because the function
of such a supervisory section is to promote the smooth operation of
the ministry in question. The past records of the German officials
involved tend, therefore, to be minimized.[92]

Within a few days a decision on the case came from General Muller:
Meinzolt would remain as State Commissioner for Education in Bavaria.
For once, E&RA had won a battle.

Perhaps the officer most concerned over the unhappy developments at
the universities was John Taylor. With reports flooding in to Berlin about
the vast extent of denazification in the universities, he was fearful that the
highest echelons of Military Government would conclude that all of the
rumors and denunciations were altogether true. The chief of Policy Enforcement Branch in Berlin had submitted a report on December 12 that
made precisely that point and recommended continued strenuous measures
to assure that those dismissed would never again teach in universities in
the U.S. Zone. A typical recommendation by a field agent on a removal
read: "It is recommended that Military Government approval be with-
drawn immediately and subject be forever prohibited to teach or speak
publicly."[93] Taylor felt the time had come to put denazification into proper
perspective, since some branches of Military Government seemed to have
concluded that it was now a goal unto itself. He reminded his superiors
that, under the new directives, definitions of guilt with regard to party
membership had tightened sharply, a fact that few seemed to have noticed.
For example, under the old MG Law No. 8, E&RA officers had never
permitted persons classified as subject to mandatory removal to remain
in office. Such persons corresponded to the present Law 104's Class I and
Class II categories, for major and lesser offenders. But the record showed
that few if any of these had been discovered still teaching in the U.S.
Zone. The old discretionary-removal categories, which corresponded to
the current Class III, IV, and V categories, had been the basis for the
vast majority of removals during the current denazification drive. Taylor
felt that blanket removal of these significantly less culpable individuals
had altered the nature of denazification. Instead of judging such individuals
categorically, he proposed that agents should review them "on an individual case basis and decisions rendered in light of (a) their former Nazi
affiliations and activities and (b) their more recent records in the German
educational service." Taylor judged Policy Enforcement's interpretations

as being "injudicious if not erroneous." Policy Enforcement held out no hope for redemption. "The view is held," Taylor countered, "that barring participation in educational work for all time would be denying the principle that a person can be reeducated. Hence this Branch does not concur in this recommendation."[94] Considering the tarnished image his branch now had in Military Government, Taylor also took the opportunity to analyze for his superiors the conditions that had caused the current crisis in the first place:

> E&RA Branch recognizes that at any given time a check on denazification of incumbents of educational positions will in all probability reveal the presence of persons who are (a) illegally employed, (b) employed due to an error in evaluation of records, and (c) employed without specific approval of MG. It is also recognized that the subject study has revealed a relatively high percentage of individuals falling in the above-mentioned categories. Were this not true, it would mean that the few education officers assigned to control of German higher education had done an impossible task. A year before the cessation of hostilities educational planners of MG had requested the assignment of one U.S. MG officer in each institution of higher learning in the U.S. Zone of Germany. Until adequate personnel have been assigned, it cannot be expected that even the denazification functions of this job can be effectively or adequately carried out. Incidentally, this applies not only to institutions of higher learning but should also be projected to cover county and local administrators and teachers in the lower schools.[95]

Taylor's statement rang true, and even Gordon Browning, who had purged Würzburg University, corroborated Taylor's assessment: "The severe limitation on personnel in the educational field prevents the performance of all functions needed. Omissions are inevitable with demands as heavy as they are now."[96]

No sooner had the dismissals taken place than all observers—both German and American—took note of the mood of deep pessimism that had settled on German and American educators alike. In April, 1947, Raymond J. Sontag sent his impressions of Germany to the State Department. "When I was in Germany, it seemed to me that cultural questions (using the word in the broadest German sense) were handled less satisfactorily than any other part of Military Government." Sontag feared that America's highest Occupation authorities were assuming that the minds of the Germans could be molded like clay. Such notions were worse than naive; they were counterproductive. He urged that Military Government establish as a goal the aim of winning German intellectuals' respect by recognizing their traditions and abilities. He also expressed hope that America's obviously weakened education program would be reinvigorated with able new leadership, now that John Taylor was about to leave Military Government. In effect, Sontag was telling official Washington that America's education programs for the past two years had failed and that major changes and a major new emphasis on education were needed at this eleventh hour if any hope of success was to be sustained.[97]

In Germany, the survivors at the universities began to discuss the recent events and to try to find solutions, but their mood was anything but hopeful. Rector Eduard Brenner at Erlangen, who had assumed his post just in time to usher in the denazification teams, convened several local meetings of academics and professionals to discuss future actions. Then in June, 1947, he called together a larger group, composed of university rectors, distinguished scholars, professionals, and representatives of the Church, to meet with the Bavarian ministry of education. They also invited E&RA officers to attend the meetings to hear them "discuss what they consider the threatening breakdown of cultural life and development in Germany today." Brenner disclosed to the American officers that he had called the meeting to "combat the alarming and increasing apathy of the people toward reorientation." Brenner's group was frank. "They are particularly concerned with the indifference bordering on hostility of those who even a short time ago were willing to take the initiative or cooperate in reeducation." The assembled German leadership left no doubt as to what had caused the present spiritual malaise: "Denazification bore the brunt of the attack," one of the American observers recorded, "not the law as much as the spirit. The alleged need of personnel in the cultural fields was made the vehicle for demands that those only slightly tainted and those capable of conversion should be returned to their positions. 'Denazification' was at times violently criticized. It causes insecurity and frustration."[98]

The Germans' mood six months after the purge was growing ever more downcast, and some State Department officials began to regret their earlier support of radical denazification. In February, Henry Kellermann had opted for the purge even if it temporarily impeded progress in the education program. Now he began to wonder how temporary the halt really was. By autumn ominous reports were reaching Kellermann in volume. He conveyed his concern to a department colleague, information policy officer Thomas Goldstein: "Reports received in increasing number from the field all indicate that we are about to lose the struggle for the sympathy and support of German intellectual circles in our zone." Citing an inadequate education staff and the generally low priority assigned by the United States to its reorientation program, Kellermann recommended that the State Department assemble once again a task force to consider ways to penetrate the wall of aloofness being erected by German intellectuals in the American Zone.[99]

In his reply, Goldstein reminded Kellermann of the traditional aloofness, political indifference, and elitism of German intellectuals, qualities he felt had caused them to remain inactive during the demise of the Weimar Republic. Goldstein agreed that Kellermann's proposal to study ways to improve the situation was correct, but he warned against proposing ambitious schemes to rally German intellectuals to America's cause. As he put it, "there should presumably be no ambitious program of ostentatious proportions (which would be likely to elicit skepticism from intellectuals); but recommendations should be directed at giving help where the need is most acutely felt (such as providing materials essential for the revival of academic research, etc.)."[100] In other words, the American supervisory presence should perhaps be less keenly felt, and funding for exchange programs and research should receive more attention. Thus the State Department came to the same broad conclusion that John Taylor had arrived at earlier in the year.

Denazification proved to be a source of unending dissatisfaction in Military Government. All Occupation personnel supported it in principle as indispensable to the creation of a healthier society. It was the precondition to the positive programs desired by the reconstructionists. Yet, in practice, denazification proved impossible to execute with the limited Military Government resources on hand. It was also the cause of tremendous friction once General Clay decided to transfer responsibility for its execution to the Germans. One of the sad ironies of the situation was that denazification finally ended as a "casualty" of the Cold War. Once the Soviets announced an end to denazification in their zone, Clay felt compelled to follow suit. Thus, individuals placed in the "major offender" and "offender" categories were called up hurriedly in 1948 and dismissed with nominal fines and sentences—a painful contrast to the hundreds of thousands of individuals in the "follower" category, who in 1946 and 1947 had endured endless delays and, relative to their actual involvement with National Socialism, had suffered stiffer sentences. Denazification of the universities in 1946 reflected the inequities and shortcomings of a policy that all democratically inclined Americans and Germans viewed as necessary but that all wished secretly or openly would simply go away.[101]

The long train of events, which led from Pastor Niemoeller's chilly reception at Erlangen to Henry Kellermann's gloomy prognosis at the end of 1947, demonstrated that E&RA Branch had lost control of important segments of the education-reform effort. Most observers had conceded from the beginning that the E&RA staff was too small to carry out its assignment effectively, and the situation was still bad in 1947. The few university officers allotted by Military Government were in no way capable of overseeing their respective institutions with the thoroughness demanded by higher authority in Military Government. Then, when unfavorable publicity erupted in the press, the initiative passed to the denazification apparatus of Military Government. Unencumbered by the need to maintain existing programs and urged on by the highest echelons of Military Government, the denazification teams could afford to be—and were in fact—ruthless. E&RA protests proved to be ineffectual except in a few isolated cases, as when they finally secured the retention of a valuable ally, Hans Meinzolt, in the Bavarian ministry of education.

Such occasional successes could not disguise the loss of vitality in higher education, at least in the American Zone. The year ended with predictions that America was about to lose all meaningful support from German academics and intellectuals. At the end of 1945, one E&RA officer announced that his branch was still paying a price for having such a low priority in Military Government. Little had changed since then, but now E&RA was saddled with unwelcome and generally unfavorable publicity.

Such exposure could not help but have a negative effect on informed public opinion in the United States, where E&RA was trying, with limited funds, to acquire highly qualified staff. In the spring of 1946, George Geyer departed from Military Government after four years in uniform. As a final service to Taylor and E&RA, he undertook an extensive recruiting trip across the United States. But now, in addition to confronting the familiar obstacles of limited funding and bureaucratic delays, a new element began to complicate his recruitment drive. In June, 1946, Geyer telexed back to Taylor in Berlin the results of one recent interview. "Mrs. May [was] too smart for us. She contacted five top-notch educators, some of whom took the Chicago line that the work was one-fourth opportunity to do a job, three-fourths butting head against brick wall of the red tape mill. Therefore, she wants no part of it."[102] Geyer later claimed that, despite this problem, the quality of those who did join E&RA generally remained high. On the other hand, John Taylor had noted during the crisis in Munich that they had not been able to secure the expert that E&RA needed in higher education. William G. Carr of the National Education Association contacted highly placed officials in Washington on Geyer's behalf, claiming that Geyer "has an extremely difficult task in finding thoroughly competent people."[103]

The crisis in higher education had no sooner subsided, to be replaced by a mood of sullen apathy, than a fresh new crisis began brewing, one that threw E&RA into yet another situation where initiative passed beyond its control to other branches of Military Government. The new confrontation came over school reform in Bavaria and, by implication, in all the Länder of the U.S. Zone. At last Americans had arrived at the moment of truth—the moment when they were required to define what they meant by establishing an educational system capable of furthering democracy.

Before it was finished, the crisis over school reform brought American Military Government and the Land of Bavaria into a direct confrontation, one that went to the heart of America's basic philosophy of justifying its presence in Germany. The collision also altered decisively the nature of America's educational program, a development that few could foresee in 1947.

4

Kulturkampf *in Bavaria*

In the spring of 1946, when attention began to center on the universities, a memorandum arrived for Ambassador Robert Murphy from the Political Adviser's (POLAD) office in Munich. Parker W. Buhrman, who ran the POLAD office for Murphy in Bavaria, expressed concern: "Recent interviews with educational personnel of Military Government and of the Bavarian Government apparently indicate a lack of definite policy with respect to German education, particularly in secondary schools." Citing a lack of education officers conversant with German education except at the highest level, Buhrman remarked that American activities to date had been largely negative and that "we are concerned primarily with denazification and the removal of Nazi books." He was shocked that some officials viewed the mere act of reopening schools as sufficient, ignoring school curricula and alternative structures.

Buhrman recognized that the wide-ranging redeployment of U.S. forces had precluded continuity for the first half-year of the Occupation, but he felt that that explanation hardly remained valid. Detecting a curious lack of initiative, he discovered that American policy, as he understood it, was confined to the principle "that the rebuilding of Germany is a German problem, and as such should be handled by Germans with the least possible supervision from us."[1]

Buhrman and others shrank from allowing the Germans such broad initiative. He remarked to Murphy that after twelve years of intellectual isolation Germany was not capable, in his opinion, of coping unaided with the need to make educational changes. He also noted that "the German school system has never been as liberal as ours." The secondary schools, which demanded tuition payments, discriminated against the poor and made entrance to the universities almost impossible for them. Buhrman

110

maintained that now was the time to offer German youth "an opportunity for liberal education such as they have never had before." Apparently, he concluded, "Military Government began with no policy other than denazification of schools. What sort of policy should be installed when denazification has been completed has never been decided."[2]

Such criticisms exemplified Military Government's confusion on education policy almost a year after the Occupation had begun. Part of the reason was that the State Department's "Long-Range Policy Statement for German Reeducation" was kept officially secret until August, 1946, although it had received limited distribution at E&RA. More important, E&RA had remained a small, little-understood organization within Military Government; its goals and methods were virtually unknown outside the branch itself. John Taylor had announced at his December, 1945, staff meeting that, given Military Government's severe shortage of personnel, the German education ministry in each Land must initiate its own plans and form commissions to solve immediate and long-term problems.[3]

At the same meeting, Bavarian E&RA Chief Alfred Pundt suggested a possible danger in Taylor's planned reliance upon German experts: "Always assuming that reeducation must come from the Germans themselves," he stated to the group, "it must be pointed out that talent among the Germans who screen clear is rare." From his perspective the democratization of education in Bavaria required an inner change, centering on the relationship between teacher and pupil because of Bavaria's traditional and formal teaching methods. "These methods are to be liberalized. A more democratic and progressive teaching technique is foreseen by the Bavarian officials, but that is something which perforce must come about slowly and as a result of teacher-education programs which will require years." Pundt also reported that elementary schooling would be lengthened to nine years and that the number of humanistic *Gymnasia* would be increased to offset cutbacks by the Nazis. Each *Gymnasium* would continue to draw pupils from the elementary schools after the fourth school year. The pupils would receive six years of general curriculum, followed by three years of advanced preparation for the university. He claimed that the Bavarian people would decide the fate of the confessional schools without interference from Military Government. Finally, Bavaria's numerous teacher-training institutions would develop a more rigorous three-year curriculum to upgrade elementary-school teachers.

There were other particulars in Pundt's speech, but his summary indicated clearly that Bavaria's school system would remain substantially the same as it had been in the Weimar Republic days, preserving a two-track system of secondary and elementary schools. Pundt's remarks seemed so unexceptional that they provoked no debate among the E&RA staff gathered at Frankfurt from all parts of the zone at the end of 1945.[4]

In fact, Pundt expressed concern that the Bavarian ministry of education might be going too far with its present desire to end confessional schools in favor of *Simultanschulen* (nondenominational schools). "This obviously will find strong opposition among many of the Catholics in Bavaria," he warned and suggested that the will of the Bavarian people should determine the issue. Parker Buhrman's position just three months later represented a radical change from this.

At almost the same time that Buhrman was registering his criticisms of Military Government, General Lucius Clay received from General O. P. Echols at the CAD a report from the recently returned U.S. Education Mission to Japan, including a comment from Clay's opposite in the Far East, General Douglas MacArthur. "The report will be most helpful to my Headquarters," MacArthur wrote, "in its further efforts to assist the Japanese Government in modernizing the Japanese educational system. The report may well be studied by all educators regardless of individual aspects."[5] Clay was habitually interested in MacArthur's Occupation experience and was well aware that comparisons between the two were inevitable. Echols remarked on the American Mission's cordial reception in Japan and asked Clay to consider the possibility of receiving one in Germany. Clay immediately forwarded the Mission's report to John Taylor for his reaction.

Taylor was cool to the idea of a U.S. Education Mission to Germany. Although there were broad similarities between the Japanese and German educational systems, including the nineteenth-century pattern of elite secondary schools for a privileged minority and a mass school system, with a different curriculum, for the great majority, Germany's schools had undergone significant changes in the Weimar Republic days, and even the Nazis had extended educational opportunities somewhat, albeit adding a heavy dose of ideology. Taylor's view was that the German educational system was now in the process of reasserting itself roughly along these already established lines.

> The so-called negative aspects of present Military Government policy with respect to German educational control, by their application, tend to reestablish an already highly developed and well-articulated system of education. Hence the situation in Germany is not analogous to that in Japan. Further, U.S. policy in Germany requires German state educational authorities to produce plans for new programs as well as for proposed reforms of existing programs in the functional fields of education. These proposals are discussed with German education ministry representatives by Military Government education officers, and it is through such conferences that the positive influencing and reorienting of German education takes place.[6]

Taylor reasoned that educational surveys were undertaken for two purposes: to lay the groundwork for a new program or to evaluate an existing
program. Since E&RA's positive program—as opposed to denazification—
had scarcely begun, it would be premature to seek an evaluation at present.
Perhaps a mission would prove useful when the State Department assumed
responsibility for the Occupation, but Taylor felt that several members of
the original State Department Advisory Committee on German Reeducation, established in 1945, could accept this additional responsibility. For
the present, he concluded, "the constitution at this time of a U.S. education mission, similar to the mission to Japan, is unnecessary."[7]

Taylor's memorandum rejecting the proposal reached division level in
Military Government, where his immediate superior, Governor Sumner
Sewell, delayed, for the time being, transmitting it to Clay's office. Meanwhile, on May 1, 1946, a meeting sponsored by the State Department
convened in Washington, D.C., on the theme of "Reeducating Japan and
Germany." Among those in attendance was William G. Carr, of the National Education Association, who urged the government to send a delegation to Germany. Following the meeting, he wrote to the State
Department's Division of Central European Affairs: "I assure you that I
was quite serious in making the suggestion. From all that I can learn
regarding the situation of German education in the American Zone, it
appears that a mission could give valuable aid to the Government of the
United States."[8] Thus, pressure for a mission intensified, and cables traveled back and forth between Berlin and Washington in the early days of
May. After further discussions at OMGUS, Taylor had no choice but to
reconsider his refusal. On May 7 he submitted a new memorandum.

Taylor refused to abandon the principle "that German authorities
[should] themselves produce plans for the reorientation and reorganization
of German education" and that E&RA's role should accordingly remain
supervisory. However, he was now willing to accept a mission, with the
understanding that it "give a full and correct interpretation of our programs to the American public." In addition, it would serve to "pass judgment for the Military Government upon the soundness of the plans now
in operation, with suggestions for improvement or modification." General
Robert McClure of ICD agreed with Taylor's revised assessment, and this
time the memorandum received Clay's immediate approval.[9]

There was another precedent for an educational evaluation. Carr, who
had been a member of the mission to Japan, had been trying on behalf
of the NEA to interest the State Department in a similar mission to
Germany as early as July, 1945. Faced with a lack of official response, he
proposed the idea more forcefully in March, 1946, and reminded State
that the British Ministry of Education had already sent a commission to
the British Zone in October, 1945. "When I was in London in November,"

Carr wrote to David Harris at State's Central European desk, "I heard many favorable comments from British educators regarding the value of such a mission."[10]

By this time, however, State Department officials scarcely needed further prompting. Eugene Anderson, following discussions with War Department officials, had sent a cable to OMGUS on May 3 suggesting that such a mission would inform the American public of progress to date and provide expert advice on German education unavailable within E&RA. Taylor's second memorandum paralleled the May 3 cable closely, indicating that the E&RA chief had come under no little pressure to reconsider his position. As soon as Clay received Taylor's acceptance, he cabled directly to Washington, requesting the appearance of a U.S. Education Mission to Germany.[11]

With the passage of time, and following the advice of Secretary of State Byrnes and Secretary of War Patterson, Taylor's initially small mission mushroomed. To the three knowledgeable veterans of the now-defunct State Department Advisory Committee five newcomers were added; ultimately, the mission was made up of eleven individuals. Hans Speier from ADO had suggested from the first that in selecting members "it will be extremely important to have a certain number of persons on this mission who are not only experts in a particular field of education but are thoroughly familiar with the political situation in Germany." He also desired to "prepare the members of the mission most carefully for their job" by presenting them with key documents, directives, instructions, and statistical data as a background to what had been accomplished to date. Then Secretary of War Patterson recommended that the mission include "women, Catholic and other sectarian advisers, and proper geographic representation." In addition, Dean Acheson at the State Department contended "that the members should be of national distinction in the field of educational work."[12]

Thus the qualifications for mission members grew more complex, and, as State and War department officials began to recruit experts, Speier's advice that intimate knowledge of Germany be paramount took second place to considerations of national prominence. Prior to the Mission's departure, Secretary of War Patterson received a background memo indicating that members had been selected on the basis of "their national distinction and knowledge of wide areas of education, their technical experience in one or more fields, their statesmanship in educational affairs, and full comprehension of the relationship between education and society." Thus, the composition of the Mission was in marked contrast to the one envisaged by Taylor. Undoubtedly competent, its members were, with few exceptions, conversant primarily with American educational experience. Chairman George Zook was originally a professor of European history who became a university president and later a U.S. Commissioner of Education. Earl McGrath, also a U.S. Commissioner of Education, was a specialist in educational administration, first at the University of Buffalo and then at the University of Iowa. Helen White, a professor of English at Wisconsin, was also representing the AAUW and UNESCO. Bess Goodykoontz, from the U.S. Office of Education, specialized in elementary education. The Textile Workers' Union sent Lawrence Rogin to inspect adult education, and Henry Hill, president of Peabody College in Tennessee, would evaluate teacher-training institutions. A YMCA official, Paul Limbert, served as an expert on youth activities, and Felix Newton Pitt, diocesan superintendent of schools for Louisville, Kentucky, provided expertise in Catholic education. There were some familiar faces too. Reinhold Niebuhr and Eugene Anderson continued their involvement, stemming from the Advisory Committee of 1945, and T. V. Smith, who had engineered Taylor's elevation as E&RA chief in 1944, also agreed to go to Germany. Except for the last three members, the Mission displayed no intimate acquaintance with European education. Selection of the members had not been accomplished without controversy. Patterson was not pleased with Zook as chairman, complaining that he was "a high-pressure salesman and not an educator." Patterson claimed that they were sending "a political mission and not an educational mission." But it was too late to make changes on the eve of departure. Later some observers referred to the results—unfairly—as the "Zook Report."[13]

After several days of briefings in Washington by Assistant Secretary of State Benton and other officials, the Mission flew to Berlin, where it entered on another round of background briefings by Taylor and his E&RA staff. There followed a month-long inspection tour of the three major Länder in the U.S. Zone: Bavaria, Greater Hesse, and Württemberg-Baden, with briefings en route by education officials from Bremen Enclave and Berlin Sector. The Mission inspected institutions at all levels of learning and consulted German and American staffs as well as other divisions of Military Government involved in the reeducation effort. Then, on September 21, the Mission personally delivered a copy of its report to General Clay, who thanked the members for their work. The Mission then returned to Washington for a press conference with William Benton. The Mission Report was made public on October 12.

The report demonstrated a thoughtful analysis of the ills besetting German society in general and education in particular, and it was properly cognizant of the damaging effects imposed by war and poverty. The Mission's central concern was the revitalization of democracy, a subject to which many lengthy paragraphs were devoted. The members conceded that any definition of the overworked word was likely to cause dissatisfaction, and they tied its development to many complex changes among

Germans in their work, family structure, religion, and culture. However, they emphasized that education was vital for the development of democratic living: "The school is central to this enterprise," they announced. It would exert profound influence on the rest of an individual's life. Therefore, the Mission thought it imperative that certain changes occur.[14]

While mindful of E&RA's extensive work in restarting the educational system, the Mission noted that currently German education resembled the pre-1933 structure. The Germans still retained separate tracks for elementary and secondary education, with sharply differing curricula. After the fourth school year of the *Grundschule*, or common foundation school, a 10 percent minority split off from the other elementary-school pupils to enter one of several types of secondary school: a humanistic *Gymnasium*; an *Oberrealschule*, with a more modern curriculum; or possibly a catch-up *Aufbauschule*, for late bloomers and the geographically disadvantaged (children from rural areas). Parents paid tuition and expenses for this elite secondary education, and its demanding curriculum emphasized classical languages and other special learning that qualified its recipients for the *Abitur* and university studies (and, by the same token, virtually eliminated the chance of a university career for those who did *not* receive it). Even among the chosen few, an 80 percent attrition rate resulted in the advance of a mere 2 percent of the school-age population to the university level.

Ninety percent of all pupils remained in the *Volksschule*, or elementary school, where, after eight years of general education, they entered vocational training, either part-time in a *Berufschule* or full-time in a *Fachschule* or *Realschule* before taking a job. The Mission expressed its awareness that a debate had raged in Germany ever since 1920 over the merits of the system but that no major changes had resulted. "Now the battle for free democratic education must be taken up again," its members announced, and they presented their own solution to the problem.[15]

Starting with the premise that the school is the "primary agency for the democratization of Germany," the Mission claimed that a multitrack system inevitably produces inequality: "This system cultivates attitudes of superiority in one small group and inferiority in the majority of the members of German society, making possible the submission and lack of self-determination upon which authoritarian leadership has thrived." The Mission believed such a division made it impossible for all pupils to share a common culture. Therefore, it posed a formidable obstacle to creating a democratic society, especially since a child's career choice was essentially made for him by the age of ten. Structural change was, therefore, essential: "To an extent not true heretofore, elementary, secondary, and vocational schools should be united to form a comprehensive school system for all children and youth below the university level."[16]

While there were many other recommendations in the Mission Report, the proposal to create comprehensive secondary schools as the guarantor of a democratic spirit in education was undoubtedly the most significant. The members claimed that the terms "elementary" and "secondary" should not mean two types or qualities of education but rather two consecutive levels, as was the case in America. Therefore, they proposed six years of elementary schooling in the *Grundschule* for all youngsters, regardless of "sex, social class, race, vocation, or professional intention." However, the Mission conceded the need to allow special groupings for certain subjects and proposed that pupils could begin foreign languages on a voluntary basis as early as the fifth year. Upon completing elementary school, all pupils would enter the tuition-free secondary school, in which "an elastic organization of the curriculum in core subjects and elective courses" would provide the necessary differentiation for vocational or professional preparation of pupils.[17]

Other particulars of the Mission Report included an initial common-core curriculum for all pupils, regardless of ability, plus a greater emphasis on the social sciences, "which should contribute perhaps the major share to the development of democratic citizenship." The experts suggested that teacher-training programs be raised to university status in light of the profound changes contemplated for elementary and secondary education. They also suggested the creation of nonpartisan youth organizations and exposure of German teachers to teaching practices in democratic nations. At the university level they hoped to break down an ingrown, narrowly scholastic outlook among faculty and students by opening the universities to broader social groupings and by creating "broadly representative advisory bodies" to recommend curricula more in accord with changed social conditions. The last hinted at the board of trustees commonly found in American universities. They recommended the inclusion of general-education requirements in university curricula, plus student government and discussion groups to enhance the concept of responsible leadership. There were many other proposals of a more technical or specific nature, as well as some general criticisms of existing practices. For example, the Report condemned as "artificial" the confining of women to the "Kinder, Küche, Kirche" formula, which had reduced those worthy functions to "antidemocratic sterilities."[18]

The Mission Report also commented on the accomplishments of America's reeducation effort to date and, not surprisingly, found them wanting. The Report stated openly that E&RA "must necessarily have the right of veto over undemocratic proposals of the Land education ministries," and, since it was charged with "the hardest and most important task facing Military Government in Germany today," E&RA should attain division status, with double its current personnel strength. The State and War departments could help by appointing a standing advisory committee to coordinate the efforts of all American agencies concerned with educational policy and operations in Germany. Finally, the Mission concluded that the United States would have to devote greater resources than it had been willing to commit to date to the education program. Their recommendations ran the gamut from increased allocations of paper for educational publications to provisions for expanded audiovisual media, more generous import allowances for scholarly works, and significantly greater resources for reviving Germans' cultural contacts abroad. "It is recommended that the program be supplemented by the provision of funds for bringing carefully selected German students, teachers, and other cultural leaders to the United States for a period of training."[19]

While many provisions of the Mission Report were sound, there was no denying the fact that it departed substantially from the earlier "Long-Range Policy Statement for German Reeducation," which had maintained that the reconstruction of Germany's cultural life "must be in large measure the work of the Germans themselves." That document claimed that American plans for German educational change must "make maximum use of those German resources" in order to be successful. Although it had been prepared at the State Department in May, 1945, the statement was not published until August 21, 1946, on the eve of the Mission's departure for Germany. Thus, the shift in attitude appeared both sudden and profound. Some private groups and individuals within the U.S. Government had always believed that direct controls were necessary if German education was to change significantly, and Parker Buhrman's advice in March, 1946, typified such thinking. The Mission Report, issued on October 12, gave official recognition to this attitude.

Assistant Secretary of State Benton, who received the Report on the Mission's return, was not pleased with certain sections. In a "letter of transmittal" to Secretary of State Byrnes he took issue with its central recommendation: the restructuring of elementary and secondary schools. "I do not believe," he wrote, "that democratic practice requires the integration of vocational education with general secondary education under the same roof, as the Mission recommends." Benton suggested instead that liberal courses could be added to a curriculum to inculcate attitudes of political responsibility without radically altering Germany's traditional educational structure. He also questioned the proposal to establish separate pedagogical faculties at the university level. Were that to happen, the training of secondary-school teachers might "be relegated to special faculties of no great competence instead of being made, as it should be, a major responsibility of all faculties in all the major universities."[20]

Thus a debate immediately began over the findings of the Mission Report. The State Department received numerous comments from American educators as individuals and groups, with the majority supporting the findings of the Mission. Willard B. Spalding, superintendent of schools for Portland, Oregon, was angered by Benton's critical letter of transmittal. "If Secretary of State Byrnes, for whom the report is really intended, has time to digest the full report himself, all will be well," Spalding wrote in a widely distributed rebuttal of Benton's position. "But Mr. Byrnes is a very busy man, and the probabilities are that he will have to content himself with the digest of it as interpreted in Mr. Benton's letter of transmittal." Spalding noted that Benton offered no evidence to support his contentions and that his eighteen years as an advertising executive, followed by another eighteen years in administration at the University of Chicago, hardly qualified him to challenge the collective wisdom of the Mission. "In recommending to his chief that the recommendation for the comprehensive high school be ignored, Mr. Benton has taken out of the report the one recommendation of the Mission that would achieve the end it sought. To perpetuate the purely vocational school will be to channel the education of the poorer classes into the trades." By differing with the Report, Benton had issued a challenge to American educational leadership, "a challenge," Spalding concluded, "which should not go unanswered."[21] Nor was Spalding alone. Benton's letter sparked a host of criticisms by other education experts.

One of Benton's assistants tried to blunt Spalding's anger with the assurance that the assistant secretary had found the report "excellent" and that Assistant Secretary John Hilldring was reviewing the entire Report, as were War Department and Military Government officials. Benton's remarks, the reply claimed, were not to be interpreted as a statement of official U.S. policy, and the assistant secretary had had "no desire to substitute his own ideas, as you suggest in your analysis."[22] But, in truth, Benton's opinion carried great weight within the State Department, and his personal views on the Mission Report were even more pronounced than his public statements indicated. He wrote to a friend and former economic adviser for Military Government, Laird Bell: "I was somewhat more critical of the report than my transmittal letter indicated—particularly what seemed to me a tendency to fasten on the German educational system all the details of the American system." He informed Bell that the State Department would now proceed with policy formulation, "growing out of Doctor Zook's report and my letter of transmittal to the Secretary."[23] Henry Leverich, at ADO, discussed the Report and Benton's criticisms with State's foremost expert on Central European affairs, James Riddleberger. Leverich reported back to Benton, "I can only say that he agrees fully with the analysis of the Report as contained in your report to the Secretary. I went over the draft of this letter very carefully with Riddleberger, and we were in complete agreement with regard to it."[24] Influential

State Department officials were not enthusiastic with the conclusions of the mission they had helped to sponsor.

A few private citizens also challenged the validity of the Report. Shortly after its release, a letter appeared in the *New York Times*. Mr. K. A. Mayr, son of a humble bank clerk in Germany and now an American citizen, took issue with the Mission's assertion that the path to higher education had been limited to individuals of wealth and higher social position. He stated that he had entered a university simply by passing the necessary examinations. "Tuition fees were small and did not have to be paid if the means were not available. Higher education depended almost exclusively on ability," he maintained.[25] Mayr was the first but by no means the last German émigré to take issue with the Mission Report. Other prominent groups, most notably thirteen professors from the University of Chicago, began work on a reply, which they published a year later at a critical stage in negotiations between Military Government and Bavarian authorities. The debate on the Mission Report proved to be as protracted as it was hard-fought.

The strong structural differences between the German and American public educational systems almost inevitably led to some misconceptions on the part of the Mission staff. The *Volksschule* curriculum was not merely vocational and practical as an outside observer might at first assume. Like the secondary schools, it too imparted general knowledge as well as skills, although twelve years of National Socialism had certainly obscured that fact. There was also a tendency to view the *Gymnasia* as private schools, on the order of the American academies and the British public schools. In fact they were public institutions that, as K. A. Mayr had noted, did not demand high tuition. Lower-middle-class families could afford to attend if they so chose, although, given the upper-middle-class aura surrounding some *Gymnasia*, many poorer families did not avail themselves of the opportunity. One phenomenon that completely escaped the Mission, as it would most non-Germans, was connected with the high attrition rate at the *Gymnasium* level. On the surface, an 80 percent dropout rate looked alarming and wasteful. However, there was a common tradition in lower-middle-class German families to send their sons—less frequently their daughters—to the *Gymnasium* or equivalent higher school up until the last three years, which were, in reality, the years of advanced preparation for the universities. These *einjährig-Freiwilligen* (one year voluntary pupils) were satisfied to receive the undoubtedly sound education at the *Gymnasium*, and they did not become "dropouts" in the American sense because they or their families had not envisaged a university career for them in the first place. Even in Germany the phenomenon caused confusion in educational surveys and literature, and it is not surprising that the Mission failed to take it into account.

If the subject of comprehensive schools and teacher training sparked controversy, the Mission's recommendation to strengthen E&RA and America's cultural programs prompted general agreement. State and War department officials concurred, but approval in Washington did not automatically produce changes in Military Government operations. Because of severe budgetary limitations, OMGUS was faced with personnel freezes and reductions at the very moment the Report appeared. A "Reduction of Personnel" memorandum circulated among all Land directors on September 26, 1946. Alarmed, John Taylor met with Clay's assistant, General Clarence Adcock, to try to exempt E&RA from the cutback. He seemed successful at first. On October 4 Adcock announced "that it is not the desire of this Headquarters to reduce personnel in the field of Education and Religious Affairs." They prepared a cable, with Clay's authorization, which was to be sent to all Land directors, but OMGUS's Manpower Board had to give its approval first.[26] Unable to produce the additional financial resources and faced with a serious budgetary crunch, the Manpower Board withheld its support. Ironically, on the same day the Mission Report appeared, E&RA received this message: "Manpower Board has not lifted freeze off Religious Affairs; hence attached cable is not approved."[27] While the higher echelons of Military Government might establish a distinction between education officers and religious affairs officers, E&RA did not. In practice, each staff member carried two or three assignments, so that such distinctions proved to be artificial. The looming issue of confessional schools would blur such distinctions even further.

Many observers confirmed independently the need for expanding America's education staff in Germany. Eugene Anderson estimated in a report to Leverich at ADO that, in attempting the more positive goals of reconstruction, Military Government would require an educational organization "at least double the size of the present one," and he also recommended that a "large number of American experts be sent to the Zone for a few months or a year or the like." Anderson had praise for the highly qualified staff presently with E&RA, but he recommended that they "be employed for a definite number of years and not be subject to dismissal at a moment's notice, as at present."[28]

At the War Department, too, concern mounted over E&RA's expanding responsibilities in the face of personnel freezes. Lieutenant Colonel Robert McRae, chief of the CAD's Reorientation Branch, conferred with Taylor and his staff in Berlin on January 16, 1947. He agreed that E&RA personnel strength was deficient in all areas, even in the newly adopted Visiting Experts Program. McRae promised to raise the matter with Clay and to try to elevate E&RA to division status at last.[29] Subsequently, McRae presented a report of his findings to General Clay. "I realize," he stated, "that the question of personnel is of vital importance at the present time in view of the theater effort to meet the manpower restrictions imposed as a result of budgetary limitations." However, he was able to present Clay with some good news: "That this work is of increasing importance is evidenced by a budget for FY 48 [fiscal year 1948] three times as large as the one for FY 47."[30]

McRae had come independently to the same conclusions as Anderson had. He felt that E&RA was "as presently constituted not adequate for the Mission Report's plans." He also described an ominous new factor: "In connection with the personnel problem I am told that it is increasingly difficult to obtain sufficient high-level German personnel for work with the American staffs and to be trained to take an active role among their own people in efforts at democratization." If the trend continued, McRae predicted that it could paralyze the entire education program. As if those problems were not enough, McRae reminded Clay that Taylor was leaving Military Government in April, 1947, to become president of the University of Louisville. He feared that finding a replacement would be even more difficult than the fruitless attempt in 1945. "If such a person is found," he warned, "I believe it will be difficult to persuade him to accept a position of Branch Chief." The Mission Report had commented adversely on E&RA's low status, and this in itself would complicate future recruiting efforts. "That report was unduly circulated in the U.S. and has been read by many U.S. educators. I would, therefore, recommend that E&RA be raised to division status."[31]

Despite the sympathy of War and State department representatives and the understanding from Clay and other highly placed personnel about E&RA's neglected status, little help was available in the terrible winter of 1946–47. Clay had more immediate problems to worry about as the Occupation concluded its second year. The German people, already weakened by years of inadequate food and shelter, now had to endure one of the coldest winters on record in a time of world-wide food shortage. Lucius Clay's Herculean task was to fend off mass starvation in the first half of 1947. The dilemma he faced was demonstrated starkly by a twelve-year-old schoolgirl in Nuremberg. When asked to write an essay on the theme "The Most Beautiful Day of My Life," she responded: "February 17, 1947, when my brother died and I inherited his overcoat, his shoes, and his woolen jacket."[32] Clay had lived with such tragedy on a national scale for many months. A year earlier he had reminded John Hilldring that "cold and hungry people are not interested in the philosophy of life."[33] Sheer survival was still the highest priority in 1947. In fact, with its budget seriously unbalanced by the food crisis, Military Government had to endure a general staff reduction of 10 percent, which also eliminated all adult education specialists from E&RA's table of organization.[34] The education staff finally achieved division status when funding in the next fiscal year permitted the change to take effect in March, 1948. For most of 1947 there were fifty individuals in E&RA, a staff strength scarcely larger than what it had been in 1945. The villain, if there was one, was general lack of interest in the U.S. Congress and among the public for funding Occupation costs. The War Department's well-known ineptness in trying to secure appropriations for nonmilitary programs only exacerbated the problem, and the harsh realities of the Occupation blocked action on even the noncontroversial recommendations of the Mission Report.

As for the controversial provisions concerning school structure, the Germans offered their reply within a week of the Report's release in October, 1946. At a meeting of all the education ministers of the U.S. Zone in Hohenwerder in Hesse, a Bavarian Social Democrat, Franz Fendt, submitted a plan for zone-wide consideration "which he feels to be properly suited for use in Germany." Fendt envisaged three separate classifications of pupils. The first would consist of gifted youngsters who were fit to pursue "academic and theoretical studies." Fendt was confident that trained teachers could identify this group by the age of ten. The second category would include pupils who were competent to engage in practical industrial employment; they would be identifiable by the age of twelve. In the third group would be those who displayed an aptitude "for craftsmanship or who indicate ability only to handle manual labor"; they would emerge clearly by the age of fourteen. Fendt's educational structure, corresponding to these categories, was a three-track system that began with a four-year comprehensive elementary school for all youngsters. Then, exceptional children would be transferred to a pro-*Gymnasium* for six years, whereupon "those who continue to be outstanding in their studies continue their work in the *Gymnasium* for three years and then are entered in the university." The second category would remain in elementary school for six years and would then transfer to a *Mittelschule* for an education roughly equivalent to that of an American high school before entering a three-year *Fachschule* for specialized education. If recognized as late bloomers, they could enter a university, on probationary status until they passed a qualifying examination to become regular students. The third category would continue in elementary school for eight years and then attend a trade school for three years before seeking employment. Any late bloomers in this group would also be permitted to transfer to more gifted groups and, finally, to the university on a provisional and then regular basis. Acting Education Minister Franz Schramm of Greater Hesse was also preparing a more flexible school structure.[35]

Consul General Wilkinson, commenting to Murphy on Fendt's plan, noted that the theory behind the plan was that each citizen was to receive a type of education for which he was best qualified. "Therefore progress in the school under his plan and continued study would both depend upon the scholastic ability of the student as well as his innate intelligence, in contrast to the American system, in which educational progress is determined almost entirely upon his passing the required examination regardless of his inherent tendencies toward one type of training or another." Murphy transmitted the plan to the State Department, along with the information that Fendt's plan had been rejected by the other education ministers at Hohenwerder. "Nor," he added, "would it probably have received the required approval from Military Government if it had been adopted." In his opinion the rejected plan was "largely a reiteration of time-worn European educational policies," which, he felt, "does not give promise of developing the type of democratic educational system which it is desired to see introduced into postwar Germany." Instead, Military Government should insist on a program that offered equal educational opportunities for German children "regardless of religious, racial, or political backgrounds or economic conditions." Murphy's conclusion was unequivocal: "Dr. Fendt's plan obviously does not represent a forward step in this direction."[36]

Since the other German educational leaders had no use for Fendt's plan and Military Government was equally displeased but for the opposite reasons, it was obvious that in the aftermath of the Mission Report the two sides were farther apart from a solution than at any other time in the Occupation. As it was, Fendt, an educational moderate, was also politically vulnerable. He had scarcely returned to Munich with his rejected plan before being replaced as education minister by a member of the dominant Christian Social Union (CSU).

The new Minister of Culture and Education, Dr. Dr. Alois Hundhammer, was a formidable man. A leading figure in the conservative Bavarian Peasants' Party in Weimar days, he represented that blend of Bavarian conservatism and Church loyalty that clashed head-on with the Nazis' anticlericalism and suspicion of Bavarian particularism. He had been committed to a concentration camp for a short time after the Nazis seized power. Upon his release, he led a humble life, managing a shoe store and lapsing into obscurity for the duration of the Third Reich until Allied victory gave him a second lease on political life in 1945. Hundhammer became the majority whip for the CSU in the Bavarian Landtag and quickly earned respect as a shrewd political strategist. His elevation to the Bavarian cabinet as education minister in December, 1946, was to have a profound impact on the development of school reform throughout the U.S. Zone during the remainder of the Occupation. The American education staffs had expected that if resistance to school reform occurred it would appear first and foremost in the traditionally conservative and authoritarian Land of Bavaria. Alois Hundhammer more than fulfilled their expectations.[37]

At about the same that time the Bavarian education minister settled into his new post, John Taylor was returning to Germany after a hurried Christmas visit to Louisville. Taylor had held a relatively neutral position on the nature of school reform and had stated repeatedly that, in accordance with directives and policy statements from his government, the Germans would be accorded maximum responsibility for producing their own educational programs as long as these were in accord with the general aim of creating a democratic society. Thoroughly familiar with the educational debates of the Weimar Republic, he felt that the flexible Weimar system represented a good start that could now be bettered. "Our suggestions to the Germans," he recalled much later, "were to go a little further than they had done under the Weimar Republic with the *Aufbauschule* and make it possible for the gifted youngster to enter secondary schools and then go on to the university."[38] That position was compatible with Franz Fendt's stillborn plan, but by the end of 1946 Taylor's position changed.

During the final months of Taylor's administration of E&RA, Clay cabled a directive to all American Land directors on January 10, 1947, requiring each education ministry to submit a statement of general educational aims by April 1 and a detailed long-term plan by July 1. Clay warned that Military Government would evaluate plans on the basis of certain principles that OMGUS held to be indispensable for the democratization of German education. Some of the specific requirements were unexceptionable: the inclusion of social studies in the curricula, school attendance through the fifteenth year, the creation of kindergartens, and the like. However, Clay specifically required a comprehensive school system. "Two-track systems and overlapping of schools [are] to be eliminated," he stated. "Elementary and secondary [are] to mean two consecutive levels, not two different types or qualities of education." Clay's January 10 directive was sent at the instigation of and with full support from John Taylor and from his deputy, Alexander. The E&RA leadership had come to the conclusion that eighteen months after the surrender it was time to begin applying pressure on the German educational ministries to move forward with educational planning rather than to rely on the reemergence of the old systems. Simultaneously with the issuance of Clay's January directive the final draft of the Military Government Regulations (MGRs) came under discussion, including Title 8: "Control and Supervision of Education." E&RA officials referred to them as MGR 8s. By incorporating the particulars of Clay's January 10 directive into the MGR 8s, the E&RA staff had encountered a difference of opinion with Henry Parkman, the director of Civil Administration Division at OMGUS. Noting that Clay had begun granting the Germans local political responsibility since the previous autumn, Parkman informed Clay and the education staff that "the occupation mission with respect to democratization will be satisfied if the German ministries, for example, should decide to continue or re-establish the two-track system with all its overlapping." The E&RA reply was that, by requiring statements of aims, objectives, and long-range programs from the German educational authorities, the MGR 8s were "doing exactly what had to be done in order to reach the point in the development of general government and political party mechanics which has been so successfuly attained." But it was Parkman who fired the parting shot: "It will be noted that the DMG [Clay] emphasizes a minimum deviation from the policy of turning over full responsibility to the Germans." Undeterred by Parkman's legal opinion, the E&RA leadership gave wide publicity to issuance of Clay's January 10 directive and to the imminent acceptance of the MGR 8s.[39]

To emphasize the point of the new directives, Taylor and Alexander paid visits to Munich, Stuttgart, and Wiesbaden in February to deliver the message to the ministries of education for Bavaria, Greater Hesse, and Württemberg-Baden. It was Taylor's most important policy statement of the Occupation. "Our goal is the democratization of Germany," he declared from the outset. Since each individual was to assume responsibility for acts performed by representatives of the state, it followed that "the education of all toward a civic consciousness and attitude is, therefore, the highest and most indispensable prerequisite." A democracy functions best when it helps each individual to attain his or her highest development. "The directives which we recently transmitted to you by telegraph," Taylor stated, "are built upon these points of view." He assured his listeners that the United States wanted unity of reform for the various states, a remark that hinted at E&RA's decision to submit reform proposals to the Allied Control Council in Berlin for four-power approval.

The plan Taylor then unfolded bore a striking similarity to the features of the Mission Report. Elementary schools were to be extended to six years for all school-age children. "Each child will proceed from this school into a higher school, which is a 'higher' school only in the sense that it goes further. Thus, the overlapping of the elementary and higher schools ceases." Taylor's proposal for secondary schools was to construct a unified "higher" school with several branches, all of which contained a core curriculum for general education. One branch of the new secondary school would be an "academic" branch within the larger school structure and would remain relatively small. Taylor proposed that it have "a common three-year substructure and a three-year differentiated upper section." It was in the last three years of the academic branch that gifted pupils would continue Germany's gymnasial tradition. "This upper section gives wide possibilities for the cultivation of the humanities, which I appreciate even as you do," Taylor reminded his German listeners. "However, I do not think they can be properly cultivated only in a school of eight to nine classes in which about forty percent of the lessons are dedicated to the ancient languages, as a plan recently submitted to us suggested." Alongside the academic branch were the larger vocationally oriented branches, which would educate 90 percent or more of the pupils. While that arrangement might have been interpreted as meaning the existence of a separate institution, Taylor made it clear that such differentiation was not his intent: "In order to lay stress on the equality of the academic and the nonacademic branches, it is desired that they, wherever possible, be combined in *one* school."[40]

John Taylor was too well acquainted with German educational thinking to presume that his suggestions would be received enthusiastically. In order to forestall at least some of the expected criticisms, he enumerated five major obstacles, which could, he felt, "with good will be surmounted." Such a system presupposed free tuition and "ample . . . grants-in-aid" for all children. The new system would also require larger consolidated schools in order to function properly, as had been the experience in the United States. Therefore, confessional schools posed a stumbling block. Taylor felt that, where such schools predominated, "there exists the danger of a weak, small school." He concluded: "I hope that both confessions will come to a friendly agreement to avoid this difficulty or danger." Private schools other than experimental institutions would have to cease operations. However, the biggest obstacle of all to his proposals was the weight of German educational tradition. "Families whose members have received for generations a classical education set their hearts on it and think it superior to any other education. Please, however, look at the facts! The high school in the old German sense, the privileged school, is an injustice to the masses of the German people and an anachronism in a democratically emerging world."[41]

In close agreement with the Mission Report, Taylor envisaged a massive effort to upgrade teacher-training institutions to university status—a logical necessity if secondary education was to be radically altered. There were many other particulars, such as his desire to eliminate the exclusive social bias in student bodies at universities, to change the universities' guild-like constitutions, and to "end their neglect of social sciences and education for citizenship" by introducing general-studies requirements. Taylor's speech reflected the Mission Report in many other details by emphasizing social studies and civics in school curricula, full-time schooling through the age of fifteen, improved health care, creation of student self-government, and the like. However, the core of his argument lay in his recommendations for comprehensive schools, for the elimination of confessional schools, and for reorganization of teacher training. Those were bold initiatives to advocate for an educational system that had fought similar battles in the past, a fact that he knew better than any other

American except Alexander. The question was whether Taylor and Military Government were now ordering such changes or merely proposing them.

In his speech, Taylor described Clay's January 10 cable on school plans as a directive and, therefore, presumably an order. Always precise in his use of language—Taylor too had studied his Latin diligently—he repeatedly employed the emphatic verb form "shall" in his speech: "The *structure* of the school *shall* be organically unified."[42] The word sounded repeatedly through his speech. Yet, at other times his position seemed open to debate, as when he called for unified secondary schools "whenever possible." He also ended his address by saying, "I have the conviction that you willingly follow our basic, democratic proposals and await your suggestions for their implementation." Later, Taylor claimed never to have decreed reforms to the Germans but to have urged proposals instead.[43] Certainly his speech demonstrated ambivalence and the fine line he had to walk between his own more flexible views and the generally tough stance Military Government had taken after the recent denazification wave in the U.S. Zone. It was significant that at one point in his speech Taylor saw fit to remind his German listeners of the traditionally nationalistic and militaristic tenor of the universities. He admitted that Military Government might have committed mistakes in ordering such large numbers of dismissals, but he maintained that individual injustices would be corrected. "However," he added, "the big error was not the de-Nazification but the acceptance of the Nazi doctrine and the lack of civic courage of too many university teachers. Do not forget that!" Yet in his privately expressed opinions about the recent denazification effort Taylor was noticeably more sympathetic to the Germans. He had complained bitterly to his superiors just a few weeks earlier about a tendency on the part of Military Government to treat denazification as a goal unto itself that left no hope of redemption for victims of the purge.[44] Under pressure from the Mission Report and its prestigious advocates, from his more militant deputy and former major professor, R. T. Alexander, and from a more unyielding position by Military Government, Taylor appeared in his February speech to have crossed the line from a position of giving advice to one of issuing orders. On March 14, 1947, most of the particulars of the Mission Report and Clay's January 10, 1947, directive found their way into the MGR 8s.

In contrast to the increasing boldness of American authorities in taking the initiative in education reform, the British were in the process of transferring authority over education to the Germans in their zone between January and April, 1947. Sir Robert Birley arrived from Eton to direct Great Britain's Education Branch and adopted a policy of flexibility on most of the issues upon which the Americans were now taking a harder line. The nature of secondary schools, the burden of tuition costs, and the future of confessional schools were all areas in which the British were inclined to move cautiously and to effect compromises, depending on the attitudes taken by their German opposites. As one of Birley's coworkers once mentioned: "Sending Sir Robert to Germany to democratize education was a bit like sending the Pope to Dublin to oversee family planning."[45] While the British Education Branch and America's E&RA had shown certain similarities in their thinking and methods during the first year and a half of the Occupation, they began to diverge noticeably in the next eighteen months.

On April 1, 1948, Alois Hundhammer submitted the first school-reform proposal in the U.S. Zone. In so doing, he shocked America's education staff back into reality. In no particular did the Bavarian education minister adhere to Clay's January 10 directive or to the MGR 8s. In place of the comprehensive school, he reaffirmed the traditional multitrack system. He ignored all suggestions for upgrading teacher-training institutions, preferring instead to retain Bavaria's thirty-odd teacher-training schools, which accepted fourteen-year-olds for a four- or five-year course in elementary-school teaching. Further, Hundhammer expected Bavarian schoolteachers to declare their religious faith either as Protestants or as Catholics, which presumably would eliminate Jews or agnostics from consideration.[46] Thus, a vast gulf opened immediately between the American and Bavarian positions on education reform. As Consul General Wilkinson remarked, "Although he is perfectly sincere and honest, the consensus of opinion in Munich is that his educational ideas are so 'old-fashioned' as to be dangerous." There was some talk among the American officers that Hundhammer's reactionary position might have weakened his political stature among the more youthful wing of the CSU, but they quickly conceded that such opposition was negligible. Since the April 1 deadline had originally been set for the offering of general aims, not concrete plans, by the German ministries, Hundhammer would have until summer to produce an entirely different plan. But no one in Military Government believed that such a change would occur under his leadership. Walter Bergman, chief of Bavarian E&RA, proposed that, "should the new program of the Ministry of Education, which is to be submitted by July 1, 1947, fail to meet the approval of Military Government authorities, steps will be taken to remove Hundhammer from office."[47]

At OMGUS, G. H. Garde, of the Adjutant General's office in Berlin, dispatched a toughly worded communiqué to Hundhammer about his plan, informing him that "both the tone of the communication and the order are unsatisfactory." Instead of a workable plan, Hundhammer had sent excuses as to why his ministry could not "put into effect the basic principles which were laid down by Military Government for the reorganization of education in the American Zone." Hundhammer had claimed in his April 1 communication that it was "the ever evident desire of the present minister and his staff to make fundamental revisions in the character of Bavarian education." Garde countered that it was the consensus of E&RA experts and of Military Government officials in general that the April 1 proposal did "not reflect any great desire whatever to make fundamental revisions."[48] The lines of battle were forming fast in Bavaria, the Land that all observers now realized was the linchpin for educational reform in the U.S. Zone.

Following John Taylor's long-expected departure from Military Government on April 23, 1947, the way was clear for Richard Thomas Alexander to take charge of E&RA. His personality was markedly different from Taylor's, and his methods for accomplishing tasks were far more vigorous than any his former student, Taylor, would have dared use. At the same time, Alexander was not in an enviable position. He had inherited the post of E&RA chief against his own will, against Taylor's advice, and against Clay's desire. A search to find a successor had by now been going on for months, but it had produced no results. McRae's predictions, made in January, were proving to be altogether too accurate. Alexander was forced, as acting chief, to handle a growing confrontation with Bavarian educational authorities and to accept ever-increasing administrative responsibilities because of the addition of the Visiting Experts program to an already overburdened staff. He had also had to accept the general 10 percent personnel reduction along with the rest of Military Government in order to stay within the slender budget allotments for fiscal year 1947.

Thus, with responsibilities mounting and a confrontation over school reform clouding its future after an already damaging involvement with denazification, the E&RA staff was experiencing a notable slump in morale in 1947. Calling his headquarters staff together, Alexander deplored the present situation and announced that General Clay was angered over the impasse over Bavarian school reform. Alexander also conceded that his efforts to exempt E&RA from the impending force reductions had been unsuccessful. According to the minutes of the meeting, "Dr. Alexander said that he did not know how many positions he could get back for this office and outlined his plans for an increase in the field." The new chief returned constantly to the theme of morale: "Everyone was advised that it was his own personal responsibility to keep up his morale without worrying about the vagaries of the Army, as there is much uncertainty in any program which the Army sets up."

Alexander also attacked the German educational profession. The minutes record him as stating "that there are very few Germans who know how to do the thing we want done. . . . They have never acted democratically as an administrative body." The teachers, he complained, felt that reform was not their affair—that only the highest educational leadership should accept responsibility and initiative for educational change.

Alexander observed that in Bavaria the teaching rank-and-file did not understand the nature of American proposals and assumed that when Military Government recommended the creation of consolidated schools it would spell the end of the village school. Where the Occupation authorities called for curriculum changes, German teachers assumed that meant the disappearance of Greek and Latin. "Some irresponsible member of the staff has done much damage by giving them [the Bavarians] misinformation," Alexander thundered. He expressed anger with Bavaria's E&RA chief: "Dr. Bergman," the minutes continued, "was given to understand that he, too, was at fault, as he had passed the program and had approved most points of it." Alexander was not successful on that day in lifting the E&RA staff's morale to any noticeable degree.[49]

"Tom" Alexander, as he was known to his friends and many admirers, was not blind to his own faults. As he confided to another prominent educator, Agnes Snyder, after completing a year as acting chief of E&RA: "In the last year I have been able to get a good many things done here by main strength and awkwardness plus a bad disposition!!"[50] Alexander's long-time deputy, Levi Gresh, reflected the mixture of admiration and consternation he inspired among his subordinates. Following his return to the United States, Gresh wrote to a friend in Military Government about Alexander: "I never did understand that chap, and yet one must admire the old boy. You ought to be his deputy for eighteen months. Then you would know what I mean."[51] Alexander had never been enthusiastic about taking on the responsibility of being E&RA chief, a fact he disclosed repeatedly to his friends in correspondence during his term of office. He referred often to a desire to return to the United States to resume his duties as a teacher, a calling to which he brought a rare ability.[52] It was part of a larger tragedy that at this crucial stage America's educational effort in Germany fell upon a man temperamentally unsuited to the task but whose sense of responsibility overrode his own better instincts. General Clay was about to reap the consequences of not acquiring the cultural adviser State and War department officials had urged upon him a year earlier.

As part of his strategy of increasing pressure upon the Bavarian educational authorities to accept American proposals, Alexander redoubled efforts to secure agreement on an educational directive from the Allied Control Council. A four-power ruling would buttress his contention that the American directives were widely accepted and would destroy any arguments the Bavarians might muster that they were being subjected to unusual pressure or were being forced to accept narrowly conceived principles. Thus, after many months of haggling, the Allied Control Authority (ACA) Directive No. 54 finally appeared on June 25, 1947, as "Basic Principles for Democratization of Education in Germany." To a remarkable degree ACA Directive 54 was the American plan as described in the Mission Report and Taylor's February speech to the education ministries. Much of the wording closely followed the American documents. It was, therefore, presumably a notable American victory and a powerful support for their widening conflict with the Bavarians. However, the directive suggested changes; it did not order them.[53]

On the same day that ACA Directive 54 appeared, Bavarian IA&C Director Al D. Sims sent a menacing memorandum to Minister President Hans Ehard and to Hundhammer informing them that Military Government was "observing current curriculum plans with keen interest." He noted that no effort had been made by the Bavarian authorities to respond to the Americans' call for the inclusion of social-studies courses or civics in their plan and warned that a veto was likely if changes did not occur. "The Minister of Education will realize that, while these words of warning are blunt and directly to the point, they are presented thus to forestall further embarrassment to him that might ensue from the presentation of another curriculum that is likely to be disapproved by Military Government."[54] With tough language from its Bavarian staff and with unanimous support from the other occupying powers, American Military Government seemed to have placed Bavaria's minister of education in a tight spot, with little recourse but to submit as gracefully as he could.

However, the situation was not as promising as it appeared. First, it was widely acknowledged that directives from the Allied Control Council carried no force except as they coincided with the wishes of the occupying power. Sir Robert Birley recalled his activities with the Education Committee at the ACC: "There we passed splendid resolutions about 'democratic' education which did not matter at all, as we all had different ideas about what was meant by democracy."[55] John Taylor could hardly complain about such cavalier treatment of ACA Directive 54. He felt exactly the same way about other ACA rulings.[56]

As for Alois Hundhammer's reactions to intimidation, he answered by introducing a measure to permit the reinstitution of corporal punishment by teachers against unruly pupils in Bavarian schools. Widely known as the *Prügelstrafe*, it was enacted after stormy debates in the Bavarian Landtag in July, 1947, during which the Social Democrats and Free Democrats bitterly opposed the bill and the Christian Democrats as stoutly supported it.[57] Although the measure lent him a measure of notoriety he had not experienced before, Alois Hundhammer clearly demonstrated that he was not easily intimidated. He also demonstrated his ability to introduce a controversial measure despite strong resistance within Bavarian party politics and, for that matter, despite the objections of the moderate wing of his own party, the CSU.

For a short time, some American observers in Military Government and at the consulate general in Munich pinned their hopes on a proposal submitted by Jean Stock of the Social Democratic Party, but in the meantime Hundhammer had secured a delay in the submission deadline until October 1. As the summer waned, it became obvious that the Social Democrats did not have the political influence to put through an educational plan and that any plan that might pass through the Bavarian Landtag would need Hundhammer's approval. As the majority whip and one of the two or three most powerful political figures in Bavaria, Hundhammer exerted far more influence than his mere cabinet rank of education minister might suggest.

Through the summer and fall of 1947, Hundhammer and Minister President Ehard received a steady stream of communications from Military Government officials concerned with school reform. Alexander at E&RA, OMGUS, kept up the pressure with detailed directives on what the October 1 plan should contain. Even Clay discussed the particulars of the plan with Ehard and Hundhammer during a brief stopover in Munich. Bavarian E&RA's host division, IA&C, and its director Al D. Sims took an active role in the negotiations. And Land Director General Walter G. Muller was a frequent participant in the increasing tempo of negotiations with Ehard and the Bavarian educational authorities. Conspicuous by the subordinate role he played in the discussions was the one person in Military Government who should have been the central figure in the school-reform context: Bavarian E&RA Chief Walter Bergman. Alexander's open criticism of Bergman's vacillation at the time Hundhammer submitted his first plan in April suggested that Bergman had lost the confidence of the senior E&RA staff in Berlin and that the slack was being taken up by individuals elsewhere than in the E&RA staff in Bavaria. It was in the autumn of 1947, when a showdown came over Bavarian school reform, that E&RA's inherent weakness within Military Government showed itself most clearly.

On October 1, Hundhammer submitted his second proposal to Military Government. He delivered it personally to Military Government authorities and expressed the hope that this time it would receive a satisfactory response. The effect of Plan II, as the Americans labeled it, was electrifying. IA&C Director Sims forwarded a critique of Plan II to OMGUS within a few days of its submission, strongly condemning it for retaining a multitrack system that still separated pupils according to ability at the age of ten. Sims acknowledged that Plan II was more flexible than its predecessor, but that flexibility did not compensate for the fact that it still ignored the January 10 directive to eliminate multitrack and overlapping school structures.[58]

However, another keen observer for the Americans in Bavaria disagreed sharply with Sims's condemnation. Sam E. Woods, the new consul general in Munich, took a more flexible approach. Woods, too, had long acquaintance with Germany. In fact it was he who had personally taken possession of Hitler's "Plan Barbarossa" in a Berlin movie theater in January, 1941, and had dispatched it to President Roosevelt at great personal risk. In contrast to Sims, Woods took the view that "the new plan is rather liberal in comparison with the April Plan and previous statements made by Dr. Hundhammer and members of his Ministry." Plan II provided for including civics courses and health instruction in the curricula, as demanded by E&RA. It acknowledged the necessity for free tuition in secondary schools for children of poor parents, and even the multitrack system was not as rigid as it might appear. Woods pointed to the more flexible provision that allowed a crossover into the university track for pupils from the fifth through the seventh school years. The new plan also provided for a special qualifying examination for pupils who had not entered the gymnasial track but who desired at a later date to attempt a university education. To be sure, there were serious omissions in Plan II, and these would require negotiation. According to Plan II, pupils would still have to pay for their textbooks, and the Church would continue to exert influence because of the maintenance of confessional schools; moreover, the Bavarians had not budged on prohibiting coeducation for boys and girls after the fourth school year. Despite these differences, Woods counseled acceptance, stating that Plan II was "a decided step toward liberalization of Bavarian education." He was not sure what position Bavarian E&RA had taken, but, despite Plan II's shortcomings, he felt compelled to offer some advice: "It should be kept in mind . . . that Military Government will not be able, and possibly should not try, to impose an entirely American system of education on people who apparently neither understand nor desire it."[59]

Tensions between E&RA and the Bavarian ministry of education had long existed, but now they approached the breaking point. The Americans felt strengthened in their position by criticisms of Hundhammer in the Bavarian press, which mounted in intensity with each passing week. Muzzled by Goebbels' heavy-handed apparatus for twelve years, the Bavarian papers seemed exhilarated by the right to criticize government ministers, especially one who saw fit to reintroduce corporal punishment for schoolchildren. Articles appeared in the humor magazine *Der Simpl*, in the *Süddeutsche Zeitung*, and in the provincial papers pillorying Hundhammer for his excessive nationalism and conservatism. They alleged that his devout Catholicism had led him into religious bigotry and that he delighted in the use of brutality. It was further alleged that he had approved a textbook with a militaristic poem about Frederick the Great and that he was, therefore, still indulging in the Nazis' hysterical *Fredericus Rex* cult. The Coburg *Neue Presse* published a photograph of an eight-year-old schoolboy with a conspicuous lack of hair on one side of his head; it transpired that the boy's teacher had grabbed a lock of his hair with less-than-judicious force and had removed an entire swatch. The accompanying article laid responsibility for the deed directly at Hundhammer's feet. Even the American-controlled newspaper, the *Neue Zeitung*, reprinted a caricature of Hundhammer from *Der Simpl* that insinuated that only Catholic academics had a chance of returning to their university posts.[60]

Alois Hundhammer was incensed. He pressed a libel suit against the *Simpl* and bitterly condemned Military Government for allowing a publication it controlled to reprint what he felt was a scurrilous caricature of himself. Further, he took to the airwaves on October 17, 1947, and in a lengthy address to the Bavarian people engaged in an exhaustive refutation of every allegation that had appeared in the press. It did little good. On the following day the *Süddeutsche Zeitung* answered with an editorial entitled *"Schweige und Arbeite"* (Shut Up and Work). With characteristic restraint Sam Woods remarked, "It would appear to be greater political wisdom were Dr. Hundhammer to ignore these petty attacks and devote all of his time to his duties as *Kultusminister*."[61] However, despite rough treatment by Bavaria's newly liberated press, Alois Hundhammer was in no way weakened politically, as some officials at Military Government blithely assumed.

Diligently involved in recording the deepening crisis, Woods reported a few weeks later that "at a meeting of high-ranking American officials attended by Dr. Josef Mueller, Christian Social Union Chairman for Bavaria and Deputy Minister President, it was decided that the difficulties experienced by Military Government in the institution of a reasonably democratic school plan for Bavaria could be eliminated only by arranging for the dismissal of Dr. Alois Hundhammer, Bavarian Minister of Culture." The initiative for such action was not provided by E&RA staff members. Woods added: "Education officials of the Office of Military Government for Bavaria have indicated their concurrence in this decision."[62] Instead, it was pressure from Clay's headquarters and from E&RA, OMGUS, where the conviction was growing that Hundhammer must go.

In mid-November, only a few days after the crucial meeting between Military Government and Bavarian officials, Clay wrote directly to Minister President Ehard to say that Plan II in no way matched the features demanded in his January 10 directive. He reaffirmed his commitment to the elimination of multitrack, overlapping school systems, and he was adamant about the need to upgrade teacher training. "Of course I am aware of the difficulties of a reorganization of the Bavarian schools under prevailing conditions," Clay wrote. "However, I do find it disappointing that in the past year in Bavaria alone no progress appears to have been made in establishing modern, democratic educational procedures. I must request you to give this problem your immediate and personal attention. I hope you will agree with me that equality of opportunity in education is essential to a sound democracy. That we must have."[63]

On December 1 Alexander followed Clay's lead with a sharply worded memo to Bergman: "You will inform the Bavarian Minister of Education that his proposals are either lacking or unsatisfactory. . . . The time has come for your office to exercise a prompt enforcement of MGR and ACA directives with respect to education."[64] Neither Clay nor Alexander was satisfied with the performance of Bavarian E&RA to date, or with Military Government in Bavaria in general, to produce progress toward education reform.

To be chief of E&RA in Munich meant trouble for anyone unlucky enough to shoulder the assignment. Walter G. Bergman was the fourth Military Government officer in that troubled position since the Occupation had begun. His background seemed to suit him ideally for the job. With a doctorate in education from the University of Michigan, he had acquired several years of teaching and administrative experience at Wayne State University, followed by ten years as the senior research director of Detroit public schools. During the war Bergman served first as a civil-affairs officer and then became director of education programs for UNRRA for a year following the surrender. He had also served in the Rhineland Occupation in 1919 and 1920. Taylor and E&RA had felt lucky to acquire his services.[65] Yet, despite all his experience and expertise, Walter Bergman seemed unable to control the direction of education affairs in Bavaria. He had barely assumed his post at the end of May, 1946, when the denazification crisis in higher education broke out anew. During those troublesome events in the summer and autumn of 1946, Bergman had had to accept initiatives and directives from other quarters of Military Government. General Clay, John Taylor, General Muller, and, for a short time, E. Y. Hartshorne had played a more prominent role in handling the denazification crisis than he had. However, that situation could be explained by his fresh arrival in E&RA and his need to acquaint himself with the intricacies of Bavarian politics. By 1947, however, after Hundhammer's April 1 plan arrived at OMGUS, confidence in Bergman at higher headquarters had begun to wane. Not only Alexander but Clay as well began to feel concern about Military Government's handling of negotiations with the intransigent Bavarians.

With matters at an impasse in the autumn of 1947, Clay decided that Bavarian Military Goverment needed investigation and possibly a shakeup of personnel in order to get negotiations moving again. Consequently, James R. Newman, Land director in Greater Hesse, loaned Clay his civil-affairs expert, Lieutenant Colonel William R. Swarm, to observe operations in Bavarian Military Government and to make recommendations. With school reform stalled, morale in Bavarian E&RA was not good. Fear was widespread at OMGUS that the Americans in Munich were not speaking with one voice to the Bavarians on school reform. One rumor held that because Muller was a devout Catholic and perhaps a sentimental veteran of the post-World War I Rhineland Occupation he was not pressing forward with negotiations on school reform energetically and was secretly encouraging the Bavarians to continue their stalling tactics. Muller, a veteran military man, gave Swarm a chilly reception. He quickly realized that the sudden appearance of another senior military officer in his command area without his foreknowledge meant trouble. After offering Swarm the command of a detachment in the delightful—and remote—Bavarian Forest, Muller gracefully accepted Swarm's refusal and confirmed his appointment as deputy director in Al D. Sims' IA&C Division.

After about ten days of observing conditions in OMGB, Swarm wrote a lengthy memorandum to OMGUS for Clay, dispelling the rumors about Muller and other individuals in Military Government but confirming that the crisis in which the Americans found themselves was serious. To a degree unsuspected at OMGUS, the Catholic leadership in Bavaria, and especially Michael Cardinal Faulhaber, were unhappy about the American proposals because of the doubtful future of confessional schools. Swarm urged Military Government in Berlin to realize that Church opposition to American initiatives had strengthened Hundhammer's position manyfold and that menacing directives and memoranda were not likely to intimidate Bavaria's educational or religious leadership. If Military Government were willing to engage in acts of violence and intimidation comparable to what the Nazis had done, then they might cow the Bavarians into submission. Only then would a school reform occur in Bavaria that accorded with the wishes of E&RA in Berlin.[66] Swarm's inference was clear. A democracy like the United States could not act in that fashion. Therefore, compromise would be necessary.

In hopes of getting negotiations moving forward again, Clay rotated some personnel out of OMGB, including General Muller, but Swarm's analysis had been correct. The arrival of a new Land director, the former governor of Michigan, Murray D. Van Wagoner, produced no change whatever in the Bavarians' position. In fact, Van Wagoner's arrival complicated matters. Muller had been General Patton's highly regarded supply officer in wartime, and in the Occupation he had earned the Bavarians' respect as an intelligent, informed administrator in local affairs.[67] Van Wagoner, on the other hand, had had no experience in Germany whatsoever. Clay had appointed him to the position because in the past he had obtained excellent results from employing other former state governors or high officials—men like Sumner Sewell at IA&C in Berlin and Charles M. LaFollette as Land director in Württemberg-Baden. But with Van Wagoner his good luck came to an end. The new Land director depended heavily on his aides, Edward Kennedy and Clarence Bolds, for advice during the frequently tense negotiations that followed. The education officers in Bavaria were frequently in despair at how poorly informed Van Wagoner was on affairs in Germany. At times he moved too boldly. For example, he immediately crossed swords with Alexander over personnel appointments in the E&RA staff in Munich but at other times proved indecisive. Several months later Van Wagoner compounded the error by appointing a former social-work specialist, Louis Miniclier, as acting director of IA&C in Bavaria, a post that gave him overall responsibility for education affairs and a powerful voice in the school-reform negotiations with Bavarian authorities. Most observers agreed that this decision, too, was a mistake by Van Wagoner.[68]

Even more important than doubtful personnel choices and instabilities was the lack of consensus on goals and methods among the E&RA staff in Munich. Following Bergman's departure, two individuals rose to prominence in the Munich office: Martin Mayes and Charles J. Falk. Mayes had been Bergman's deputy until the latter's departure in December, 1945. With a 1933 doctorate in philosophy from Heidelberg University and publishing experience in his native Missouri, he had helped Military Government license reliable publishers before joining Bavarian E&RA in September, 1946.[69] Of all the E&RA staff in Munich, Mayes entertained the strongest private doubts about the wisdom of imposing educational directives on the Bavarians, in part because he knew and admired the pre-1933 educational system and in part because he feared that dictated reforms would fail. Mayes did not want to accept Hundhammer's proposals *in toto*, and he agreed with his E&RA colleagues in Munich and Berlin that on some principles, such as the introduction of free textbooks and tuition, there could be no compromise.[70] Intimately acquainted with the dynamics of Bavarian politics, he recognized early the formidable position Hundhammer had built, not only in education but in Bavarian politics generally, and he wanted to avoid a confrontation if possible. He found support among several other members of the E&RA staff, including Marion Edman, an elementary-school specialist, Clifton Winn, Bavarian E&RA's senior officer in higher education, and James Eagan, a religious-affairs specialist.[71] William Swarm and General Muller had adopted similar positions.

Charles J. Falk also brought considerable talents to his job as secondary-education specialist for E&RA in Munich. A respected professor of education at San Diego State College, Falk arrived in Germany in the autumn of 1946. When he was first hired in June, John Taylor had assigned Falk to a secondary-education slot with E&RA in Württemberg-Baden. However, in the intricate shuffling of personnel, Falk's name was entered on the list of experts for Bavaria, and so he had arrived in Munich several weeks before Hundhammer became education minister. Falk proved to be an energetic and resourceful staff member, and his striking personality allowed him to meet Mayes as an equal. He was also able, unlike Mayes, to achieve a harmonious relationship with Alexander in Berlin. Falk strongly advocated the position outlined in Clay's January directive, in the MGR 8s, and in ACA Directive 54. He was a natural ally for Alexander and for Alexander's likeminded German assistant at E&RA, OMGUS, Dr. Erich Hylla. He had his admirers and supporters in E&RA and in Military Government as well. Falk played a prominent role in the negotiations that followed the rejection of Hundhammer's Plan II in the autumn of 1947.[72]

As the weeks passed, the Bavarian Catholic Church and the Vatican began to take a more active role in the discussions between E&RA and the ministry of education in Munich. Hundhammer, Bishop Aloysius Muench (an American-born representative for the Vatican), and Cardinal Faulhaber all supported the continuation of the confessional schools. As Charles Falk's prominence in the negotiations grew, the Bavarian clergy revealed their discovery that Charles J. Falk was a former priest and that his wife was a former nun, who had joined him in Munich with their two daughters. This fact made the Bavarians' stance even stiffer as the drama of school reform in South Germany unfolded.[73]

As discussions continued into December, word arrived at E&RA headquarters in Berlin of demoralization among the E&RA staff in Bavaria. Alexander finally dispatched a trusted deputy, Dr. Mildred English, to Munich to investigate. During a meeting with Mayes, Falk, and several other staff members about personnel woes, she took special note of their urgent plea to find a permanent chief for E&RA: "They asked me to get Dr. Alexander to agree and said they would all work with Mayes and try to hold things together but to *push* getting a chief." Then, in the midst of the discussion, James Eagan, their religious-affairs specialist, interrupted to say that another Church representative and ecclesiastical adviser to Military Government, Father Stanley Bertke, wished to speak to Charles Falk about school-reform plans. Some of the staff suggested that Falk avoid yet another confrontation, but he refused. English, more than mildly concerned, reported that "Bertke was saying it is Falk's criticism of the school-reform plans that is holding things up, that Falk has reasons of *his own*." Furious that his past was known to the Bavarians, she suspected treachery: "Who told Bertke [that] Falk wrote the criticism of the reform plans?" she asked Alexander. "Falk says that for seventeen years the Catholics have been following and checking on him—in America and now over here."[74]

Exactly how the Bavarians learned of Falk's religious past was never made clear, although the frequent contact between Cardinal Spellman's office and Cardinal Faulhaber made that the likeliest channel for such information. Far more important than the method of exposure was the fact that, now that the Bavarian educational and religious authorities were fully aware of his past, Falk was no longer useful as a key negotiator. Yet, no changes occurred in the Bavarian E&RA's negotiating team. During the crucial months ahead, many of the E&RA personnel were unaware of Falk's background, but Alexander and English were fully aware.[75] As late as May, 1948, after fifteen months of deadlock with the Bavarians, IA&C's acting director, Louis Miniclier, put in an urgent request to Deputy Land Director Clarence Bolds for a promotion for Falk as an incentive to keep him in Bavaria. "I believe you and the Governor [Van Wagoner] are both fully aware of the fact that at this time Dr. Falk is the only person in the Education Branch capable of offering any real degree of leadership."[76] Even the able new secondary-education specialist in Bavaria, Lawrence G. Derthick, who was destined to become a U.S. Commissioner of Education, expressed praise for Falk. He wrote to Alexander in May, 1948: "With respect to Dr. Falk, I previously knew of your confidence in him and I found that everyone, including Dr. Wells, was anxious to have him stay another year."[77] To his credit, Charles Falk decided that, despite the confidence his superiors placed in him, his presence in Bavaria was counterproductive. He returned to the United States in June, 1948.[78]

The Bavarians were well aware that there was no consensus among the Americans on an ideal school-reform plan. On December 16, 1947, Mildred English attended a bargaining session between E&RA staff and Bavarian education officials, including Hundhammer. After Father Bertke walked into the meeting, unannounced, English demanded angrily when he had joined the E&RA staff, but Bertke was undaunted. In her discussion with the rest of the senior staff, English became ever more concerned. Marion Edman, a teacher-training expert from Wayne State University, confessed frankly to English "that the Germans in the Bavarian Ministry have laughed at Clay's orders because he sends things back disapproved and extends the time. So long as this happens, they will do nothing because they think they can continue to delay." Some of the Munich education staff feared that even in the highest echelons of Military Government the unyielding public position on school reform was not matched by a similar inner conviction. English reported to Alexander that Falk was already inclined to return home. Falk claimed that Herman Wells not only referred to some of the particulars of Clay's January 10 directive as "educational gadgets" but said that Clay felt they were too. However, English reported, in subsequent conversations Wells had assured Falk that "he did not mean to leave that impression, he felt sure Clay would stand pat on that." But Falk had already disclosed his fears to Al D. Sims and others, so that rumors of indecisiveness in the highest echelons of Military Government were added to the realities of the staff's own lack of cohesiveness and the Bavarians' unyielding posture.[79]

There were other reasons for alarm as well. English discovered that none of the subordinate staff was aware of Bergman's resignation or dismissal from E&RA (no one was sure which was the case), and the staff as a whole exhibited the classic symptoms of a dispirited, leaderless organization. "I urged general staff meetings for the entire staff," she reported to Alexander, "to keep them informed as to what is going on. As matters stand now, no one has stated why Bergman isn't there or what's cooking." She noted that little effort had been made to introduce new staff members to the situation and that there was apparent lack of uniform understanding of the MGRs. "I suggested to Falk and Mayes that they get the MGRs and go over them with the staff. . . . I also told them I felt it would be one good way of bringing unity into their group and to build morale."[80]

But no improvement occurred in succeeding weeks. By late January, when yet another deadline approached for Hundhammer to submit an acceptable reform bill, Dr. Leo J. Brueckner, a teacher-training specialist at E&RA, OMGUS, traveled to Munich. Brueckner reported that the atmosphere at Bavarian E&RA had, if anything, worsened since Mildred English's visit in December. At a meeting of E&RA and other high Military Government officials with Hundhammer's ministry, the education staff had prepared a chart to describe the school structure they felt was best for the Bavarians. Brueckner was horrified by what followed: "Many questions were asked by the Germans about points they wished to have clarified. Different individuals for MG attempted to answer each question, and on a number they were not in agreement. The ensuing discussion must have been confusing to the Germans. At times the exchange among the MG people was quite heated." Almost as bad as the open dissension among the Americans was the climate of fear that permeated the staff, especially since Brueckner, a representative from OMGUS, was now present. "In my opinion," he continued, "confusion was multiplied by the discussion. Subsequently nothing was done to follow up by MG to clarify the thinking of the Bavarian officials on points still not clear." Brueckner had hoped to attend a session of the Bavarian Landtag at which Hundhammer would present his newest plan, but, when the E&RA staff begged him to stay away, he did not insist. "The attitude of fear so frequently evident in MG discussions in Munich is most unwholesome," he concluded.[81]

By contrast, Hundhammer methodically prepared his own strategy. At two critical meetings between Bavarian E&RA and Hundhammer on December 16 and 17, the Americans' negotiating stance stiffened perceptibly. Even on seemingly minor details, such as the publication schedule for textbooks, an air of suspicion prevailed. Mildred English noted that Religious Affairs Specialist James Eagan was preparing to confront Hundhammer at the first of the two meetings. Upon hearing a complaint from representatives of the Evangelical Church that they did not have sufficient religion textbooks, "Mr. Eagan asked for the records, saying if he can show Hundhammer that his Schulbuchverlag, which he controls, had not submitted requests for religious books, he could make it hard for him," English recorded. Eagan was as good as his word. He criticized the education minister roundly, despite Hundhammer's protests that religious books had had Military Government's lowest printing priority and that he had received criticism from other Military Government officials for publishing too many of them already. Eagan persisted in examining the details until finally, in exasperation, Hundhammer stated that he was simply not informed on exactly how many copies were contained in each individual press run and that he would have to investigate the matter further. To this Eagan replied: "The present situation is, however, not satisfactory."[82]

The turning point in the negotiations came finally on the following day, when Hundhammer received R. T. Alexander's forceful memorandum of December 1 to Bavarian E&RA demanding execution of a school reform in accordance with Clay's January 10 directive and ACA Directive 54. Until then Hundhammer had bargained and debated over the American proposals and had offered copious reasons why the Bavarians could not accept them either on financial grounds or on philosophical grounds. Confronted now with Alexander's adamant directive, Hundhammer finally asked if Military Government was negotiating on the points of their reform plan or was issuing orders. When he received the reply that Military Government expected compliance with its directives, Hundhammer rose to his feet and stated: "I am a soldier; I know how to take orders."[83] A new phase had begun in the confrontation between Germans and Americans on school reform; it went to the heart of the relationship between the occupier and the occupied.

Within a short time, Hundhammer informed Minister President Ehard of the decisive meeting. Ehard also received a confirming letter on December 23 from Van Wagoner, stating that Hundhammer's Plan II had been found unacceptable because it had not observed the particulars of the January 10, MGR 8, and ACA 54 directives. "The Minister of Education is hereby required to implement Military Government regulations and directives and to include the full implementation in the reform proposal due 1 February 1948," Van Wagoner ordered.[84] Hans Ehard was dismayed. He conveyed to Van Wagoner his disappointment that the American initiatives must now be considered orders. "The Bavarian Government did not hold the opinion that . . . concerning the question of school reform it is bound to the instructions of Military Government in all details, the more so as these points have repeatedly been frankly discussed in negotiations with officers of Military Government." Instead, his government had expected to pose alternatives: "to make other proposals and to hint at the impracticality of some points, provided that a definite democratization of the school system, which is likewise the objective of the Bavarian Government, is kept in mind."[85]

Hundhammer no longer tried to debate with E&RA representatives. He conferred with them on the details they wanted to incorporate in the third plan, due on February 1. His activities aimed at giving Military Government a plan it could no longer fault. At the same time, he began a publicity compaign to put the facts as he saw them before the Bavarian people. On January 21, 1948, in a radio address, he provided his own account of what had developed in his lengthy discussions with Military Government. Referring to "notable hesitations," not only on the part of Bavarians but also in several of the Länder in the British Zone, the education minister listed five areas of disagreement. Transfers from elementary to secondary school would take place after the sixth year rather than after the fourth. Existing secondary schools would be dissolved in favor of a one-track school that would allow variable combinations of subjects but would have "a rather uniform curriculum." Qualification for teacher training would require an *Abitur*, and all such training would rise to university status. "This applies even to teachers of technical subjects, such as cooking, needlework, etc." The Bavarians would have to establish kindergartens for the four-to-six-year-olds as part of the regular school system, and all children would be required to take an additional year of schooling through the age of fifteen. He described the orders for free tuition and textbooks as applying "even for children of wealthy parents" and reminded his radio listeners that such radical departures in payment "are matters concerning more the Minister of Finance and the taxpayer than the Minister of Education." It was a shrewdly composed message, hinting at enormous costs for the impoverished Bavarian people, the raising of training standards to impractical levels for large numbers of teachers, and the destruction of a prized German institution, the *Gymnasium*. As evidence that, before the receipt of the American orders, his own position had been notable for its reasonableness, Hundhammer cited support from many quarters, including the rector of Munich University, the president of the Bavarian Academy of Science, Catholic bishops, leading Evangelical representatives, and the budget committee of the Bavarian Landtag. Even more disastrous for the American position was Hundhammer's revelation that Assistant Secretary of State William Benton had expressed similar reservations a year before, especially on the changes in secondary education. More recently thirteen esteemed professors at the University of Chicago, led by a former Military Government legal counsel, Max Rheinstein, had issued a manifesto in October, 1947, which the education minister felt was in close accord with his own reform proposals of the previous April and October. "I could almost have written these paragraphs myself," he announced. He dwelled on financial difficulties at length, adding that "the last word about the way of carrying out these orders will be at the disposal of the Landtag," and he ended with an appeal for the public to understand that "not the external form of the school system, but the spirit of the teachers" was what would rebuild democratic and morally responsible human beings.[86]

Hundhammer also embarked on a program of information dissemination among the leading educational institutions of Bavaria. He had already distributed his October 1 plan throughout leading education circles, including the rectors of the universities and other institutions of higher learning. Now, with the rejection of Plan II, he encouraged Bavarians of all classes and callings to respond to recent developments. The Bavarian people needed scant prodding. Correspondence poured into the ministry of education approving his reservations and expressing alarm at the consequences that would stem from the American proposals. Typical was a letter from the faculty and rectorate of the Philosophical-Theological Seminary at Freising, which not only circulated within the ministry of education but was sent to all other Bavarian educational institutions. This group said that its members did not attempt to deny the abundant evils of their National Socialist past and that they welcomed reconstruction of their educational system to broaden the avenues of advancement for gifted children. However, at the core of their argument was a defense of the traditional secondary school: "It is especially necessary to guard the humanistic Gymnasium against the dangers posed by dissolving its lower grades and raising an artificially unified structure of secondary education." To do this, they claimed, would be to destroy a unique institution, which, as the repository of West European culture, had also earned educational esteem in North America as well. The Freising proclamation asked the ministry of education "to leave nothing undone in order to press the Occupation Authorities in the realm of school reform to raise the level of education and to maintain the humanistic Gymnasium."[87] Its authors added that their policy was solidly backed by the other institutions of higher learning in Bavaria and by a zone-wide movement, headquartered in Münster (British Zone), called the "Friends of School Reform."

The Friends of School Reform had organized at the end of 1947 to assert German cultural unity, which, they claimed, was endangered by the widely divergent educational proposals being made by the three Western powers. Led by rectors Lehnartz and Kroll of Münster and Cologne universities, respectively, the Friends entered a strong protest against transferring the lower grades from the secondary schools to the unified *Volksschulen* because such action "would leave the most impressionable years of youth unused." They issued a call to representatives from the universities, schools, churches, and the business community "to build action committees immediately in view of the current crisis in education which would present a plan for the solving of one of the most important issues of our day."[88]

The response was instantaneous. In a much-publicized move, over two hundred of Bavaria's most prestigious scholars, scientists, and educational leaders issued a "Declaration of School Reform" in support of the Bavarian Ministry of Education. Indubitable democrats like Georg Hohmann and Karl Vossler, the current and former rectors of Munich University, joined hands with distinguished but discredited men of learning like Mario San Nicolo and Wilhelm Prinz von Isenburg, who, because of denazification, were currently banned from teaching by Military Government. There was no disputing the fact that Alois Hundhammer had, despite his notoriety, succeeded in welding Bavarians of widely differing views together on the issue of school reform. Their declaration expressed "gravest concern for the future of our educational institutions." Central to their protests was the objection that Germany's humanistic *Gymnasium* would lose its cherished position at the center of the educational structure. Such action would strike against the classical languages at a time when "the call should be made and heeded to breathe new life into the values of antiquity and Christianity, the two most important foundations of Western Civilization."[89]

On January 31, 1948, Hundhammer submitted his third plan for school reform, but he also affixed to it a "Preliminary Remark," in which he made it abundantly clear that the new plan was not his but one prepared by his ministry under orders of Military Government. "No statesman," he declared, "with a sense of responsibility could answer for abandoning the peculiar nature and value of our educational system in favor of a system which has proved its merits across the sea." He still maintained that the mission of the traditional educational system had been "to preserve the qualities and values of Western civilization, which is rooted in antiquity and Christianity," and he reminded Military Government that Bavarians supported his position, including Michael Cardinal Faulhaber and all the other individuals and institutions to whom he had alluded in his radio broadcast of the previous week. The similarity between Hundhammer's remarks and the various petitions was not lost on the E&RA staff. He then presented the Americans with a plan that exactly reflected their thinking. In its externals the new plan appeared to be a complete victory for the position taken by R. T. Alexander and Charles Falk. In his final sentence, however, Hundhammer remarked: "I should not fail to draw your attention to the fact that, considering the course which events have already taken on this subject in the Bavarian Landtag, a decision with respect to the various issues in dispute is likely to encounter considerable difficulties. It is indeed possible that the plan will not be approved."[90]

The trap was sprung. Actually, the members of the education staff in Munich were well aware of growing public support for Hundhammer and rightly suspected that he was orchestrating opposition among the public. After his radio address the E&RA staff considered their next move. Charles Falk was incensed by the one-sidedness of Hundhammer's remarks and decided that the only effective way to combat his hostile interpretations to the Bavarian people was for the Americans to take their case before the public. In a series of twenty-eight questions and answers on school reform, Falk tried to expose the insinuations and obstacles he felt Hundhammer had unfairly inserted into the debate. It was Military Government's first public statement on the subject of school reform, and, while it earned Falk high praise among E&RA officials at OMGUS, it had no appreciable effect in lessening Bavarian public support for Hundhammer. One of the particular points Falk made was that the purpose of the American proposals was to offer equal educational opportunities to all Bavarian youth. He countered the most emotional argument—the dissolving of the *Gymnasium*—by stating that "the training of pupils whose gifts and desires lead them to advanced work in mathematics, science, and languages will continue. It can be even better than it was before. The only requirement here is that, before entrance into a Gymnasium type of program, all children be given six years of general education in a Grundschule or Volksschule. After the Grundschule, the Gymnasium may continue for six, seven, or even eight years, if Bavarians so desire." Falk did the same for Hundhammer's other arguments, including teacher training, the study of classical languages, and the costs involved in introducing changes, which he estimated as amounting to only one-sixtieth of the Bavarian budget. The document, while cleverly conceived, was simply too little and too late.[91]

Unable to stem the education minister's renewed support, the Occupation authorities paused to consider what options were open to them. For a brief time in November, following the rejection of Hundhammer's Plan II, Consul Sam Woods had proposed "that the removal of Dr. Hundhammer from his position is an advisable step, since his continuing as Minister of Culture could jeopardize the future of Bavarian education." But, by January, Woods concluded that if any party to the conflict was in danger, it was Military Government. "Hundhammer," Woods observed

who has and who deserves the reputation of a clever politician, might be attempting to maneuver Military Government into a practically untenable position in that he expects the educational plan, when submitted to the Landtag, to be refused by that body. This could very well result in an impasse, since the Landtag, having spoken for the people as the elected representative body of Bavaria, could then accuse Military Government of being undemocratic in any attempt to override the Landtag's decision.[92]

Woods was merely stating the obvious. Most of the education officers were only too painfully aware of their own vulnerability and of Hundhammer's seemingly impregnable position. Acting Chief Mayes flew to Berlin in February to attend a branch chiefs' meeting, along with Alexander and Wells. There was considerable indignation at OMGUS about Hundhammer's recent move. It was repeatedly suggested that Military Government's Bavarian gadfly simply be removed. But Mayes thought it important to explain to his colleagues that the plan "was not as they would like to have it but that Hundhammer was more firmly entrenched in the Bavarian political structure than ever." Other branch chiefs were not inclined to be intimidated. Harry Wann, of Greater Hesse, was indignant and felt that Hundhammer's adoption of the American plan and his not-so-subtle hint that he would engineer its defeat in the Landtag represented "rank impertinence." Harold Crabill, from Bremen Enclave, stated that Hundhammer's preliminary remark "could almost be considered justification for ordering his dismissal."

For once Alexander was inclined to act cautiously in Bavaria. He smelled a rat. If Hundhammer were to introduce the proposals into the Landtag and secure their passage all at once, the result could be far worse than if he had engineered their defeat. The changes contemplated by Alexander's office—and they were profound changes, despite any publicity to the contrary—could all be nullified and discredited if the Bavarian ministry attempted to implement them immediately. As the minutes indicated: "Dr. Alexander said he thought we should be very careful with reference to the speed with which the program is to be carried out. We ought to emphasize first the training of teachers, then inner work on curricula, etc. We don't want the thing to move too fast, as there is always the possibility of failure when a project is rushed into." Wells decided that his fiery education chief was substantially correct in his strategy this time. "Dr. Wells," the minutes continued, "said he thought we should make the kind of reply that takes the most wind out of Hundhammer's sails." They agreed that one or two of the less ambitious parts of the new "Bavarian" plan should be instituted first. For example, instead of changing the elementary-school structure for the coming September, they should instead concentrate on upgrading teacher training.[93]

One reason for Alexander's circumspection was his awareness that Hundhammer's arguments had proved so persuasive to the Bavarians. He was also acutely embarrassed by the education minister's references to

Benton and the thirteen American professors led by Max Rheinstein, whose criticisms of the Mission Report had strengthened Hundhammer's hand. Alexander had known about the Chicago report since November, when his immediate superior received a copy from Robert Murphy, with the handwritten comment: "I think E&RA should mull this over carefully."[94] The E&RA chief was furious. He replied: "It is the expression of a group of German educators educated in Germany and thinking like Germans on the German education question." Their arguments were identical to those he had confronted in Bavaria and elsewhere for the last year and a half. "This paper could very well have been prepared by Dr. Hundhammer," Alexander continued. "In brief, the document proposes no changes whatever in German education. It represents the old German and European point of view of school and privileged classes. OMGUS policy on education is very much to the contrary." Since the report had not actually been addressed to him, Alexander decided that he should not reply to it officially, although he would do so if asked. "In the meantime," he concluded, "we have enough German documents of the same nature to contend with."[95]

Thus, with their positions hopelessly estranged, Hundhammer and Alexander prepared their next moves warily. Following the meeting of branch chiefs in Berlin, Alexander forwarded a memorandum to Bavarian E&RA formally suggesting what their next steps should be. "This Headquarters advises urgently that your office examine very carefully the schedule of implementation proposed by the Bavarian Minister of Education, in order to avoid a hurried implementation of the school reform, which would result in confusion and failure." He warned further that the new plan, while certainly acceptable from the American point of view, also had a conspicuous omission: there was no timetable for implementation whatsoever.[96]

In fact, Hundhammer had not chosen the strategy that Alexander had expected. Instead, he returned to the well-tested method of delay and inaction that had carried him so successfully through 1947. By the end of February it had become apparent to Mayes and Falk that Hundhammer's failure to introduce any portion of the American-approved measures into the Landtag was effectively killing any chance of school reform in 1948. The Bavarian Landtag was scheduled to convene through early June. Therefore, legislation, in order to be effective for the September school openings, would have to secure approval prior to June 3. In a lengthy memorandum to his division director, Mayes drew up a list of incidents in Military Government's long-standing dispute with Hundhammer, ending with the conclusion that "the case for noncompliance and disagreement with Military Government directives and regulations is complete."[97] By mid-March, the acting director of IA&C, Louis Miniclier, recommended "taking aggressive action in order to assure passage and implementation of a Military Government ordered and approved school reform."[98] Accordingly, John Bradford, chief of Governmental Structure Branch, OMGB, considered the problem of how to produce some results. "Military Government could now present a plan of implementation to the Minister of Education, with set deadlines and orders for accomplishment," he wrote to Mayes. "However, I believe this will again be unavailing. The Minister will oppose future directives of Military Government, as he has before, with arguments of evasion . . . all with the aim of playing for time." Bradford returned to the position Military Government had considered following its rejection of Plan II in October, 1947: "I believe there cannot be any success at all unless the Minister of Education is removed without further ado." He suggested that Military Government draw up a bill of particulars against Hundhammer, then call a meeting with Ehard and Van Wagoner as witnesses and present the charges. If that still produced no change in Hundhammer's attitude, "it should be recommended to OMGUS that he be removed."[99]

Falk enthusiastically endorsed Bradford's position, but more and more Military Government officials were entering the fray. Paul Moeller, a member of IA&C's Research Branch, analyzed the situation after surveying "more than one hundred political and other opinion leaders in Bavaria." He found that there was, in fact, Bavarian support for some of the particulars of the American reform proposals but that resentment remained high that the reform was to be accomplished on orders from Occupation authorities. He also noted that the Bavarian people had ambivalent feelings about their education minister. The right wing of the CSU and influential leaders of the Church hierarchy backed Hundhammer solidly, but reactions outside that group were mixed: "The Landtag debates and other public statements have demonstrated . . . that people have joined the ranks of Dr. Hundhammer's opposition who do not share his ideology and the resulting campaign against the reform. These people, while denouncing Dr. Hundhammer's reactionary views, support him on principle in protest against Military Government pressure." Moeller catalogued Hundhammer's undoubted success in instilling most Bavarians with the fear that the American proposals "contemplated elimination of humanistic education," although the respondents cited many other details, including the problem of expense. Moeller regarded the American situation as better in some ways than it had been in 1947. "The present determined foreign policy of the United States has probably enhanced the prestige of Military Government during recent weeks. The food situation shows signs of improvement. The Germans might actually begin to realize that they need us more than we need them." These welcome developments, if given a chance to ripen, could help produce a healthier climate between Military

Government and the Bavarians. Moeller agreed wholeheartedly that Hundhammer was the central figure in blocking progress on a school bill, but he doubted that Military Government could find a replacement who would be any more kindly disposed to the reforms the Americans desired. In fact, Hundhammer, if dismissed as education minister, would be more dangerous than ever: "he would remain CSU whip," Moeller reasoned; "his removal would rally the Bavarians to the last man, not without apparent justification, in an anti-Military Government campaign. Antagonism would be accentuated and would render execution of the school reform virtually impossible."[100]

Moeller's viewpoint prevailed. Van Wagoner called a meeting with Ehard and Hundhammer for April 1 and elicited a promise to implement the school plan in six specific points, and Hundhammer confirmed this promise on April 5, at a luncheon with Ehard, Van Wagoner, and their staffs at Munich's Haus der Kunst. As a token of the improved relationship, Van Wagoner gave Hundhammer an exit visa "to visit Rome and the Vatican in the interest of Military Government." The crisis at last seemed on its way to a resolution. To be sure, the first implementation objective was no longer Alexander's ambitious scheme for changing teacher training by September 1. Instead, Military Government secured agreement from Hundhammer and Ehard that free tuition and textbooks would become the first objective, and the Ministry of Education would include an item for 5.9 million Reichsmarks in its budget for that purpose. The Bavarian educational authorities would also set up commissions to lay plans for creating six-year elementary schools for the 1949 school year and for university-level teacher-training institutions on about the same schedule.[101]

A month later the agreement began to unravel. In a conference with Herman Wells, Ehard, and other officials, Hundhammer claimed that one of the six points of the April 1 understanding could not be accomplished as promised. Plans to elevate the vocational teacher-training institute in Munich to university level by September, 1948, were not feasible, he claimed. The American officials grudgingly assented to a delay but asked Hundhammer to convey to Van Wagoner in writing his inability to live up to the agreement. Hundhammer agreed. However, his next announcement produced a new outburst of indignation among the Americans. Hundhammer stated that because of the costs involved he would also be forced to withdraw his promise to institute free tuition and textbooks. If he won on this point, Hundhammer would prevent any implementation of school reform in 1948. Sensing the anger rising within the American delegation, Ehard decided that his education minister had finally gone too far. He overruled Hundhammer and promised Wells and Military Government that he would prepare legislation for the Landtag to enact this particular reform.[102]

However, instead of accepting Ehard's decision as final, Hundhammer continued to announce that he could not support free tuition and textbooks. He also informed high Church officials, such as Munich's Bishop Johannes Neuhaeusler, of that fact. When the education staff confronted him again on the subject and demanded a written statement from him that he could not support the twin measures, Hundhammer refused. That decision probably saved him his office, but his defiance was beginning to wear thin the collective patience of Military Government. Thus, when Hundhammer requested a second exit visa to attend a conference at The Hague, he received a curt no, with the explanation that he would be too busy securing passage of free tuition and textbooks in the Landtag to allow him any time to travel. Uninformed on what Military Government's future course of action might be and fearful of his imminent dismissal, Hundhammer for once appeared to moderate his stand. He pushed the measures through his ministry with dispatch and presented them to the Landtag in time to be considered for implementation the following autumn.[103]

In fact he was not as insecure in his position as recent events seemed to indicate. Other observers in Military Government, among them Lieutenant Colonel Paul Burns of the Civil Administration Division, noted that the CSU's more moderate wing, led by Josef Mueller, stood opposed to Ehard and Hundhammer but that it would be a mistake to assume that Ehard might appoint a more moderate successor. The reason for a conservative choice was simple: Ehard did not want to add another Mueller advocate to his cabinet and thus tip the scales in the latter's favor. With elections scheduled for the end of May, such an action might topple Ehard from power. Burns also reminded his colleague that, if Military Government were to dismiss Hundhammer anyway, there was a good chance that "Hundhammer [would] continue to play behind the scenes, whether proscribed by Military Government or not, just as Schaeffer played from 1946 to 1948." In any case, Burns considered that school reform would be dead if Hundhammer were removed from office, "unless Military Government makes public an exceptionally strong and convincing exposé of Hundhammer's activities and just as strong and convincing a case for the merits of the plan."[104]

Falk was inclined to accept the risks. If the impending elections failed to dislodge Hundhammer, then "the Minister President should be asked to replace Dr. Hundhammer now as Minister of Education," he declared to the education staff on May 26. However, Falk's position became less convincing to his superiors when analysts from other branches of Military Government made their opinions known. Finally, Louis Miniclier, one of Falk's strongest supporters, conceded that the status quo must be maintained at least until June, when the free tuition and textbook measures would be presented to the Landtag. "However," Miniclier added, "it is suggested that the Military Governor and his political and cultural advisers study this attached source material [Falk's analysis]. It is the opinion of the writer that action may be required by the Military Governor in the foreseeable future."[105] Miniclier's opinions did not always carry much weight with the education staff, but in this instance he judged the situation correctly.

During the spring of 1948, while Hundhammer's fate was being debated within Military Government, striking changes were occurring within the education staff in Berlin. On March 1, E&RA finally attained division status and became known as Education and Cultural Relations Division (E&CR), in belated recognition of its importance within Military Government. The new title also reflected the increased attention being paid to cultural programs and exchange programs beyond the limited scope of formal education. The addition of important new personalities to the division put an end to undisputed control by R. T. Alexander. At a meeting of branch chiefs and education personnel in February, Alexander announced some of the changes that were about to occur. "He first introduced Colonel Lenzner to the group and told them that under the new organization [Lenzner] would be Acting Director and, later, Deputy Director of the Division of Education and Cultural Relations."[106] Emil Lenzner, a German-born American, was a professional soldier and West Point graduate who had earned respect at OMGUS. Now that Herman Wells had achieved greater familiarity with his duties as cultural adviser, the two new leaders were able to add vigor and flexibility to the fledgling division. Some of the Bavarian education staff had felt that Alexander and his German assistants— Erich Hylla, for example—had exacerbated a delicate situation by failing to recognize the Bavarians' ancient aversion toward orders made in Berlin, whether these came from Occupation authorities or from fellow Germans. Lenzner was acutely conscious of the cleavages between north and south Germans, and he conveyed that consciousness to Wells.

For the time being, however, Alexander continued to play a forceful role in educational affairs. At the March meeting he thundered against Van Wagoner's recent appointment of Louis Miniclier as director of IA&C in Munich. "Dr. Alexander said it disturbed him greatly that when we are trying to build up our educational program Mr. Miniclier had been put in as Chief in Bavaria without this office being consulted."[107] Mayes was also present at the March meeting in his capacity as acting chief. When he heard that Alexander was sending an acclaimed education expert, Lawrence G. Derthick, to Berlin Sector in the spring, he immediately asked that Derthick be allowed to come to Munich for an interview. "Dr. Alexander said that this would not be done and that he was recruited for the Berlin Sector and would fill that position."[108] In the end Alexander relented. Derthick held his interview with the Bavarian education staff and established instantaneous rapport with all of the personnel. He was a committed advocate of the American school-reform proposals, and his flexible approach and diplomatic skills might have accomplished far more had he steered E&RA in 1946, before the crisis arose. He proved to be an effective spokesman in Bavarian town meetings. Because he was a realist, Derthick quickly concluded that in 1948 there were sharp limitations on how far Military Government could push reforms on the unwilling Bavarians.[109]

He was joined in Munich by another skilled and experienced Military Government officer, Charles D. Winning, who took formal command of Bavarian E&CR at Clay's personal request. Winning had proved his ability in a Military Government G-5 detachment in Mannheim at war's end. He became a deputy to Land Director William Dawson, in OMG Württemberg-Baden, and at the Länderrat. Winning stayed with Military Government's Regional Government Coordinating Office (RGCO) after Dawson's untimely death, a fact that disappointed Taylor, who had hoped to install him as Bavarian education chief in 1946. Clay urged him to take over E&CR in the summer of 1948, when the RGCO was dissolved. The Military Governor needed all the competent help he could muster in Bavaria in the summer of 1948.[110]

Any illusions that Hundhammer's political position was weakening were dispelled by the Bavarian election results of May 30. The education minister emerged as strong as ever. On July 14 the Bavarian Landtag's Budget Committee considered the proposals for free tuition and textbooks. In the meantime, however, currency reform had finally come for the West Germans, and, while it brought undeniable advantages, it also caused severe dislocations in Land budgets. Luck defeated school reform once more in Bavaria. The entire Bavarian Landtag Budget Committee, including the Social Democrats, sided with Hundhammer in claiming that currently there were no resources for funding the two measures. Bavaria's finance minister attended the meeting to assure those present that the necessary financial resources were lacking. Hundhammer sought a postponement of the bill until October 1 but also requested approval from the Budget Committee to provide emergency funds for education costs for needy children. Clifton Winn, who had been with Bavarian E&CR since 1946, recorded the decision: "The tone of the meeting was calm," he wrote. "There was no evidence of railroading tactics. All who wished were given opportunity to express their views at whatever length they desired. . . . One got the impression that all members of the committee were convinced, some reluctantly, some otherwise, of the inevitability of the decision."[111]

Murray D. Van Wagoner, however, did not believe that the fiscal situation was as serious as claimed. On July 16 he wrote to Clay: "The budgetary questions produced by currency reform, while serious, do not seem insurmountable. The consensus of this Headquarters is that the action taken by the Bavarian Landtag Budget Committee is defiant to the point of adversely affecting the prestige of the Occupation. . . . This resolution is another element in what appears to be a definite plan for delaying action whereby opponents of school reform hope to negate your order of 10 January 1947."[112]

Acting on Van Wagoner's report, Clay immediately convened a meeting on July 18 of E&CR, OMGUS, including its acting director, Milton E. Muelder, and Winning and Louis Miniclier. This time Clay was inclined to treat the Bavarian leadership harshly. He announced that the issuance of free textbooks and free tuition "does not constitute a subject for negotiation and discussion with the Bavarian authorities." The directive was sent to Munich on July 25 with the advice that, if the Bavarian Government did not comply, Military Government would requisition the necessary books and charge them to Occupation costs. Similarly, all tuition fees would be banned.[113] Accordingly, on August 4, Van Wagoner ordered Ehard to institute both measures for the approaching fall school term.

At the Landtag's Budget Committee hearing of July 14, the Church prelate, Meixner, had opened the debate with a sharp attack on the bill, claiming it would not improve the quality of education in Bavaria. In fact, Meixner's ardent criticism signaled a renewed attack on school-reform proposals by the Catholic hierarchy.[114] Cardinal Faulhaber had been particularly upset with one provision of the six points Hundhammer had promised to implement in April. If all teacher training were raised to university status, then nuns teaching in kindergartens would presumably come under the same umbrella requirement. James Eagan, E&CR's religious-affairs specialist, and Louis Miniclier promptly addressed the potential problem and in a letter to the Cardinal in May, 1948, assured him that nuns would not be required to undergo university training for the running of kindergartens. "For this kind communication I have thanked the Governor [Van Wagoner, formerly governor of Michigan] in my letter of 12 May 1948," Faulhaber stated in a later communication to the Land director.[115] However, Van Wagoner's interpretation of Faulhaber's letter was wildly optimistic. He wrote to Bishop Aloysius Muench several days later to say that university training of kindergarten teachers was "the last objection raised by Cardinal Faulhaber to school reform. This matter has been settled satisfactorily, and His Eminence has raised no further objections to school reform."[116] Van Wagoner also communicated the same information to Francis Cardinal Spellman of New York, who was following educational affairs in Bavaria closely. In an angry letter dated July 19, Cardinal Faulhaber confronted Van Wagoner on his interpretation of the May 12 letter: "In this letter I did not touch upon other questions pertaining to school reform because there was no reason for it in this connection. . . . My letter of 12 May 1948 does not offer any basis for such an assumption. Such an assumption is in unequivocal contrast to what I wrote in the name and by order of the Bavarian bishops in my letter of 7 January 1948 to His Excellency Bishop Muench against the school reform ordered by Military Government."[117]

Faulhaber now wished to inform Van Wagoner and Military Government exactly what his position was on school reform. He reminded them of his January 7 letter, in which he had stated that educational reform was "strictly part of the internal affairs of a nation." The nation was to arrange its school system in accordance with the wishes of teachers and, "above all, parents" and without interference from the occupying authority. "Such an interference, even if the intention to democratize education is given for a reason, would be absolutely contradictory to the spirit of true democracy, destroy faith in democracy and, therefore, have an effect exactly contrary to its intended purpose." Now, half a year later, with pressure from Military Government for school reform intensifying, the Bavarian Cardinal wrote: "I feel that it is my duty to repeat this warning." He also assured Van Wagoner that he had always found Hundhammer's proposals of April 1 and October 1, 1947 acceptable and that they accorded with the wishes of most Bavarians. "Both school programs were disapproved by Military Government, and this in the most abrupt manner. . . . This disapproval has left the majority of the people with the bitter impression that the Bavarian people is denied the right of self-determination relative to school reform and is subjected to a school dictatorship instead." Faulhaber was upset that Hundhammer had been forced to submit a reform bill designed by Military Government, but he was far more disturbed that, in the confrontation between the education minister and the American authorities,

> Dr. Hundhammer is accused of mixing religious affairs into the question of school reform for the purpose of securing the support of the Church for his own political aims. On its reverse side, this serious, completely unfounded accusation of the Minister contains just as serious and unfounded an accusation against the Church. The Bavarian bishops cannot put up with this accusation in silence before the public. I hereby declare that the Bavarian bishops support Education Minister Dr. Hundhammer with their fullest confidence.[118]

Cardinal Faulhaber then announced to Van Wagoner that he was sending copies of his letter not only to Bishop Muench but also to Pope Pius XII, "since," he explained, "upon a letter from Cardinal Spellman, an inquiry was sent to me from the Vatican on June 21, relative to the assertion that Cardinal Faulhaber would raise no more objections to school reform."[119] Any advantage Van Wagoner had hoped to gain from the Cardinal's May

12 letter was now in abeyance. In fact, the clumsy maneuver had roused the Catholic hierarchy to a fury, and undoubtedly the awkward situation would shortly become known not only to the Vatican but in America as well. According to Van Wagoner, Faulhaber's letter, though dated July 19, had, inexplicably, not arrived in his office until July 26. On July 28 he mailed a translation of it to Clay in Berlin. "As the Cardinal has seen fit to forward this information to such high level," he wrote the Military Governor, "I feel you should be apprised of the situation."[120]

Given the disruption in communications caused by the Russian blockade of Berlin, Clay had sent the orders instituting free tuition and textbooks by cable rather than letter on July 25. Van Wagoner might well have followed that example in forwarding Faulhaber's letter, with its highly sensitive contents. Since the Bavarian Landtag adjourned on July 31 without taking action, the Land director decided to order free textbooks and tuition as being "essential to the democratization of the Bavarian school system." Van Wagoner informed Ehard on August 4: "The time has come when Military Government cannot countenance additional delay."[121] Hans Ehard was outraged by the order and nearly resigned on the spot.

Belatedly, Clay became aware of the deepening crisis with the Catholic hierarchy. Sensing a disaster in the making, he flew out of beleaguered Berlin in mid-August to deal directly with Ehard on "neutral ground" at Frankfurt. In effect, Clay eclipsed Van Wagoner, Alexander, and Hundhammer. He respected the Bavarian leader, and Ehard had already demonstrated, earlier that spring, his willingness to overrule his truculent education minister. Thus, in a "compromise agreement" with Ehard, Clay agreed to soften Military Government's position in view of the financial crisis caused by currency reform. The two leaders devised a transitional scheme whereby the Bavarian government would pay 50 percent of the costs for tuition and books for the approaching school year, 75 percent of the costs for the following year, and the entire cost thereafter. Clay even acknowledged one of Hundhammer's old grievances by agreeing to permit wealthier parents the freedom to pay for their children's books and to make voluntary contributions in lieu of tuition fees for the improvement of schools. They agreed to modify Van Wagoner's order, and Clay put the terms in writing for Ehard at the end of the month: "I approve of the change in this order dated August 4, 1948, in the format as set forth above."[122] Nothing further was said about the other major features of the January 31 plan that Hundhammer had been forced to submit. E&CR continued to press for their implementation, and Hundhammer as stoutly resisted. Clay also moved to repair Military Government's relations with the Church. On August 29 he wrote to Robert Murphy: "At an early date could you not pay Cardinal Faulhaber a visit and have a good talk with him? I don't like this note-writing business."[123]

1

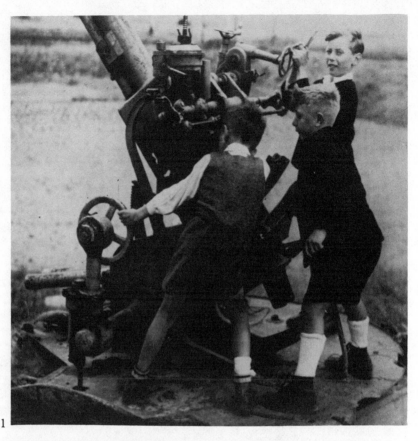

2

1. German schoolboys play with abandoned military equipment outside Koblenz, May, 1945. Worried by the presence of juveniles in the streets of the ruined cities, the U.S. Army urged E&RA officers to reopen schools quickly. Such scenes added greater urgency to the Allied goal of denazifying and demilitarizing German society. To the American public, such images were a poignant reminder of the Nazi emphasis on influencing German youth. (*U.S. National Archives*)

2. A Nazi invitation to a book-burning, issued to the students of Munich in May, 1933, reinforced fears among leading Military Government circles in 1945 that the German universities might become centers of nationalism and renascent National Socialism. (*Bayerisches Hauptstaatsarchiv München, Sammlung Rehse*)

3

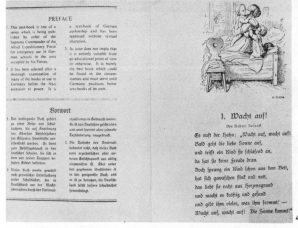

4

3. By the summer of 1944, Allied education officers discovered that National Socialism had permeated all educational literature in the schools. That fact led to the decision to produce millions of SHAEF emergency textbooks. *(U.S. Army)*

4. In order to eliminate Nazi influence from the schools, SHAEF education officers replaced existing schoolbooks with reprints of books used in the time of the Weimar Republic. This avoided charges that the Allies were introducing propaganda into the classroom; but the reprints were hardly ideal, since they, too, displayed excessive nationalism and militarism. Thus, each of the five million SHAEF textbooks carried a disclaimer in its preface. *(U.S. Army)*

5

6

5. German refugee children gather in a churchyard in Vettelsschloss in western Germany, March, 1945. Evacuation of children from the cities began on a massive scale in 1943. After the war the problem worsened when millions of Germans were evicted from eastern Europe. The resulting influx further burdened the educational systems in all four of the occupation zones. (*U.S. National Archives*)

6. The first day of school arrives for the children of Aachen, June 4, 1945. Most of these first- through fourth-graders had had no schooling for over a year because of disruptions caused by the war. (*U.S. National Archives*)

7. Aachen elementary-school pupils began classes four months earlier than elsewhere in the three western zones because the city had been under American occupation since October, 1944. Aachen's schools reopened along the same structural lines as the pre-1933 educational system. (*U.S. National Archives*)

8. A kindergarten continues to function in war-torn Aachen in the autumn of 1945. Some preschool instruction continued under G-5 Civil Affairs supervision until the formal reopening of elementary schools in June, 1945. (*U.S. Army*)

9. General Lucius D. Clay maintained responsibility for the U.S. Zone for most of the Occupation. Preoccupied with the problems of four-power control in Germany and with the need to revive the German society and economy, he did not at first assign a high priority to educational reconstruction. With the advent of the Cold War, and in light of the failures in American reeducation policies up to 1947, Clay allocated greater resources and talent to reorientation programs. (*U.S. National Archives*)

10

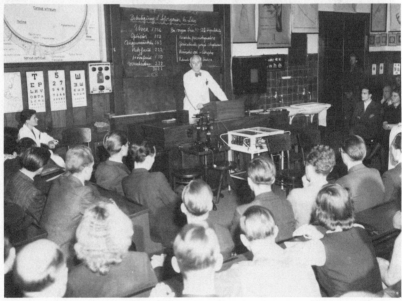

11

10. E&RA leadership convenes in Berlin in the autumn of 1946. From left to right the participants are John P. Steiner, E&RA chief in Württemberg-Baden; Vaughn R. DeLong, E&RA chief in Greater Hesse; Walter Bergman, E&RA chief in Bavaria; Harold H. Crabill, E&RA chief in Bremen; R. T. Alexander, deputy E&RA chief at OMGUS (until April, 1947); and Fritz Karsen, E&RA higher-education specialist at OMGUS. (*U.S. National Archives*)

11. The rebirth of German higher education begins with the reopening of the medical school at Heidelberg University in August, 1945. Here, Dr. Engelking, dean of the medical school, lectures to three hundred former Wehrmacht doctors, now enrolled in a refresher course. Malnutrition and disease provided a strong incentive to train medical personnel as quickly as possible. (*U.S. Army*)

1

12. The Johann Wolfgang Goethe University reopens in Frankfurt am Main in February, 1946. The hurried reopening of medical schools put pressure on German university authorities and Military Government to revive full university operations as much as a year earlier than originally planned. By mid-1946, charges in the American press of incomplete denazification at the universities led General Clay to order a second purge. (*U.S. National Archives*)

13. German students gather among the ruins of their university in 1946. Universities in large cities, such as Munich and Frankfurt, suffered severe damage in the war, whereas Heidelberg, Marburg, and Erlangen emerged unscathed. Overcrowding was universal, given the demand by veterans to resume their studies. With the lifting of the Nazis' 10 percent enrollment ceiling, women could enter the universities in significant numbers for the first time since 1933. (*U.S. National Archives*)

14. Alois Hundhammer, Bavaria's minister of education from December, 1946, until the end of the Occupation, was the most conservative educational leader in the U.S. Zone. Next to Minister President Ehard, Hundhammer was the most powerful figure in Bavarian politics, a fact that helps explain his ability to resist Military Government demands for educational change. A shrewd political campaigner, he succeeded in convincing most Bavarians that the structural changes called for by American Occupation authorities were unsuitable to local conditions. (*Amtliches Handbuch des Bayerischen Landtags, 1955*)

14

15

16

15. Herman B Wells, president of Indiana University and cultural adviser to General Clay, arrived in Berlin in November, 1947. Wells helped upgrade education to division status in Military Government and won greater support for reorientation programs from Clay and from American public and private sources. He deemphasized efforts to restructure German educational systems in favor of programs of cultural exchange, aid, and expert advice. (*U.S. National Archives*)

16. German and American education officials bid farewell to a contingent of Bavarian students departing Frankfurt am Main for the United States in 1949. By streamlining exchange procedures and marshaling public and private funds, the Americans enabled large numbers of future German leaders to travel abroad, especially to the United States, thus ending German cultural isolation for the first time in a generation. (*Kenneth Bateman*)

17. The Free University of Berlin celebrates its inaugural ceremony on December 4, 1948. The central speaker, an early supporter of the new university, was Mayor-elect Ernst Reuter. *(U.S. Army)*

18. Applicants begin registering at the Free University on August 30, 1948. Originally the result of student initiative, the fledgling university began life on a shoestring and depended heavily on public largesse, supplemented by financial support and cooperation from Military Government. *(U.S. Army)*

20

19. Alonzo G. Grace succeeded Wells as cultural adviser in mid-1948. He continued to generate much-needed publicity by organizing international education conferences, including one at Berchtesgaden with General Clay as its keynote speaker. However, Grace feared the dissolution of reorientation programs once the Occupation Statute failed to retain control of German education. He resigned from Military Government in the summer of 1949. (*U.S. Army*)

20. After a world war and universal impoverishment, German social institutions experienced a notable decline. This village school in Bickenbach near Jugenheim was typical of the decayed educational plant throughout the U.S. Zone. Village schools were a revered German educational feature, much like America's little red schoolhouse; but chances for improvement after the war were bleak, since few if any villages possessed the resources needed to rejuvenate their schools. (*Kenneth Bateman*)

21

2

21. U.S. High Commissioner John J. McCloy (center) and Colonel James R. Newman (right) attend groundbreaking ceremonies for a Hessian school being built with American assistance in June, 1952. Because McCloy was strongly committed to supporting and expanding Military Government's reorientation programs, State Department cultural-affairs officers acquiesced in the dropping of education controls from the Occupation Statute in 1949. The dramatic increase of reorientation funding in the years of the High Commission confirmed their hopes. (*Kenneth Bateman*)

22. An experimental elementary-secondary school, serving the needs of several Hessian villages near Jugenheim, the Schuldorf-Bergstrasse resulted from a proposal by Kenneth Bateman, an American teacher-training expert attached to Military Government in Hesse. It incorporated some but by no means all the features of an American regional school. Among its innovations was the construction of square classrooms to encourage democratic discussion groups. (*Kenneth Bateman*)

23

23. German pupils in the Soviet Zone demonstrate in favor of a comprehensive school in Dresden in June, 1946. The Soviets and the East
German Socialist Unity Party (SED) favored structural changes in elementary-
secondary education that paralleled American proposals, as evidenced by their
cooperation in approving a uniform school law for Berlin in 1948. However, the
two occupation powers differed sharply in their methods of introducing such
changes, especially after the Americans encountered heavy resistance in Bavaria.
(Kenneth Bateman)

Some weeks before the compromise agreement, Clay learned from a colleague, Paul Bonner, of the American Embassy in Rome, that foreign legations were receiving statements from German citizens to the effect that the Americans were engaging in intellectual mayhem by closing the humanistic *Gymnasia*. Angered, Clay composed a reply in which he indicated that his expectations with respect to German education had undergone modification since 1947. He claimed that Military Government as an adherent to ACA Directive 54 "has never in any way ordered or implied that the Humanistische Gymnasien should be abandoned. In our Zone today there are 98 full Gymnasien and 150 Realgymnasien." Indeed, the Americans were now "spending millions of dollars trying to assist in the reconstruction of the German educational system." The particulars that Clay wished to emphasize were the upgrading of elementary education, teacher training, "newer teaching methods, and the introduction of a more democratic approach to education generally." Compared to the language of the January 10, 1947, directive, the MGR 8s, and the Mission Report, Clay's position had grown more flexible with respect to the nature of elementary and secondary education. His compromise agreement with Ehard was concrete evidence of this shift in attitude.[124]

Clay's personal intervention in the Bavarian school reform crisis and Ehard's willingness to accept responsibility for the necessary implementing legislation finally established a truce in what some of the E&CR education officers in Bavaria had come to call "Tom Alexander's Kulturkampf." Had a decision rested with Alexander, who had departed from Military Government at this time, or with Hundhammer, who remained adamantly opposed to any changes, no resolution of the crisis would have occurred. Even with Clay and Ehard's intervention, the issue proved thorny. American authorities at high levels were inclined to avoid official reference to the ending of the crisis. Thus, when Henry Kellermann requested information from POLAD on Clay's successful effort in Bavaria, Jacob Beam at State Department's German-Austrian branch, advised against releasing such information to the press: "I am of the opinion," he wrote to Kellermann, "that reference to Bavarian educational reform is undesirable at this time." Beam's concern was that if the American press indulged in a campaign of jubilation at this American "victory," it could easily undermine Ehard in the ongoing negotiations. "This entire matter was awkwardly handled," he continued, "and is now a subject of General Clay's personal attention. I am sure any positive developments will be reported in due course."[125]

Beam's prognosis was correct. Hans Ehard had to overcome stout resistance from the right wing of the CSU, which, in the autumn of 1948, sought to delay passage of a law long enough for the predicted enactment of the Occupation Statute to strengthen their hand. Most Germans expected that this statute would grant them virtual sovereignty and allow them to regain control of their cultural affairs. Hundhammer, according to Sam Woods, set in motion "various maneuverings designed to impede passage of school legislation." In the end, the CSU finally had to choose between Ehard and Hundhammer on the emotional issue, and it was Ehard who emerged the winner. In a tense session of the Landtag on December 15, the CSU spokesman Dr. Steng announced that, while his party opposed the bill, "it could not, as the government party, deny passage of the agreement between Ehard and Clay."[126] On that day the Bavarian Minister President fulfilled his promise and earned the gratitude of Military Government.

There was no dramatic conclusion to the rest of the school-reform issue. Conflict continued over secondary education, teacher training, and the other items desired by the Americans, but it was a controlled deadlock; that is, it did not involve the prestige of either government or draw in the leadership of either side. Instead, the issue became, once again, the preserve of E&CR and the ministry of education, just as it had been in 1945 and 1946. Charles Winning and Lawrence Derthick continued gamely, up to the end of the Occupation and beyond, to try to institute further reforms. Winning made personal appearances before the Bavarian Landtag's Cultural-Political Affairs Committee, armed with lengthy proposals and critiques, which at times entered into minute details of language.[127] Derthick and others continued on the public circuit, addressing large crowds about the virtues of E&CR's plans. But it was all to no avail. State support for tuition and textbooks was the best that Military Government could secure, and it was questionable whether the transitional payment scheme would continue beyond 1949.

In fact, Hundhammer was unwilling to accept defeat even on the initial 50 percent arrangement for the 1948/49 school year. On January 17, 1949, several months after the tuition and textbook scheme had been put into effect, a distraught young medical student from Erlangen wrote in desperation to Van Wagoner asking for his aid. It transpired that the student was about to be dismissed from medical school because his father could not pay his tuition, which was in arrears to the total of DM 204. His father was a teacher who was currently receiving only 100 DM per month as a partial salary because the state claimed it could pay no more. Such a small sum could not feed four mouths and at the same time allow the student to continue his studies, he wrote. The student pointed out the unfairness of a situation where, with one hand, the state refused to honor its teachers' salaries and, with the other, took an absolutely rigid stance on debts owed to it. He had tried to gain understanding from the Bavarian Government but had found no one willing to accept responsibility for the situation or willing to help him. Disgusted with the "great manure pile" that was the

Bavarian Government and its self-serving officialdom, the student had finally turned to Military Government. Charles Winning, to whom the letter was given, sympathized with the young man's predicament and promised to have E&CR's university officer look into the situation. He hoped to find some alleviation but also offered some friendly advice: "Governments and their practices are improved more readily through constructive criticism and, if possible, remedial action than by applying scurrilous epithets to them."[128] The urge to reeducate was not entirely dead.

The student's predicament was hardly unique. By early spring a pattern of partial payment or nonpayment of teachers' salaries had become recognizable. This indicated that Hundhammer was attempting to renege on the Clay-Ehard compromise by disrupting salary payments and thus producing pressure on parents to pay all tuition and book costs after all. Sam Woods recorded the fact that "although the local communities have paid one half of the tuition for secondary schools, the Land government has made reimbursement to only part of the communities. Some of the teachers have not been paid for some time, and considerable resentment has resulted. It is felt by Military Government officials as well as by the Consulate General that the failure to pay the local communities was intentional on the part of Hundhammer." Parents in some school districts complained that they had come under strong pressure to "voluntarily" pay for textbooks. After the evidence had accumulated for several months, Military Government began a quiet investigation in April, but it was not quiet enough. "Hundhammer apparently heard of this," Woods continued, "and at once paid all of the money due to the communities through the month of April."[129] Thus, a game of cat-and-mouse ensued on finances and on many other day-to-day issues. For example, the German definition of denazification as a rehabilitative process won out in the end, and the minister of education sent scores of letters to E&CR at the end of 1948 and in 1949 to inform Military Government of the reinstatement of previously dismissed faculty. Most were confirmed as a matter of course, but by no means all. On such occasions Winning would inform Hundhammer that the individual in question did not "possess the positive political, liberal, and moral qualities needed to assist in the development of democracy in Germany."[130] Accordingly, the education minister was ordered to dismiss the faculty member in question, even though the end of Military Government was clearly in sight. There was scant good will remaining between the two educational bureaucracies.

One reason the Americans were inclined to deal sharply with Hundhammer was their lack of faith in his claim that financial impoverishment made state payment of tuition and textbooks impossible. At the very time he had been withholding funds from communities, he had begun to move toward the establishment of another university for Bavaria. In February, 1949, the student government association (ASTA) at Erlangen appealed directly to the State Department, claiming that the founding of yet another university was wholly uncalled for at a time when there was a severe shortage of funds and staff for the existing universities.[131] The inconsistency in Hundhammer's behavior was not lost on Henry Kellermann. "It would seem remarkable," he wrote to General Edgar Hume at the CAD, "that, in view of its previous protestation of lack of funds, the Bavarian Government should now have the means for defraying the expenditures involved in the founding of a new university." Kellermann urged CAD to investigate the matter, and if, as seemed likely, the Erlangen students' allegations proved correct, then CAD should bring the matter to Military Government's attention.[132]

The students' protestations were only one indication that Alois Hundhammer was still a controversial figure in German educational circles. By his refusal to countenance any change, he had stirred discontent and antagonism among his German peers as well as among students. His reinstitution of corporal punishment in 1947 and the wave of adverse press reaction that followed were merely the beginning. In February, 1948, at the height of the school-reform crisis, the education ministers and higher staff from the various Länder gathered at a zone-wide conference of the Länderrat Education Commission to consider matters of common concern. Obviously the Bavarian reform proposals were central to their thinking. Ministers Erwin Stein from Greater Hesse and Theodor Bäuerle from Württemberg-Baden conferred with American experts, including higher-education specialist Fritz Karsen and Vaughn DeLong from Greater Hesse. However, the Bavarian delegate, who announced that he would represent Hundhammer, was a subordinate officer, Dr. Dieter Sattler. For the most part the meeting was congenial, and there was even a general expression of sympathy among the German participants for the plight of the Bavarian contingent in the aftermath of the American-imposed reform bill.

However, when Sattler requested that Hundhammer be given the chair of the zonal Working Group on School Reform, all congeniality vanished. As Heinz Guradze, an observer for the RGCO, noted: "On this occasion Minister Stein, in the name of the committee, bitterly complained of Minister Hundhammer's absence from committee meetings. Of four meetings, Minister Hundhammer had attended only the one held in Munich and, even then, had been absent part of the time, Minister Stein said. Minister Bäuerle pleaded with Herr Sattler to prevail upon his chief to attend the meetings."[133] Stein, Bäuerle, and their ministries were not alone in their distaste for Hundhammer's educational ideals and his strongly political maneuvers. During the Bavarian school crisis the American negotiators had experienced great frustration that Hundhammer had constantly interrupted important meetings to attend sessions of the Landtag. Eventually, other German educational leaders were inclined to associate with him no more than was minimally necessary. In the autumn of 1948, while Hundhammer was trying to combat the implementation of free tuition and textbooks in Bavaria, the university rectors of the three Western zones scheduled a meeting at Würzburg in northern Bavaria. There was some sentiment not to invite the controversial Bavarian education minister at all, but, as Rector Kroll of Cologne University observed, "It would not look at all well if we have two ministers as guests from other Länder without at least having communicated with the host minister." Rector Rösser of Marburg University agreed and conveyed Rector Martin's acquiescence as well. All education ministers would have to be invited. "Only in this fashion could a subsequently ugly situation be avoided," Rösser concluded.[134]

Given the ambivalence of Germany's educational leadership toward their most conservative peer, it was, in retrospect, a tragedy that Bavarian issues and personalities came together as they did. During most of the Occupation, the American education staff in Bavaria was too divided and too weak to assume the initiative in leading Bavarian school reform, and power had passed to forceful leaders like R. T. Alexander or to incautious or ill-informed figures in Bavarian Military Government, like Van Wagoner. The confrontation need not have been inevitable; Taylor beforehand and Wells afterward avoided one. The Bavarian crisis had worsened when Military Government concluded that its own authority was at stake. There had always been a strain of opinion in America that the victor should decide the course of education reform for the German people. However, America's official planning agencies had unanimously avoided that temptation in 1944 and 1945 even though they had been separated from each other by vast spaces and poor communications. Their conclusion then was that German initiative and German cooperation were imperative if a successful and lasting reform of education was to occur. From that premise they also concluded that the Germans should draw on their own cultural tradition in producing new plans. To be sure, private groups and isolated public officials had continued to propose a more coercive course of action, reasoning that the Germans must have educational models from the victor in order to produce an educational system in keeping with a democratic society. However, such groups and individuals achieved no influence until the U.S. Education Mission produced its report in the autumn of 1946. Its influence could be seen in the shift in attitude that John Taylor adopted in his last months with Military Government, a shift that was reinforced by apparent inactivity on the part of the respective education ministries of the Länder. However, R. T. Alexander's elevation by default to the leadership of the education staff of Military Government sharply altered the manner in which America attempted to fulfill the goal of education reform.

Following an inspection tour of the U.S. Zone in April, 1947, Raymond J. Sontag offered some advice to the State Department in selecting a new leader for America's education effort. He warned State Department officials that the tradition of tolerance and forbearance, which acted as a moderating influence on strong personalities in American academic communities, was simply not operative in occupied countries. "Here," he said, referring to the U.S. Zone, "there seems the opportunity to mold the mind of a whole people, and here there is not the steady pressure of the opinion of a closed academic community. Personalities expand like sponges in water. Truth becomes absolute and dissent becomes heresy. Scholars become embattled prophets. All this is inevitable, and any chief must expect to be attacked with unrestrained fury by subordinates who will not hesitate to enlist the support of pressure groups at home." Sontag also feared that if American educational administrators adopted a policy of suspicion or hostility toward religious groups, especially the Catholic Church, such action would result in "consolidating the ascendancy of reactionaries in German Christian political life."[135]

While some portions of Sontag's memorandum were not borne out by events (he predicted a new splintering of political parties), his cautionary statement about the dangers of appointing a willful, unrestrained education chief proved uncannily correct. R. T. Alexander steered a bold course in Bavaria long after the dangers of a confrontation had become apparent. His provocative support of controversial figures like Charles Falk, despite inevitable Church hostility, showed poor judgment at the very least. In the end he ensured a collision with a reactionary figure solidly backed by the Catholic hierarchy, which in its wrath did not fail to draw on support from pressure groups in America. Alois Hundhammer proved to be everything Sontag feared he would be—and more. Bavarian school reform produced a confrontation of such proportions that for a time the credibility of Military Government became tied to its outcome. In the end it required the combined efforts of two men of good will, Lucius Clay and Hans Ehard, to offset the harmful effects caused by Alexander and Hundhammer.

The confrontation that took place in Bavaria was not typical of developments in other Länder, although events in Munich inevitably influenced what happened throughout the U.S. Zone and, for that matter, in the French and British zones. The Bavarians were proud of their cultural and educational traditions even as they were fond of their peculiarly Bavarian political past. But particularism was not unique to Bavaria, as the Americans quickly discovered. In Greater Hesse, Württemberg-Baden, Bremen, and Berlin the inhabitants cherished their own traditions, preserved their own expectations, and presented political and economic conditions that had no equivalent anywhere else. In 1945 Germany's cultural diversity offered the Americans unique challenges in each Land of the U.S. Zone.

5

Around the Zone

In planning for German educational reform at war's end, the United States and American military forces in Europe encountered a major difficulty—great enough, in fact, to necessitate changes in their operational plans. Initially they had assumed the continued existence of a central German government, which they would be able to control with a modest complement of education officers. This assumption seemed logical, since the National Socialists had created a ministry of education in Berlin, similar to other centralized agencies of the Hitler governmental apparatus. However, in May, 1945, it became apparent that no centralized educational agency, let alone a central government, had survived. Military Government would have to operate on a local level until the emergency period of denazification and other punitive measures was over. The Americans also discovered that there was no desire on the part of the German people to rebuild a tight-knit bureaucracy, and the educators were, on the whole, relieved at this. However, as chaos ended and Military Government began functioning on the local level, the customs and traditions of each Land returned to life. This neoparticularist tendency was most apparent in the confrontation that took place in Bavaria over education reform, but it was found throughout the zone. It was perhaps asking too much of American planners to recall that, until seventy years before, "Germany" was merely a geographic expression—to paraphrase Metternich. Nevertheless, the Americans, especially those headquartered at OMGUS in Berlin, began to encounter the problem that had bedeviled German civil servants since the time of Bismarck: Berlin may decide, but the Land will interpret the decision.

John W. Taylor was familiar with the diversity of educational traditions in Germany, having led graduate students from Columbia to numerous

German cities in the time of the Weimar Republic; but during his tenure as chief of E&RA in Berlin he did not confront the problem of German cultural and education diversity head-on because the years 1945 and 1946 were mostly a time of emergency operations. Taylor became sensitive to the dangers of overcentralization when pressure built up in 1946 to send a U.S. Education Mission to Germany, similar to the one that had just visited Japan. He warned that "the situation in Germany is not analogous to that in Japan": Japan's system was highly centralized, Germany's was not. Taylor maintained that the German educational system had lost much of its rigidity during the Weimar days. He stated further that Military Government's controls until mid-1946 tended "to reestablish an already highly developed and well-articulated system of education." Therefore, E&RA headquarters in Berlin did not expect to change the Land educational systems except by providing broad guidelines, such as the MGR 8s. Initiative lay with the Germans on the Land level. Taylor continued: "Further, U.S. policy in Germany requires German state educational authorities to produce plans for new programs as well as for proposed reforms of existing programs in the functional fields of education." Land E&RA officers then discussed the plans with local German officials, and Taylor felt it was on that level that "the positive influencing and reorienting of German education actively takes place" (see p. 112, above). Taylor's immediate superiors persuaded him not to send so strong a memorandum to Clay, and he grudgingly accepted the Education Mission. However, Taylor's perceptions reveal his sensitivity to the tradition of decentralized education in Germany.

R. T. Alexander was just as aware of the problem. His experience in Germany dated back to the *Kaiserreich*. However, Alexander was unwilling to leave the initiative for reform to German educational and political authorities, and, as the events in Bavaria revealed, the views of American education authorities in Berlin were entirely different from German attitudes in Munich. To a certain extent the MGR 8s and, certainly, Clay's January, 1947, directive demanded plans that would produce a uniform educational structure in all Länder in the U.S. Zone. Alexander energetically pursued this goal and invoked the name of the Allied Control Authority to pressure the Land education ministries. Yet the results of his efforts to produce structural change were disappointing, and the saga of education reform that unfolded in Bavaria presaged events in the neighboring Länder.

The sequence of events was similar in all of the Länder except Berlin, which was under four-power control. During the first year of the Occupation a handful of American educators in each Land struggled to oversee the reestablishment of existing educational systems in a time of universal shortages, denazification, poor morale, and chaos. The end of 1946 saw a quickening of the pace toward some kind of reform in the wake of the Education Mission, General Clay's directive, and a zone-wide tour by Taylor and Alexander. Throughout 1947 the Land ministries complied— with varying degrees of willingness—and by October each had produced a set of general aims and specific plans. Although the German public had left the debate to professional educators up to this time, it began to take a livelier interest in the autumn of 1947, when protests against structural changes grew in size and intensity. As pressure from E&RA, OMGUS, and some Land education officers intensified, relationships between E&RA officers and their German opposites in the education ministries deterio- rated. The inevitable pressure took its toll. Walter Bergman resigned his post in Munich in December, 1947, to be followed by several other key American education officers soon after. Tardily, the Americans awakened to the fact that the goals they espoused were regarded almost universally by the German public as exclusively American. Despite an eleventh-hour effort at winning public approval, the Americans faced rising hostility to any structural change. The Bavarians' successful delaying tactics received widespread attention, as did public comments by such key American civilians as Robert Hutchins. The result was a widespread halt in reform efforts. Democratic procedure proved to be an effective block to further structural change; each Landtag either rejected or pigeonholed school- reform bills with a political adeptness the Americans could scarcely fault. Portions of the various reform packages were passed by the spring of 1949, but in almost every case they were significantly modified or else were enacted with such extended implementation schedules that their future was uncertain. The only clear-cut American victory was the enactment of laws providing for free tuition and textbooks.

As a rule, American initiatives experienced a warmer reception in Länder that possessed their own traditions of educational change. Greater Hesse was perhaps the best example, followed closely by Bremen. Württemberg-Baden lay somewhere between Bavaria and Greater Hesse, although its education minister was more willing to consider reforms than Alois Hundhammer. Berlin, too, had a rich tradition of educational in- novation. It was also in Berlin that political parties attempted openly to impose their views on educational structure, countering the Americans' claim that education should remain outside politics. In three of the U.S. Länder the policies of neighboring zones exerted considerable influence on developments in the American-controlled territory. Thus, in Bremen the education officers had to reckon with developments in the British Zone. In Stuttgart the E&RA staff had to balance its principles against the day that Württemberg-Baden would reunite with the half of its territory that was now controlled by the French. Finally, in Berlin the Americans experienced the perplexing phenomenon of Soviet and German Communist leadership, which had similar structural ideals but used utterly different methods.

Although a relatively favorable climate for educational change existed in Länder other than Bavaria, that fact did not dissuade German educational traditionalists from campaigning against the proposed changes. They showed great ingenuity in delaying reforms while at the same time galvanizing public opposition. By 1948 the results of their labors were manifest. Educational reform came to be associated in the public eye almost exclusively with American initiatives, and the Land governments faced heavy pressure to resist change of any kind. Increasingly in the last year of Military Government, the Americans turned toward the provision of material aid and other reorientation programs aimed at influencing the Germans indirectly. The experiences of E&RA officers around the zone served to remind them of German educational diversity and to warn them that the foreigner is *ipso facto* at a disadvantage in domestic political debate.

Greater Hesse

If Bavaria proved to be the most intransigent Land with respect to educational change, Greater Hesse acquired the reputation of being the most progressive. The reasons for this divergence were due in part to the nature of Hessian society and to peculiarities within the Land Military Government. If any of the Länder could be viewed as a counterpoise to Bavaria, it was above all Hesse, with a roughly comparable population and political prominence.

Greater Hesse was a new creation in May, 1945. Land Hesse, Hesse-Nassau, and Frankfurt-am-Main were merged together, amalgamating peoples of varying religious, cultural, and political persuasions into one state. Consequently, Greater Hesse was less homogeneous and more fragmented than conservative Bavaria. It had four political parties—Christian Democrats, Social Democrats, Liberal Democrats, and Communists—all of whom expected recognition from the Land ministries.

Within Military Government in Hesse (OMGH), more flexible personalities and a less-threatening atmosphere eased OMGH relations with the Hessians. Land Director James R. Newman, a former school superintendent, developed a more sympathetic stance toward his E&RA Branch. Newman did not have to face obstinate indigenous leaders like Bavaria's Fritz Schaeffer. Neither did he have to contend with reactionaries like Alois Hundhammer or influential Church leaders like Cardinal Faulhaber. Newman's opposites, Karl Geiler (the first Minister President) and Christian Stock (his successor) were hardly straw men, but there was a healthier give-and-take in Wiesbaden than in Munich. Newman displayed no conspicuous talents as Land director, but he never had to confront the severe crises that toppled Walter Muller. He was also fortunate in directing a staff that contained such able men as Ernest K. Neuman and Francis Sheehan. On the functional level, E&RA in Hesse achieved greater consensus in its aims than the badly divided staff in Munich. Staff turnover was less frequent, though hardly nonexistent, and morale among E&RA officers in Hesse was, for the most part, higher than in Bavaria.[1]

The first education chief for Military Government in Greater Hesse was Lieutenant Colonel James F. Bursch, formerly an assistant school superintendent in Sacramento, California. He worked with civil-affairs G-5 teams in Hesse in the spring and summer of 1945. The pressures encountered in administering a people experiencing total defeat were tremendous, and there was little recognition for the work. Bursch became chief of E&RA with a staff of only four in October, 1945, when OMGUS formally came into existence. In December an official report on E&RA organizations expressed concern over low morale among its officers and cited Bursch as the most conspicuous example of neglect by the military establishment: "Major Bursch . . . most outstanding officer in the field, 30 months in grade."[2] Unbelievably, Bursch was only a part-time education officer during the emergency period. As an official report noted, he was "placed on orders as President of an intermediate Military Court, which necessitated his spending at least two days a week studying and preparing cases and another two days presiding over the court in the actual trial of the cases."[3]

The immediate tasks were as daunting in Hesse as they were everywhere else. The first year of the Occupation witnessed the usual programs of denazification, vetting of textbooks, and repair of school buildings. It soon became apparent that the E&RA staff's initial hopes of using existing German administrative machinery to execute its directives were unrealistic. In many cases the celebrated German bureaucratic efficiency proved mythical, and education officers often had to institute procedures directly. No thought was given at this stage to ambitious restructuring. Opening the existing system by October seemed an impossibility.[4]

Denazification eliminated, on the average, 52 percent of the elementary-school teachers in Hesse. Nearly 600,000 textbooks were slated for pulping, but the education staff could distribute only half that number of SHAEF emergency textbooks. The Americans also distributed a "comprehensive syllabus of instruction for each subject to be taught, the outline of a curriculum of instruction purged of every Nazi and militaristic element." The results of denazification were sometimes appalling. Teacher-pupil ratios of 1:80 and even 1:120 were common, with instructors teaching three shifts per day. The necessary first efforts would have been difficult with a full staff, but "the task of supervising, directing, and guiding the whole program," an official report observed, "was accomplished with a staff of two Education Officers and one Enlisted Man."[5]

Bursch's deputy, and a key education officer in Hesse, was Vaughn R. DeLong, formerly a school administrator in Oil City, Pennsylvania. During the war DeLong had joined a G-5 team, survived the Bulge in 1944, and crossed the Rhine into Hesse in April, 1945. As a detachment leader he administered an entire *Kreis* in the chaotic months before and after the final defeat. In that capacity he managed to meet several key Hessian educational leaders who later played significant roles in the school-reform debates. Georg Morgenstern, a prominent teacher-training specialist from Weilburg, in Hesse, and Franz Schramm, destined to be the first initiator of school reform in Hesse, were favorably impressed by DeLong when he saved a valuable library collection at Weilburg and participated in emergency teacher-training programs in the summer of 1945.[6]

It is significant that DeLong's career spanned virtually the entire Occupation, a longevity matched in the U.S. Zone by few other educational officers. He did not receive the leading spot in Hessian E&RA until 1948, but he was always a leading presence, performing as deputy director or as acting director for the first education chiefs: James Bursch and Harry A. Wann. He earned respect as a diplomat in the counsels of E&RA in Wiesbaden. This quality was sorely needed in the years ahead.

Among the education officers of the U.S. Zone, Hesse generally had a reputation for cooperation. However, the Hessians and Americans at first appeared to be entering a confrontation fully one year before the collison occurred in Bavaria. The first minister president in Hesse was Karl Geiler, formerly a professor of law at Heidelberg and seemingly an ideal new leader for the fledgling democratic state. Geiler had greeted the Nazis' seizure of power with coolness, as did his Jewish wife. Forced out of his academic post in 1939, he resumed private practice in Mannheim and quietly survived the war. He claimed no party allegiance in 1945, and because of Hesse's complex four-party system he was unable to form his coalition cabinet until November 1, 1945. One of his CDU cabinet choices was another law professor, Franz Böhm, who became the first education minister. Military Government officers had the right to review the candidates selected for cabinet posts by Geiler, and the E&RA staff was especially concerned about Böhm's nomination: "twenty-seven applicants recommended by four anti-Nazi German consultants were interviewed by Military Government before an Acting Minister of Education was chosen for Greater Hesse."[7] Despite these elaborate precautions, the results were hardly satisfactory. Böhm was temperamentally unsuited to the job and lacked political acumen. Within days he had alienated important elements in the Hessian political world with his controversial personnel choices and his reactionary educational philosophy. Bursch was equally piqued. Böhm favored retaining multitrack secondary schools and devoted the bulk of his energies to defending the classical humanistic *Gymnasium*. He frequently invoked the sacred name of Pestalozzi and claimed that secondary teachers had urged him to isolate gifted pupils at the earliest possible age so that they would not be held back by the less gifted. He expected the latter to benefit from being able to spread their wings in the absence of more formidable competition. "I think that was the spirit of Pestalozzi," he proclaimed. "And it is that spirit that prevails among most of our teachers in spite of those destructive twelve years, especially in our elementary schools."[8]

Böhm's other pronouncements were hardly less compromising. He concluded that, if an amalgamation of schools must take place, it should be based on the *Christliche Einheitsschule* (Christian Unified School). That concept did not appeal to the Socialists and Communists. The Catholics were also opposed, although for different reasons. Pressure intensified on Geiler to replace Böhm. From the start Bursch had conceded Geiler's right to form his own cabinet. Unimpressed with the Americans' selections, Geiler persisted in supporting Böhm even though the latter's lack of previous administrative experience was painfully evident. Bursch was convinced that such experience was indispensable in an infant ministry, and he also complained that Geiler was ignoring the opinions of the other political parties in making Böhm his choice.[9]

Franz Böhm led a short but exciting career as Hesse's first minister of education. He persisted in making personnel choices without consulting the Americans. An official report concluded: "In forming and appointing the Ministry of Education, Minister Böhm proved his incompetence." His staff selections possessed few professional qualifications. Even Böhm conceded that he chose many of them because of political pressure. The exception was Franz Schramm, who had demonstrated great proficiency in organizing teacher-training workshops earlier that summer and who was now in charge of secondary education. Certainly Böhm's first actions were provocative, although hardly more so than Hundhammer's, two years later in Bavaria. The difference was that Hundhammer held political power while Böhm was a political neophyte. In January, 1946, matters worsened when he delivered a radio address in favor of the traditional educational system. Bursch was infuriated that Böhm delivered his opinions "as if they were the official policy of the German Government, without previous notification to the Education Division." The speech also sparked heated protests among many German listeners. When asked to provide Military Government with an outline of the aims and purposes of his ministry, Böhm simply offered a copy of his controversial radio speech. Thereupon Bursch informed Newman of "the complete rupture of confidence between the Chief of the Education Division and the Minister of Education and his deputy."[10] Simultaneously, a crisis threatened Geiler's entire regime in the wake of the municipal elections of January, 1946, when the victorious Social Democrats wanted to displace Geiler. The Communists readily joined forces with the SPD and attacked Böhm as the outstanding example of a minister who was incompatible with the new political and social realities.[11]

Recognizing the inevitable, Böhm resigned before Newman acted, thus ending the incipient crisis. Despite SPD pressure, Newman preferred to keep Geiler in office until the Landtag elections that autumn. Apparently the only person who regretted Böhm's departure was Geiler, who commented: "The decision of the SPD has affected me less than the loss of Minister Böhm, whose sudden resignation was demanded by American Military Government because certain points of difference arose between him and the gentlemen of the education section."[12]

Franz Schramm, a former *Oberstudiendirektor* for Geisenheim and the only professional educator on Böhm's staff, proved to be a fortunate replacement for Böhm. DeLong had met him at an emergency teacher-training conference in the Rheingau, and they had established good rapport after DeLong made a conciliatory speech asking for cooperation between Germans and Americans in rebuilding the Hessian educational system.[13] Schramm was destined to guide the ministry through a difficult year of continuous dislocations, shortages, and crises. The Americans' confidence in him was mirrored in a secret report: "Franz Schramm. Progressive Catholic. Excellent leader. Very able administrator. Has a profound conception of democracy as it could apply to Germany. He won the complete loyalty of all his staff members during his period of office. Thoroughly dependable and quick in carrying out plans."[14]

A month after he had assumed his duties, Schramm issued a directive banning corporal punishment in the schools. By September, 1946, with the entire educational system functioning again, he had prepared a school-reform proposal in time for consideration by the new Landtag. Schramm called his new creation a *Deutsche Einheitsschule* (German Unified School). However, his conception of what was unified or comprehensive varied from the models envisaged by his American counterparts. For example, he proposed that the first four grades, or *Grundstufe*, should retain a common curriculum for all, after which a *Mittelstufe* of four grades would permit some differentiation of pupils into two categories: deductive-theoretical and inductive-practical. However, he was careful to arrange fifth- and sixth-year curricula so as to allow for easy transfer. Latin instruction began in the seventh year for the first group. The more practically oriented pupils began with modern languages. At the end of the eighth year a sharp differentiation occurred, when three distinct groups emerged from the *Mittelstufe* into the *Oberstufe*. One group within the *Oberstufe* provided three or four years of vocational training. A second group provided four years of training for business. The third resembled the old *Gymnasium*, and its curriculum was subdivided into classical languages, modern languages, or science and mathematics. These three subdivisions corresponded to the old *Humanistisches Gymnasium, Realgymnasium*, and *Oberrealschule*.[15] Schramm hoped to construct several six-year *Aufbauschulen*, or accelerated-learning schools, for late bloomers and geographically disadvantaged (i.e., rural) pupils. In order to minimize social differences among the types of schools, Schramm wanted to put all of Hesse's pupils, regardless of ability, under one school roof, and he suggested, as a practical expedient, that large "school centers" be built amid the ruins of the burned-out cities.[16]

While Schramm was readying his plan, a debate occurred in the Hessian constitutional assembly. One of the more prominent political spokesmen at that summer gathering in Wiesbaden was Erwin Stein, a founding member of the Christian Democratic Party in Hesse. He advocated a new spirit of humanity, tolerance, and democracy for the school system but cautioned that parents and the Church (both Evangelical and Catholic) must work closely with the professional school leadership in effecting reform. He proclaimed his readiness to work with Christian unified, confessional, or lay schools, depending on the parents' wishes. Other spokesmen, such as Ludwig Metzger of the SPD, strongly advocated nonconfessional schools, as did the Communist deputy, Konrad von der Schmitt. Only the Liberal Democrat, Ernst Landgrebe, stoutly defended confessional schools. He also spoke forcefully on behalf of the traditional multitrack system. The discussions led the Hessian deputies to end separation of Catholics and Protestants in the schoolroom. They also supported free tuition and textbooks as a guarantor of greater class equality in education.[17] The contrast with Bavaria was striking. It was at this time that most American observers concluded that Hesse was in the forefront of school reform in the U.S. Zone.

The Schramm plan attracted wide attention. A surviving arm of America's wartime OSS, the Office of Institutional Research (OIR), issued a report in June, 1947, that rated Schramm's plan and Franz Fendt's scheme in Bavaria as the two most important proposals in the U.S. Zone. However, the OSS observers were not fully convinced of the democratic features of either plan: "These reform plans appear to be only partially suited to eliminating the traditional class divisions in the German school system," they averred. "The cleavage between the types of education, although slightly less sharp, will still exist. Children would attend school together for only four years and be forced to choose their future vocation at age ten. Finally, the possibility of transfer from one type of education to the other will be very remote in practice, although transfer is theoretically facilitated under these plans."[18] Neither Franz Fendt nor Franz Schramm survived in office long enough to test his plan.

In Hesse the 1946 Landtag elections strengthened the Communists and Liberals on the left and right, forcing the Social Democrats and Christian Democrats into a "great coalition," which dominated Hessian politics until 1950. Compromise and caution were a necessity with the power of the Land so broadly distributed among four groups. There was also a desire for cooperation to alleviate the terrible privations that had come with defeat. The Hessians' class lines had become as blurred in 1945 as they would ever be. Conscious of these realities, Minister President Christian Stock of the SPD gave four of nine cabinet posts to the CDU. Although Franz Schramm had earned the respect of his coworkers in the education ministry and in E&RA, he was not a political power in the CDU. Erwin Stein, on the other hand, was a leading Christian Democrat; so, when Stock convened his first cabinet on January 6, 1947, it was Stein, not Schramm, who held responsibility for cultural and educational affairs.

The E&RA staff also experienced a shakeup at this time. In June, 1946, James Bursch accepted an offer to become superintendent of schools in Sacramento, California, and Vaughn DeLong became acting E&RA chief in Wiesbaden, to serve until Military Government recruiters could find a new chief. But George Geyer was experiencing difficulty in attracting educational talent in the United States, and, because of the crisis over denazification in Munich, Bavarian E&RA was uppermost in Taylor's and Geyer's minds. Thus, when one highly qualified individual joined E&RA only under the condition that he serve in Berlin, Taylor readily agreed. "We might later get him into Bavaria," he added.[19] E&RA in Wiesbaden remained understaffed.

Besides scarcity of qualified administrative talent, the Americans were also plagued by overlapping powers of appointment between E&RA in Berlin and the Land directors. This dual authority caused considerable mischief in Bavaria, and it was also a factor in Wiesbaden. For example, the E&RA staff was determined to prevent the retention of a junior officer, Ida Elzey, but James Newman was determined to keep her on the rolls. Taylor informed Geyer: "Neither DeLong nor I would approve her civilianization, but Newman has told her she may remain as long as she likes in military status."[20] Irritating as such disagreements were, Taylor had to admit that Hesse was still not his gravest problem: "Württemberg-Baden," he admitted to Geyer, "is the weakest of the lot."[21]

By December, 1946, the lack of a permanent chief in Hesse was becoming intolerable. The Hessians were about to form a new government, and the E&RA staff would have to prepare for action soon. Finally, Alfred Pundt, who had once served as education chief in Bavaria and who now reappeared as a state-side recruiter for E&RA, sent word that Dr. Harry

A. Wann, an administrator for the New Jersey Department of Education, was available. Recruitment's message to Berlin read: "Wann knows no German language or history but struck me as a good administrator and willing to learn. He will go, but it will be necessary to inform him definitely soon." Taylor was not certain. "Don't know about Wann," he replied, "although Dr. Alexander says they were together in Turkey thirty years ago. Will check with DeLong and Newman."[22]

Newman was impatient, after the long delay, and brushed aside any reservations. Thus Harry A. Wann, about whom little was known except that he spoke no German, became the third chief of E&RA in Hesse at the same time as Erwin Stein became the Land's third postwar minister of education.

Immediately, both the Hessian Ministry and E&RA were faced with major decisions. General Clay's January 10 directive had already made the rounds of the Länder, as had the Mission Report. Alexander expected the Hessians to provide statements of basic aims in April, 1947, to be followed that summer by detailed plans. All of this had to be done on top of the day-to-day demands of an educational system that was functioning with insufficient resources and staff at a time when the punitive aspects of the Occupation predominated. Thus, the daily letters that the newly arrived Harry Wann wrote to Erwin Stein did not, at first, reflect concern with broad educational goals. A typical letter reads: "Dr. Albrecht, Frankfurt, Launitzstr. 8 II, a former party member who had no work, is giving lessons in languages." What was Stein prepared to do in this case of imperfect denazification? Another letter described a lazy but enterprising instructor in the new capital: "A teacher in the Hebbel-Schule, Wiesbaden, is reported to have held no classes for the past two weeks, but sits around smoking cigarettes, which he obtains from the schoolchildren, whom he sends out to collect cigarette butts."[23]

Prior to Wann's arrival, DeLong had been extraordinarily active in the absence of a permanent executive for E&RA. His accomplishments included the formulation of the first plan to utilize visiting American experts to study specific problems in the Land educational system.[24] Together with the university rectors and E&RA staff, he had worked feverishly in 1946 to complete the denazification of the institutions of higher learning in order to forestall a complete shutdown of the universities.[25] In the lower schools DeLong perceived a worrisome lack of concern among the Hessian people about the need for change, and he hit on a clever means of dramatizing the situation. In November, 1946, E&RA distributed a questionnaire among the schoolchildren of Marburg about their recent National Socialist past. The results were sobering. When asked "Do you believe that National Socialism was a bad idea or a good idea which was carried out badly?" only 3.5 percent of the children found National Socialism to be a bad idea. Over 51 percent felt it was a good idea but badly executed. Nearly 45 percent were undecided. There were many other questions dealing with the nature of fascism, anti-Semitism and other aspects of totalitarianism. The answers to these were similar and produced widespread concern among the adult population. As one of his first acts Stein ordered instructors to provide an accurate historical treatment of the Third Reich.[26] Thus, Harry Wann inherited a post with solid accomplishments and promising precedents. He also retained DeLong as his deputy director.

An important gathering of Hessian and American education officials assembled in Wiesbaden in February, 1947, to discuss school reforms. The participants included John Taylor, whose tour of duty was coming to an end, and R. T. Alexander. Erwin Stein was on hand, as was Willy Viehweg, his deputy at the ministry. DeLong was also an active participant. Taylor led off with an address in which he advocated the reforms proposed in the Mission Report; at its conclusion he asked for a response.[27]

"I am pleased to affirm," Stein answered, "that the basic concepts on educational policy as presented by Dr. Taylor are the same as mine." Stein agreed that the negative goals of denazification and demilitarization were insufficient and that reforms must aim at "a moral democratic renovation of the people." He intended to create a "differentiated *Einheitsschule*," and he visualized the admission of pupils solely on the basis of their abilities, talents, and interests rather than class or income. Stein's response actually devoted little time to elementary- and secondary-school structure or curriculum design. Administrative problems concerned him more. For example, he wanted to give school superintendents greater autonomy. Other goals included a ninth school year for all pupils, uniform teacher training, and permanent adoption of free textbooks and tuition. It was a conciliatory rejoinder to Taylor's remarks, and in spirit and tone it was far more sympathetic to the Americans than anything heard in Munich.[28]

John Taylor was impressed: "I have already had similar discussions in Württemberg-Baden and in Bavaria, and I find that there is more response here in Hesse and that more steps have been taken in the direction we would like than in any other place." Taylor agreed that future reforms depended, in the final analysis, on German initiatives: "I would like to say that there is no idea on the part of the American Education Division of Military Government to impose any school reform in any Land of our Zone." His chief concern was the "*Überschneidung* and the *Zweiheit* between secondary and elementary schools."[29] In fact, Stein's statement on elementary- and secondary-school structure was ambiguous. Willy Viehweg, too, refused any definite commitment: "We will begin with a common elementary school, which probably—as it seems now—will be of six years' duration. The final word on this matter will be spoken by the Landtag." Viehweg visualized the future secondary school as a "*wei-*

terführende" rather than an exclusively *"höhere"* Schule. But he admitted that this new form would retain two or three branches, one of which would lead to the *Abitur* and university studies. He predicted that, because of the restricted Hessian budget, relatively few pupils would enter this ambitious curriculum. The *Aufbauschule* was an important feature of the contemplated reforms, as was ease of transfer from one branch to another. Viehweg admonished the Americans not to allow any centralized agency, such as the education committee of the Länderrat, to control education reform because it would become yet another bureaucratic echelon incapable of understanding the needs of Hessians as opposed to Bavarians or other Länder.[30]

The February 20 meeting was a fair indicator of the harmonious relationship between the Hessian education ministry and E&RA leadership, both at OMGUS and in Wiesbaden. Quickly, Stein organized a number of committees composed of ministry representatives and acknowledged education specialists. The panels studied the feasibility of a six-year elementary school, curriculum offerings, and teacher-training institutions, among other things. The Americans were impressed with this purposeful activity and with the quality of the staff who congregated around Stein. The Americans rated his deputy, Willy Viehweg, as "an idealist, thoroughly able. Has a profound grasp of the youth problem in Germany, of the German school system's reflecting sociological changes, and of highly technical German school matters. He has the complete admiration and confidence of every member of the staff in the Ministry of Education. He is industrious to the point of ruining his own health. He is deserving of every bit of support the Occupation can give."[31]

The Americans were scarcely less enthusiastic about another official, Franz Hilker, a ministry authority on Catholic education who had served as adviser to the American Education Mission during its tour of Hesse. Hilker was no stranger to American educational institutions: "Educated at Columbia University," an E&RA report announced; "German delegate on the committee for education in the League of Nations at Geneva after the First World War. . . . Is one of the most progressive and forward-looking thinkers in all of the State of Hesse. . . . He is the type of leader, especially in Catholic circles, who is so necessary to the democratic development of Germany."[32]

Wann was most impressed with Stein, and, after a few months, he communicated his praise. "It has been a pleasure," he wrote on April 1, 1947,

> to work with you on the many problems involved in connection with the reconstruction of the school system of Hesse. . . . I have had an opportunity to observe your leadership in the selection of personnel,

in the organization of your staff, your leadership in public relations, and to exchange thinking on the general problems of education. I consider that Land Hesse is fortunate in having one of your capacity, clear thinking, and leadership ability head the Ministry in these difficult times. I want to assure you of my complete confidence in your leadership and of the full cooperation of my Division in helping develop the educational opportunities in Land Hesse to the highest degree possible.[33]

In the spring of 1947 the pace of discussions quickened when sixty American education experts arrived to aid the ministry and to bolster the ranks of E&RA. Wann was pleased with the performance of many if not all of these consultants and noted that faculty from the University of Wisconsin were making a particulary notable contribution. He identified the contributions of Professor Burr Phillips, Bernice Leary, and Mary Kelty among the experts and also recognized Howard W. Becker, a permanent member of the E&RA staff in higher education, as making an outstanding effort.[34]

One consequence of so much diversity of effort by twenty reform committees was that the deadline for detailed reform plans, originally ordered for June 1, 1947, proved impossible to meet. Stein was well aware that the Bavarians had received an extension from E&RA, OMGUS. Now he asked Wann for similar treatment: "It is known to Military Government that the Hessian Work Seminar 'Die Neue Schule' is thoroughly and ardently working upon the school reformation, on school curricula, and textbooks. I would like to wait for the results of that work, so that I may base upon them my decisions."[35] Wann supported Stein's request to Alexander, but Stein was taking no chances and arrived in Berlin in mid-June to plead his case directly. He preceded his Berlin visit with a directive to retain free tuition and textbooks in Hesse in the absence of any Landtag legislation, a move that ensured a friendly reception from Alexander. Following the Marburg school survey, he had also moved quickly to change curricular offerings, and he hinted that he intended to drop a proposed teacher-training college in Fulda "because it is too strongly under the influence of the Catholic Church."[36] Alexander promptly granted the extension. Stein appeared to be a kindred spirit and the most advanced education minister in the zone.

Through the summer and early fall of 1947, Hesse's twenty education committees refined their reform proposals. However, what the Americans in their exuberance tended to overlook was the committees' advisory status. Thus, the general committee on school reform, which formed the core of the reform effort, discovered that Stein would accept only some of their proposals; he would not forward their plan unchanged to Military Government. The various committees had been organized in accordance with the provisions of the Military Government Regulations, which stipulated that "new school laws will be developed democratically." In order to ensure democratic processes and to prevent enactment of reform legislation favored only by professional groups rather than the public, the education ministry, at Military Government's urging had also formed a *Hauptausschuss*, or central committee, composed of members of the general public, to review the work of the twenty professional committees. They were expected to "weigh carefully the recommendations of the professional committees, to ascertain that they meet the principles as laid down in the Military Government Regulations, that they meet the needs of today's children, and that they are practical." If disagreements arose, the *Hauptausschuss* was to return the recommendations to the professional groups for further consideration.[37]

In practice, however, the complicated review machinery began to work in ways the Americans had not foreseen. On September 8 the *Hauptausschuss* considered the work of the three professional committees that dealt with general schools, trade schools, and academic schools. The three had finally arrived at a draft solution for this core problem of the German educational structure, and now they wanted approval by the *Hauptausschuss*. "However," Harry Wann complained to Erwin Stein, "when the report was read, it was immediately attacked by guests who had not been in on the previous months of discussion and could not be expected in one meeting to be oriented on all which the committees had considered over a period of months." Only twenty-six persons out of forty-seven committee members were available on the day of the crucial review. Furthermore, there had been twenty-nine guests. "Fully 75 percent of the entire debate time was consumed by the guests," Wann complained. Worse, they had created a committee of five persons "to resolve points of view which had previously been amply considered and resolved by the committees (properly authorized) for this responsibility." This new committee of five was dominated by nonprofessionals from the *Hauptausschuss*. Not one specialist on elementary schools was a member.[38]

Angered by this unexpected turn, Wann informed Stein that only formally designated committees should make recommendations and that the *Hauptausschuss* was to confine its review to the practicability of proposals. Furthermore, this committee was to determine whether or not the draft conformed to the ten principles embodied in the MGRs, the Mission Report, and Clay's January 10 directive. Wann stopped short of closing the meetings of the *Hauptausschuss* to the public. "Guests should be encouraged at all committee meetings," he allowed, "but it should be remembered that the committees are deliberative bodies and that the limited debate time should be reserved for members of the committees." True, specialists could deliver reports on technical points, and individuals could, "if desired, be asked to present a viewpoint (not to enter a debate)." Wann feared that the older generation was dominating the proceedings, and he recommended that the ministry add "at least two outstanding teachers or administrators between the ages of twenty-five and thirty-five to each committee as regular members."[39]

Erwin Stein drew a different conclusion from the incident. He thought it indicated that among the general public there was a far more serious division over the direction of school reform than the professional educators had been willing to admit. He therefore, in October, submitted a school-reform proposal to Military Government that did not follow the exact recommendations of his professionals. The incident of September 8 had been a signal that no politician could ignore: school reform had become a sensitive issue in Hesse. Whereas his professional committees were prepared to institute a six-year elementary school with a common curriculum, as Military Government wanted, Stein was now inclined to retain certain features of the old system, including early differentiation. His October 1 proposal permitted the teaching of Latin to fifth-year pupils, as had always been done in the *Gymnasia*. This decision should not have come as a surprise. As early as the February meeting with Taylor and Alexander, Stein had qualified his acceptance of the comprehensive school by defending the principle of differentiation. His current plan was to allow foreign-language instruction, including Latin, in grades five, seven, or nine.[40] It was a flexible system, to be sure, but Harry Wann was not pleased.

"From the standpoint of cost and administration," he wrote in a summary of the October 1 draft,

> this proposal seems entirely impractical. An elective subject in the fifth grade means again a differentiation within the elementary school and a selection of students which differs from the present system only to the extent that it is proposed that the students will be housed in the same building. The election of a language either in grades 5, 6, or 7 would entail parallel courses of the language throughout the school system. While this might be feasible in the large school system, it would be exceedingly expensive, and, in the smaller schools, it would be entirely impractical.

Wann had to admit that Stein's school-reform proposals were a step in the right direction, but they fell short of Military Government expectations.[41]

During the discussions that ensued, it became apparent that the organization of the education ministry, with its twenty professional committees plus the quarrelsome *Hauptausschuss*, was a hindrance to reform rather than an aid. The Americans muted their stand about the democratic process and showed interest, instead, in streamlining the bureaucratic mechanism. Thus the creation of a *Landesschulbeirat*, or Land School Advisory Board, resulted from the new discussions that autumn. It was to be an enlarged committee, of forty individuals, organized along E&RA lines for ease of coordination with Wann's staff. It was to be an autonomous body of acknowledged experts who would receive financial assistance from Military Government but would have no formal ties or obligations to the Americans. Wann even secured funds to serve daily hot lunches to the hardworking committee members. The *Landesschulbeirat* was expected to handle school-reform proposals for the ministry, operating under Stein's overall leadership. Yet it was not an internal committee of the ministry. It could negotiate with the E&RA staff, and it was to be headed by a professor of education, Dr. Heinrich Wilhelm Haupt. The *Landesschulbeirat* formally came into existence on November 28, 1947.[42]

Wann was enthusiastic about future prospects: "We expect that within the next few weeks the committees will develop plans and programs for the implementation of changes which will be agreeable to Minister Stein, acceptable to Military Government, and practical, even in the present situation."[43] It was noteworthy that Wann appointed DeLong as the chief American to negotiate with the *Landesschulbeirat*.[44] Wann's confidence in other members of his E&RA staff, however, diminished greatly after the sudden halt to progress that fall. He intimated as much in his correspondence to former colleagues back in the United States. To a friend, Charles Hamilton, he confided, "My chief problem during the past year was to secure from the States competent personnel."[45]

However, there were other observers in Hesse who criticized Wann's performance and held him responsible for a notable decline of morale in the Wiesbaden staff. Hayes Beall, a youth-activities specialist and friend of Alexander, spent several months in Wiesbaden observing the progress of reforms there. Because of Wann's inability to demonstrate openness and frankness, Beall observed, "the greater part of the E&RA staff began to hear criticisms of their work which had been made to visitors and bystanders, along with assertions that they would soon be replaced."[46] In fact, several staff in secondary, vocational, and adult education left Wiesbaden that autumn, as Beall had foreseen. Six replacements began arriving at the end of 1947, to be followed by another half-dozen recruits in the final year of Military Government operations.[47] Beall's prediction of high turnover was accurate. He was worried about the lag time between dismissals and the arrival of replacements. "The criticism I offered to both Dr. James R. Newman and Dr. Wann," Beall continued,

was that the latter's personnel policy had seriously impaired the morale—and therefore the working efficiency—of most of his staff and had consequently reduced their effectiveness, whereas a policy of support and encouragement would have produced far better results in the interim between February [1947] and the arrival of the desired replacements. I further said to Newman and Wann that I could not comprehend how a man with an experience of so many years in personnel work could handle people so ineptly.[48]

Even more disturbing was the revelation that Wann had disclosed his personnel problems to Erwin Stein. "When Minister Stein voiced some criticisms," Beall stated, "of what he thought the summer camping program might be—based on Stein's unfamiliarity with the work of his own staff—we found Wann quickly agreeing with him and then coming back to take credit for the work when the camping program showed good results. As matters stand, Wann is one of the loneliest and most unhappy people in Wiesbaden. No one has confidence in him; his policy has isolated him on all sides." Beall traced the problem to James Newman's eagerness to fill the E&RA director's spot, but events had changed the Land director's mind: "I happen to know that Newman is more than ready to welcome your help in correcting matters in Wiesbaden."[49]

It was a disturbing report, and Alexander did not dispute its facts. "As you know," he replied to Beall, "I did not make the appointment and cannot do much about changing it until I am definitely asked to take a step in that direction." Alexander promised to speak to Newman, but the best he could do for the present was to announce that he had recruited "three or four very fine people in recent weeks" for Hesse.[50] In fact, the Land director was the key officer in each Land, and without Newman's active cooperation little could be done. Alexander was preoccupied by the confrontation in Bavaria, and his relationship with Clay was deteriorating as education reform around the zone became increasingly controversial. Alexander knew well that Wann's position did not depend on the judgment of anyone in E&RA in Berlin.

As the autumn nights of 1947 lengthened, so did the gloom about prospects for rapid passage of school reform in Hesse. A quick victory there would influence the other Länder. Similarly, a defeat in Hesse would have strong repercussions. At an E&RA branch chiefs' meeting in Wiesbaden that November, the Americans expressed concern over Stein's performance, although they conceded that it was politically understandable. Instead of accepting all of his committees' recommendations, including Latin instruction starting in the seventh year, Stein had tried to win the traditionalists by allowing classical languages to begin in the fifth school year. "He tried to present a plan which would satisfy everyone," the minutes of the meeting recorded; "consequently, Dr. Wann does not feel it will satisfy anyone."[51] Wann proved correct in his assessment.

Harry Wann pondered his next move. His staff examined Stein's proposal in minute detail, and on December 8, 1947, he sent a detailed criticism to Stein. E&RA's demands were straightforward: "The schools will be organized on the basis of an *Einheitsschule* with six years' undifferentiated elementary school."[52] Wann expected the newly erected *Landesschulbeirat* "to develop a plan of reorganization of the school to conform to this pattern." He also established a timetable for the creation of the detailed reform plan. It was to be in Military Government's hands by April 1, and it was to be in operation in the autumn of 1948. This tough new stance paralleled the combative mood of education officers in the other Länder and a corresponding stiffening of resistance on the part of the German education ministries. DeLong had remained sanguine about progress in Hesse that fall, but by early 1948 his own doubts began to surface. On February 9 he visited a zone-wide conference on cultural affairs at nearby Schönberg in the Taunus Mountains. He was sobered by what he heard. "It was a great shock to the undersigned," he confided to Alexander "to learn that all Länder contemplated continuing with the present system at the beginning of the new school year in October; in other words, they expect as usual to have a new group of students leave the elementary school at the end of the fourth year and enter one of the Höhere Schulen." DeLong also worried about "the extent to which the finance ministers in each Land can—perhaps will—hinder certain aspects of school reform. This matter seems to be so serious that perhaps OMGUS should make a study of the matter and perhaps suggest concerted action by the Länder."[53] DeLong's concerns proved to be well founded when, in midsummer, 1948, currency reform became a reality.

Notes of pessimism echoed through the education offices in the winter of 1947/48. One official report conceded: "The chronic problem of secondary-teacher and parent opposition to school reform represents one of the biggest actual potential hurdles in Hesse as in other Länder."[54] Another report on Bavarian school reform admitted that this southernmost Land had strong moral support in Hesse, as indicated in a survey of March, 1948: "A discouraging aspect of the survey findings was the fact that very few of the teachers' interviews—including those seemingly in accord with the proposed reform—evidence any genuine understanding of the basic principles of the reform plan. Most of them felt that no real need existed for any fundamental changes in the education system and that the Stein reform program constituted simply an unnecessary and unwelcome burden imposed upon them by dictatorial superiors."[55]

Some Military Government education officers reacted keenly to the growing German criticism. Many, like William L. Wrinkle, had come to the zone with considerable zeal for the American reform effort but soon fell prey to inner doubts. Wrinkle enjoyed a close relationship with Alexander and after several months in Wiesbaden prepared a series of confidential memoranda for the E&RA director, which he also shared with DeLong and Wann. One of his basic concerns was that American educational philosophy and institutions, while appropriate for the United States, "may not be the best for Germany." The point seemed obvious. "Yet," he admitted, "I wasn't aware until last Wednesday that there was a strong possibility I might be merely mouthing words and unconsciously behaving quite differently on the basis of prejudices I brought over from the States." Wrinkle had begun as an ardent advocate of the undifferentiated six-year elementary school followed by three years of middle school and capped by three years of advanced schooling. It was possible to argue in favor of such a plan as psychologically a more favorable form of progression for pupils, but the most common justification he had heard in E&RA circles was that it was "merely a mechanical expedient which looks good because it automatically eliminates the possibility of early differentiation." Originally, Wrinkle had wanted structural change because leaving the traditional system in place would make it more difficult to introduce changes in the traditional curricula. However, he decided, on closer examination, that to justify a radical reorganization solely because it aided curricular change was shaky grounds for so fundamental an alteration of the Hessian school system. Reluctantly he turned his attention back to the American junior high school and decided that that peculiarly American institution "was largely the result of this expediency type of thinking." Such schools had developed rapidly because they were administratively feasible and were popular with the public. Yet, experience had demonstrated, according to the National Survey of Secondary Education of 1932, that it was the size of a high school, not the pattern of organization, that contributed most to determining the quality and variety of the curriculum offerings. "Should we make the same mistake in Germany that was made in the States?" Wrinkle asked. "Or if 'mistake' is not the best word, should we kid ourselves into believing that we have done something to improve German education if what is done does not involve a fundamental improvement?"

Wrinkle conceded that the German village system was unlike anything found in the United States, a fact that could affect the quality of secondary schools. Was centralization of grades beyond the sixth school year more conducive to high-quality secondary schools than centralization above the fourth school year? Possibly the answer lay in centralization above the eighth school year. "I don't know," Wrinkle confessed; "I know of no one who knows. Only close examination of enrollment figures and geographic patterns, trends made ever more complex by the influx of refugees, could provide such answers." To demand a six-year elementary school now might force every village to enlarge its school—an expensive undertaking in those hungry times. Wrinkle felt it might be better to retain four undifferentiated elementary grades and thus limit expansion efforts to less numerous but more centralized structures for grades five and above.[56]

Wrinkle had also detected other biases among his American colleagues. E&RA officers were, he felt, a preselected group who disdained what he called a "faculty psychology." They were distrustful of a certain lack of social reality in American institutions of higher learning. This distrust was not necessarily bad, but Wrinkle feared that it prejudiced E&RA officers in a crucial way. Foreign-language instruction in America occurred largely in the colleges and universities and was not taught as a functional subject. Language instructors were, as a consequence, arrayed squarely in the camp of "faculty psychology"—which the functionalists distrusted. "A group of American educational functionalists, therefore, unless they would be careful, would have a tendency to think of foreign languages in Europe with the same prejudiced point of view as they show in America." It followed that American reform plans would tend to minimize or delay foreign languages in school curricula. "See how the six-year undifferentiated elementary school provides a slick partial solution?" Wrinkle asked. "Maybe we haven't looked at the foreign languages as Europeans have to look at them. I think we should."[57]

Germany had become a minor power in world affairs virtually overnight, Wrinkle observed. Its geographic position was also such that it must now become a two-language nation. To be sure, not everyone must learn a second language, but certainly the commercial and professional classes had to do so. The second language might be English or, perhaps, Russian. The choice was not so important at this stage. In any case, the Americans had to encourage the German children's facility in languages, which meant introducing foreign languages as early as practicable. Wrinkle admitted that it was entirely possible that such a stage might come before the seventh school year. He hoped (although he admitted that he lacked statistical information) that the Germans could incorporate the first foreign language into the general curriculum. Then, at a later stage, linguistically gifted pupils could undertake a more intensive language curriculum. "This would be in violation of the principle of the undifferentiated elementary-school curriculum, but it is a totally different brand of differentiation from the current practice of differentiation on the basis of premature vocational choice."[58]

Wrinkle's doubts about American reform goals were not meant for general distribution and did not become the basis of a general discussion among the general E&RA staff. Neither was it the subject of discussion with Stein and his ministry. Nevertheless, his speculations reflected the freer atmosphere and less dogmatic stance of the education officers in Greater Hesse. Leading personalities on both sides showed a greater capacity for compromise and a genuine desire for reform. The *Landesschul-beirat* proved to be a more practical deliberative body than the twenty-odd committees of 1947, and DeLong came to respect its chairman, Professor Heinrich W. Haupt, as an intelligent and tireless leader. The *Landesschul-beirat* was able to achieve better recognition among the Hessian public, and DeLong, at least, felt that it emphasized German initiative in the school-reform debate at a time when German critics were charging that the reforms were a purely American initiative.[59] He claimed that there was a strong desire on the part of the E&RA staff to acquaint members of the *Landesschulbeirat* and the education ministry with the American proposals and to discuss them openly as equals. The Hessian and American educational experts maintained cordial ties that held even during the later tense negotiations in 1948—a pleasant contrast to the frosty encounters in Munich.

However, discussions between E&RA and the ministry were bound to be controversial, and none more so than the ones concerned with the sensitive issue of teacher training. This was the subject of early discussions because of the need to supply large numbers of teachers in the emergency period. Before the war Hesse had had teacher-training colleges at Weilburg, near Giessen, and at Jugenheim, near Darmstadt. Then the Nazis had closed them in favor of five *Lehrerbildungsanstalten*, or LBAs, which were easier to control. Following the war, E&RA officers revived the two colleges and opened temporary teacher-training centers in Frankfurt, Fulda, Fried-berg, and Eltville. No one considered the latter as anything more than emergency centers. DeLong had already gained some experience with the Weilburg college when he entered the town in 1945 and established his G-5 headquarters there. After closing the Weilburg college, the Nazis had stripped it to outfit their overtly political LBAs, but they had ignored the library of 50,000 volumes, regarding it as politically unacceptable. DeLong had helped the former rector, Georg Morgenstern, save the collection from the weary GIs who were busily commandeering the building, thus en-dearing himself to Morgenstern. DeLong's support for Weilburg and the arrival in 1948 of Kenneth Bateman, a teacher-training expert assigned to provide expertise for Jugenheim, measurably helped the recovery of the two permanent institutions and created a store of good will between Americans and Hessians in teacher training that endured long after the Occupation had ended.[60]

As early as May, 1946, the E&RA staff had called on the education ministry to prepare long-range plans for teacher training. The planning was to be done in democratic fashion, so the ministry called on experts, including the leaders of Weilburg and Jugenheim, for advice. This initia-tive produced several meetings between ministry officials and experts, who then issued a series of reports. By the end of June the Hessians had come to several tentative conclusions. They were especially concerned that future teachers be more broadly educated than was traditionally the case. There was much talk about democratic teacher training and inner reform. The Hessians also devoted attention to practical needs, such as accelerated training schedules to replace the generally overage teachers. They braced themselves for the influx of refugee children and speculated on how many permanent institutions they should maintain after the emergency period.[61] Significantly, the ministry did not discuss the discrepancies in professional training between elementary and secondary teaching in Hesse. Nor were they alone in this. In his first annual report in June, 1946, DeLong discussed emergency training at length and noted that the ministry was considering a third permanent teacher-training college in North Hesse. Conspicuous by its absence was any mention of the need to make the contemplated institution or existing ones comparable in quality to the universities or to affiliate them in any way with the universities.[62] However, within weeks the U.S. Education Mission changed all that. E&RA plans, issued after publication of the Mission Report, called for just such an elevation of teacher-training institutions.

In February, 1947, during Taylor and Alexander's visit to Hesse, DeLong asked Taylor whether or not teacher-training institutions were to be raised to university status. The minutes recorded a simple "yes" from Taylor.[63] Stein spoke vaguely about eliminating the traditional sharp distinctions between elementary- and secondary-school teachers, but his deputy, Willy Viehweg, was more specific. He announced that the new teacher-training institutions in Hesse were to be called "pedagogical institutes." "We deliberately chose the title Pedagogical Institute," he said, "in order to raise them to the same status of other, comparable institutions possessing connections to the universities. . . . I stated earlier that we shall no longer have any differentiation among the secondary schools, and we shall no longer have so much differentiation among the types of teachers."[64] The tone of Viehweg's remarks gave hope that Americans and Hessians would quickly agree on a teacher-training law, but it became a casualty when efforts to produce a school bill stalled in the autumn of 1947.

Interest in teacher training in Hesse extended beyond the ministry and the E&RA staff. Since the stated goal of Americans and Hessians alike had been to upgrade teacher education to university status, the education officers desired to limit the number of such institutions so that scarce resources could be utilized most efficiently. A prime example of expensive duplication was Bavaria's thirty-five colleges.[65] American estimates of the number of teacher-training institutions needed in Hesse varied. A 1947 E&RA report estimated that four institutions might be required, including two new centers at Fulda and Giessen.[66] Then, as progress in education reform languished, the teacher-training proposal became an additional sore point between the ministry and E&RA. In early 1948 a newcomer to Wiesbaden, Eugene Robert Fair, formerly dean of Illinois State Teachers College in Carbondale, commented on the lack of progress: "In an otherwise basically cordial cooperation, Ministry officials, in presenting their teacher-training budget to the Landtag, persist in recommending too many small institutions, so that university-level teacher education still is far from becoming a reality."[67] Fair had hopes of providing an existing institution with generous financial support to demonstrate to the Hessians what intelligent concentration of resources could achieve. He wrote to colleagues in the United States, soliciting aid and teaching staff for Weilburg Pedagogical Institute: "We have realistic hopes of making this institution outstanding in every way," he announced to one friend. Fair confided that the Rockefeller Foundation was willing to provide sizable grants to Weilburg for research in child growth and development.[68]

However, the education ministry, instead of following the Americans' lead, was still considering other institutions; in this they were yielding to pressure to build a permanent teacher-training institution in northern Hesse's predominantly Catholic region. The logical site was Fulda, which had housed an emergency training center and was also the home of a seminary for priests and a college of music. The bishop of Fulda was eager to have a pedagogical institute there, and he was not alone in making that wish known. A familiar figure in the Bavarian school-reform debate appeared in Hesse in late 1947. Father Stanley Bertke was touring the zone to advise E&RA officers on confessional schools and religious education. Following the revelations about Charles Falk in Munich, Bertke had little reason to expect cooperation from R. T. Alexander, and he became suspicious when he learned that E&RA was withholding permission for the Fulda project, pending submission of a teacher-training law to the Hessian Landtag. Dumont Kenny, E&RA's religious-affairs chief in Wiesbaden, discussed the issue with Bertke at length. He denied that there was any move afoot to sabotage the creation of another teacher-training institution. Kenny and the E&RA staff emphatically disclaimed any intent to hold the Fulda project hostage to the passage of the law.[69]

Bertke was not convinced and appealed directly to Robert Murphy. He complained that there was religious discrimination in the case and that he had received no satisfaction from E&RA officials, either in Wiesbaden or Berlin. Bertke's case was simple: "A third of the population of Greater Hesse is Catholic," he told Murphy. "The two teacher-training schools already approved are in non-Catholic regions. Fulda is in a Catholic region. The Catholics, a third of the population, want one of the three teacher-training schools to be in a Catholic region." Bertke reminded Murphy that the Catholic bishops of Hesse were behind the Fulda project, and he claimed that Stein, the minister of education, also supported it.[70]

Alexander refused to believe that Stein supported the Fulda proposal. Several months earlier Stein had discussed the issue while in Berlin, visiting the E&RA leadership, and the minutes of the meeting recorded that "Dr. Stein is in favor of dropping the teacher-training institution at Fulda because it is too strongly under the influence of the Catholic Church. He thinks that this institution should be in Kassel."[71] Consequently, when Robert Murphy forwarded Bertke's objections to Alexander without naming the author, E&RA's irascible education chief offered a stinging rebuttal. "Assuming that it is written by Father Bertke," he wrote back to Murphy, "we do not care to communicate with him through your office. . . . He has been attached to this division as liaison officer and knows where he can get full answers to all his questions."[72]

Alexander confirmed the fact that no new teacher-training institution would be approved in Hesse until an acceptable teacher-training law had been passed, but he flatly denied Bertke's accusation. "No religious considerations entered into nonapproval of the school at Fulda, since the teacher-training institutions in Hesse are nondenominational and religion has nothing at all to do with the matter. It seems that Father Bertke is the one who has tried to inject religious elements into the question."[73]

Robert Murphy defused the confrontation as best he could, relaying the substance rather than the actual remarks of Alexander to the ecclesiastical adviser. For the record he noted that "Father Bertke is convinced that there is religious discrimination in this matter, regardless of the remarks made by Dr. Alexander."[74] For their part, the E&RA staff in Wiesbaden were convinced that Bertke had exceeded his mandate in the Fulda affair. Eugene Fair, for one, claimed that "unwarranted interference of a high-placed American ecclesiastical adviser to General Clay in itself has bordered upon sabotage of E&CR efforts to keep Hesse's plan for teacher education open for evaluation on its professional merits exclusively."[75]

Still, no teacher-training law was immediately forthcoming. It was inexorably bound up in the general discussion and debate concerning school reform, and, as DeLong observed to Wann in February, 1948, a general pattern of resistance against reform proposals was now emerging. "It seems more and more evident that our program is not moving forward in the ministry," he told his chief. Teacher-training legislation had made no progress since August, 1946; school reorganization had been at a standstill since October, 1947. "Committees are meeting," he observed, "but no conclusions are reached." The free-tuition law was stalled in the Landtag, and no implementation schedule existed for any reform. DeLong recommended another meeting with Stein to establish clear-cut deadlines and to renew discussions on all aspects of reform.[76] The meeting duly took place, and the E&RA staff informed Stein that it expected to see a detailed plan by April 1, 1948.

Erwin Stein simply ignored the deadline, and the education officers, faced with noncooperation, backed down. They then shifted tactics and on April 19 requested the education minister "to furnish information from several *Kreise* which would show exactly the situation relative to teachers, pupils, and buildings, [assuming that] no fifth-school-year pupils were admitted to the *Mittelschulen* or *Höhere Schulen* in October of this year."[77] Since it took several months to acquire the necessary information on the representative school districts, no further meetings between E&RA and the ministry took place until mid-July, 1948. Then the pace of events quickened again.

On July 15, one day after Stein had supplied the desired statistical evidence, DeLong attended a zonal E&CR conference headed by Alexander. Despite the ministry's recent compliance, DeLong was afraid the Hessians lacked any desire to submit a plan in the near future. Stein, he said, "will postpone it again and again for various reasons, arguing that changes must be made in the plan before submission can be effected. Education Division, OMGH, therefore plans to have an order issued by the Director of OMG Hesse to retain all fifth-grade pupils in the elementary schools this October."[78] DeLong and the E&RA staff were convinced now that James Newman must apply direct pressure on Stein. At this decisive moment, with the Bavarian crisis at its height, DeLong announced an important new round of discussions with the Hessians.[79]

The conferences took place between July 17 and 26. Statistical information from the three representative *Kreise* indicated to DeLong that the retention of fifth-year pupils in elementary schools was feasible. Therefore, even before the concluding meeting with Stein and the ministry, scheduled for July 26, he set about obtaining a direct order for Hessian school reform. At this critical juncture Harry Wann was in Washington, D.C., on a recruiting trip, so DeLong had to inform Wann by letter of his major decision: "Following our zonal conference Thursday and Friday, I was more than ever convinced that this is the only method by which we will achieve the goal established in the directives. I talked to Dr. Alexander about the matter, and he agreed in principle that our Land should issue such a directive."[80]

On July 20 the American staff obtained Stein's latest proposal. "We feel that the draft is no better than Stein's proposal of last September," Delong complained to Wann. "It seems very evident that he would start Latin in the fifth grade as an elective subject and that those pupils who started in the fifth grade would have third-year Latin in the seventh grade and would be given another foreign language. This is no change from the present system."[81]

Meanwhile, DeLong's draft order was moving through the echelons of Military Government in Hesse at the same time that he was discussing his next steps with the new E&CR director, Alonzo G. Grace. "Dr. Grace was here for several hours on Wednesday on his way to Berlin," DeLong informed his chief. "He read the draft of this directive and approved very highly the idea of taking such action. I then discussed the matter with Dr. Alexander in Nuremberg on Thursday. He went over it carefully and is also a hundred percent behind it."[82] Still, DeLong hesitated. He had called for a dinner meeting with the ministry to examine once again what had been discussed so often before in the hope of avoiding so drastic a step. "We shall discuss the details of this directive with all concerned at that time," DeLong stated. He detected a new militant mood in Military Government, and he informed Wann that, "as a general comment, I wish to say that I have the feeling that OMGUS policy will be much stiffer from this time on."[83]

DeLong attached great importance to the July 26 dinner meeting. He told Stein and the ministry staff of his anxieties about growing public hostility. "It seems to us," he stated, "that if it does not take place *this* year, then the school reform in Hesse will lose another year or even more. It also seems to us that within the last year the opposition against school reform has grown." Parents of secondary-school children were in the forefront of the protest movement, apparently because they feared a lowering of the quality of secondary education. DeLong would permit limited differentiation alongside a common-core curriculum, but this early differentiation should not become a prerequisite for advancement in succeeding grades. "Latin," DeLong claimed, "is being used, in effect, as an intelligence test." A year earlier the various school committees had recommended including English as a core subject in the six-year elementary school. Now, in 1948, the new statistical evidence bolstered that arrangement. Its opponents within the ministry claimed that there were not enough language teachers, and they were raising other, purely technical, objections against this fundamental change.[84] DeLong questioned their motives. He had already warned his colleagues at OMGUS about divisions within Stein's staff: "The greatest difficulty," he told Alexander, "is the lack of unity in the German Ministry. The minister, who is not a professional school man, refuses very often the suggestions and advice of competent members of his staff and disagrees with the proposals of the committees. This and division of opinion between the other members of the Ministry mean a serious retardation of work."[85]

Not to be outdone, Erwin Stein mustered several telling arguments in defense of his staff at the dinner meeting, and he reminded the Americans that, ultimately, the Hessian Landtag must pass the school bill. He reminded the E&RA staff that the Hessians had taken a leading role in school reform to date. It was he, not the Americans, who had chosen the three school districts for the statistical studies on which the entire school-reform estimates would be based. He singled out the hardworking *Landesschulbeirat* for praise, noting that it was unmatched in any other Land. This committee was examining the total problem of school reform, including structure, curricula, teacher training, and much more. "If we see school reform in terms of external organization only, then this reorganization will fail," Stein declared, "and people will lose confidence in school reform and school reorganization." He pointed out that as education minister he must always consider the political mood in Hesse. To ride in the face of it would be to court disaster. "The Landtag would regard this as an offense to its rights and would take me to task," he warned. If school reorganization came in 1948, Stein claimed, it would do so only on direct American orders, and he felt that his Land deserved better treatment than that. "Hesse is not Bavaria," he reminded DeLong. "Therefore, I am sure that the Landtag will give the decision early enough so that during the next few months we can make the necessary preparations to meet the requirements formally and organizationally for 1949."[86]

Stein's position during the long exchange of opinions that evening was hardly one of complete opposition. He could accept the six-year elementary school, "but within each grade there should be a certain differentiation," he persisted. "The teacher will soon find out which of his students are more gifted." Stein stuck to his position that, while English was an obvious first choice, Latin should continue to be taught, starting in the fifth year. Moreover, he felt that Hesse's parents, who felt keenly about Germany's Western heritage, should have some say in the pupils' language curricula. Especially in the larger cities, Latin should remain as the first foreign language.[87]

By this time a hint of irritation had crept into the discussions. DeLong's patience was beginning to wear thin: "What Minister Stein said has been said over and over again in all the committee meetings." He reminded everyone present that the requirement for the six-year elementary school was now "a requirement of Military Government"; as such, it was like any other vital directive, such as denazification or currency reform. DeLong tried to pose the issue as a joint E&RA–ministry problem imposed by higher military authority. "And it is the purpose of this meeting," he added, "to find out how we can work together to carry out this order given to *us*, not necessarily to *you*." However, he revealed that a decision must be forthcoming by the following week. Failing an acceptable bill, the Americans would impose their own reorganization.[88]

It was an exhausting meeting, for the parties deliberated at length over statistics and the other minutiae inevitably associated with so sweeping a reform proposal. The Americans demonstrated the feasibility of the reforms they wanted. The Hessians as energetically pointed out the practical problems that stood in the way. DeLong pointed to the progress of school reform in Bremen and Berlin, where laws were nearly complete. But H. W. Haupt of the *Landesschulbeirat* countered that school reform was a long-term process, as demonstrated by the slow but steady progress of Sweden toward reform. In Hesse, too, they wanted to progress in such a way that "future generations, perhaps not under the supervision of Military Government, will carry on what was started because it was good." Each side spoke bluntly now. DeLong clung tenaciously to the main point: "What assurances do we have that the school reorganization [will] be in operation by 1949?" he asked.[89] In the end, the Hessians withheld any assurances. DeLong decided to act.

He requested a meeting with James Newman and discussed a school directive with Newman's chief aides, E. K. Neuman and Francis Sheehan. He also kept Wann informed of events. DeLong confided to his absent chief that "the real element which blocks the progress on this matter is the emotional element. I am convinced that this will not change—ever."[90] Finally, on August 4, DeLong, Newman, and his aides met with Minister President Christian Stock and Education Minister Stein. After recounting the lack of progress, the Americans issued a direct order:

> Therefore, you are directed to take the necessary steps to insure that no beginning fifth-year pupils will be admitted to the Mittelschule or the Höhere Schule in the first school year beginning after the date of this directive, or in succeeding years, and that no beginning sixth-year pupils will be admitted to the Mittelschule or the Höhere Schule in the second school year beginning after the date of this directive or in succeeding years.[91]

Hesse, which had made the greatest progress in school reform in the Occupation, became the first Land to receive a direct order instituting a structural reorganization. Stein won only one concession: the beginning of the new school year would be shifted from October to April so that the directive would go into effect in the spring of 1949. Two days later a more intimate gathering took place in Newman's office, and DeLong later recorded that "all [E&RA] members were of the same opinion, and E. K. and Sheehan were convinced that if the action is to be taken, it should be taken at once."[92]

DeLong desired quick action because of what he felt were unmistakable signs of a gathering reaction against school reform. He reported to Wann in Washington: "The Bavarian Government is somewhat in arms to think that they have been ordered to furnish free textbooks. A newspaper item yesterday stated that the Germans in the Koblenz area felt that their rights were invaded when the French told them they could not have confessional teacher training. Such is the current attitude. It emphasizes more than ever the fact that we are going to have to take some strong measures and to take them immediately."[93]

DeLong's attempts to keep Wann abreast of events were commendable, but, as events proved, they were wasted effort. While in the United States, Wann received a job offer to conduct a survey of public schools in Washington, D.C. To everyone's amazement he accepted on the spot and never returned to Hesse.[94] "I believe his interest ended when he left Germany," DeLong confided to a colleague, and he never mentioned Wann's name again.[95] Thus DeLong became acting director of E&CR for the second time in his career, and he was soon elevated to the top post. There were many on the staff who wished it had happened much sooner.

Events outside Hesse made Newman's August directive obsolete. Within a few days General Clay flew to Frankfurt and concluded his compromise agreement with Hans Ehard. With the break in the storm in Bavaria, a relaxation of tensions also occurred in Hesse, although Newman's order remained in effect. Nevertheless, both sides resumed their customary good relations. Within a few weeks, Stein wrote to a visiting expert, Burr Phillips from Madison, Wisconsin, thanking him for his contributions: "Whereas you pointed to the good collaboration between you and my staff, both in this ministry and in the *Landesschulbeirat*, I beg to emphasize with a feeling of sincere gratitude that such collaboration is, to a great extent, due to your understanding and always helpful cooperation."[96]

Despite such expressions of good will by the professionals, prospects in the political arena worsened. In mid-1948 one Military Government analyst summarized public attitudes toward the education debate in these words: "Nobody knows a damn thing about school reform, but they sure are against it."[97] In an effort to counter the trend toward protest, which they felt was fed by ignorance, DeLong, Haupt, and Stein, as the chief protagonists in Hessian school reform, participated in a radio debate in late autumn. It proved to be anything but a polite minuet. The radio commentator (whose name never appeared in the Military Government transcript) insinuated that the *Landesschulbeirat* was merely a Military Government vehicle with which to Americanize the German schools. Stein took strenuous exception, explaining that the committee included "school specialists and educators of every kind and representatives of all the population" acting as an advisory group to him and "independent of the contests of the political parties." DeLong added that, since "a mere copying of American institutions would be of doubtful result," the Americans had limited their expectations to the principles of Allied Control Authority Directive 54. This was, of course, precisely where the E&RA officials and Hessian education leaders had disagreed in private, but Haupt, as the chairman of the *Landesschulbeirat*, attempted to minimize the differences by stating that the members of his *Landesschulbeirat* were "only obliged to regard those general basic principles which are in agreement with the thought of old school reform in Germany." He also reaffirmed that his members could "work out details and additions freely and independently of the Ministry of Culture as well as Military Government." The moderator asked the participants to explain the ACA Directive point by point, and when, later, Stein reverted to general statements about creating a new spirit of ethical consciousness, the commentator zeroed in on the central point: Was Hesse to have the four-, six-, or eight-year elementary school "around which so much opposition to school reform is developing?" Stein refused to commit himself, saying that structural form was not the crucial question: "Rather," he stated, "it is the inner spirit of the schools, the person, his worth, dignity, and the meaning of his life." By this time DeLong was willing to speak more directly to the commentator's sharp probing. He referred to studies conducted in Bremen before 1933, which showed an attrition rate of seven out of eight pupils in the secondary schools, a trend corroborated by other German studies made in the same period. DeLong indicated that such attrition represented a heavy expense to the state. Inspired, perhaps, by DeLong's bluntness, Haupt addressed the issue more boldly. He claimed that a flexible two-track system—one that allowed for easy transfer—would not mean, as DeLong was arguing, the return of social privilege to education. Haupt found Stein agreeing emphatically with him as the broadcast came to an end. Thus the radio debate produced no consensus about the nature of school reform.[98]

Public debate continued to mount in intensity as the weeks passed, and by the end of November, 1948, with no progress in sight, DeLong grew restive. He called together the ministry and E&RA staffs for another marathon meeting on November 29. Despite the friendly tone at the outset, DeLong made it clear that he expected a draft proposal from Stein that would include six-year undifferentiated elementary schools with no specialized offerings of foreign languages, i.e., no Latin: "This order *must* be carried out," he stated.[99]

Eugene Fair complained that the Hessian public was as yet unaware that the six-year school was required to begin in April, 1949. "In July you told us that if you only had time to plan for the opening of the new school year in 1949, all the difficulties could be taken into account," he said. Now, an uninformed public would be easy prey for the opposition. DeLong recounted, a little later, his own experiences with public-discussion groups: "I have been in forums where only five or six people have spoken," he related, "but they spoke in such a way that the man with the elementary education did not dare to enter the discussion. In such a situation it is possible for a few people to block democracy."[100]

Two months earlier, OMGUS had organized an interzonal meeting in Berchtesgaden to discuss the future of education reform, with General Clay in attendance. Now DeLong spelled out the significance of the Military Governor's participation. The general, DeLong announced, "told us that in the course of the Occupation other divisions would get smaller or disappear. But education divisions would certainly be as large as they are now, and the last day of the Occupation would be very much concerned with education still."[101]

Undaunted, the German educators again reminded DeLong of the need to consider political realities in the Landtag. Stein stated—correctly—that he had often called for new educational aims and was now readying his own draft law. If he had chosen the easiest course, he would simply have forwarded Newman's August 9 directive to the Landtag and let it suffer whatever fate the political representatives had in mind for it. "But then we no longer have a German school reform," he stated. "At that point we have an American school reform." Stein was facing ever greater difficulty convincing his own citizens that he was not simply doing the Americans' bidding. He wanted time and the right to do it his way. "Do trust us," he pleaded, "we who are in responsible positions and who from inner conviction and with all our heart favor school reform and who want to see it accomplished with completely democratic freedom."[102]

At this point DeLong, displaying a rare degree of impatience, retorted that the Americans had ordered the dismantling of dangerous German war industries and that "your German school system is just as dangerous as those war-materials factories."[103] Those were strong words. Fortunately, Willy Viehweg leaped into the breach and announced that in many public discussions he and the Hessian educational leadership had repeatedly rejected the status quo. "I said that we in Hesse have . . . started with a given, namely, that we want a school reform with schools for the masses and not for secondary schools to preserve their old privileges."[104] He also noted that this statement always elicited applause from German audiences. Viehweg then argued that a school reform ordered in 1949 would require many exceptions if it were to have any chance to succeed. If they tried for 1950 instead, the school reorganization would be universal and would stand a much better chance of succeeding.

Kenneth Bateman, an American teacher-training expert stationed in Wiesbaden, made the only practical suggestion that long evening for breaking the deadlock. He proposed a select committee of "persons who will be responsible for the execution who will then make recommendations to Mr. DeLong and Minister Stein." The result was an agreement by both parties to form a Committee of Eight, evenly divided between Americans and Germans. The members would schedule weekly meetings and submit their findings to their superiors by January, 1949, on a precise plan to be presented to the Landtag. "I am willing at this time," DeLong announced, "to guarantee that I, as the Director of the E&CR Division, will accept the recommendation and shall forward it to Dr. Newman."[105]

While the Committee of Eight—four Americans and four Germans—engaged in prolonged discussions, Stein and the other ministry officials went on the stump to build support among the distrustful public. They had good reason to be active. On the day following the late-night E&RA–ministry meeting, the CDU Landtag representatives issued a statement: "The CDU fraction is of the opinion that the approved elementary-school system, approved for forty years, should not be abandoned without pressing reasons." They favored the retention of the existing four-year elementary school, the continuation of Latin instruction, and the preservation of the humanistic *Gymnasium*.[106] Stein, as a member of the CDU, was in a difficult position.

Karl Rieser, an education ministry official, had not spoken out during the sometimes bitter discussions of November 29, but now he was willing to offer his viewpoint candidly to the public. In a CDU membership meeting in Frankfurt, Rieser claimed that only the socialists and communists were in favor of the six-year elementary school and that they openly viewed Military Government as their ally. A report of the meeting recorded also that Rieser "sharply criticized the way the Americans negotiate with the German governmental authorities." He stated that DeLong had "seriously reproached the Minister . . . for not having followed the orders of Military Government." More damaging still, he repeated DeLong's statement that the German educational system was "just as dangerous as the German armament industry." The audience bristled. Rieser charged Military Government with "constant interference," which undermined the public's confidence in its own authorities. The meeting ended with a clarion call to rally all teachers and parents against the Newman directive.[107]

Soon after this, Erwin Stein visited a CDU gathering in Kassel. There the party faithful cheered him when he thundered against school reform by directive, invoked the Hague Convention to protest U.S interference in internal German affairs, and castigated the present directive as not being German at all but rather "another" school reform. Stein aroused hoots of derision when he said that the Americans claimed that a differentiated (i.e., multitrack) school system was undemocratic. Enforcement would be "an outrage upon all talented children," he claimed, and he stated, once again, that April 1, 1950, was the earliest date that any reform could become operational. He concluded by saying that his ideal was the differentiated Swiss school system—an unimpeachably democratic system. The crowd roared its approval.[108]

However, Stein's position was by no means uniformly negative. He reminded his German audience that the Americans had made valuable contributions: "Above all, the problem concerning the selection of talented students must be solved in quite a different manner," he said. "In Germany we have completely backward methods, and the methods applied in all other countries of the world are better. One can accept many ideas for the improvement of the German school from the American and other foreign school systems, but they must correspond to the German characteristics and qualities." He also demonstrated impatience with reactionary views. When two female teachers urged a return to corporal punishment and the segregation of boys and girls, he dismissed both suggestions with a curt "No!" Worried that Stein's criticisms of the Americans would cause trouble, one CDU representative informed a Military Government observer at the meeting that "the Minister wanted to defend himself against certain reproaches which accuse him that his school policy is too much influenced by the Americans and that he adopts the American suggestions without any criticism."[109] Stein had to walk a tortuous path in the last year of Military Government operations.

Meanwhile, the Committee of Eight continued to debate the outstanding issues dividing E&CR and the ministry. The four German negotiators fought tenaciously for a delay of implementation until April 1, 1950, and, in the end, the four Americans relented.[110] But they remained determined that the Hessians approve a six-year elementary school, and in this they finally had their way. DeLong proved as good as his word and accepted the Committee's decisions. For his part, Stein obtained revocation of Newman's August directive. He also pointed out that the draft law, as amended by the Committee of Eight, was only now entering the political machinery of Hessian politics. In effect Stein was saying that from this point onward the Landtag rather than his ministry would set the final terms. Here he hinted broadly to his American opposite that he stood poised on the knife's edge: "The serious desire to meet the OMGH Director's directive within the limits of what is politically possible and admitted by the provisions of the Constitution, and to progressively shape the school in an allowed manner, was the reason why members of my ministry belonged to the Committee of Eight to work out a proposal of mediation." Stein enumerated several features in the final draft that he hoped would save the bill in the political battles to come: he had retained the teaching of Latin in the fifth school year for 1949, and he had announced that Land-wide achievement tests were to take place before April 1, 1949, in order to judge pupils' readiness for the fifth year, but that the Hessians would continue to use teacher evaluations of classroom performance and "moral attitude" to determine placement of pupils in the middle and secondary schools.[111]

Despite Stein's cautionary remarks, it appeared that there were grounds for celebrating the end of the long confrontation. On February 16, 1949, the Hessian Landtag enacted a law for free textbooks and tuition, which finalized the arrangements made first by Schramm and then by Stein. Stein's draft school law appeared to be a skillful compromise, one that, while satisfying most American demands, would still attract support from the Hessian public. His intent was to create a six-year elementary school and a secondary system with three branches. However, the Committee of Eight had successfully postponed retention of fifth-year pupils in the elementary schools until April, 1950, and of sixth-year pupils until April, 1951. Simultaneously, Stein released the draft of a teacher-training law that provided for some common training for elementary- and secondary-school teachers. The bill was surprisingly complex, allowing students the option of starting at a pedagogical institute and then transferring to a university, or they could perform the bulk of their work at a university with a one-year break at a pedagogical institute. Yet a third provision allowed students to "enter the teacher-training field after completing their eight-semester subject-matter training at the university." The Americans were apprehensive about so intricate a teacher-training bill. Nevertheless, it appeared that tangible progress was being made, and in March, 1949, a State Department dispatch praised the Hessian initiatives, seeing the passage of the law authorizing free textbooks and tuition as only "the first item in a comprehensive program of legislation designed to improve and develop the system of public education on democratic principles."[112]

However, the passage of one bill did not ensure success for the others, as DeLong was well aware. He confided to a colleague in December, 1948: "The one field which is extremely discouraging is that of getting proper legislation through the Landtag."[113] A short time later he responded to *Washington Post* correspondent Fred Hechinger's assertion that the time for basic changes in school structure had passed: "It is now 11:59, perhaps," DeLong admitted. "But there is time before 12:00 to accomplish the change if we do it properly and quickly. We are bending every effort in Hesse to this end."[114]

In 1949, Hessian school reform did not proceed in the way DeLong or even Stein had prophesied. The gathering reaction, already visible in September, 1947, mounted steadily. Traditionalists skillfully exploited fears of excessive divergences among the Land educational systems on the eve of political reintegration in the West. Debate over the Occupation Statute occurred throughout the western zones in April and May, 1949, and, as German opponents of school reorganization well knew, it ended with defeat for those who wanted to retain American control over German education.

Unlike Alois Hundhammer, who actively orchestrated protests against school reform in Bavaria, Erwin Stein found himself caught by his own clever compromise between Military Government and the traditionalists. He had repeatedly warned the E&CR staff that the Landtag would be the arbiter of the school bill, and of course the Landtag was ultimately responsible to the Hessian public. Influential groups like the *Landesverband Hessen für Höheren Schulen*, an organization of secondary-school teachers, had publicly endorsed differentiated schools in September, 1947. Now the reaction gathered strength. Bishop Albert Stohr of Mainz spoke out against six-year elementary schools in June, 1949, at the very moment Stein's compromise package was entering the Landtag. Already in March, all four Hessian universities had issued a joint communiqué in favor of the four-year elementary school; the six-year system, it said, would handicap intellectually gifted children. Spokesmen for higher education stoutly defended the *Aufbauschule* as adequate for late bloomers and geographically disadvantaged pupils.[115] Thus in Hesse the conservative forces orchestrated their protests just as they had in Bavaria. It seemed to make little difference whether the education minister was leading the movement or trying to brake it. In the end, Hesse did not advance much beyond Bavaria as far as the structural form of its elementary and secondary schools was concerned. By the spring of 1949, when their control over education was about to lapse, it became apparent that any changes the Americans might effect would have to be done on an advisory basis and through indirect means, such as cultural exchanges, aid programs, and visiting experts. E&RA in Hesse had performed well in these areas since 1947 in any case, but the termination of Military Government in 1949 spelled a dramatic increase in these operations in the HICOG era.

It was apparent to many education officers in the spring of 1949 that any overt attempts at restructuring education were counterproductive. With the new change in emphasis in U.S. education programs, Vaughn DeLong, who had spent the entire Occupation in Hesse, transferred to the United States as a State Department official to administer the vastly expanded exchange programs projected for the 1950s.

The controversy that developed between E&RA and the Hessian education ministry in 1948 was in many ways an aberration that temporarily clouded one of the most effective working relationships between Germans and Americans in the Occupation. The education officers in Wiesbaden found a more willing audience for their ideas there than in Bavaria. As long as the two parties forged their ideas cooperatively and as long as the Americans operated under the formula of advice and assistance, all went well. The E&RA staff sought change through example and support, as is indicated by their ability to generate financial and other practical support for the Land educational system. It was a happy coincidence that Land

Director James Newman, a former school administrator, enabled his education officers to aid their Hessian colleagues on a scale unmatched in the other Länder of the U.S. Zone. Once the political debate over structural change had abated, concrete results were not long in coming. At the end of 1948 the Hessians began to publish their own journal on educational innovation, with American support, and the *Hessische Beiträge zur Schulreform* received wide attention in Hessian educational circles. In the following decades Hessians pioneered in replacing one-room village schools with higher-quality regional *Mittelpunktschulen*. They were also among the first to erect an experimental comprehensive school, which gathered all school types, from kindergarten through secondary and vocational education, into one unified school complex, the famed Schuldorf-Bergstrasse. Schramm and Stein had contemplated such institutions, but it was Kenneth Bateman, a former E&RA staff member, who saw the project through to completion in the 1950s. Greater Hesse and West Berlin continued to be the two Länder in the Federal Republic with the strongest records for producing innovative school structures.[116] Consequently, the cries of pessimism that had sounded loudly among the E&CR staff in 1948 proved unfounded. For Vaughn DeLong and others, the stalling of structural reform must have appeared to be a discouraging repetition of events in Munich, but, once education retreated from the highly visible political arena, parallels with Bavaria ceased.

Hesse provided instructive contrasts to Bavaria because of its more balanced party structure, its less conservative social and educational traditions, its greater heterogeneity, and the diminished influence of the major churches. But in the end the problem remained one of foreigners attempting to restructure education in a state to which they had already granted internal political sovereignty. Military Government could not order the Hessian Landtag to produce reforms any more than it could order reforms from the Bavarian Landtag and still claim that it was acting democratically. Thus, General Clay's decision, early in the Occupation, to revive German political institutions came back to haunt the education officers later in the Occupation. Contrary to all the talk about their being numbed politically by the Nazis and therefore incapable of acting in a democratic fashion, the Germans recognized their new power early—and used it.

Bremen

The ancient Hanseatic town of Bremen—with its normally prosperous, industrious population, its statue of Roland, reminding visitors of past glories, and its tradition of progressive education—was a sad spectacle by the end of the war. The Allies had pounded 80 percent of the town into rubble. Only two school buildings had escaped harm. German school officials and the handful of American education officers were so desperate in their effort to ready the school system for operations by October, 1945, that they required every schoolchild to obtain a pane of glass to provide the rickety buildings with some protection against the elements.[117]

The Americans had received Bremen and its environs from the British Zone as an entrepôt for supplying U.S. needs in south Germany. After the American and British armies sorted themselves out, Civil Affairs Detachment E2C2, headed by Colonel Bion Welker, set up headquarters in the wrecked town, which was soon teeming with an infantry division and the U.S. Navy's Bremen Port Command.[118] With the formal establishment of OMGUS in October, 1945, it became necessary to reorganize the detached territory along the same lines as the other Länder of the U.S. Zone. Thomas F. Dunn became the city's first Land director, and he remained in office until he was replaced by Captain Charles R. Jeffs, U.S.N., at the end of 1948. Both leaders cooperated closely with the education staff in the course of Military Government operations in Bremen.

Early E&RA activities followed the pattern seen elsewhere in the U.S. Zone. The G-5 civil-affairs detachment managed, with the help of large numbers of German school officials, Special Branch, and other elements of Military Government, to begin the first painful tasks. The detachment's chief education officer was Harold H. Crabill, an Indiana high-school teacher who later earned a doctorate and joined the department of education at Indiana University. Denazification produced serious shortages of teachers. The requisitioning of buildings for the use of U.S. military units added to the acute scarcity of classrooms. During these emergency operations in 1945, Crabill and his fellow officers had little time to worry about the future structure of the city's educational system. Bremen immediately lost two-fifths of its teachers. Teacher-pupil ratios soared to 1:100, and the age composition of the teachers in Bremen climbed sharply. Of 880 school teachers vetted by the end of November, 1945, fully 474 received dismissal notices, effectively eliminating the younger adults from Bremen's teaching ranks. The average age of male teachers was fifty-three; for women it was forty-six. Over 200 of the staff were above the age of sixty, and ten stalwart septuagenarians were still functioning in the classroom.[119]

Because Bremen lay in close proximity to the British Zone, its citizens could compare the denazification procedures employed by the two powers. In a conference of Bremen school authorities on October 1, 1945, a Military Government observer noted the Germans' dismay: "It aggravates matters," he wrote, "that measures concerning the dismissal of personnel are apparently much more strictly carried through in the American-occupied territories than under the English Military Government."[120] The school authorities, headed by Christian Paulmann, hoped that Military Government would soon allow the reinstatement of former party members "who, though members of the Nazi Party, had in their hearts never been Nazis." It was wishful thinking. A year later another Military Government report observed that the situation was, if anything, worse. "The effects of the American denazification policy are beginning to be painfully visible," it concluded. "There is a great scarcity of younger teachers, and a large number of able young teachers are transferring from the Bremen school system to those of the British Zone."[121]

Discouraging as such trends were, the Bremen educational system benefited from one undeniable advantage. Social Democrat Christian Paulmann, the city's senator for education and culture, proved to be a driving force for a more flexible system, and Bremen rivaled Greater Hesse as the most progressive Land in its intended school reforms. Paulmann had been an education official in the Weimar Republic and was renowned for his desire to create a more flexible, egalitarian school system. In 1933 the Nazis had promptly dismissed him, along with other well-known Social Democrats, like Wilhelm Kaisen, who later became Bremen's senior German official in the Occupation. The two men had much in common as survivers of the Third Reich, and they worked well together in the difficult days following the war. Clay rated Kaisen as one of the most talented SPD leaders in the U.S. Zone.[122]

Paulmann proved willing to take on unpopular tasks early in the Occupation. By December, 1945, he and his revived Bremen school board had acquired permission to set up a special committee to review denazification procedures for schoolteachers. On the one hand it dismissed several teachers who, though they had passed muster on the *Fragebogen*, were considered by the committee to have been too tainted by the recently deposed regime. But the committee also recommended "appeals in a number of cases of dismissals." It convinced Military Government officers that lumping all minor Nazi bureaucrats, such as air wardens and disaster-relief officials, into the automatic-dismissal categories was too extreme. In November, 1945, a report duly noted that "During the month 47 teachers were thus retained, who would otherwise have been dismissed." By December 3, the secondary schools followed the elementary schools into operation, so that the Bremen school system was functioning again, however precariously, six months after the conclusion of peace.[123]

Christian Paulmann was not afraid to voice his opinions bluntly at a time when Military Government operated by direct order. In October he voiced his concern for the need to produce school reforms that would mesh with reforms elsewhere. Stressing the need for realism, he said that it was unwise to try to "effect a complete disorganization of the uniform German school system. At a later date the uniformity of the German school system would be a fact again, and all present steps therefore ought to be considered from this point of view."[124] Paulmann was keeping a close watch on developments in the nearby British Zone.

There were no universities in Bremen, but Crabill personally opened the city's teacher-training college on December 1, a ceremony that took place in "one of the famous Bremen 'Progressive Schools' which had been closed by the Nazis in 1933," according to an official account.[125] Thus, by degrees, Bremen, like the other Länder of the zone, slowly and painfully brought its educational system back to life. That autumn Paulmann and Crabill agreed to create an emergency one-year course for politically un-tainted teachers. As a later report observed: "Bremen had always had a highly developed school system, and, therefore, it was difficult for the school authorities to contemplate putting untrained teachers in the schools." From four hundred *Abiturienten* the authorities chose 160 finalists above the age of twenty-four with general educational achievement so that the emergency curriculum could concentrate on educational theory and practice. They favored male candidates because of the significant imbal-ance between the sexes in the current teaching ranks. Following a final examination at the end of the course, the survivors would undergo a probationary year, "during which time the young teacher must prove his ability under the supervision of an experienced supervisor." Thereafter, Paulmann and his staff expected to reopen a normal three-year curriculum in Bremen's expanded pedagogical institute, an event that did not, in fact, take place until October, 1947.[126] Nevertheless, the emergency teacher-training program was typical of the well-planned measures Paulmann in-stituted in the face of enormous pressures to increase the teaching ranks immediately.

In the following spring Major Harold Crabill became once again Dr. Crabill and permanent E&RA branch chief at Bremen. His minuscule staff continued to fill two and sometimes three slots in the OMGUS table of organization—a handicap that Crabill was never able to eliminate despite his many bitter complaints to E&RA in Berlin. A few additional recruits filtered in after E&RA became a civilian rather than an Army organization, but the Bremen E&RA staff never exceeded five or six individuals.[127]

When the emergency phase of operations ended that fall and the effects of the Mission Report became increasingly apparent, expectations rose that Bremen would adopt a comprehensive school law in 1947. When it came time for the Bremen school authorities to submit a set of general aims and proposals for school reform, following General Clay's January 10, 1947, directive, Paulmann and his colleagues conferred with the E&RA elementary-education specialist, Ernest Flatow. The first meeting concen-trated on the need to upgrade education for elementary-school teachers, who, the conferees decided, "need a far more thorough training, especially with a view to psychological subjects, since the elementary schools rep-

resent the basis for all schoolwork. Great responsibility lies in the hands
of the elementary teacher as to child guidance and help for decisions on
special education in scientific, economic, musical, and vocational subjects."[128]

A week later a second conference covered a wider area of concerns than
teacher training. In view of the complex course that school reform eventually took in Bremen, it is noteworthy that Paulmann and his colleagues
initiated internal discussions on school reform as early as 1946. As the
minutes of the conference recorded: "The reconstruction of the German
school system along the lines General Clay suggests in his directive had
been under discussion in previous meetings, since Bremen school authorities have already advocated the same ideas." The Bremen school
authorities were advocating such features as the six-year elementary school
with a common curriculum, including the introduction of English in the
fifth year, and a three-year intermediate school with some variations on
a core curriculum, including the introduction of Latin in the seventh
school year. The final segment was expected to be more differentiated,
with four branches leading pupils to practical, vocational, business, or
scientific/scholarly pursuits. The discussions covered curriculum content
and social studies, so that Bremen's educational leadership appeared to
back both Clay's January directive and the Mission Report. Yet the cautionary remarks of the Bremen authorities were as important as the principles they espoused. As the minutes of the January 20 conference duly
recorded, "it is hardly to be expected that school authorities from other
parts of Germany will be in the same conformity with General Clay's
directive." The Bremen leadership proposed to forward supplementary
reports, along with their general education aims, to OMGUS to explain
"the educational, psychological and sociological situation which made for
the attitude adopted by the Bremen school authorities." Paulmann and his
colleagues were especially concerned that their city's tradition of progressive education should not be interpreted by E&RA as typical of German
conditions. They also avoided commitments to any early implementation
of their ideals because of the great shortages of teachers, plant, and equipment. Paulmann continued to express concern about altering the Bremen
school system to a degree unusual in northern Germany: "For reasons of
a uniform school policy, negotiations should be initiated with school authorities at Hannover and Hamburg in order to secure the establishment
of an elementary school comprising six grades for northern Germany.
Senator Paulmann will discuss these questions with Minister Adolf
Grimme and Senator Landahl at the next meeting of the Zonal Educational
Council."[129]

By April Paulmann was able to submit the general statement of aims
required by OMGUS. It received a hearty welcome in Berlin. Alexander

wrote back: "This office wishes to compliment the authorities in Bremen on the proposals thus far made, since they indicate a trend in the right direction in accordance with the principles set forth in our cable of 8 January 1947." Other, unnamed, consultants at OMGUS, who had observed the activities of the Bremen school authorities, were equally enthusiastic. One expert noted: "While in Bremen I attended two three-hour sessions with some fifteen school officials who were formulating administrative principles in procedure on the Bremen school system. I was highly impressed with the intelligence, earnestness, and thoroughly democratic attitude of the entire group. Therefore, I feel that the present statement is an accurate presentation of the real ideas and sentiments of the school administration." Another commentator observed: "The proposed school organization closely parallels that in the United States and seems to be designed to attain the most desirable goals of such a system." Clearly, Alexander and his staff were enthusiastic about the prospects in Bremen. The aims included a 6-3-3 plan with a common elementary curriculum and a flexible middle school. The Bremen authorities were also prepared to institute free tuition and textbooks, coeducation, and university-level teacher training.[130]

Understandably, Harold Crabill was pleased: "Many of the accomplishments have been made possible because of the good relationships existing between the Military Government education staff and the German Ministry of Education," he announced. "The weekly and at times semiweekly meetings between the two staffs since December, 1946, have materially aided in bringing about a better understanding of the problems faced, the goals sought, and the means to be employed in achieving the immediate and ultimate ends."[131]

Christian Paulmann, like all other responsible German education ministers in the zone, had to play a delicate balancing act between the Americans and his own constituents. Although senators were chosen by the *Bürgerschaft*, or city parliament, rather than by direct popular election, Paulmann was in no way insulated from public opinion, and he also had to reckon with the mood of the *Bürgerschaft*, which had chosen him. In addition to this balancing act was Paulmann's stated goal of implementing reforms that would coordinate with initiatives in the British Zone. While some American educators wistfully hoped that Bremen could implement its ambitious reform program as early as autumn, 1947, Crabill knew better. He admitted that the public was the ultimate arbiter of school reform, and in Bremen the public was as yet largely uninformed. "The entire matter of adequately informing the public about its schools needs to be considered," he concluded in the summer of 1947. "Newspapers, radio, and other media should be employed to bring to the people a large body of information about their educational system."[132]

Judged by the plans discussed and the aims submitted, the Bremen authorities seemed to have taken a striking lead in achieving school reforms; but, smoothly though it had begun, the reform effort suddenly came to a halt. The first indication of trouble occurred in July, 1947, during debates concerning the Bremen Constitution. Two draft articles dealing with education had caught the eye of political leaders concerned with religion and the schools. Article 29 appeared to be deliberately ambiguous: "Private schools require state licensing. Further details will be given by law." Article 32 stated, further, that "The general educational public schools are community (nonconfessional) schools where an undenominational instruction in Bible history is given." The law permitted the teaching of biblical history to children on a voluntary basis, depending on the parents' decision. Moreover, the organized churches had the right to offer religious instruction outside the schools.[133]

Neither Catholics nor Evangelicals were satisfied with the draft proposals, and they organized to protest. On August 10 a demonstration of five thousand Bremen Catholics condemned the city's draft constitution as being "more radical, godless, and dictatorial than the constitutions of the other German states." The Catholics were especially unhappy, fearing the proposed articles would deprive them of state-supported confessional schools, a right they had won in 1907. By the turn of the century Bremen had absorbed a sizable influx of Catholic migrant workers, and the number of private parochial schools had expanded steadily. The city schools were largely Evangelical, reflecting Bremen's traditional Protestantism. Subsidies to the Catholic schools were modest at first, but inflation in the Weimar Republic escalated costs so rapidly that by 1933 the city was paying for most of the Catholic teachers' salaries and school operating budgets. The Concordat of 1933 seemed to guarantee state-supported denominational schools, but in 1938 the Nazis, by threatening to end all subsidies, acquired the Catholic schools outright; in return, all teachers, including nuns, were paid as civil servants. The Catholics had had no recourse, and Bremen's confessional schools had ceased to be confessional. Now, nine years later, the issue was once again of burning concern. The Evangelicals were also troubled by articles 29 and 32, but they took special aim at the issue of religious education. Limiting instruction to a nondenominational history of the Bible would, they felt, leave too much initiative to the individual instructor, whose lessons might "be given in a Christian manner or simply be given as fairytales." The Protestants preferred to end religious instruction in the schools if the alternative were nondenominational instruction.[134]

Meanwhile, a familiar figure had appeared in Bremen. Father Stanley Bertke held several conferences with church groups in August, 1947, and then negotiated with Paulmann, Crabill, and other education officials. Paulmann agreed that the Catholics had ceded their schools in 1938 only under heavy pressure and had so informed the Bremen senate in 1945. His advice then had been to return the schools to the Catholic Church, but the *Bürgerschaft* had not acted and the schools had remained state property. "From a legal point of view," Paulmann informed Bertke, "the treaty [of 1938] is valid; from a moral point of view, perhaps not. I do not hesitate to acknowledge that the Catholics acted under pressure." There were plans to annul the old treaty, but Paulmann could not foretell the outcome in a state where, given strong SPD and KPD influence, the critical shortage of schools made it politically difficult to relinquish any property. Besides, a transfer now would see the Catholics simply repossessing many bombed-out ruins.[135]

Stanley Bertke remained suspicious and reminded the conference of Paulmann's earlier statement that "the only desirable thing that Hitler did was the closing of the confessional schools." Paulmann confirmed that he had made the statement but claimed to have uttered it in the context that "the unifying element is superior to the differentiating one." Bertke then obtained a promise from Paulmann that the Catholics could again operate private schools in Bremen if they so desired. However, Paulmann stipulated that they had to conform to the requirements established for the public schools. The senator also promised to work for specific guarantees in the constitution. Soon after this, Bertke spoke to various church organizations and political parties, but he could find no tangible evidence of religious discrimination. An E&RA officer recorded Bertke's conclusions: "He made no official report but stated unofficially that religious instruction was being made a political football." Within days of Bertke's departure, Bremen's four political parties conferred for a final time on the touchy subject. They altered the constitution to guarantee the right to confessional schools and, in deference to the Evangelicals, inserted a passage stating that Bible history "will be given on a Christian basis." With those changes, both churches dropped their opposition, and the new constitution became law in October, 1947.[136]

Once broken, the momentum for school reform seemed never to recover in Bremen. By October, 1947, the Bavarians' intransigence on school reform gave new heart to traditionalists elsewhere. Faced with these warning signals, Crabill appeared less confident while attending an E&RA branch chiefs meeting in Wiesbaden that November. He conceded that Bremen's secondary-school teachers were now stoutly defending differentiated curricula and that his relations with Paulmann, once so cordial, had cooled perceptibly. Despite Military Government prodding, Paulmann was not pursuing a program of public enlightenment on school reform, with the result that the Bremen population remained ignorant of the real issues. Crabill announced that his staff was preparing to hold another round of conferences soon with the Bremen educational authorities, and he hoped to see passage of a school bill in 1948. Despite the recent disappointments, he was convinced that, with increasing awareness of the issues, popular resistance would cease.[137]

As the winter of 1947/48 progressed, it became apparent that, far from reconciling any differences, Crabill and Paulmann were disagreeing with each other frequently and on a wide range of issues. The Bremen authorities were not attaching the same urgency to the program of public information as Crabill. A few miles away, in the British Zone, the Control Commission (British Element) had chosen in January, 1947, to drop its control function in education, and the Land education ministers had therefore recovered almost complete authority in their own domain. Confronted with these facts, Crabill sent a position paper to Land Director Thomas F. Dunn in January, 1948, outlining his views on the intended reforms.

Crabill reminded Dunn that the educational system exercised a vital, long-lasting influence on the development of all Germans as individuals. "Hence," he stated, "the whole educational system is of the utmost importance to our mission in molding the next generation at the same time as we are controlling and seeking to influence the present one." Were the Americans to discontinue their supervisory role in education in favor of renewed sovereignty by the Germans? "NO, WE CANNOT," Crabill thundered. "Even in Land Bremen, the most progressive area of the U.S. Zone (educationally speaking), there is insufficient enlightened leadership." The Germans might pay lip service to the abstractions of freedom and democracy but institute no democratic practice in their children's education. Crabill's response to those who maintained that the Germans must educate themselves was sharply negative: "In the light of the facts, this is high-sounding nonsense and utterly incompatible with our mission." Crabill charged that Military Government had ignored educational reform so long that it had reverted to its old organizational pattern. "In 1945, we were in a position to order any changes in organization or practice which we desired," he reminded Dunn, "and such orders would have been carried out." It was painful, he said, to watch the Germans grope toward their own reforms like "blind men." The best Crabill could say for the policy of advice and assistance was that it would "produce more sincere and lasting results than merely imposing changes 'By Order.'" But that policy would necessarily require significant increases in American personnel over a long span of time. He estimated that the Americans would have to retain control until 1950 and then maintain a close inspection system for many years thereafter.[138]

Crabill's opinions galvanized Dunn into action. In a sharply worded communiqué to Paulmann, the Land director took the senator to task for his recent selection of controversial new school officials. "It is of particular interest to Military Government," Dunn complained, "that these same persons are among the most active opponents of the school reform required by Military Government and planned by your office." Dunn recognized that Paulmann could choose his own personnel as long as they possessed the positive qualities needed to develop a democratic society, but he doubted the senator's wisdom. To emphasize the point, he issued a blunt warning: "Repeated mistakes on your part in the selection of personnel for appointment, or retention of persons in leading positions who actively oppose Military Government policies, can even endanger your own position."[139]

Christian Paulmann, who had endured twelve years of Hitler's rule, was not intimidated by strong language from Thomas Dunn. No sooner had he received the Land director's reproach than he leveled a criticism of his own. By coincidence the *Neue Zeitung*—a newspaper overtly controlled by the Americans—had just published an article on school reform in which Adolf Grimme was misquoted. Grimme, the education minister of Lower Saxony, was cited as speaking out against the six-year elementary school. Paulmann was astonished at his colleague's seeming about-face and phoned Hannover immediately. "Thereupon, I was informed by Herr Grimme personally," he related to Crabill, "that he had never made such an utterance in the Landtag and which, as I would know, did not correspond to his principal opinion." Paulmann feared that the offending article would cause mischief at home. "In the struggle about the question of the six-year elementary school that has also arisen in Bremen, this false report of the American paper in Germany has caused great bewilderment. It is known that Minister Grimme professes the same political party as I do. Now the point of view of Minister Grimme is pitted against my own and against me, even though I have always advocated the six-year elementary school."[140]

Paulmann had remained attentive to developments in the British Zone. From both the German and British perspectives, education reform there had increasingly diverged from American practices in 1947, and Paulmann was caught by this separation of policy. From the first he had attended British Zone education conferences to keep abreast of activities in the rest of northern Germany. The *Neue Zeitung* gaffe of January, 1948, was particularly painful for him because, of all the Land education ministers in North Germany, Grimme was closest to him in methods and spirit. On the other hand, school-reform efforts in the other British Länder were serving as a warning to Paulmann of dangers to be avoided, and they, too, influenced his tactics in 1948.

The extremes he was trying to avoid arose in Hamburg and Schleswig-Holstein, where the SPD held a strong position and where dislocations resulting from heavy refugee concentrations and widespread poverty were particularly noticeable. Heinrich Landahl in Hamburg and Wilhelm Kuklinski in Schleswig-Holstein were loyal socialists who sincerely believed that school reform would act as a corrective of past social evils. Many features of the laws that they and their party pushed through the SPD-dominated Land assemblies contained innovations the Americans could also support, although the model in both instances was Britain's 1944 Education Act rather than Allied Control Authority Directive 54 or America's Mission Report. The most significant features included six-year elementary schools followed by three secondary branches: academic, technical, and practical, with safeguards to ensure ease of transfer among them. The laws of the two states were by no means identical, but the broad outlines were similar. In Schleswig-Holstein, for example, the partisan reformers pushed through a tough teacher-training law that included elaborate safeguards for equal training of elementary- and secondary-school teachers in *Pädagogischen Hochschulen*. In Hamburg, Landahl attached teacher training to the university and tried in other respects to accommodate local traditions by allowing certain suburbs to retain their traditional confessional schools. However, in each Land the school laws had triggered harsh reactions among the traditionalists. In Hamburg the university faculty and the secondary teachers' *Gymnasialverein* accused supporters of reform of blatant partisan politics and of ignoring the CDU minority viewpoint. The British authorities were appalled to see the legislation instituted with almost no public participation. Later, when the socialists lost their local majorities in the early 1950s, their CDU rivals simply annulled the two school laws.[141]

North Rhine and Westphalia merged after a time, and their most prominent education minister, Josef Schnippenköter, succeeded, with the help of his dominant CDU faction, in fastening a traditional educational system on this most populous of German Länder. The system looked much like the pre-1933 model: it included separate tracks starting in the fifth year, Latin for the gymnasial pupils, confessional schools, and no coeducation whatsoever. Schnippenköter's plan was nearly as traditional as Alois Hundhammer's, and in northern Germany it was easily the most conservative program of education reform.[142]

It fell to Adolf Grimme to establish education reforms between these extremes. Prussia's last socialist education minister before Hitler, Grimme was also a former classics instructor who disdained the role of professional educational administrator. He preferred to be viewed as a Christian humanist. Like Stein in Greater Hesse, he was fortunate in initiating reforms in a composite state where new educational laws appeared as an attractive alternative to disparate local systems. Grimme's plan called for modification of earlier educational practice, which, he felt, by burdening pupils with excessive facts and specialized skills, had discouraged independent thinking and moral judgment. His proposed six-year elementary school had a common curriculum, with English as the first foreign language. The three branches of secondary education—academic, practical, and technical—were flexible, especially since he deferred Latin until the seventh school year. Nevertheless, Grimme was an enthusiast for Latin instruction and chose the novel argument that more rather than fewer pupils should learn it. He claimed that Latin taught precision and helped develop the mind. Under the usual plan, gifted pupils were compelled to take it from their fifth year on in order to remain competitive, but many refugee children had been unable to begin that early. If instruction were deferred to the seventh year—where, it was hoped, the instruction would be superior—even more pupils could begin classical studies. This change also ensured greater ease of transfer among the branches. It was an argument the traditionalists had not encountered before, and it was central to what came to be called the *niedersächsischer Zug*, or "Lower Saxon current," which coursed through the reform debate in northern Germany. By no means all of Grimme's ideas survived the contest between reformers and traditionalists. His proposals to merge the *Mittelschule* with the quasi-gymnasial *Oberschule* found little support, and neither did his suggestion for a thirteenth-year *Philosophikum*, or tutorial year, for gymnasial students, to replace the usual *Oberprima*. Many traditionalists eyed his deferral of Latin with the darkest suspicion. Nevertheless, Grimme received recognition for his ability to steer a middle way, as did Günther Rönnebeck, who succeeded him as education minister in 1948, when Grimme left to assume leadership of Northwest German Radio. The best that can be said is that many of Grimme's reforms survived, in contrast to the bolder reforms attempted in Hamburg and Schleswig-Holstein.[143]

The British education officers deliberately chose a less obtrusive role in the education-reform debates in their zone. Far more numerous than their American counterparts and thus more widely dispersed among the German educational leadership, they hoped to exert influence informally, through frequent contact and practical advice. By relinquishing control over the educational systems at an early date, they compelled their Germans to accept full responsibility for reforms so that shortcomings could not be charged to a foreign military government. This approach enabled them to avoid clashes with the German authorities, and it minimized the political repercussions among the German public, who might otherwise have raised the specter of foreign interference. The disadvantage was, of course, that, in attempting less, the British could not stop the return of conservative educational structures, such as Schnippenköter's solution in North Rhine–Westphalia, which the traditionalists used successfully to roll back reform legislation elsewhere in the early 1950s. Britain's education chief, Sir Robert Birley, had tried in vain to get the German educational authorities in his zone to coordinate more fully and to produce consensus legislation. Thus, when he learned of Wilhelm Kuklinski's reform package in Schleswig, Birley praised its progressive features, but he also urged the education minister to negotiate with his opposition; he also suggested that Kuklinski might telephone the education minister in North Rhine–Westphalia to make sure that the timing of his own bill would not embarrass reform efforts in that more conservative Land. Nothing came of the suggestion.[144]

Yet, the advice had been apt, and Christian Paulmann was attempting to practice this kind of coordination when the Bremen school proposals took shape in 1948. Harold Crabill and R. T. Alexander were not immediately concerned with coordination among the Länder or with consensus politics to the degree that Birley and the British education officers were. With the contest in Bavaria approaching crisis proportions in 1948, they were anxious to show tangible progress on school reform somewhere, and Bremen's draft proposals seemed to show the most promise. Out of desperation, Crabill applied pressure on his education minister in a manner not seen during the earlier years of the Occupation, when the two had worked so amicably together.

Crabill was not trying to replace Paulmann, whom he respected. He acknowledged to Dunn that the senator was personally supportive of school reform. The chief problem lay elsewhere. "While the Senator and the *Schulräte* favor the plan, many teachers and principals do not. Therefore, the Senator and his assistants are looking to us for help in explaining the plan and winning support for it."[145] But not all Americans agreed with Crabill. A few weeks later one education officer wrote in dismay, "Opponents of school reform are making great propaganda here from the statements of American educators in the faculty of Chicago University."[146] Events in South Germany were also having an effect on school reform in Bremen. Elizabeth Means, a curriculum specialist at Bremen, announced to a zonal E&CR meeting in May, 1948, that public opinion in Bremen had stiffened and that secondary-school teachers and parents were in the forefront of the fight. "The program has been stalled," she declared. "The CDU is opposed, and they are waiting for Bavaria, feeling that, if Bavaria gets by and it isn't forced there, it can't be forced in Bremen."[147] Crabill, too, feared the Bavarian influence, claiming that "conservative elements" in Bremen were receiving "aid and comfort from the situation in Bavaria— mainly on the six-year school."[148]

The situation in Bremen in mid-1948 was perplexing. Here the Americans encountered an educational leadership that, despite important exceptions, was more sympathetic to their own principles than any other educational authority in the zone. Yet school-reform legislation was not forthcoming because a small but vociferous minority had found a way to frustrate both Paulmann and E&CR. The secret of the conservatives' success lay in a legal complication embodied in the Bremen constitution. The heart of the problem was the *Reichsschulpflichtgesetz*, or compulsory-education law, passed by the Nazis on July 6, 1938. The details of the law were not unusual; the National Socialists had simply retained most of the features of the traditional German multitrack school structure, including the four-year elementary school. What was important about the law was that it was prior legislation and now had to be superseded by another law. The Bremen constitution decreed that new legislation before the *Bürgerschaft* required only a simple majority but that bills designed to replace existing legislation required a two-thirds majority. Undeniably, Bremen's school system was functioning along the lines of the old law, although it was not, to be sure, educating Bremen's children in the spirit of National Socialism, as the first sentence of the 1938 law urged.

On February 3, 1948, Christian Paulmann consulted the Bremen senate's chief legal adviser for an opinion and promptly received word that the 1938 law was still in effect. Bremen's new school law would therefore require a two-thirds majority for passage.[149] Harold Crabill was incredulous. He immediately contacted OMG Bremen's Legal Division only to discover that they, too, agreed that the law was still operative. Paulmann would have to attract a large majority in order to enact his school legislation. Legal counsel Robert Johnson confirmed that Military Government condemned all Nazi laws, "but," he observed, "no one has ever determined just what is a Nazi law." Johnson agreed that the first sentence of the 1938 law was inadmissible, but the rest of the legislation contained no such taint. "In my opinion," he continued, "the rest of the law should remain in force and effect unless modified or repealed by the legislative body of Land Bremen." Johnson added that Legal Division's powers were "very limited" and, in fact, were largely confined to deciding whether German legislation infringed Military Government policy. If Crabill wanted to rescind the 1938 law, Johnson's sole advice was to try to get action at OMGUS headquarters in Berlin.[150]

Crabill immediately phoned Alexander, imploring him to move the bureaucratic machinery. Alexander was willing to send his own opinion, but no official position ever arrived from higher legal counsel in Berlin. A year later Crabill was still trying to obtain a legal response from Alexander's successors, Milton Muelder and John Riedl. He explained to them that Alexander "is thought to have referred it to the Legal Committee of OMGUS headquarters, but, since nothing has ever been done about it officially, it may be assumed that it was either referred only by telephone or personal conference or that correspondence on the subject has somehow become lost."[151]

Suddenly the prospects for a Bremen school law dimmed. Paulmann knew well that he could produce a simple majority with the combined votes of the SPD and KPD, but the CDU and Bremen's second conservative party, the *Bremische Demokratische Verein* (BDV), could prevent a two-thirds majority. That simple fact goes far to explain his actions in 1948 and 1949. Crabill, Dunn, and other Military Government leaders were aware of the legal complication, but the Americans badly needed a success in 1948. Given this context it is not surprising that Thomas Dunn, the Land director, began to put pressure on Wilhelm Kaisen for the first time. In May he wrote the senior senator: "While it is gratifying to this office to know that the school-reform plan prepared by the Land Department of Education has been approved by OMGUS headquarters and commended as the best plan submitted in the U.S. Zone, it is self-evident that a good plan is of no value unless it is carried out." He complained that reorganization had been "unnecessarily and inexcusably delayed." Now he wanted to see some legislation enacted for the following school year, which meant April, 1949.[152]

Harold Crabill and his staff met frequently with Paulmann's staff that summer. Crabill tried to accommodate his German opposites as best he could while maintaining heavy pressure to produce legislation. Thus, as a concession to the school principals, he was busily searching for typewriters for the threadbare school administration. For the language instructors he attempted to secure a set of hard-to-find English-language readers in use in the British Zone. Fortunately, the education authorities in Bremen were showing no signs of joining the city's educational conservatives, and one official from a secondary school told Crabill that if he was looking for precedents for the six-year elementary school, Bremerhaven would serve well. The port city had had over twenty years of experience with such schools and with an unusual four-year *Aufbau* program.[153]

Then in September, 1948, Paulmann decided on a change of tactics. At a meeting of the *Bürgerschaft*'s Education Committee he secured approval for four separate education bills, claiming that it would be easier and more manageable to secure passage for each piece of legislation separately. The American education officers approved. The hostility of the two conservative political parties was intense, and it was mounting among the secondary-school teachers and parents. They were well aware that the trend was not working in E&CR's favor. To be sure, the topic was now receiving extensive coverage in the press, radio, and other public forums, but it was also proving to be highly controversial.[154] In the midst of these developments, Thomas Dunn offered a gesture of good will that he hoped would shore up Paulmann's precarious position: "It is the wish of this Headquarters to do everything possible within U.S. policy to assist you in the rehabilitation of the school system and in the implementation of the school-reform plan which has been devised and approved for Land Bremen. Approval of the reinstatement of teachers falls within this category." Dunn, with Crabill's concurrence, had decided to accelerate the denazification procedures to allow the reinstatement of 150 badly needed teachers. Dunn was making the offer to "serve as evidence of good will on the part of Military Government and help to remove the feeling on the part of some Bremen education personnel that Military Government policy is not in the best interests of the Bremen schools and Bremen children."[155]

No sooner had the Americans made the reinstatements than Special Branch announced that it had uncovered serious irregularities in the denazification of the teachers at Bremerhaven. Paulmann and Crabill learned that either an American officer or the German authorities—no one knew who was to blame—had failed to carry out the dismissals. E&RA had been stretched far too thin to oversee compliance, and now, in the summer of 1948, Military Government was compelled to dismiss twenty-nine teachers on the eve of the opening of fall classes.[156]

Crabill gamely attended a meeting of Bremerhaven school principals and tried to explain the circumstances and soothe as best he could the hard feelings his unpopular action had inevitably engendered. He promised to handle the denazification cases expeditiously and indicated that, where possible, Military Government would reinstate the released personnel promptly. He was agreeably surprised at the mild reaction of the principals, but he also knew that there might be trouble elsewhere. "There is considerable evidence," he informed Dunn, "to indicate that the noise about this situation is being made by persons seeking to exploit the situation politically to their own advantage."[157]

The reaction was not slow in coming. Soon the "Central Parents Committee of Bremen High Schools" held a widely publicized meeting and forwarded two resolutions to Military Government. They demanded nothing less than the complete return of control of education and educational personnel to German hands and noted "with deep concern the fact that all Bremen schools after more than three years of reconstruction efforts are still provided with a wholly insufficient number of teachers."[158] By this time a note of testiness had crept into OMG Bremen's relations with the city population. Thus, a few days later, when a traveling cabaret team known as the *"Hinterlassenen"* (Survivors) presented a satirical performance in Bremen, Thomas Dunn closed it down for making slanderous references to Military Government. The E&CR theater chief noted that the new group simply shifted to nearby Hamburg, where it continued its "impudent slanderings of U.S. policy with the blessings of the British Theatre Officer."[159]

With the approach of winter, the E&CR staff increased its efforts to publicize the reform proposals. Floyd Hines of the secondary-education section announced at a zonal E&CR meeting that his division had conducted numerous conferences with school officials and had instituted a weekly public forum. Public attendance was so great that they had actually been forced to turn some citizens away.[160] Then two prominent figures in the school-reform controversy disappeared from the city. Thomas Dunn left Military Government for the United States, to be replaced by Captain Charles R. Jeffs. Christian Paulmann also departed on a trip to the United States, to observe American educational practice at first hand. He was scheduled to return to Bremen at year's end. Paulmann gave Crabill assurances that legislation would be forthcoming immediately upon his return. "He gave me his solemn word of honor," Crabill recounted to Jeffs, "that this law would be passed as soon as he returned from the United States and that the six-year elementary school would actually be begun at Easter, 1949."[161]

Paulmann returned to Bremen on schedule, but no school bill was forthcoming. Finally, in mid-January, Crabill began to panic. Time was running perilously short if the school reforms were to materialize in 1949. Then he discovered that the senator was redrafting the entire school law and that he had returned to his original strategy of submitting the entire set of changes to the *Bürgerschaft* as one reform package. "Despite Senator Paulmann's assurances to the contrary," Crabill fretted, "I am sure that the redraft will occasion some objections, debates, and conflicts in the legislative body and probably stir new organized opposition amongst the conservative school people." Paulmann remained confident of passage; by clearing each point of the bill with the political parties beforehand, he felt he could beat the April deadline. But Crabill was not reassured, and he advised Jeffs that "Our task now is to keep in close touch with developments and assure ourselves that each point in the law is satisfactory from the standpoint of Military Government policy and to keep snapping at his heels in order to bring it to an early completion." Crabill felt that, if no school law was forthcoming within six weeks, Military Government must impose a reform by direct order.[162]

Paulmann entered a marathon session with the political factions and by late February was able to hand Crabill a copy of his final draft. Crabill was not pleased with what he read. He informed the Legal Office that the bill "has been considerably watered down since the last draft which I have seen." Some provisions would bar the education senator from issuing instructions without approval from the *Bürgerschaft*'s School Deputation. Even more disturbing than this surrender of authority was the fact that the new bill read more like a declaration of intent than a binding law. True, the bill was to become law on April 1, 1949, and it stated that Bremen would provide six-year elementary schools; but the final draft omitted any schedule of implementation. Other hard-won features, such as a ninth school year for all pupils and a broadening of the vocational schools' general curriculum from eight to sixteen hours per week, also depended on the *Bürgerschaft*'s initiative. Crabill conceded that the draft still espoused a democratic educational philosophy. "However," he observed, "it does not provide positively for the implementation of that philosophy but rather makes it *possible* to implement the philosophy *if* the school authorities wish to do so." Crabill had little faith in the nascent democracy of Bremen. "Therefore, everything depends upon the desire, the courage, and the strength of the incumbent Senator," he complained. Crabill accused Paulmann of straddling the political fence between opponents of school reform and E&CR. "It had been his [Paulmann's] position as well as that of Bürgermeister Kaisen that the school law must be widely supported rather than passed by a small left-wing majority. The opponents of the legislation have exploited this attitude to the full in forcing concessions."[163]

Charles Jeffs began consulting with Paulmann directly to let the senator know the importance he attached to the reform measures. Crabill also kept abreast of developments and made no secret of how he felt about Paulmann's recent actions: "It is desired expressly to point out that Senator Paulmann has broken faith with me in this matter." Crabill was still disgruntled that an entirely new draft and a new strategy for implementation were in the offing. "To assist him over his difficulties, I made one concession after another, including the reinstatement of 150 teachers," Crabill complained. Now rumors were circulating that Paulmann had agreed, during his conferences with the right-wing parties, to defer the six-year elementary school until 1950. "Hence it appears that Senator Paulmann has broken faith not only with Military Government but with his own Party and with his coworkers on the School Board as well."[164]

Crabill's frustration was perhaps understandable, since the work of three years appeared to be going down the drain. But Paulmann was also facing a difficult political battle. Neither man had any illusions about the intentions of the educational conservatives in the *Bürgerschaft*, one of whom had been quoted in a recent school-reform debate as saying: "If we win time, we win everything."[165]

Paulmann's political moves were still governed by the need to forge the two-thirds majority. Crabill, for his part, tried desperately, one last time, to get action on this vexing legal technicality. For a short time he seemed to make progress when OMG Bremen's new legal adviser, Norman Metal, agreed that the 1938 school law should be declared invalid. But, like his predecessor, Metal balked at acting alone. Once again Crabill implored the E&CR staff at OMGUS for help. "The awkward situation," he told Milton Muelder and John Riedl "is that apparently the Law is a stumbling block to School Legislation only in Land Bremen and not in the other Länder because of the provisions of the Bremen Constitution or the cleverness of our BDV Senator for Law and Justice. The nature of the situation leaves the initiative in the hands of the German Government, which means that rightly or wrongly their interpretation will prevail unless definite action is taken by Military Government." By this time Crabill had become suspicious that even Paulmann was hiding behind the 1938 law. "It is the personal belief of the undersigned," he confided, "that the Draft was rewritten to include provisions which were in conflict as a deliberate political move."[166]

To be sure, Kaisen and Paulmann saw the matter in a different light, and Kaisen at least was able to discuss the matter with a distinguished visitor to Bremen in March, 1949. George F. Kennan was making a tour of inspection to gauge the results of four years of occupation. In an evening gathering at the residence of the American consul for Bremen, Maurice Altaffer, Kaisen complained that while he and his party wanted school reforms, including the six-year elementary school, they desired to introduce it gradually, so as to accustom the parents to the sweeping changes. Kaisen recalled asking Military Government for a transition period. "The answer was no." (Kennan later recorded: "They had to do it right now.") After listening to Kaisen's complaints, the famous guest finally asked who was responsible for conducting negotiations from the American side. Upon learning that it was Harold Crabill, Kennan inquired about his background. Altaffer stated vaguely that he had been a high-school teacher in Indiana. When Kennan then asked whether Crabill was a man of understanding and competence, he noted a strange reaction: "The consul was taken aback by this question. [Crabill] was, he replied, a good high-school teacher in Indiana."[167]

This assessment was not entirely fair to Harold H. Crabill, who had, after all, left a post at Indiana University. Nevertheless, Altaffer's opinion did point to a certain inflexibility on the part of the Bremen E&CR chief with regard to German educational values. Perhaps it was inevitable that his frustration was greatest because, of all the E&CR chiefs, he had come closest to overseeing the passage of reforms most nearly in accord with expressed American ideals. However, he had a hard time coming to grips with the political realities that Kaisen and Paulmann faced daily, and he sometimes expected too much from a society still recovering from a disastrous defeat. Thus, another of his schemes, namely the creation of a new university in Bremen, was an unrealistic undertaking, doomed by lack of resources. Yet it diverted much of his energy and succeeded in alienating Fritz Karsen and other high-ranking education officers at OMGUS.[168] It was not German education leaders alone who disappointed this exacting man. And if anyone believed fervently in an American mission in Occupied Germany, it was Harold H. Crabill.

In any case, Crabill's belligerence ultimately had little effect on Christian Paulmann. The Bremen Democratic People's Party (BDV) succeeded, as rumors indicated it would, in wresting from Paulmann a final concession, namely, the deferring of the six-year elementary school until April, 1950. The new legislation also declared that the old Reich law of 1938 was now void, thus preserving the legalism that a two-thirds majority had been necessary to pass the new law.[169]

The Bremen school law went far toward satisfying the goals espoused by the Americans and expressed in ACA Directive 54. The six-year elementary school offered a common curriculum, including English instruction for all in the fifth year. Latin instruction did not begin until the seventh school year. The general "secondary school" permitted sharp differentiation, based largely on four traditional models that had been much in evidence in Bremen in earlier times. Branch A offered three years of full-time general instruction plus three years of vocational education. Branch B gave four years of full-time general curriculum followed by two years of vocational training, which corresponded to the old Prussian *Mittelschule* or to Bremen's traditional *Oberbau*. Branch C was a commercial school offering three years of instruction, with an emphasis on economics, to pupils from either Branch A or Branch B. This, too, was an ancient education feature, reflecting Bremen's prominent role in trade and commerce. Branch D was the *Oberschule,* with three subdivisions for ancient languages, modern languages, and science and mathematics. The whole package was made more palatable to the Americans by the provision that "the various Branches of the Secondary School should be collected in one building." Thus, the law that passed on April 1, 1949, declared an intent. The Americans would now have to have faith that Paulmann and the *Bürgerschaft* would carry out its provisions.[170]

With the passage of the school law in Bremen in the final months of Military Government operations, it became obvious that further overt attempts to change the school structure would be unavailing. The tasks at hand were now of a different nature, centering largely on coordinating the newly enhanced aid and exchange programs and the stocking of libraries and textbook and curriculum centers. Faced with this change in emphasis, Harold Crabill joined the growing number of education chiefs who embarked on other careers in the summer of 1949. He had told his coworkers and superiors that he considered a control function by the Americans to be indispensable. His departure was consistent with his beliefs.

The Bremen experience indicated that a Land with a tradition of educational innovation was prepared to accept American proposals that accorded with its own values without the rancor of a more tradition-bound Land like Bavaria. Even so, there were sharp limitations on how far even the citizens of Bremen were prepared to change the structure of their schools. First, they were by no means immune to feeling resentment at being pressured by a foreign government. The declaration of the thirteen University of Chicago faculty members and reports of the Bavarians' spirited resistance were eagerly received in the port city. There was also no denying the fact that opponents of school reform in the two conservative parties had found a clever legal device with which to thwart change. This opposition also proved skillful in selling its point of view to the public. Once again the course of the reform debate demonstrated that in a democratically conducted contest for the minds of German citizens concerning their children's education, the Americans fared poorly. It would have taken an unusual degree of detachment to examine so emotion-stirring an issue without noticing which language the speaker was using.

Finally, Bremen was inevitably affected by the pace of education reform in the Länder of the neighboring British Zone. From the start Paulmann had declared his intention of coordinating his reform proposals with developments elsewhere in northern Germany, and, by and large, he succeeded in keeping his city's legislation in line with developments in Lower Saxony. Certainly, divergences between British and American education policy caused some difficulties. The problem surfaced again painfully in the denazification effort, which had a negative effect on the supply of capable teachers in Bremen. Resentment at the Americans' retention of a control function over education long after the British had formally adopted an advisory position prompted further unfavorable comparison, which the Bremen citizens were not slow to make.

Württemberg-Baden

In southwest Germany, American Military Government confronted a unique problem: it faced the reality of sharing the administration of a territory evenly divided between two sovereign powers. The two traditional rivals in south Germany, Baden and Württemberg, had always had a common north-south border, but in 1945 the Americans and French divided the two states from east to west. North Württemberg and North Baden became an American-occupied Land, and Württemberg-Hohenzollern and South Baden fell under French control. This forced and unnatural separation of the territories inevitably caused significant problems for the two occupying powers. America's Office of Military Government for Württemberg-Baden (OMGWB) discovered quickly that it had a difficult territory to administer. Its E&RA Branch also confronted administrative problems associated with the peculiar division. In 1948 the imminent reintegration of the twin territories brought the contrasts between French and American educational policy painfully into view.

Despite the awkwardness that was implicit in sharing power with France, there were compelling reasons for creating a French occupation zone. The State Department was eager for France to reassert itself in European affairs, and General Eisenhower raised no objection to a French presence in Germany. In the north they received a territory that fanned out westward behind Koblenz. Eisenhower would gladly have given the French all of Baden and Württemberg, but his staff realized that his headquarters at Frankfurt-am-Main required access to a Rhine port at Mannheim and to the Autobahn routes through Karlsruhe. Thus, North Württemberg and North Baden came under American control. What resulted was an odd hourglass-shaped French Zone, which pleased no one. Reluctantly, the French agreed to the shift only in mid-July. This was, then, the last major realignment of territories among the occupying powers.[171]

Soon an American civil-affairs detachment, under Colonel William W. Dawson, established its Land headquarters in Stuttgart and then organized a subordinate capital for North Baden, first in Mannheim and then in Karlsruhe. Dawson also became OMGWB's first Land director. Formerly a law professor at Case Western Reserve University in Ohio, he was, by common consent, the ablest of General Clay's Land directors. Much of his energy went into the creation of the Länderrat early in the Occupation. Unfortunately, he died midway through the Occupation. He was succeeded by Charles LaFollette of Wisconsin.[172]

One of the first education officers in Stuttgart was Captain John P. Steiner, formerly a school superintendent in Portales, New Mexico. Steiner received the chief E&RA slot at Stuttgart, and a succession of junior officers, including Walter Bergman, conducted school surveys in North Baden. At first the education officers were G-5 detachment officers, who set the denazification machinery in motion, surveyed building damage, and succeeded, with German help, in reopening the schools by October 1.

The French, who had occupied Stuttgart from April, 1945, until their grudging exit in July, had already appointed Professor Carlo Schmidt as head of a new ministry of education on June 15, but, when the Americans arrived, Schmidt moved south with the French to their new headquarters at Tübingen, where he became the first minister president. Fortunately, the Americans were able to locate a prestigious replacement, the famed historian and journalist Theodor Heuss. They also added a respected educator as Heuss's deputy, Professor Theodor Bäuerle, a noted pioneer in adult education and, before 1933, a sometime associate of R. T. Alexander's. Heuss and Bäuerle both had impeccable anti-fascist credentials and between them lent integrity and professionalism to the fledgling ministry of education. They organized the educational structure into five divisions, of which the most important was the public-school division. This was further subdivided into four sections: adult education and youth activities, elementary education, secondary education, and vocational education. Each section reported directly to the deputy minister, Theodor Bäuerle.[173]

In the Heuss-Bäuerle plan, teacher-training fell within the domain of the elementary- and secondary-education sections. For the Americans, teacher training was a higher-education function. Thus the administrative gears of the two bureaucracies meshed imperfectly. At first the defect was not apparent. During the first six months of the Occupation, the education ministry devoted the bulk of its energies to planning and organization, since the local Kreis (county) educational systems followed orders directly from their local Military Government detachments. After January 1, 1946, the local German education offices operated only under Land education-ministry auspices, subject to Land E&RA supervision.

Most of the E&RA staff had been professional educators in civilian life. For example, Captain Harold Robinson, formerly a school principal in the Midwest, headed E&RA's Schools Branch. The other branches included comparable personnel for institutions of higher learning, teacher training, youth activities, and religious affairs—conforming to the E&RA pattern elsewhere. There were also a few field officers, including a post for a historian and classicist, Earl Crum, at the Land's solitary university, Heidelberg. Richard G. Banks, who served as Steiner's deputy for long periods and then as acting director, was not happy with E&RA's organization in the new Land: "In many ways," he commented later, "it was at cross-purposes with the traditional German organization, as, for example, in teacher training, which normally came under the German elementary school section."[174]

If organization proved faulty, the sheer lack of E&RA officers caused equally severe problems. Besides supervising denazification of teachers and learning materials, inspecting libraries, schools, and youth organizations, and carrying on all the usual watchdog activities, they had to ready the entire system for renewed operations in October. The Land had a population of about 3.6 million people by the end of 1945, including 700,000 hapless refugees. On October 1, after prodigies of E&RA and ministry effort, 306,000 pupils, or 70 percent of the elementary-school population, began classes. By year's end the figure had risen to 90 percent. The teacher-pupil ratio stood at 1:91 on the average but sometimes approached 1:150. Theodor Heuss estimated a shortage of 4,000 teachers following the purge. By contrast, the Land secondary schools, which opened in December, included 34,000 pupils, and the teacher-pupil ratio was 1:47. Early reports indicated that the school system was barely functioning amid conditions of universal undernourishment, poor discipline, and substandard instruction, but there was little the American education staff could do about it. The acting director, Richard Banks, recalled working for several months with "only one staff member for the entire education field, including the public school system, private schools, one university, twelve teacher-training institutes, and six technical, agricultural, and art colleges."[175] In June, 1946, the staff was expanded to four. By 1948 the authorized strength of the enlarged E&CR Division rose to a paper strength of twenty-two, although in practice fewer than half that number were on hand. Banks and Steiner encountered difficulty in recruiting high-quality educators to come to Germany, and John Taylor conceded that filling slots for Württemberg-Baden was difficult. "This outfit is the weakest of the lot," he complained to George Geyer at the Pentagon in May, 1946, and he displayed a list of canceled positions and unsuccessful attempts at filling existing ones.[176]

Despite its rural setting, the Land had lost half its school space as the result of war damage. This, coupled with the emergency use of surviving space for hospitals, barracks, refugee camps, and orphanages, meant that three-fourths of the Land's school buildings were unavailable. Lack of coal and window glass further reduced operations, so that in every school district some classes were forced to meet in private homes and even in taverns.[177]

Denazification removed 65 percent of the teachers, a somewhat higher average than in other Länder. The survivors were elderly teachers between fifty-five and sixty years of age. The education ministry therefore rapidly organized emergency teacher-training facilities and courses for hurriedly mobilized replacements and young school helpers. Experienced teachers led these makeshift classes on weekends. The Americans suffered no illusions about the results of such crude training and admitted that expedients of this kind "did great damage to educational standards."[178]

Teacher training became an early sore point between E&RA and the education ministry. Bäuerle and others tried to convince the Americans that many of the dismissed teachers would eventually be reinstated and that it was folly to train new teaching ranks in such large numbers; those being reinstated would combine with the new arrivals to create a serious oversupply. "As it turned out," Banks conceded, "the German authorities were right."[179] Nearly two-thirds of the dismissed teachers returned to their jobs by 1948. Teacher-training problems among secondary-school teachers were less severe. Higher prestige and salaries continued to attract educated persons from other professions. "As a consequence of this situation," Banks observed, "very little attention was paid to the training of secondary teachers during the emergency period."[180]

As early as January, 1947, with the establishment of Clay's directive, the E&RA staff in Stuttgart was theoretically expected to order the ministry to produce a statement of general aims for education reform. In fact the emergency period, as Banks judged it in Württemberg-Baden, continued through all of 1946, so that little long-range planning was possible. Beginning in April, 1946, Banks directed the E&RA division when John Steiner returned to the United States on a lengthy leave of absence, and he was in charge when the U.S. Education Mission toured the zone in August and September of 1946. Its findings initially carried great weight in Stuttgart. Referring to the Mission Report later, Banks stated: "Here was not another pronouncement of the occupying powers but rather a considered statement from a group of nonpartisan educators."[181] Whether the German educators were of the same opinion is less certain, but they exhibited an intense interest in the Mission Report. Bäuerle distributed copies to every teacher in Württemberg-Baden. Impressed with the Report's recommendation that U.S. education staffs be enlarged, the E&RA officers in Stuttgart prepared eagerly to receive visiting American experts to augment their small staff. Banks deplored the continuing shortage of regulars but admitted that "it was difficult to employ outstanding educators for continued service in Germany, since most of them had long-standing full-time commitments."[182] In his words, the regular education officers were "so burdened with administrative problems that they had little time to spend in scholarly planning with German educators."[183] Few of the E&RA staff claimed to be educational specialists. They were, by training, practical administrators and were not inclined to speculate about contending philosophies of education.

When John Taylor and R. T. Alexander toured the zone in February, 1947, they visited the E&RA staff and Bäuerle's ministry in Stuttgart to deliver the message contained in both General Clay's January 10 directive and the Mission Report. Thus, in early 1947, E&RA at Stuttgart, like E&RA staffs in the other Länder, began to exert pressure on the Land education ministry. Fortunately, Steiner and Banks had managed to develop a cordial relationship with their German counterparts during the emergency period and had tried to deal with Bäuerle and his staff as equals. As early as December, 1945, Steiner had called on his fellow officers to accord "more dignity and authority to the top Germans chosen to run the educational systems of the . . . U.S. Zone."[184] Steiner practiced his beliefs in his daily interactions with Heuss, Bäuerle, and the ministry. This spirit of equality manifested itself in many little ways. Neither Steiner nor Banks ever ordered the appearance of the ministry's staff. If the Americans desired a meeting, they made a point of calling on their German opposites. The German staff responded in kind, so that, despite the tensions surrounding denazification and school reform, the two educational bureaucracies largely preserved a cordial relationship.[185] Steiner's approach echoed the informal style of the British education officers.

In the spring of 1946, Banks and another E&RA staff member, Paul Bodenman, were returning from a conference in Wiesbaden when they accidentally discovered a vast collection of U.S. Army dictionaries, text-books, and other educational works in a warehouse near Mannheim. The works were originally intended for a million-man army of occupation that never materialized, and the Army had decided to jettison the unwanted collection. Using the time-honored methods of the military scrounger, Banks and Bodenman quickly transferred 2.5 million volumes to Stuttgart, where Bäuerle's ministry distributed the best of the materials to schools and English-speaking teachers. They pulped the rest to produce millions of desperately needed notebooks and drawing pads for schoolchildren. The thrifty Germans even dismantled the thousands of sturdy wooden packing cases to use in making emergency repairs on their dilapidated school buildings. Much later, the Pentagon gave its assent to the already completed distribution—much to the relief of Colonel Dawson and the E&RA branch. E&RA's aid, even in the emergency period, extended to such minutiae as school feeding programs and teachers' workshops, where the participants received badly needed supplemental food rations. The lack of an adequate operational budget hampered Steiner's ability to match the generosity of the E&RA staff in Wiesbaden. Nevertheless, relations between German and American educators in Württemberg-Baden were marked by respect and, for the most part, a friendliness comparable to that seen in Hesse and Bremen.[186]

Although the Land education ministry had already begun to address such issues as curriculum development, textbook preparation, and im-proved social studies during the emergency phase, the day finally arrived when both parties had to come to terms over the core issue of school structure and the related problem of teacher training. Predictably, Theodor Bäuerle preferred to concentrate on inner or spiritual reform before tack-ling the politically sensitive issue of structural change, but by 1947 the American officers dismissed such proposals as offering "too nebulous a result to expect from a Military Government sponsored reform pro-gram."[187] Structural changes were more easily measurable than spiritual reforms.

Bowing to the demand for concrete goals, Bäuerle submitted a set of acceptable general aims in April, 1947. He was willing to raise the general school-leaving age to fifteen. As a gesture to the traditionalists, he added a year to the secondary-school curriculum, returning it to the pre-1933 thirteen-year gymnasial program. More striking was his proposal to in-crease elementary schooling from four years to six, "with only slight dif-ferentiation of the curriculum during the fifth and sixth years." The reform also envisaged a *Mittelstufe* of three years, having a more sharply differ-entiated curriculum, followed by a four-year *Oberstufe* for those intending to enter the university. This last level was expected to provide five sub-tracks in classical languages, modern languages, mathematics and science, business studies, and the performing arts. Bäuerle proposed raising elementary-school training to university status so as to place elementary-school teachers on a comparable professional basis with secondary-school teachers. There was little in the general aims that the Americans found objectionable except that it was "of a more general nature than Military Government has expected," and they waited for the ministry to offer specific plans.[188]

In the meantime, personnel changes within the education ministry were beginning to affect the reform effort. Theodor Heuss had left the ministry in 1946 to start the Land's first postwar newspaper and to direct the south German wing of what became the Free Democratic Party. Since Theodor Bäuerle was nonpolitical, and since a CDU-sponsored education minister stood a better chance of pushing legislation through the Landtag, the education ministry received a new director at the beginning of 1947, Wilhelm Simpfendörfer. Simpfendörfer had a long record of involvement in politics, dating back to the Weimar Republic—too long, as it turned out. Shortly after his appointment, the *Stuttgarter Zeitung* announced that, as a Reichstag deputy in 1933, Simpfendörfer had voted for the Enabling Act that gave Hitler dictatorial powers. The ensuing outcry finally forced Simpfendörfer's ouster in March, 1947. Since the CDU could not name an acceptable replacement, Bäuerle took over as the permanent education minister.[189] For a time it appeared that there might even be advantages to his lack of political alignment, but after the submission of his detailed education plans in October, 1947, E&RA discovered that there were drawbacks in not having a spokesman with political power.

The more detailed October plan appeared at the time to calm American anxieties, and a contemporary report called it "a decided improvement over the plan submitted on April 1, 1947." Both the Stuttgart office and OMGUS expressed their approval, but, as Banks later observed, their jubilation was premature. "Military Government," he confessed, "rather naively accepted it as though it would soon become an accomplished fact."[190] In reality the struggle had barely begun. Closer observation revealed that there was no timetable for implementation of the various features, and opposition had already begun to form when the ministry pieced its detailed plan together between April and October of 1947. Bäuerle had activated a "School Planning Commission" that spring, with representatives from among the *Schulräte* (school superintendents), teacher-training institutions, elementary schools, secondary schools, universities, and the two churches. There was also an advisory body for the committee, with members from the political parties, trade unions, industry, government, and the professions, so that most of the important segments of Land society had a hand in the discussions. Unfortunately, as the result of its well-intended diversity, the newly constituted committee accomplished little. Its first meeting in fact accomplished nothing at all. As one report indicated: "A lively debate developed as to the merits of the proposed plan." The same observer noted that two distinct groups coalesced, with "the six-year elementary school and the differentiated high school proving special targets of attack by the secondary-school representatives, whereas the elementary-school delegates warmly defended these proposals as fundamental to any real school reform." At this acrimonious first meeting the ministry already found itself caught between two angry forces. If it changed its proposals to appease the secondary-school faction, it faced the ire of the elementary-school forces; yet to continue on the present course would insure the implacable opposition of the secondary-school teachers. "In either event," the observer concluded, "the prospects for a speedy implementation of a school reform are somewhat remote."[191]

Following Bäuerle's submission of the October plan, events began to take a familiar turn. Some American observers felt that the new plan was still too vague. One intelligence estimate claimed that it "proved to be no more than a further extension of the original general statement." In a parallel move to Hesse's *Landesschulbeirat* Bäuerle's ministry formed a general committee or *Hauptausschuss* in November, 1947, to prepare detailed implementation plans for the formal proposal. No less than twenty subcommittees materialized to examine specific issues. Approximately two hundred prominent educators throughout the Land labored on the proposals, and in April, 1948, the *Hauptausschuss* completed its detailed plan. One unusual procedure was that the committee submitted its findings directly to E&RA without working through the education ministry. The latest proposal came to be called the Caselmann Plan, after Committee Chairman Christian Caselmann, who was also the Land director of secondary-school teacher training and formerly a gymnasial instructor. While respecting the independence of the *Hauptausschuss*, E&RA had hoped to offer it material support, but in this it was thwarted by the lack of a meaningful budget until mid-1948. After that, Clay's decision to earmark income from American-directed publications, such as the *Neue Zeitung*, allowed greater flexibility to the Land E&RA staffs, which could now offer grants-in-aid for worthwhile education projects. As Banks noted, "this move greatly increased the field of operations of the E&RA division, which previously had been without local budgets."[192]

The Caselmann proposal had emerged from months of fractious negotiation at about the time that four-power control in Germany ground to a halt following the failure of the Foreign Ministers' Conference in London in December, 1947. Therefore, the theme of unity haunted the Germans. At a conference of education ministers in Stuttgart the following February, Theodor Bäuerle called on his fellow education ministers to agree on "a common basis for the rebuilding of our school and educational system."

Bäuerle was worried about the lack of coordination in even the Western zones. "It is amazing how rapidly all contact can be lost," he warned, and he asked his colleagues to agree to unify their cultural policy in line with similar efforts at coordination in economics and politics.[193] His remarks were not intended as a plea for the traditional multitrack system. In speeches to the subcommittees of the *Hauptausschuss* that winter he spoke angrily about disparities between the elementary and the secondary schools. To one group he said, "Too much is done for the talented students, too little for the less talented or ungifted." To another he claimed that reforms aimed at diminishing differentiation "will not destroy German culture as is claimed; it will make German culture available to more Germans."[194] However, his opinions were of a personal nature, and, because of his background in adult education, no one construed his remarks as emanating from a specific political party or faction.

One of the curious developments with regard to education policy in Württemberg-Baden was that for long it remained outside public view, among the blocs of elementary- and secondary-school teachers and university leadership. True, the Social Democrats and the Communists officially declared in favor of school reform but offered little practical support. The Christian Democrats had as yet shown no great antipathy. Only the smaller, more conservative, Deutsche Volkspartei, or DVP, had rejected it outright. Even the two churches were slow to take sides, and Military Government postal intercepts of the correspondence of a leading Protestant church leader, Bishop Asmussen, indicated that the Protestant hierarchy was not inclined to enter the debate. The faculty at Heidelberg had, by contrast, condemned the projected reforms, claiming that students entering the university would be insufficiently prepared in classical languages. One intelligence analyst suggested that such public opinion as existed was hostile and that the proposed reforms were being seen as American models forced on the Germans. Other estimates indicated that the elementary-school faction had begun to rally support for the reforms in the fall of 1947, and in several school conventions this group publicly endorsed structural change. Its arguments generally paralleled those presented by Minister Bäuerle: segregation of pupils into sharply differentiated schools would perpetuate class biases in education.[195]

With time, the debate moved beyond the confines of the professionals into the public forum. The elementary- and secondary-school factions battled each other, brandishing statistical evidence to capture public opinion. The latter group used it to show that significantly lowered tuition costs for secondary-school pupils had eliminated class privilege. The former countered that such figures ignored the tremendous sacrifices that impoverished parents had to make to pay for transporting their children to school and for supporting them for a longer period of time. The political parties soon dropped any pretense of neutrality. Thus, when a Social Democratic deputy in the Landtag attacked the bourgeois atmosphere among students at Heidelberg, he drew heavy criticism from Theodor Heuss who expressed dismay that differences between elementary- and secondary-school teachers were being exploited "for purposes of class warfare."[196]

In Mannheim, Military Government officials observed particularly acrimonious confrontations between professional educators and the public. Elementary-school spokesmen accused secondary-school teachers of prejudicing their pupils against reform and then setting them on their parents to pressure the government to abandon structural change. The traditionalists accused their attackers of acting as "collaborators of the occupation forces and therefore traitors to their fatherland."

Thus, public debate on school reform in Württemberg-Baden came late, but it did not lack fury. It is therefore ironic to read a Military Government assessment of the situation in January, 1948, that "despite the strength of the power-entrenched forces which oppose school reform in this Land, favorable sentiment appears to be growing." Citing public apathy, support from Bäuerle and most of his staff, and a low profile by the churches, Military Government's intelligence analysts professed optimism. Their only worry was that the April 1 plan might not be comprehensive enough.[197]

Christian Caselmann and his *Hauptausschuss* usually convened without American participation. "E&RA staff members carefully refrain from attendance at committee meetings but hold themselves ready to advise as necessary," stated one observer, who noted that this practice contrasted with negotiating practice in Hesse.[198] Then, on January 23, 1948, Payne Templeton of E&RA's Schools Branch accepted Caselmann's invitation to attend a session. He experienced a rude awakening. Although pleased with some proposals, he was so dismayed by others that he later demanded "a careful written statement of the tentative reform plan presented to us orally by you at the meeting last Friday." Templeton warned Caselmann that E&RA chief Richard Banks and other senior staff members would study the proposals closely. The problem was that Caselmann had announced his committee's decision to return to a four-year elementary school structure, and Templeton was unhappy. "As you know," he reminded Caselmann, "we are somewhat doubtful of any plan which might tend to segregate pupils as early as the fifth grade, unless such process of selection can be shown to be only tentative, with opportunities in later grades for pupils to cross over to the courses leading to the university." He then reiterated his stand that the new plan should consist of a "six-year *Grundschule* and of a centralized three-year *Mittelstufe*, with flexible provisions for differentiation according to ability and interest."[199]

Banks was well aware of the tensions between the educational circles in the Land and assumed that the committee chairman was trying to minimize controversy. "The Caselmann plan is apparently designed to interfere as little as possible with existing administrative and structural arrangements," he observed to Minister Bäuerle, "and to cause as little change as possible in the curriculum of the secondary school in the hope that a spirit of inner change will arise to complete the reform."[200] For the E&RA division, that approach was simply inadequate by 1948. As Banks saw the situation, "there will need to be a sharp reorganization of school structure if Germany's future educational needs are to be adequately met." Banks reaffirmed what Templeton had stated earlier: "There is no magic in the six-year *Grundschule* or in any other form of school organization, but it is our considered opinion that the six-year *Grundschule* is the needed vehicle for educational reorganization in Württemberg-Baden and elsewhere in Germany." Banks recommended a two-year transition period to achieve that change, and he reminded Bäuerle of progress elsewhere. "You are aware, of course, that despite some opposition, the six-year *Grundschule* is planned for the other Länder. Although Württemberg-Baden should not be expected to follow slavishly the practices of other Länder, a sharp departure in a fundamental feature would certainly require careful explanation." Banks also cited Alexander's December 1, 1947, memorandum to the Bavarian E&RA office and education ministry, in which he reminded them that ACA Directive 54 "specifically prohibits dual or triple-track systems."[201]

Banks conceded that in some American schools differentiation of a kind existed in the form of learning groups based on general mental ability, but he said that all pupils in those instances used the same curricula, learning materials, and teachers and that classes were of equal size. Gifted pupils received additional tasks, and the system was marked by great flexibility and easy transfer. The Caselmann proposal contrasted strongly with that system, which was not, in any event, the normal American pattern. Now the *Hauptausschuss* appeared to be advocating a sharp differentiation in the fifth year in major portions of the curriculum, such as languages, science, mathematics, and history. These accounted for three-fourths of the curriculum, and the textbooks in each instance were expected to vary considerably for the gifted pupils. "In other words," Banks wrote, "the general curriculum and its specialized arrangements for grades five to eight would be little changed from the existing practice." Admittedly, there were attractive features, such as the committee's intent to enter all pupils into the *Mittelstufe*, and the E&RA staff were impressed by the Germans' desire to produce a unified school administration up through the secondary level. But that in no way compensated for the undesirable feature, so that, if the *Hauptausschuss* persisted with its plan, Military Government would announce "disapproval of the selective principles in the *Mittelstufe* as presented by Mr. Caselmann." Banks informed Bäuerle: "We regret that there appears to be a fundamental difference of viewpoint between the head committee [*Hauptausschuss*] and U.S. Military Government."[202]

Undaunted, Caselmann submitted his plan anyway, and although the final version added more desirable features, such as easier transfer by means of examination, it still retained the four-year elementary school followed by the more highly differentiated four-year *Mittelstufe*. At this time John Steiner returned to Württemberg-Baden to replace Banks, who was rotating home for a new assignment. Steiner expressed sympathy for the education minister's difficult position: "We in Military Government are fully aware of the difficulties you are faced with in preparing a plan of school reform which will satisfy both Military Government and the Germans themselves. Not only are the economic and financial conditions a problem, but there are also the traditions of centuries, which have become a part of the popular attitude, and there is the opposition of groups and classes who fear the effects of change."[203]

By trying to minimize changes in the traditional structure, Christian Caselmann apparently fell between two stools. Among the Germans he was unable to attract converts from either traditionalists or reformers, and, despite Steiner's sympathetic stand, the Americans were not about to accept the Caselmann Plan. Harold Robinson, E&RA's vocational expert, doubted the success of the *Hauptausschuss* in insuring equal input from representatives of elementary, secondary, and vocational education groups. He maintained that the committee's primary strength resided with the secondary school faction. Therefore, the 4-4 plan aroused especially strong suspicion among elementary-school representatives. For his own reasons, Bäuerle was equally dissatisfied, and within a few weeks he, too, informed the *Hauptausschuss* that their plan was unacceptable. He expected them to return to a 6-3-3 structural plan (or 6-3-4 if they intended to resurrect the traditional thirteenth year). By this time the E&RA staff had begun to observe sharp cleavages within the ministry. "Vocational people in the ministry are very much in favor of reform," Robinson noted, "to a greater extent than we are ourselves."[204]

Bäuerle officially informed Steiner of his decision to disapprove the plan in July, 1948. Following deliberations with the Landtag's cultural-political committee and with his own ministry staff, he announced that "the eight-year *Hauptschule* has been discarded, whilst the six-year differentiated *Grundschule* has been accepted." The return to a six-year school did not mean that the Land was acceding to American demands. Rather, the Landtag committee and Bäuerle had come to the conclusion that a full plenary session of the Landtag would veto undifferentiated plans. Therefore, he hoped that, by reverting to a six-year elementary school with some differentiation, he could still pass the narrow straits between E&RA and his own traditionalists. He informed Steiner that "the fifth school year is to be regarded as an *Auslesejahr*, and the differentiation shall be carried through at Easter of each year." Furthermore, he had decided that, because the ministry anticipated greater autonomy for local school districts, the deferring of differentiation of pupils should be decided on a local-option basis.

Despite these gestures to the traditionalists, Bäuerle's optimism began to fade in the summer of 1948. Like the other Länder, Württemberg-Baden was suffering an acute financial crisis, induced in part by currency reform. The impoverished Land government was operating under alarming deficits. Just as important to the education minister were the peculiar circumstances of his rump Land. He reminded Steiner once again of "the dismemberment of our two Länder, Württemberg-Baden, and the differing school policies of the [two] occupation forces." Anything his ministry implemented now would "be subject to new review and new deliberations by the future common Landtag. This fact demands most serious consideration . . . today."[205] Steiner agreed with this assessment and reminded a group of E&CR directors, meeting in Stuttgart, "of the peculiar situation of his Land and of the possibility of the future amalgamation of the separated parts of Württemberg-Baden." The new E&CR director from OMGUS, Alonzo Grace, and John Taylor, who had returned to the zone for a quick inspection, were sobered by Steiner's remark that he did "not believe it would be wise to force ACA Directive 54 on Württemberg-Baden at this time."[206]

Events began to unfold as Steiner had feared and as Bäuerle had predicted. Public opposition gathered strength in the fall of 1948, and it was at this time that old fears about Theodor Bäuerle's lack of political strength came back to haunt the supporters of school reform. The Americans recognized clearly that Bäuerle and his staff were hardworking and utterly conscientious, "but," as one intelligence analyst stated, "none of them appears to have the burning conviction and drive that would be necessary to overcome the stubborn opposition."[207] James Wilkinson, the consul general at Stuttgart, now took stock of events. "Prospects for early passage of the proposed legislation are not bright," he conceded. Bäuerle had shifted tactics by introducing seven separate bills, including legislation for school reorganization, compulsory attendance, free textbooks and tuition, and teacher training, but not one of the bills was making any progress. Wilkinson estimated that Württemberg-Baden was running a deficit of $300,000 per day, and the bill for free tuition and books alone came to DM 19 million ($6 million), a seemingly intolerable burden. Worse, Bäuerle's relations with the Land finance minister had plummeted, with the result that the latter initially rejected all of Bäuerle's bills. A second delay occurred when Bäuerle departed for the United States for several weeks, during which time his proposed legislation remained frozen in various government committees.[207] After his return, Bäuerle expected to bypass the finance minister and appeal directly to the Land cabinet, but, as one Military Government observer noted sadly: "The cabinet will support the Finance Minister."[208] Paradoxically, this depressing situation resulted in part from a strongly worded communication by General Clay, urging the Land governments to balance their budgets in the aftermath of currency reform.[209]

As if these political woes were not enough, the E&CR staff began to find new faults in Bäuerle's latest proposals. One staff officer declared that the school bill suffered from the same problem as the October, 1947, bill: "This bill is very short and general," he complained. "Under such a measure a progressive ministry could work out an improved school system, but without forward-looking leadership the results would amount to very little."[210]

True to his word, Bäuerle had returned to the six-year elementary school with limited differentiation in the fifth year. Because of budgetary considerations the new bill omitted mention of a ninth school year, which was part of the earlier proposals. The Americans then predicted that cutting the final segment of the *Volksschule* from three years to two would make it "stand out awkwardly."[211] The bill provided for easier transfer through examination, and it encouraged the smaller villages to produce comprehensive schools. Nevertheless, continued differentiation remained a serious sticking point for the Americans. In other areas the bill showed considerable promise; it proposed curricular changes (with greater attention to social studies), improved examination regulations, health education, and much more. The ministry expected it to go into effect by September, 1949. Vague as the Americans found its structural features, they recognized that it showed some real promise, and, in contrast to other contemplated reforms, it was a concrete bill.

However, such vital fields as teacher training had not yet achieved the status of draft legislation. The diminutive Land had no less than eleven institutions for training elementary teachers, and trying to produce a bill to raise them to university status proved difficult.[212] The Americans had thought of reducing the number to three institutions in order to concentrate resources and produce higher-quality centers. Greater Hesse was an obvious model. Unfortunately, teacher-training legislation ran afoul of the dissension between the Land's polarized elementary- and secondary-school factions and so got nowhere. Other proposals—for school administration, experimental private schools, and school finances—were not yet ready for draft legislation.

Given this snail's pace, Steiner's staff was growing apprehensive at year's end and noted that "opposition to all of these measures is gradually developing, especially among the educated, among those with the 'akademische Bildung.' The opposition centers upon the six-year Grundschule but is extending to the idea of connecting secondary-school teacher training with the training of other types of teachers." Simultaneously, the Catholic Association of Karlsruhe abandoned its neutral stance and joined forces with the traditionalists against the intended reforms. A CDU women's group in Karlsruhe condemned the pending legislation as "intellectual dismantling."[213]

Looming above this battle at the end of 1948 was the impending merger of Württemberg-Baden with the adjoining French Zone territories to the south. "There is a certain degree of justification," one intelligence analyst conceded, "for delaying enactment of school reform and large-scale changes in any field immediately prior to the expected merger of Württemberg-Baden with its French-zone counterparts." Of all the occupying powers, the French had launched the strongest effort to control the German educational system. In the autumn of 1948 Steiner and several of his staff visited their French counterparts in Württemberg-Hohenzollern to see what progress the French had made. It was a sobering lesson in how much the two nations' educational policies diverged. "The American participants returned with a definite conviction that the differences between U.S. and French occupation policy on education are so great that evolution of a policy acceptable for the entire area would present serious problems," one official account warned.[214]

Undeniably, the French had placed great emphasis on closer cultural ties between France and the area of Germany they controlled. They required French as the first foreign language of all pupils. Aspirants to the university had to pass a French language examination. Every secondary school had an education officer to teach the French language and literature. The same officers doubled as community youth leaders and oversaw sports activities and cultural events. French Military Government sponsored large summer-camp programs for the young people of their zone and mingled them with French, Swiss, and other European youth on a scale that dwarfed American programs.[215] They were especially generous in their treatment of university students, whom they sent abroad in large numbers, both to France and to French-speaking Switzerland. They "reopened" the University of Mainz after a century's inactivity and structured it as they saw fit, thus neatly skirting any internal squabbles they might have encountered at the two existing universities, at Tübingen and Freiburg-im-Breisgau. Knowing the Germans to be voracious readers, the French flooded their zone with high-quality French literature, both in French and in German translation, providing generous subsidies not only for these works but for popular journals as well; they also made a special point of sending their best films to all the commercial theaters.[216]

In contrast to American reform efforts, the French programs did not attempt to alter significantly the structure of the educational systems in their zone. In fact, they felt it was in everyone's best interest to sharply limit the number of university entrants. Consequently, less than 10 percent of the school-age population entered the secondary schools in the first place. In this one point the German and French educators agreed, and so the traditional multitrack system remained in place, with the bulk of the pupils remaining in the *Volksschule* for eight years. The French Zone's school administration became highly centralized, in contrast to American efforts to give greater autonomy to *Kreis*, or local, boards.[217] The French even organized the *Abitur* examinations centrally, not wishing to leave them to the discretion of local districts or secondary schools. Concerned about overcrowding at the universities, the French used their centralized *Abitur* examinations as a tool for limiting student enrollments. For example, of 890 *Abitur* recipients in South Baden in 1947, only 147 received permission to enter the university. In the Palatinate only 87 were chosen from a total of 612 candidates. The system proved to be an effective *numerus clausus*. It also stirred strong resentment among the Germans.[218]

Aware of dissatisfaction within the teaching profession, the French directly controlled all training institutions. They established three teacher-training colleges and handpicked the faculty, student body, and curriculum. The students undertook a four-year course of studies, all of which was free. The French charged tuition and all other training expenses to occupation costs. In fact, the chief reason for the far more intensive French programs and larger staff was that they were categorized as occupation costs, to be borne by the Land population. The French also derived certain natural advantages from their common border with Germany. They had easy access to their zone and a large pool of Alsatian French, whose perfect German allowed them to communicate easily with their German opposites, often using the same or a similar dialect. The Americans and French also differed sharply in numerous minor ways. Whereas the latter were willing to give direct orders to change curricular content and to impose textbooks in sensitive areas, such as history, the Americans preferred to allow the Germans to develop their own curricula, with matching learning aids. The French used Swiss history texts and émigré works, a course of action the Americans had rejected as early as 1944. About the only area of general agreement between the Americans and the French was that both advocated free textbooks and tuition in their respective zones.[219] There was thus reason for grave concern about the problems that would arise when the two neighboring Länder were reintegrated.

The French had been signatories to ACA Directive 54 and were, theoretically, committed to the same general principles as the Americans; but, as one intelligence officer noted, the French could not be expected to accept American policy, because "it would involve their relinquishing use of the school system to disseminate French culture." On the other hand, the E&CR personnel were loath to accept French policy; they felt "it would mean discarding three years' work toward democratization of education." Even a compromise between the two starkly differing systems would place education in a reunited Land Württemberg-Baden on a different basis from the rest of the U.S. Zone. The E&CR Division could only urge support of ACA Directive 54 for all three Western zones—an unlikely development, as they well knew.[220]

Despite the undeniable energy with which the French directed education in their zone, there were growing signs by the autumn of 1948 that their efforts might come to naught as soon as occupation controls were lifted. Dorothy Barker, an American consular official in French-controlled Baden-Baden, admired the French cultural programs but reached some pessimistic conclusions about the future. She noted that the centralized *Abitur*, the *numerus clausus*, and the tightly controlled teacher-training centers were causing unexpected reactions: "The Germans attempt to boycott or circumvent them," she reported. The one attempt by the French to limit the harsher effects of differentiation to some degree (by amalgamating all secondary schools into a general *Gymnasium*) was also meeting resistance. Barker also noted that, even within the French Zone, differing educational policies from Land to Land ensured future problems. In Württemberg-Hohenzollern, for example, the electorate openly favored denominational schools, unlike the other Länder. The French were facing the same strong opposition from older educators that the American E&CR officers had encountered, with the added disadvantage that the German ministries of education in French-controlled territory were openly at odds with their French Military Government counterparts. Barker understood from French education officials that the Germans were hoping "that the occupation will be ended before any radical departures are made from the status quo." These officials also admitted that French Military Government had "not progressed any further toward realizing the objectives of Directive No. 54 in the French Zone than [the Americans had] in the American Zone."[221]

Barker's reports of growing German resistance were soon reinforced by intelligence reports of secret meetings between German education leaders in Württemberg-Hohenzollern, hosted by Education Minister Albert Sauer. The French were fearful that German conversations about a proposed education bureau in Frankfurt to coordinate meetings among Land education ministers were merely the first step toward a centralized bureaucracy to control trizonal education policy. Theodor Bäuerle had also attended the Ravensburg meeting, but, as an intelligence report from December, 1948, indicates, even he refused to discuss the proceedings in the French Zone with his American colleagues.[222] Richard Banks commented on a phenomenon he had observed in the French Zone—something that had no counterpart, as he saw it, in his own: "Stern and authoritarian as the French education officer may be, he is looked down upon by the other French for his friendliness toward the enemy." Thus, given the traditional frictions between the two peoples, the lot of the French education officer was unenviable, especially in the aftermath of a long war and the French people's bitter experiences with four years of German occupation.[223]

For the E&CR staff in Württemberg-Baden time had already run out; though technically they were still in control of the Land educational structure, they could accomplish very little. John Steiner had never used coercive powers, except in the initial emergency period—and then only for pressing technical or practical matters. He therefore took issue with Milton Muelder, deputy director of E&CR, OMGUS, when Muelder, in August 1948, proposed that they order free tuition and textbooks for Württemberg-Baden even as they were doing for Bavaria. Steiner remarked that the time for strong-arm methods was past, but "Dr. Muelder," the minutes of their meeting recorded, "stated that as of 1 September 1948 it will be increasingly difficult to accomplish anything by direct order."[224]

And so it proved. Steiner kept urging Bäuerle and his ministry to submit their draft legislation, which they did in the final winter of Military Government operations. However, Bäuerle's feud with the finance ministry continued unabated, and the bills remained frozen in the governmental machinery throughout the spring of 1949. By then the failure of the education officers and their backers to retain a control mechanism in the impending Occupation Statute made it plain that the reforms the Americans and French had worked for in such contrasting ways would come to little. In Württemberg-Baden, at least, the differing policies of the neighboring occupying powers had had a paralyzing effect on reform efforts in the twin Länder.

Other conditions peculiar to America's rump state also stymied reform. The inability of the Germans to install an education minister with political influence impaired progress, as did the polarization of the elementary and secondary teachers into two camps. E&CR had begun its campaign of public enlightenment only in the autumn of 1948—far too late to be effective. One observer noted at the time: "MG education experts are conducting forums and seminars in order to build up 'grass roots' support for reform, but at best it will take a long time for this comparatively small number of crusaders to win over enough people to swing the balance."[225]

In fact, the time for such campaigns of enlightenment was past, and Württemberg-Baden, like the other Länder, successfully delayed the American-supported reform measures until the end of Military Government operations. Finally, the Americans' observation that the Land would undergo a painful period of educational adjustment, once the artificially separated Länder were rejoined, proved entirely accurate.

Berlin

Berlin was unique in the American Occupation experience. Surrounded by the Soviet Zone and governed by an unwieldy four-power control mechanism, the once-imperial city felt the weight of military control most heavily. Even with the best will, four-power cooperation would have been difficult, and it became obvious during the Occupation that good will was a dwindling commodity among the former allies. Berlin's city government included an assembly and an executive known as the Magistrat, which operated under the control of an Allied Kommandatura, or four-power control authority. There were also specialized committees of the Kommandatura, among them a diminutive Education Committee, or AKEC, which met fortnightly and wielded overall control of educational programs in all four sectors of the city. Execution of policy was the responsibility of the Berlin *Volksbildungsamt*, or Public Education Department of the Magistrat. Subordinate to this was the *Hauptschulamt*, or Main School Office, whose head came to be recognized as a de facto deputy to the head of the *Volksbildungsamt*. In Berlin's highly political atmosphere, party affiliations played a vital role in this education administration.

United States forces were not able to enter Berlin until July 4, 1945. On their arrival, they found that the Soviets had been busy in the weeks since the armistice. The Soviet Military Administration (SMA) decided to reopen schools at the first opportunity and was busily purging teachers and administration toward that end. The usual conditions of widespread damage, shortages, and hunger abounded. Only a quarter of the city schools had escaped damage, and many of these were being requisitioned for emergency use. The Russians dismissed fifty-nine of the sixty members on the *Hauptschulamt*, retaining only Karl Sothmann, a Social Democrat. Sothmann said that most of the executives had not been active Nazis, but the Soviets viewed them as typical Prussian civil servants, who "would have been an eternal deadweight hampering any progressive ideas."[226] Another Soviet nominee, Karl Schulze of the SPD, felt that National Socialist influence still survived in the teaching ranks and that a sharp purge was imperative. The Soviets dismissed a quarter of all teaching and administrative staff members in Berlin. U.S. Military Government removed an additional six hundred teachers from its sector. Soviet desires for education controls were intense: Schulze announced plans to register all schoolchildren in order to identify former youth leaders—"not to make them suffer," he claimed, "but to enable the authorities to watch and supervise them." They hoped to alleviate the teacher shortage with anti-fascist emergency aides, who would be paired with experienced instructors.[227]

The hurried reopenings resulted in a stopgap curriculum. Administrators, instructors, and older pupils were expected to repair school buildings and to remove all National Socialist books and Nazi insignia. Others were to engage in gardening projects, to prepare for the hungry winter ahead. The youngest children organized games. No books were available, so a Russian offer of educational films seemed timely. Instruction was necessarily confined to the basics, and reading lessons could be gleaned only from newspapers or classical German literature.[228]

A triumvirate of German communists, Paul Wandel, Otto Winzer, and Ernst Wildangel, ran the *Volksbildungsamt* and *Hauptschulamt* for the first year and a half of the Occupation and continued to influence the direction of Berlin school reform thereafter. When the Kommandatura's Education Committee met for the first time, on August 13, 1945, it was faced in many respects with a *fait accompli* by the Soviet administration and the communist-led German party of the Eastern Zone: the Socialist Unity Party (SED). The Russians had already ordered the Berlin school authorities to prepare a reorganization of the city schools. At the first meeting of the AKEC the representatives announced that the Soviets' action "was approved and that such order was thereby issued by the Allied Kommandatura Education Committee." However, the AKEC membership also established that German school authorities were henceforward to submit policy decisions to the AKEC for approval rather than to the Soviets alone.[229] The initial changes were of a broad nature, based on such general directives as the Potsdam Declaration.[230]

There were other early disagreements, too, as when the Soviets took exclusive control of Humboldt University despite protests by the three Western powers. This unilateral decision ultimately led to the creation of another university, but at the time it appeared to be an isolated incident.[231] Steadily, the committee produced other agreements: expanded hot-lunch programs, a teacher-training institution, and city-wide religious instruction in the schools. By July, 1946, it had approved summer-camp programs, extra rations for children, and permission for refugee families to return to Berlin. However, the Soviets reacted suspiciously when American Army units organized youth-assistance programs in the summer of 1946. U.S. representatives to the AKEC protested, in turn, when the *Volksbildungsamt* approved trade-union and political-party involvement in adult-education programs.[232]

Despite this give-and-take, most observers conceded that, until the municipal elections of November, 1946, the Soviets held "undisputed control over the city administration, in the Education Department as well as in other branches, since all influential posts had been filled before the arrival in Berlin of the other three Allies." But the fall elections strengthened the parties of the moderate left and center. The Social Democrats, especially, had the best claim to positions of leadership, and for the first time the Soviets witnessed challenges to SED control. That trend produced a stormy relationship between the AKEC and the Berlin education agencies after the 1946 elections.[233]

Long before the November elections the Soviets and SED had produced a comprehensive school law for the Soviet Zone. It was largely the product of a Dr. Heise and a group of SED educators working in the *Zentralverwaltung für Volksbildung* in Berlin. The final draft received SMA (Soviet Military Administration) approval before being distributed to the individual Länder of the zone for formal acceptance. There were to be no private schools of any kind. The law stated unequivocally that "Education in schools is exclusively the responsibility of the state." This also implied strict separation of church and state in education, a fact that made approval by the rump CDU and LDP factions all the more remarkable and prompted an American intelligence analyst to opine: "Coercion by SED and SMA is a clear possibility."[234]

The core of the new law was its provision of "an organically composed (*organisch gegliedertes*) democratic school system—the democratic *Einheitsschule*." The plan called for an eight-year *Grundschule* with a common-core curriculum plus four more years of an *Oberschule* for the gifted, distinct from the vocational three-year branch. The SED plan of 1946 permitted some differentiation in the seventh and eighth school years for languages, science, and mathematics. All pupils would begin two foreign languages, including Russian. Significant differentiation was to take place only at the beginning of the ninth year. The *Oberschule* led to the university and permitted specialization in languages, science, and mathematics. The *Grundschule* was completely free. The *Oberschule* was also free for children whose parents earned less than 250 Reichsmarks per month. The plan appeared even to the Americans to offer equal educational opportunity for all. Nevertheless, there were some at E&RA, OMGUS, who doubted its practicality and were critical of its language-instruction features: "The Russian Zone plan of an eight-year elementary school with two foreign languages for all elementary-school children takes into account neither the lack of trained teachers nor the lack of ability of a considerable number of elementary-school children to profit by foreign-language instruction."[235]

The Soviet-SED plan also provided for a unified teacher-training program and claimed that "a teacher qualified in a specific subject will teach in the *Grundschule* as well as the *Oberschule*." The Heise plan found precedents for the *Einheitsschule* in the Thuringian Schools of the Weimar Republic days. It quickly received enthusiastic endorsement from Wildangel and Wandel in the *Volksbildungsamt* in Berlin, and they began to plan similar reforms for all city schools. Some American observers openly applauded the more visible features of the plan. "There can be no question," one analyst observed, "that the new school system offers a degree of equality of educational opportunities, at least in principle, as has not been known in Germany until now." They did note that the new curriculum, especially in history, was avowedly Marxist, but, as an intelligence report on the new law concluded, "It may be said that this machinery set in place under the new school law is technically suited to the democratization of education."[236]

By June, 1946, Ernst Wildangel, the dominant figure in the *Volksbildungsamt*, pushed energetically for identical school reforms in Berlin, but at the June 24 meeting of the AKEC the American representative, Professor Adolph Zucker, protested Wildangel's initiatives. Zucker had learned indirectly that the *Volksbildungsamt* had, with Magistrat approval, prohibited the registering of fifth-year pupils, a preliminary move to extend elementary schools to six years or more. Zucker favored this reform, but the dictatorial methods being used left him uneasy. "This constitutes putting into effect an eight-year *Einheitsschule*," Zucker announced, "and means a large reform in the school plan which has been taken without consulting the Committee." Other recent moves toward reform also had an irregular look, since the Magistrat had given only verbal orders to date. The Soviets pleaded ignorance of the entire affair. The French replied evasively, claiming that the arrangements were only a matter of "administrative expediency." However, the British member backed Zucker, and together they blocked de facto school reform.[237] At the following meeting of the AKEC, Wildangel appeared, and Zucker repeated his objections. "It is [the same as] the plan in the States," he admitted, [but the] move is . . . a very quick and drastic one here. The order of the Magistrat, preventing students from signing up for the fifth year, is too sudden." The Soviet representative, Colonel Sudakov, protested Zucker's attitude, claiming that the plan clearly gave pupils equal opportunity of education.[238] The Americans did not deny that; what they were objecting to was the high-handed administrative procedure. All members of the AKEC were quick to defend the committee's authority over the German school administration. School reform, if it came to Berlin, would require the unanimous approval of the AKEC.

The city elections in November enabled the Social Democrats to place their expert, Dr. Siegfried Nestriepke, in charge of the *Volksbildungsamt*. Thus began a struggle for control of the educational administration, which hitherto had been SED-oriented. Nestriepke, as one U.S. education officer noted, "undertook an extensive reorganization of his department, aiming at an administration which would be more efficient and more completely under his own control."[239] The new chief assumed that it was his privilege to rearrange the *Volksbildungsamt*, but by February, 1947, the Soviets mounted an intense campaign against him. The trouble had begun when he presented his reorganization plan to the AKEC and, almost as an afterthought, indicated his willingness to "accept the wishes and advice which may possibly be transmitted to me." But then he made a provocative announcement: "However, I would request you to understand my viewpoint, already expressed to you, that such changes in the administrative structure do not require the approval of the Allied Kommandatura."[240]

Nestriepke's actions ensured Soviet wrath and weakened his position with the AKEC. Thereafter the Soviets pressed continuously for his ouster, and in this they were supported to some degree by the French representative. Finally, in July, 1947, the Soviets had their way, but their luck with Nestriepke's SPD successor, Walter May, was scarcely better. For months they refused to confirm him, with the result that progress toward a school bill ceased, "because," as one American officer recorded, "the Soviet member refused to consider any documents coming in under his [May's] signature." The Soviets finally relented when May agreed to retain Wildangel as chief of the *Hauptschulamt*. Wildangel claimed the status of deputy to May, although the Western representatives on the AKEC never recognized him as such.[241]

The Cold War inevitably had an effect on the operations of the AKEC, as it did on Kommandatura activities in general. The result was spasmodic progress and frequent stalemate. In April, 1948, the AKEC agreed to ban corporal punishment in the schools and approved uniform administration of libraries and evening schools. Yet, when the committee invited Berlin's nonpolitical cultural organizations to apply for city-wide operations, the Soviets rejected all but twenty-three of the three hundred applications, claiming that fascistic elements posed too great a danger.[242]

Given the unevenness of the AKEC's success and the divisions within the *Volksbildungsamt*, it was scarcely short of miraculous that a school bill actually did emerge in Berlin. Walter May and his "deputy," Wildangel, were responsible for the draft school bill, which then became the subject of lengthy debates in the city assembly and in the Magistrat. Like the legislation passed in the Soviet Zone, to which it showed many similarities, the Berlin bill came closest to meeting the American ideals embodied in ACA Directive 54. The city assembly approved the draft on November 13, 1947, and this was followed shortly by Magistrat acceptance. Support came from the SED, SPD, and even the LDP, over the opposition of the CDU. While attractive in many ways, the draft also contained several controversial proposals, which provoked lengthy discussions in the AKEC. The bill's central feature was its provision of an eight-year elementary school, followed by two branches, for vocational and academic preparation, respectively. Like the Soviet Zone law, the Berlin bill proposed the abolition of private schools. This provision caused considerable debate between Americans and Soviets—a debate in which the British took a strong stand on the side of the Americans.

The British and American representatives viewed the closing of all private schools as unduly harsh. To eliminate all private schools was to remove any choice of education. The British objected that a completely unified system could become totalitarian. Moreover, private schools had served as pioneers of experimental education in Germany. Alone among the negotiators, the Americans spoke out in defense of denominational education. Private schools offered a choice to "parents who wish that their children should have the character-building influence of Christian or ethical teaching."[243] At first the Soviets were unmoved, claiming that private schools allowed too much individual initiative to the instructor. The French countered that tight regulations and standards imposed by the Magistrat would curb such dangers, and eventually the Soviets agreed to a British proposal to continue the operation of private schools and to make provision in the bill for "a small additional number which may be authorized in accordance with existing procedure." The number of pupils involved was in any case small. The American negotiator, John Sala, estimated that there were only 686 pupils in private schools in the American Sector out of a school-age population of 132,000. But, if the numbers were small, the principle was great, according to Sala. The Soviets finally conceded the point.[244]

Sala also sought to improve the haphazard quality of religious instruction in the city schools. Under current practice, church representatives, rather than full-time teachers, made daily rounds, offering religious instruction at odd hours of the school day. Most reports indicated that these ecclesiastical personnel were proving to be poor pedagogues. If religious instruction was to continue, Sala felt, the bill should ensure that the instructors were well qualified. On this point, however, he could gain no support from the other national representatives, despite strong appeals.

Given the tenacity of E&RA's defense of private schools and its greater emphasis on religious instruction, it was ironic for the American education staff in Berlin to receive from Francis Cardinal Spellman through Robert Murphy the urgent admonition to veto any measure that did not permit private schools. Spellman reminded the American representatives at the AKEC that passage of such a law would be "denying fundamental democratic rights." Robert Murphy assembled background information on the negotiations in order to reassure the Cardinal. He pointed out that the move to eliminate all private education in Berlin was German and had come originally from three out of four political parties in Berlin; only the CDU had supported continuation of private schools. Now Murphy could point to promising initiatives in the Kommandatura, such as a British proposal to permit private schools to continue operations and even slightly to expand their share of education in Berlin.[245] Murphy's optimism proved accurate. In mid-January, 1948, the four representatives of the AKEC resolved the problem by permitting the private schools, presently approved by the Kommandatura, to continue to operate. The Soviets even conceded the possibility of allowing a small number of additional private schools to open. This four-power understanding eliminated a major obstacle to reform.

Resolution of the outstanding problems of Berlin school reform came about in a curious way. In 1947 the chief Soviet negotiator to the AKEC was, normally, Sergei Shabalov, whom Sala and the other representatives found exceedingly combative and prone to engage in irksome debate over nonessentials. By fluke or design—no one knew which—he was absent from Berlin in December, 1947, and January, 1948, when the crucial features of the school bill received Kommandatura attention. His youthful deputy, First Lieutenant Almasov, took over the duties of senior Soviet representative, and with his arrival the Americans received a pleasant surprise. John Sala afterwards described the new atmosphere at the AKEC as follows: "The approach of all Committee members to this proposed law has been business-like in an effort to expedite it," he wrote. "This is largely due to the fact that the Soviet member has been out of town and that his deputy is a keen individual, willing to make small compromises."[246]

Sala and the E&RA Branch in Berlin were surprised to discover that the latest city proposals still contained provisions that, if unchanged, would make likely the early separation of vocationally oriented and academically oriented youngsters. Sala pointed out to the members of the AKEC and to Wildangel that approximately 8 percent of the pupils were entering the academic four-year *Oberstufe*, where they were effectively separated from the great majority in the vocational branch. However, de facto differentiation was occurring earlier. Those who hoped to enter the *Oberstufe* had to elect Latin in the seventh year, and this meant that they had to make a career decision two years before they would leave the eight-year elementary curriculum.[247] Paul Shafer, another representative on the AKEC, enthusiastically endorsed most of the bill but shared Sala's view that differentiation, as presently proposed, would limit flexibility. "Educators think it is possible to go from one track to another up to the sixth year," he informed other E&RA chiefs.[248] In effect, the small (8 percent) minority and their parents had to make their choice at the end of the sixth year.

On December 22, 1947, Sala stated to the AKEC that his main objection to the bill was "not that there should be different courses for children with various gifts, but that they should be split from each other." Subsequently he urged the committee, May, and Wildangel to reorganize the plan in such a way that the two types of education would take place under the same roof. There were certain core subjects that pupils from both branches could take together and that could be taught by a common teaching staff, assuming that vocational and academic teachers met comparable training standards. (Equality of teacher training was a sensitive issue which the Committee explored only later.)

As the lengthy meeting continued, Sala and Almasov returned to the issue of physical separation of gifted pupils from the majority. The Soviet representative questioned Sala's opinions, wondering if "the mechanical gathering under one roof would liquidate the split between the groups." The American claimed that it was German custom to "split individuals into groups which never touch each other," and he considered this type of segregation to be "very dangerous." The minutes of the meeting reveal that Almasov was listening to Sala's argument with interest: "The Soviet member found this to be a very deep question, concerned not only with the decentralization of education, but of all German life." He could not commit himself to any immediate position but gave a sympathetic hearing when Sala explained the possibilities of bringing the branches together. Sala claimed "that practically all the courses given in the *Berufsschule* are also given in the *Oberstufe*," and he didn't see why it was not possible to combine them. The E&RA representatives had spoken previously to Wildangel and other city officials about the matter. Wildangel admitted that his major problem was resistance from secondary-school teachers, who claimed that such proposals would be the death of the *Gymnasium*. He also pointed out that "there was a considerable lack of unity in the school office." However, he was willing to return to his own administration with the outline of the discussions at the AKEC, to see if they could resolve the issue.[249]

As originally proposed, Paragraph 20 of the bill would have continued the traditional separation of the vocational and academic branches because of the Germans' assumption that vast differences in preparation between teachers of practical as opposed to academic subjects would make it more or less impossible to create a common-core curriculum. Thus, the attractiveness of putting the two branches under one roof was no longer apparent. The American reaction was to encourage changes in teacher training so as to eliminate the striking differences in pay, prestige, and training between vocational and academic teachers. As J. C. Thompson, who replaced Sala, later reported, this idea impressed the Germans:

> The U.S. member's suggestion to eliminate the cleavage between the academic and practical branches, which existed after the sixth grade

even under the proposed law, caused surprise and at first suspicion to the head of the Main School Office [Wildangel] and also to the Soviet representative. The former learned to his amazement that in the United States teachers of vocational subjects were on a professional level and received the same pay as academic teachers of similar experience, and that students of the two branches held courses in common.[250]

The American proposal now received Soviet approval and acceptance by a committee of German educators. Paragraph 25 of the bill required that all teachers, regardless of their field, must show three years of "attendance at a college or a recognized teacher-training college or department." With the inclusion of Paragraph 25, the members of the AKEC returned to the original problem of separate tracking. As J. C. Thompson duly recorded, "Paragraph 20 was amended and the elimination of the traditional two-track educational system was assured."[251]

In the meantime, Professor Shabalov had returned to Berlin, and several months of intense negotiations were required to work out the final language of the bill. There was some justice in the Americans' irritation with Shabalov. For example, the provision for a few private schools in Paragraph 2 of the bill became the subject of protracted negotiations. All members agreed that private schools already licensed by the Kommandatura could continue operations, but the language for adding a few extra schools provoked endless discussion:

SOVIETS: I had in mind the change of the word "small quantity" to "limited quantity."

BRITISH: Does the Soviet Member mean he would prefer "small" to "limited"?

SOVIETS: Yes, in the same manner as was proposed the last time.

BRITISH: Yes, I don't mind. I merely changed "small" to "limited" because, while in English it makes almost no difference, the word in the English text of the minutes said "limited," that is all. But I am perfectly willing to make it "small" instead of "limited."

U.S.:   I personally have no objection to the change of wording. I imagine that a dictionary of synonyms would give "limited" as a definition for "small" or "small" for "limited." It is just a question of policy, Mr. Chairman; that is all.[252]

The AKEC finally settled on "small."

At one point the Soviets suggested resolving the private-school impasse by issuing a Kommandatura order for extra private schools, but the Americans felt that such a move was legally questionable if the proposed School Law expressly forbade private schools.[253] The Soviets finally yielded, but, in exchange, the draft law was changed to read: "The School

Authority must make provision that valuable progressive pedagogical ideas will be given a chance to stand their test in public schools." The Soviets were determined to see public schools enter the field of experimental education rather than leave this initiative solely to the private sector.[254]

The Berlin School Law went into effect on June 1, 1948. It proved to be one of the last united actions of the Kommandatura. Within days the blockade began, and the rapid dissociation of the Western sectors from the East followed. Ironically, it was the first comprehensive school bill to be passed in any territory under American administration. The bill provided many other features besides radical restructuring. Free tuition and textbooks, compulsory education to age eighteen, coeducation, and much more set it apart from the older school systems. Unlike bills being prepared in other Länder, the Berlin law also provided a set of principles and guidelines for history-teaching for grades five through twelve, a detail that reflected the political nature of school reform in the former capital.

As early as the summer of 1946, when the Magistrat and educational administration were still under strong Soviet influence, the AKEC pondered a set of directives for history instruction similar to those employed in the Soviet Zone. Wildangel and his SED colleagues in the city school administration had endorsed them enthusiastically. Since 1945 the former capital's schools had offered no history instruction whatsoever, so that all representatives on the AKEC favored a speedy resumption. However, Wildangel's proposals drew immediate fire from the American negotiators. E&RA Branch Chief J. C. Thompson commented later: "As these directives reflected a very definite and one-sided interpretation of the course and causes of history and were therefore not acceptable in the light of American policy, the American representative refused his assent to their use in Berlin."[255] Other American education officers in Berlin were even more candid. At zonal meetings of E&RA officers they dismissed the plan of the *Hauptschulamt* as being "the set-up of history instruction as it is in the Soviet Zone."[256] There followed a protracted round of negotiations within the AKEC to establish some course of action. First, the AKEC organized a History Subcommittee to establish guidelines. Then, in the spring of 1947, it established a German committee for history in the Berlin Magistrat, which operated under a mandate from the Kommandatura. However, as political tensions escalated within the Magistrat, its membership grew reluctant to issue detailed instructions for history textbooks and courses. As a result, no history instruction was possible in Berlin until the final resolution of the problem many months later—in mid-1948. In an effort to make some progress, the E&RA staff of OMG Berlin Sector provided a grant-in-aid to a commission of German historians and instructors to prepare detailed plans and textbooks. They worked within the broad framework established by the AKEC's History Subcommittee and eventually produced materials for grades five through twelve. They also produced a series of eight textbooks, which were to be published in quantity for schoolchildren in all four sectors.[257]

Progress was necessarily slow because of disagreements among the four powers on the AKEC. The Americans objected to what they saw as the Soviets' tendency "to fix the basic causes for historical change in economic factors and the control of the means of production." However, the Soviets did not torpedo the American initiative in creating a history commission composed of Germans. American financial support had allowed the German scholars valuable release time to carry out the difficult assignment of producing a curriculum that would satisfy all four occupying powers. In March, 1948, John Sala prepared to negotiate at the AKEC on the proposed reforms. He informed the deputy commandant of OMG Berlin Sector that his foremost objective now was to remind the other parties that the history project was, above all, a German project—that the financial assistance it was receiving from OMGUS was only incidental. Sala also revealed that the Military Governor himself had urged his E&CR staff to drive that point home to the city's population: "General Clay has expressed concern that the German public shall not receive the impression that the Americans are taking a direct hand in introducing their own viewpoints into German education." Earlier the Soviet representative had proposed that the AKEC itself produce the history textbooks, a move the Americans vetoed. "Needless to say," Sala continued, "this would put a policy-making body into the field of operations and is entirely impractical."[258]

Sala had a strong argument. The members of the AKEC had had enormous difficulty in agreeing on distribution of existing textbooks, much less trying to produce their own. By the end of 1946, disagreements on textbooks mounted. Paul Shafer presented the AKEC with a criticism from E&RA of a proposed text, "Du und die Welt" (You and the World). Shafer and his colleagues praised its high quality but were displeased with a chapter on the Russian Revolution of 1917. Shafer explained at length that it was not E&RA's intention to "belittle or minimize the importance of the Revolution of 1917." Their objection was that "the presentation of a division of society into classes to German children is not desirable in the American view." The Soviet representative, Colonel Sudakov, protested that the offending chapter simply described Lenin's leadership of the Revolution, with help from workers and soldiers. "If this were to be suppressed," Sudakov replied, "the facts of the French Revolution, the writings of Stendhal and Hugo, as well as any facts of American and British history could not be presented to Germans either." Shafer countered that to put all merchants in the same class and in the same bad light—which the offending text did—was to ignore the fact that the middle class had been in the vanguard of other revolutions and had benefited all members of society.[259] The discussion led nowhere, but it was at least courteous. One year later, amidst the Cold War, the atmosphere on the AKEC was entirely different.

By October, 1947, Paul Shafer had become the Soviet delegation's *bête noire*. They desired to publish six books by famous authors such as Mark Twain and Jack London, as well as speeches by Stalin. Shafer objected that the foreword to each of these books was "full of criticism and propaganda against the Western democracies" and that "the materialist philosophy of the Soviet leaders is cited as an example against the way of life of the Western democracies." The Soviets bitterly attacked Shafer, labeling his attacks an arrogant attempt to make the British and French march to his tune: "Mr. Shafer," the Soviet representative complained, "wishes to force on everyone his own way of thinking."[260] In the following March the situation deteriorated even further when the Americans discovered that a book by Ernst Hoffmann, an SED textbook-writer for the *Zentralverwaltung für Volksbildung* (Central Education Administration), was being distributed without AKEC permission. Ostensibly the volume commemorated the centenary of the German Revolution of 1848, but its foreword directly attacked the Americans, and John Sala demanded its immediate removal, plus disciplinary action against Hoffmann and the publishers.[261] The Soviets retorted that Hoffmann's foreword carried "just accusations against the American reaction, imperialists, and certain German politicians." The AKEC had, like other four-power organizations, changed from a control agency to a forum for the exchange of insults and accusations. However, the history-curriculum project was so far advanced that no nation wished to take the blame for preventing its implementation. That summer J. C. Thompson reported to his E&CR superiors: "The final program was approved by the Education Committee and sent to the Magistrat on 30 June 1948."[262]

Thus Berlin, the cockpit of the Cold War, became the one place in Germany where educational reforms achieved striking departures from past German practices. The major initiative for the reforms came from the Soviets—along with their kindred spirits, the SED—and from the Americans. Both powers were more committed to the provisions of ACA Directive 54 than either the French or the British, and in Berlin the political lines were more clearly drawn than in the other Länder of the Western zones. Thus, when the socialists, especially the Social Democrats, secured control of the Berlin government after the November, 1946, elections, it was possible for them to formulate their own reform proposals, subject only to Kommandatura review. A spirit of *vae victis* (woe to the conquered) did not fully pervade the new socialist city administration, but there was far less willingness to accommodate the views of the Christian Democrats than was the case in Bremen or Greater Hesse, where the Social Democrats also wielded considerable power. The reform process had had its moments of irony, as when the Americans vetoed an attempt by the SED-controlled *Volksbildungsamt* to issue a school reform in 1946 even though it accorded with the Americans' point of view. The same phenomenon occurred at the end of 1947, when the issue of private schools arose. The Americans, with British and French approval, argued that a "democracy recognizes not only the will of the majority, but also the rights of the minority."[263]

Yet, out of the discussions for Berlin school reform there emerged an understanding between the Americans and Soviets on several core provisions, such as minimizing the differentiation of school types, standardizing the quality and status of teacher training, and creating greater curricular flexibility for the pupils. Thus there was a certain sadness in the fact that, at the very moment when the principal actors in the Cold War were drawing apart on a wide range of issues, they could still unite over educational reform and social-studies curriculum. The passage of a Berlin School Law on June 1, 1948, and of a standardized history curriculum on June 30 occurred at the very moment when barriers were going up all around the beleaguered city.

Progress in educational reform proved not to be a harbinger of renewed understanding but a final flickering of Allied cooperation. For the Germans caught in the breakdown of the four-power machinery, confusing and dangerous times were at hand. In September, 1948, the Soviets placed a military officer and his secretary in Walter May's office in the *Volksbildungsamt*, where "they kept a close watch on May's activities and the functions of his office, asked numerous pointed questions, and concerned themselves particularly with the files of the Secretariat, the Personnel, and the Sports Sections," according to an E&CR report.[264] May complained to American authorities that his nominal deputy, Wildangel, was conspiring with the Soviets to break up the *Volksbildungsamt*. He predicted that the Magistrat would remove Wildangel and that the Soviets would suspend May in return. As another E&CR report indicated: "In anticipation of such an action, therefore, May transferred his headquarters and all important files of the Public Education Department to the British Section, and about 50 percent of the department personnel followed him." The breakup of Berlin's fragile governing machinery had begun.[265]

Passage of the Berlin School Law established no discernible trend elsewhere. Most Germans viewed events in Berlin as peculiar to that divided city. If it signified anything, the Berlin experience confirmed the truth that prior traditions of experimentation in school reform could combine with a stronger socialist representation to overpower traditionalist sentiment. The political forum in Berlin was, by any estimation, far from peaceful, and the winner imposed his principles on the loser.

Conclusion

The drift of events in the various Länder of the U.S. Zone tended to confirm the Bavarian victory in halting structural change in the summer of 1948. Differences in educational tradition and political factors unique to each Land produced a set of circumstances different from the direct confrontation in Munich, but in the end the outcome was, with the notable exception of Berlin, much the same. By 1949 most E&CR directors recognized the futility of attempting further overt changes in the structure of education. In each instance a rising tide of public opposition, led by traditionalists, swamped E&CR's campaigns of public enlightenment. There was a growing sense among German political figures that the impending formation of the Federal Republic would see them recover their cultural sovereignty, and they were right. The Occupation Statute, which was passed in May, 1949, omitted education controls. Thus, any lingering E&CR influence would have to be exercised according to the formula evolved during wartime planning: advice and assistance. There would be no executive decrees.

The cumulative effect of American efforts to change the German educational system was not as meager as the outcome of the 1947–49 debate over school structure might suggest. In Greater Hesse, Bremen, and West Berlin discussions continued over the nature and design of the school system, and experimentation, often of a high order, occurred after the Occupation ended. In the Länder with traditions of educational innovation dating back to the Kaiserreich, the American initiatives fell on more receptive ears, and the German educational community quietly continued the Americans' work after the Americans themselves had departed and political passions had cooled. Elsewhere, as in Bavaria or Baden-Württemberg, more traditional methods prevailed, and sentiment for an *Einheitsschule* was correspondingly weaker.

John Taylor had simply uttered the truth when he warned his superiors not to assume that Germany was like Japan. Far from exhibiting centralizing tendencies, the Germans tended to be suspicious of national bureaucracies after their sobering experience with National Socialism, and nowhere was the return to local authority more clearly apparent than in the field of education. It is scarcely an exaggeration to refer to a neoparticularist sentiment in the postwar period. Taylor was correct in predicting that the American education staff would have to negotiate on the Land level if there was to be any chance of success. R. T. Alexander either forgot or decided to ignore this elementary fact of German history. The need to yield to local circumstances and traditions if they expected results was already recognized in America's overall directive for Germany, JCS 1779, which became effective in July, 1947. The heightened attention paid to cultural and educational goals in the Occupation also included explicit recognition of diversity in German education. The U.S. Government, JCS 1779 proclaimed, "believes that there should be no forcible break in the cultural unity of Germany, but recognizes the spiritual value of the regional traditions of Germany and wishes to foster them."[266] R. T. Alexander was not inclined to refer to JCS 1779; he preferred to base his efforts on Clay's January 10, 1947, Directive, the MGR 8s, and ACA Directive 54.

It is scarcely surprising that the American education officers who entered their assignments with knowledge of German educational traditions, language, and history fared better than those who concentrated single-mindedly on specific models of reform. The American experience suggests that reorientation programs are highly demanding. They require personnel of the highest caliber, able to treat with local leaders diplomatically and on an equal footing. The American experience also suggests that those who want radical change—and educational restructuring *is* radical—must abandon democratic methods. Those who would cherish democracy must be prepared to jettison radical change. The education debate was also buffeted by major developments outside the field of education; the return of local political authority to the Länder in late 1946 is one example, the currency reform in June, 1948, is another. The early predictions of American policy planners that reeducation would depend on a multiplicity of factors therefore came true; for the revival of local political forums insured a collision once Alexander and Taylor convinced Clay to issue his January 10, 1947, education directives, while currency reform dealt an economic blow to structural change that its opponents quickly capitalized on in the summer of 1948. E&CR and its programs fitted only imperfectly into Military Government operations.

To the Americans' credit, they did not attempt to work secretively or to encourage enactment of reforms before the distracted German public was aware of their implications. Tempting as it must have been to avoid political controversy, the E&CR officers insisted on broad public discussion so that the reforms would have the approval of the citizenry. This decision was not only just; it was wise, as the unhappy fate of Hamburg's school law suggests. With the scales tipping perceptibly against them by the summer of 1948, the more perceptive E&CR directors began to shift the emphasis away from programs for structural alterations to programs of assistance, such as personnel exchanges, information exchange, textbook and curriculum centers, the provision of visiting experts, and other efforts to put an end to the Germans' cultural isolation. Such programs, though they had come into existence as early as 1947, had languished for lack of funds and support. But what had been at best a complementary function in America's reeducation undertakings in the first half of the Occupation began to assume major importance from 1948 onward. Although only imperfectly understood at the time, these newer programs of material assistance proved in the long run to be the most potent tools for influencing key groups within German society. With the structural debate finally settled in the traditionalists' favor, and with denazification largely if imperfectly complete by 1948, the stage was set for the great shift from overt reeducation to the subtler approach of reorientation.

From "Reeducation" to Reorientation

"Reeducation" was a word coined in wartime. It reflected the bitterness engendered by total war and was reinforced by the grim revelations of death camps in the spring of 1945. At the moment of peace no one deemed it too strong. Thus the State Department's long-range planning group was known as the Advisory Committee on German Reeducation. That title accorded well with the Allies' statements of intent at Potsdam and with Paragraph 14 of America's JCS 1067, which had called for denazification, demilitarization, and democratization of the German educational system. But when the educational system began to function again, however shakily, after the initial wave of denazification, the term began to strike many as too one-dimensional. Taylor and his E&RA staff grew less inclined to use the word and began to replace it with the gentler term "reorientation." Reorientation implied a greater emphasis on exposure to alternative systems and on material assistance. The War Department also shifted to the new term; in 1946, when it established a new unit concerned with educational reconstruction, it called it the "Reorientation Branch." Similarly, E&RA officers tended to drop *Umerziehung* from their German vocabulary, replacing it with the more positive sounding *Wiederaufbau*.

In practical terms the shift from reeducation to reorientation proved difficult to achieve. The principle of reorientation received recognition by planning groups as early as 1945, but concrete directives for cultural and educational exchanges and for extensive aid programs emerged only at the end of 1946. Worse, America's first efforts to implement such programs in the following year were largely ineffective because of insufficient funding, faulty administration, and, not least, skepticism about their value in the highest echelons of Military Government. But by the end of 1947, when the Cold War came more sharply into focus, an awareness dawned that cultural assistance and exchange programs were valuable components in the effort to achieve educational reform in Germany. New leadership arrived in Military Government, capable of mastering the complex problems involved and of mustering new resources to make reorientation rather than reeducation the keystone of the American educational effort in occupied Germany. The result was that the string of defeats and disappointments that plagued American educational personnel until the end of 1947 were, in the last years of the Occupation, increasingly replaced by successes. The decision to support the Free University in Berlin was the most dramatic example of America's role in helping to reconstruct German education. Less visible but ultimately even more influential was the blossoming of a genuine cultural-exchange program, starting in 1948, which pointed to a promising future as the Occupation ended. Despite this hopeful trend, Military Government ceased operations on a note of uncertainty in 1949, when American educational leadership launched a drive to retain a control function over German education for an indefinite period. The effort failed.

Some New Programs

The notion of altering the German educational system indirectly, through programs of assistance and exposure to alternatives, was as old as the concept of reeducation itself. In 1943 the State Department's General Advisory Committee spoke of the need for American assistance to Axis nations as part of the postwar reconstruction. They desired the reintegration of German cultural life into the Western intellectual community. When first assigned to the task of planning reeducation in January, 1945, Archibald MacLeish considered some practical means of ending the Germans' isolation: "It is assumed that an effort will be made to replace books removed by the Nazis and to make available, by acquisition or otherwise, books that will refute and counter Nazi doctrines."[1]

The State Department's Advisory Committee on German Reeducation stated, in its Long-range Policy Statement on German Reeducation, the need "to restore as soon as possible the cultural relations between Germany and other nations." The committee also proposed to "introduce an affirmative program of reorientation in harmony with democratic principles."[2]

Even the more militant private organizations concerned with educational change in Germany recognized the principle. Paul Tillich's refugee-oriented Council for a Democratic Germany concluded that "the new German education must be integrated in the framework of European and international education." Once the German educational system had reactivated "international contacts and intellectual exchange," the Council forecast that "foreign scholars will be of great value." Further, "Lecture trips and courses by individual scholars, the making available of supplies of foreign books and teaching materials, will greatly facilitate the reconstruction of German education and international understanding." The Council spoke of creating international universities, with a "resulting international exchange of students," to help dissipate lingering chauvinism.[3] There was, therefore, common agreement among public and private agencies in America that a successful reeducation program must promote the exchange of ideas, information, and persons between Germany and the United States.

During the opening phases of the Occupation, denazification and the progressive reopening of educational institutions took precedence, and little more was heard of the concept of programs of assistance and interchange until Eugene Anderson, of the State Department's Area Division for Occupied Areas (ADO), pondered the problem in April, 1946. He sent a memo to several colleagues at ADO: Henry P. Leverich, Hans Speier, and Assistant Secretary of State John Hilldring, who had recently left the War Department's CAD. Anderson posited three requisites for a successful reorientation program. First, it would need the "full cooperation and participation of expert personnel in United States schools, press, radio, and other informational and cultural institutions." Second, American experts would have to explain it face-to-face to Germans "in sufficient detail to adapt those parts useful for their own life." Third, a workable program might have to identify "certain psychological attitudes of the Germans, such as political docility and authoritarianism, which our program should aim to influence in a democratic way."[4]

Anderson's exploratory memo contemplated an involved scheme of advisory bodies and study groups of educational experts in both the United States and Germany to exchange ideas and distribute reports aimed at rectifying the Germans' national deficiencies. However, he admitted that "No blueprint for precise use in Germany can be prepared in this country." He did not feel that dispatching American experts to Germany could or should solve the entire problem: "A too rigid program might defeat its own purpose," he warned. Instead, the Americans should stock the nascent U.S. textbook and information libraries with large selections of publications. He also proposed the use of radio, press, and documentary films. "The cumulative effect," he hoped, "might be sufficient to stimulate the Germans to bring about some changes in their previous ways." He informed his colleagues at ADO, following his discussions with War Department officers, that the CAD was attempting to secure funding to send about 250 visiting experts to Germany and Austria in the next fiscal year.[5] Though somewhat rough-hewn, Anderson's proposals laid the first practical groundwork for the visiting-experts program for Germany, which made its debut in February, 1947.

Anderson also proposed to Leverich and Speier a scheme to bring German leaders and students to the United States; they would come "under the auspices of specific private institutions or organizations, which would also pay all expenses." Public funding so soon after the war might arouse public criticism in the United States. To counter this, Anderson visualized a massive undertaking, going far beyond formal education circles. The compaign to secure sponsors would encompass prominent individuals in the labor movement, press and publishing, social welfare, medicine, and religion. Private organizations like the American Friends Service Committee, church organizations, and trade unions could act as host organizations for three-month stays for German leaders and one-year visits for students. There was already a precedent, for the Federal Council of Churches had decided to invite Pastor Martin Niemoeller to America. Potential participants should be "of well-known anti-Nazi standing" in order to avert criticism or incidents. He hoped that the Occupation authorities could also streamline procedures for shipping publications to Germany by charitable organizations.[6]

Even in this exploratory stage, Anderson was encouraged to discover private groups in the United States willing to provide funds for education programs of this nature. "I am told that the Overlander Trust or the Carl Schurz Foundation has nearly $200,000 accumulated for use in cultural relations with Germany," he said. "I am fairly confident that other organizations will have funds for similar purposes." With promising private resources available, Anderson felt it would be wise to set up an official government body to coordinate the activities of government and private organizations. Anderson's twin proposals of April, 1946, represented, in rudimentary form, the Visiting Experts and Cultural Exchange programs, which eventually came into being in 1947.[7]

It was George Zook's Education Mission to Germany that gave a powerful impetus to Anderson's proposals. Anderson accompanied the Mission's ten educational leaders during their month-long inspection tour of the American Zone in the summer of 1946. His contribution to the Mission Report of October 12 centered on Point 8, "American Aid to Germany." The Report advocated the allocation of facilities, equipment, and material support to improve teaching conditions, especially at the universities, which were functioning "amidst the darkened ruins of once great cities." A chronic shortage of basic educational supplies was effectively thwarting important segments of educational programs. "Restrictions on the importation of books, paper, journals, and other instruments of culture should be modified," the Report stated. However, the Mission's major recommendation was to revive German cultural contacts abroad: "The United States has a unique opportunity to influence the fundamental reorientation of the German education program in the direction of democratic goals and procedures." Existing programs should continue, but the Mission explicitly recommended that they "be supplemented by the provision of funds for bringing carefully selected German students, leaders, and other cultural leaders to the United States for a period of training." They envisaged a coordinating body in Washington to serve as a clearinghouse and liaison for government agencies and private organizations. It would recruit Americans for cultural work in Germany and make it possible for Germans to visit the United States. The same organization might funnel privately supported cultural aid and materials to German institutions.[8]

The Mission Report buttressed the State Department's reconstructionist stance on reorientation programs, with the result that SWNCC Directive 269/8 received official acceptance on October 24, 1946, permitting the exchange of persons between Germany and the United States. Later, in July, 1947, it was modified by SWNCC 269/11 to allow exchanges between Germans in the U.S. Zone with other countries. Meanwhile, in February, 1947, SWNCC Directive 269/10 had appeared, regulating the interchange of cultural and educational materials between the two countries. All three directives echoed the original Long-Range Policy Statement for German Reeducation, and all three implied the need for administrative mechanisms along the lines discussed by Anderson and Leverich the previous spring. SWNCC 269/8 assumed that the government would have to carry the major financial and organizational burden for exchanges, "until such time . . . as the visits may be placed largely on a private basis." The leaders of industry, the professions, education, and politics who participated would require official or other recognized sponsorship and would have to demonstrate "a satisfactory record as regards past and present political activities and affiliations and must meet established security requirements." The writers of SWNCC 269/8 inserted an additional precautionary clause: "Wherever possible, preference shall be given to persons who have demonstrated their opposition to Nazism and their belief in democratic principles." The document left the dimensions of the programs fluid, "subject to the availability of educational, informational, cultural, and other facilities and budgetary resources."[9]

While he was in Germany with the Mission group, Eugene Anderson discussed all educational programs with Taylor's E&RA staff and with German educational leadership as well. Afterward he urged a much greater effort on the part of the United States government to support its education programs in the U.S. Zone. "The German people are intellectually and morally wrecked," he informed Leverich at ADO. "They are so completely defeated that it will require the widespread and vigorous assistance of the Occupying powers to revive their intellectual life sufficiently for the Germans to come back, economically as well as politically, to anything like a healthy state within a generation." Anderson discovered similar sentiments among Allied cultural experts: "The head of the French educational work in Berlin agreed . . . that far from being any kind of menace to world peace, Germany will have to be resuscitated by outside help. He said that French political leaders regarding Germany still as a powerful enemy would only need to visit the country to be cured of this illusion."[10]

Anderson regarded the absence of a male generation between the ages of twenty-five and forty-five as critical. The educational system was being run by "tired and hungry old men." This gerontocracy was especially in evidence at the universities. "The outlook for having a professorial staff of any competence five to ten years from now in all lines . . . is so bleak that outside aid in the form of exchange professors will be absolutely essential."[11]

Anderson was especially struck by the students' obsession with making a new career. They "study with an intensity which is almost frightening," he observed. "Young people, professors, teachers, officials, are eager to have American professors, teachers, and students in all fields come to Germany. . . . Time after time Germans in positions of authority told me that their universities, their teacher-training institutions, and their schools would welcome as many professors or teachers from the United States as we could send." German initiative and energy were insufficient in the present circumstances. The victorious powers held the key to recovery, through aid and exchange programs. Anderson fully endorsed the Mission's recommendation to double the permanent staff of E&RA, and he proposed anew his scheme for preparing teams of visiting experts. Furthermore, Military Government should encourage private foundations and organizations to help promote the cultural interchanges and aid in the same fashion as CRALOG (Council of Relief Agencies Licensed to Operate in Occupied Germany).

But Anderson did not as yet see encouraging signs. Not only was E&RA drastically understaffed, but the entire reorientation program was hurt by its unclear ties with the much larger ICD. Following discussions with both staffs, Anderson concluded that "the liaison between these two groups is not as close as it might be, and the work could be improved by reorganization." Neither group was willing to accept responsibility for social welfare or problems of juvenile delinquency, and frictions had arisen over such gray areas as "overt" (American-controlled) publications, audiovisual materials, U.S. Information Centers, and translations of American educational materials.[12] This indicated that philanthropic support would

not be possible without the assumption by the United States occupation authorities of a new kind of responsibility. The authorities must act as a service agency for the activities of private individuals and organizations furthering the cultural rehabilitation of Germany.

Administrative adjustments on their part will be necessary in the
United States and in the field to handle the additional responsibility.
It is believed strongly that the full and varied democratic life of the
United States can exert its influence upon the German people only
through this cooperation between governmental and private cultural
action.[13]

Despite the urgency with which the Mission urged government support,
Anderson remained skeptical about future trends. While in Germany with
the Mission he had seen the last great wave of denazification go beyond
the control of the E&RA staff. He had also witnessed the education staff's
inability to escape the call for Military Government personnel reductions
in September despite Mission Report demands for staff increases at E&RA.
He was therefore not optimistic about ambitious schemes for cultural
exchange if they required Military Government initiative. "The present
view of Military Government toward this recommendation is not known,"
he wrote to ADO. "But past experience would indicate that Military
Government may not be very cooperative."[14]

Meanwhile, in Germany, plans moved forward rapidly to boost the
American educational presence by importing American experts, who
would apply their special skills to specific problems. The Mission members
had already received enthusiastic endorsement for an experts program
from Taylor and the E&RA field staffs. Vaughn DeLong, the E&RA chief
in Hesse, had submitted his "shopping list" to Taylor by mid-September.
DeLong's staff requested eight experts initially. Their plan was to build
a pioneering research group of three experts, including specialists in educational psychology, school administration, and educational testing. Later
on, experts could offer special skills in the training of elementary and
secondary teachers, in vocational and adult education, and in student
government. He explained in detail the problems and personalities the
visitors would encounter and suggested that they have a sound knowledge
of German schools and language. "This factor is not of absolute importance," he wrote Taylor, "but it will materially affect the results which
can be accomplished." DeLong stressed the need for experts to subscribe
to a "belief in democratic education as a necessary factor for world peace."
They would not be working with E&RA staff in Hesse so much as with
German education officials, teachers, and advanced students. After examining the educational needs of the Land at first hand, the initial research
group would "recommend certain specific research projects to be set up
immediately." Following their advice, DeLong would then request a specific expert for the designated task. For example, the vocational specialist
would experience frequent contact with his German opposites and must
therefore possess an "articulate, forceful, and persuasive personality." The
student-government expert, a woman, would have to demonstrate an

"ability to catch and hold the interest of students and also to awaken a belief in and respect for student government in older teachers, who will be definitely opposed to it."[15]

Thus Taylor began to receive the detailed information needed to obtain qualified personnel for the specialized requirements of each Land. He then sent lists of needs to Reorientation Branch (R/O) at the CAD. There Edward F. D'Arms recruited experts to meet the needs outlined in Berlin. At one point, D'Arms had located some German refugees, now U.S. citizens, as potential visiting experts, but Taylor was not enthusiastic: "We take the position that similar persons could be found here and that the experts should include indigenous Americans familiar with our culture and believing in our own democratic principles."[16] But finding indigenous Americans familiar with German education proved difficult.

Other problems delayed the visiting-experts program until February, 1947. To simplify the administration of visiting experts, OMGUS and USFA (United States Forces in Austria) had requested the War Department in October, 1946, to coordinate their two programs and thus "increase the effectiveness of the project."[17] Despite Washington's acceptance of the program that autumn, USFA's requests did not arrive in Washington until January, 1947, which slowed implementation of the project by several months. Thus, the first group of education specialists—six social scientists—did not begin to arrive until February, 1947, to inspect educational facilities and programs.[18]

During a meeting in Berlin with Robert McRae of R/O, John Taylor pointed out that the visiting-experts program would place very heavy demands for translators and clerical support on his overworked staff. McRae sympathized and promised to raise the matter with the Military Governor. But Clay was not inclined to place much emphasis on the program, and he informed General Daniel Noce at CAD that he had higher priorities. "With respect to the visiting-experts program," he wrote Noce, "our failure with this program this year gives us little basis to expect much from next year." There had been some noneducational pilot projects in 1946; these had not impressed Clay, and he was now inclined to move cautiously. "We are convinced that real value will be obtained from such experts only when they become a part of our staff employed on a semi-permanent basis at the minimum."[19] E&RA's visiting-experts program was in trouble even before it began.

A typical visiting expert began his assignment by attending orientation sessions in Washington; in Berlin he received more extensive briefings at the E&RA headquarters. The largest group of experts, which arrived in the spring of 1947, was briefed by R. T. Alexander. They then left to take up their field assignments. Walter Bergman, the E&RA chief in Bavaria, received about thirty-five experts during 1947 and reported his experiences to Berlin. The new program was, he felt, a mixed success. The extensive skills and experience advocated by Anderson, Taylor, and others were not yet clearly in evidence. "No one who does not speak German should be considered for such an assignment," Bergman stated. Moreover, it was distressing to him to find that, after so much administrative effort had been expended, an individual might be available for only a few days. "Some of our greatest difficulties arose from experts whose tour of duty was very short and who came to the Land after a long orientation period at Berlin, during which they gained the impression that the plans suggested at OMGUS, often without consultation with the Land, due to the press of time, were the definitive program."[20] Tensions between Alexander and the Bavarian staff were never far below the surface.

Some experts arrived expecting cars, chauffeurs, and interpreters as well as clerical assistance. When none of these was forthcoming, they expected the hard-pressed permanent staff to take over these chores. Bergman noticed a rising tide of irritation among the regulars, who rated their own professional qualifications on a par with those of the experts. Some specialists could not resist trying to "transplant the whole American scheme of education to Germany, an obvious impossibility." Others behaved like observers rather than advisers: "A few of the experts, who had never traveled in Germany nor seen German schools, seemed more interested in gathering information and experience than in trying to be of immediate service in Germany." One case in point was a respected professor of education from Stanford University, Paul R. Hanna, who remained in Bavaria only four days to discuss his "five-year plan" with American and German staff members. "Dr. Hanna," Bergman observed, "though a very able and well-known man, did almost nothing for Bavaria. He did not understand German nor the German educational system. His plan was considered to be a stereotyped American 'scope and sequence' plan that did not face realistically the present German situation." To be sure, there were encouraging successes to record, too; Elizabeth Donovan, for example, helped organize curriculum centers in Bavaria, and Bergman strongly requested her return in 1948.[21]

An example of an expert who had arrived too late in the Occupation to be of significant aid was Walter R. Hepner, a secondary-education specialist. He helped create a demonstration school in Munich, with a comprehensive-school curriculum, but he was unprepared for the cold response he received. "Early in my work here," he told Bergman, "it became obvious that there was no immediate readiness, to put the matter mildly, on the part of the *Kultusministerium* or of the public secondary schools in Bavaria for the launching of experimental programs directed toward comprehensive-curriculum reorganization."[22]

Greater Hesse developed one of the most ambitious visiting-experts programs in the zone. The Land received approximately fifty visitors in the spring of 1947, and afterward Harry Wann wrote enthusiastically to a benefactor of the program, President E. B. Fred of the University of Wisconsin. The Wisconsin contingent figured prominently in Hesse; it included Professor Burr Phillips, Dr. Bernice Leary, and Dr. Howard Becker, who had joined the permanent staff. Phillips worked extensively with Hesse's four teacher-training colleges in establishing social-studies curricula, and Leary conducted workshops in audiovisual methods with secondary teachers. They returned to Hesse on a later occasion, and Erwin Stein thanked Phillips personally for his contributions—a striking contrast to the reception that experts like Walter Hepner received in Munich. This pattern of mixed successes and failures was repeated in the other Länder. In Württemberg-Baden the permanent staff members were as pleased with the results of expert consulting as the staff in Hesse was. Richard Banks recorded notable contributions by Dr. DeWitt Boney, who organized workshops in elementary reading materials, and by Dr. Daniel Prescott, a specialist in childhood development. This staff also thought there were "misfits" who needed to be "weeded out," but it rated the visiting-experts program "a highly successful medium for the importation of new educational thought into Germany."[23]

Bergman felt that a more effective program would result if fewer experts spent extended periods in one place instead of touring the entire zone, as they frequently did. In this he had come to a conclusion similar to the one contained in Clay's January 31, 1947, statement to Noce. The permanent staff could then plan more carefully for the specialists, who would, it was hoped, display a greater awareness of German educational systems than the first wave had in 1947. Bergman also remarked that if the prospective expert were to receive information at home, outlining his assignment and working conditions, the program would produce better results: "If this were done," Bergman concluded, "orientation of experts in Washington would not be necessary. If the visitor is to work, particularly in a single Land, as should be the case, the orientation in Berlin could be reduced to a minimum or entirely eliminated, and the reporting period at the end of the visitor's stay could also be reduced or eliminated."[24]

The visiting-experts programs provided information and advice of high quality at all levels of the German educational system. For example, a report by Raymond Paty and Donald Cottrell made valuable suggestions on ways to render assistance to the sadly run-down universities, albeit with recommendations to restructure the universities along lines similar to American institutions of higher learning. Certainly some of the experts fulfilled all that could have been asked of them. Sigmund Neumann, one of the last visiting experts to arrive under Military Government auspices in 1949, provided several excellent analyses of the status of the social sciences in the universities. In 1947 only 50 experts traveled to Germany. The total rose to 82 in 1948, to 157 in 1949, and continued to expand in the years of the High Commissioner.[25] Moreover, the Exchange of Persons Program began to send American lecturers and scholars to Germany, thus broadening the scope of the visiting-experts program.

A recurring theme in the visiting experts' numerous reports was a call for an early end to denazification in education; Paty and Cottrell, for example, expressed this very clearly in their analysis of the universities. The experts also took the position that if Americans wanted German educational leaders to understand American educational ideals, the best course would be to send Germans to the United States. Marvin S. Pittman, a teacher-training specialist and senior administrator from Georgia Teachers College in Statesboro, wrote directly to General Noce at the CAD about the need for a new policy. "The de-Nazification program is a source of much delay, uncertainty, and irritation," he claimed. "It should be finished as soon as possible, particularly for all teachers. It is now doing our cause much harm." Pittman felt that the time for telling the Germans what they must do was at an end. "For their sake and for ours, we should now send people to rebuild them in spirit and to merit and win their confidence and friendship." Presently there was constant and irksome military restriction. "This not only is the opinion of educators but also of practically all of the military governors with whom I associated," Pittman claimed.[26]

Many visiting experts and scholars were dismayed by the bureaucratic hurdles confronting them. For example, in June, 1949, an American guest professor at Heidelberg University wanted to carry on a discussion with his German colleagues and students in a public restaurant and was dumbstruck to learn that he had to get permission from Occupation authorities to do this. Robert Ittner, a senior university officer with E&CR in Stuttgart, sympathized and forwarded a request that Military Government Circular No. 55, requiring such permission, be dropped. Milton Muelder at E&CR, OMGUS, agreed, but Clay's successor, General George Hays, denied the request. The matter, the educators learned, would best be dropped until the arrival of the High Commissioner in the following autumn.[27]

The visiting-experts program, while it had its uses, was obviously an expedient. Clay had shown himself to be unenthusiastic about it from the beginning, and the results in 1947 were not wholly encouraging. Even Alois Hundhammer saw fit to comment on its mixed success. In a conversation with Louis Miniclier in the spring of 1948, Hundhammer declared his preference for sending Germans to America. "Dr. Hundhammer," Miniclier recorded, "pointed out that there would be greater gain if Germans could be sent to the United States and recommended that experts in given fields come from the United States to lecture before professional groups and at the universities." Hundhammer also observed that experts whose visits to Germany were brief "would be somewhat tempted to impose the American ideas."[28]

General Clay had offered support for cultural exchanges in his comments on the Mission Report in late September, 1946, which he addressed to General O. P. Echols at the War Department. He fully concurred with the Mission group's statement that "German students, teachers and school officials should spend a period of training in the United States," and he referred to his recent decision to allow German theology students to travel to Switzerland and Italy for study. However, he also noted the scarcity of German foreign currency exchange,[29] and he made it clear that he was not anxious to assume sizable financial responsibilities for the program at that stage in the Occupation. In a further communication to General Noce, he observed that, "while we hope to see German students and specialists visit the United States, we believe this should be financed by private aid. We feel certain that the German student sent to the United States at government expense would be less effective on his return than if his visit were financed with private funds." Clay was bracing for further food shortages and other privations during the current cold wave in 1946/47. He had to balance social against physical needs. Paper shortages would continue, he said, but "we still believe full bellies to be a first requisite to receptive minds." Clay summarized his thinking on cultural programs in 1947: "We realize that there is almost no limit to the funds which could be expended for reorientation in Germany. However, we believe that the appropriation which we have requested, in the amount of $1,025,923, . . . will give our reorientation program a status proportionate and comparable with our overall program."[30] If a program of cultural exchange was to take place, the initiative would have to come from Washington and be funded privately rather than by OMGUS.

Following the passage of SWNCC 269/8, War and State Department officials began exploring ways to secure private funding for cultural-exchange purposes. CAD officers opened talks with Laurence Duggan of the Institute of International Education (IIE), one of several private organizations capable of serving as a clearinghouse for donations, sponsorships, and coordination with German applicants. The CAD's Reorientation Branch (R/O) would act as the government agency for handling the public funds involved and for coordinating with agencies functioning in the private sector. Once the mechanism had been created, the government could officially inaugurate cultural exchanges with Germany. Subdivisions of the State Department would help the other agencies in what was called "backstopping" procedures of policy direction and technical support; for example, they could help judge the quality of candidates and sponsoring organizations. Such precautions appeared necessary following Pastor Nie-moeller's incautious remarks on nationalism during his American tour in 1947.[31]

Initially the cultural-exchange program focused on "safe" categories of Germans, such as displaced persons and others who had been actively persecuted by the Nazis; students, clergymen, and educators; and scientists who were deemed important to the needs of the War Department. Later, as funding and the general social climate improved, the program was extended to broader groups in German society.[32] There were no exact estimates of how many Germans would be able to participate. Robert McRae, of the CAD's R/O, in his discussions with E&RA in January, 1947, spoke of public funding for between 500 and 750 Germans and no ceiling on private support. Public support, he told Taylor and Alexander, would not become available until the new fiscal year, starting in June, 1947. Private groups would have to shoulder the burden until then.[33] A few days later McRae indicated to Clay that CAD officials were projecting a reorientation budget for 1948 fully three times that of 1947, and he told Clay that General Daniel Noce "anticipates some difficulty justifying the funds . . . unless he has a letter from you reiterating the necessity for the overall amount apportioned to Germany."[34] But Clay's response was the crucial January 31 communication to Noce, which in effect, since it called for no increase in reorientation funds, placed the entire burden of cultural exchange on the private sector. Finding no support from Clay, Noce refused to request the funds from Congress. Consequently, the reorientation budget for FY 1948 carried no provision for the much-desired cultural-exchange program.

Notwithstanding Clay's decision, SWNCC 269/8 was released to the public in March, 1947, announcing the institution of an exchange of persons between the United States and Germany for the first time since the war. On April 11, Laurence Duggan, at the IIE, followed up the publicity release with requests for support from scores of colleges and universities across America.[35] The initial response was heartening. Offers of aid and sponsorship poured into Washington. Duggan had learned too late about the fate of the reorientation item in the new Military Government budget.

In Germany, too, R. T. Alexander was beginning to receive inquiries from interested American organizations. He was distressed at the budget decision and replied bluntly: "This is a very definite disappointment to us, since in my opinion it will cripple our efforts to democratize German schools. However, there is nothing for us to do now but to arrange the exchange of German teachers and young students on a private basis."[36]

The hapless reorientation officers at CAD also had to mollify disappointed would-be participants. Donald B. Watt, director of the Experiment in International Living (EIL), had conferred directly with CAD about a resumption of operations by his organization. State Department officers were enthusiastic, but Daniel Noce vetoed EIL operations, saying that the first international contacts with German youth "must be prepared with the greatest of care." Watt was stung and retorted that that was precisely the kind of care his organization was prepared to offer. His request was denied.[37]

There were frequent indications of faulty coordination between Washington and Berlin in the early stages of the exchange. On March 24, 1947, Alexander contacted Edward D'Arms to say that his office, which presumably was the best-advised unit in Military Government on the exchange program, was "working under a handicap with reference to procedures of exchange students from Germany to the United States." "It seems essential," he told D'Arms, "to outline the steps the institutions at home must take in order to exchange the students." On the German side, E&RA assumed that German institutions would select their own pool of candidates. Military Government would conduct a second screening, including a final review by the OMGUS Combined Travel Security Board. However, the program still lacked guidelines, and, the heartier the German response, the greater the confusion. Alexander felt that Reorientation Branch was responsible, and in an angry letter to President Henry Hill of Peabody Teachers College he remarked: "It has been hanging fire since last summer, but some of the fat boys in Washington do not realize the speed with which time moves." Alexander rated the exchange program as potentially the most effective means of influencing the German educational system. State teachers colleges in America could sponsor German students and raise awareness at home about reorientation programs. "I would anticipate that at first the exchange would be one-sided," he continued, "but that we would look forward to exchanging materials, ideas, students, and faculty personnel in due course of time." One scheme involved the pairing of German and American institutions: "Along the same line we recently have linked up the George School in Pennsylvania with the Gertraudenschule in Berlin, the Phillips Academy with the Arndt Gymnasium, and the Groton School with the Schorndorf Schule near Munich. What I have in the back of my head is to tie up all German secondary schools that are interested with an American secondary school."[38]

Far from proposing new projects, Laurence Duggan's International Institute of Education found itself in an increasingly embarrassing position with regard to the original one. By May, 1947, numerous colleges and universities were willing to sponsor Germans, but as yet the IIE had no candidates. In June, Edgar Fisher of the IIE wrote to Secretary of War Patterson: "Two months have now elapsed since our appeal to the institutions of higher learning," he complained, "and we are under considerable embarrassment with respect to our cooperating colleges and universities, because the War Department representatives have thus far sent us no credentials of approved students." Fisher reminded Patterson that America's centers of learning were currently overcrowded and that it was unreasonable of the government to expect them to reserve places if the War Department could not deliver the foreign students.[39] General Eberle, of CAD, replied that since government funding was unavailable the War Department had been forced to appeal to "a large number of foundations, organizations, and institutions asking for funds for this program." If the appeal was successful, the exchange could proceed. However, Eberle was not optimistic: "In view of the above-mentioned financial uncertainty, the War Department has held in abeyance the matter of securing credentials for approved students. It is not deemed advisable to arouse hope in the minds of prospective candidates until training placement can be combined with provisions for transportation and maintenance."[40]

But by the end of June it was too late to warn against raising hopes. Annoyed at such vacillation, Duggan decided to present the issue to the public. At the end of May the IIE's *News Bulletin* carried Duggan's article "Are We Serious about German Reeducation?" In it he announced: "Our Government itself is unable to implement its own policy for lack of funds." Moreover, since the budget for fiscal year 1948 omitted any public support, the situation did not appear likely to improve. Duggan wanted to know whether the War Department was really interested in strengthening democratic elements in Germany. "It almost looks as though it did not put much faith in its own policy," he said. The IIE would continue to work for the exchange of Germans to America, he added, in the hope that "in the meantime the Government itself may come to realize the indispensability of providing funds to make its own policy broadly effective."[41]

Because of the confusion, only a handful of Germans were able to benefit from the exchange program in 1947. Appropriately, one of the earliest students was Benigna Goerdeler, the daughter of Karl Goerdeler, who had perished in the resistance against Hitler. A measure of the extent of the program came in an E&RA report from Bavaria summarizing the significant events for the year 1947, just completed: only one Bavarian student had managed to get to the United States.[42] Lack of government support had effectively stymied the cultural-exchange program in 1947.

From the start the cultural-exchange program had been considered a two-way street that would allow American scholars, professional and civic leaders, and students to travel to Germany. There they would lecture, mingle, observe, and provide services. In short, they would function like the visiting experts, but less formally and on a larger scale. In 1945 and 1946 Clay had categorically forbidden the admission of American students to German universities because of the catastrophic conditions in the university towns, and that ruling remained in effect until April, 1948.[43] In the absence of government funds for the cultural-exchange program, it seemed unlikely that the program would be capable of producing significant results in reverse, namely, the placing of American exchange personnel in Germany. Then in April, 1947, rumors circulated in Washington and Berlin that President Robert Hutchins of the University of Chicago was about to offer eight senior faculty en bloc to a major German university. Alexander quickly realized the implications and used Hutchins' proposal as a lever to get help elsewhere: "I regret very much that Columbia University has thus far shown little interest in our tremendous problem here," he wrote to that university's secretary, Philip Hayden, "and hope this communication may lead to some active interest on the part of the University. One large middle-western university" he added, "is contemplating assuming the sponsorship for the University of Munich." He also reported that, for the first time, Rockefeller Foundation representatives were in the U.S. Zone, appraising the possibilities.[44]

The rumors about Hutchins were well founded. On June 4 Professor Max Rheinstein of the Chicago law faculty represented Hutchins at a series of meetings with R/O Branch in Washington. Following preliminary talks, Hutchins formally proposed "to constitute at one university a special group, whose individual members would remain with the German university for one or two semesters, so that a group of eight to ten university professors would be present at the German university for a period of about three years." The eight senior professors would be "primarily from the fields of the social sciences and the humanities." Unlike the low-profile visiting experts, Chicago's visiting scholars would teach intensively and remain highly visible. "Their primary concern would be working with young Germans intending to enter on an academic career," Hutchins stated.[45]

Hutchins estimated the cost of the project at $100,000 for salaries plus another $10,000 for books, all of it to be borne by the University of Chicago and the Rockefeller Foundation. Because of the bad living conditions in Germany, Military Government would need to assist in obtaining proper food and shelter for the eight scholars: "It is understood that American scholars cannot be expected to live in Germany unless they are provided by Military Government with suitable billets and are entitled to eat either at an officer's mess or to obtain provisions from the Commissary." That system was already functioning for Military Government personnel and their dependents and for short-term specialists. Now all that was needed was assent from the War Department. "The University will make efforts to obtain the necessary funds immediately upon receiving a definite acceptance of the plan by the War Department and Military Government," Hutchins concluded. "No such efforts can be made, however, until such definitive acceptance has been received."[46]

It was a generous offer and one that promised to generate emulation in other American institutions. Colonel R. H. Chard at CAD forwarded the details to OMGUS and informed Hutchins: "It is hoped that in the near future provisions can be made whereby American citizens working in German institutions can be billeted and provided with maintenance by Military Government."[47] Privately, the CAD was worried about the technicality of commissary support and discussed the point with Alexander in Berlin. They feared that the visiting scholars would encounter ill will if they received quarters and food that were far superior to those endured by their German colleagues. A possible compromise "might be found in allowing the American professors to purchase a reasonable amount of commissaries which could be used in connection with their messing with German units or in German families."[48]

In Berlin, the negotiations encountered obstacles immediately. Professor Richard P. McKeon, a classicist and dean of humanities at Chicago, was aiding the State Department as a representative to UNESCO. McKeon was also a close friend of William Benton and was widely respected in Washington. On July 16 he flew to Berlin to discuss the Chicago project with Clay and Alexander. The E&RA chief and McKeon urged acceptance because of the useful precedent that would be established and because the project was targeted on institutions with which the Americans had achieved the least rapport. As the minutes of the meeting indicate, "It was considered that the caliber of these men and the level at which they would work would enable the intellectual presentation of the democratic tradition to be made in a more serious philosophic form than had hitherto been attempted by the United States reorientation agencies." McKeon and Alexander also pointed to French success in sending intellectual leaders to Tübingen and Freiburg, but this was a tactical error.[49]

General Clay had endured many frictions with the French occupation authorities and was not an unqualified admirer of their methods. A comparison between the French and American zones was inappropriate, he countered, and claimed that "democratization in our zone [is] many times more successful than in the French Zone." McKeon, the minutes reveal, labeled this remark a nonsequitur, and the negotiations soured. Clay rejected the Chicago plan, stating that the Americans' unwillingness to live on the German standard of living "would be considered as a form of propaganda." If he aided even eight professors, no matter how distinguished they might be, Clay felt that he would "have to extend similar facilities to every welfare organization which desired to send a staff to Germany."[50]

Alexander listened to the arguments with growing dismay. He had explored the point with German university authorities, who assured him they would "eagerly welcome this very serious offer without expecting the

American volunteers to undergo very real disadvantages." However, Clay was unmoved. The most he would offer was three-month permits, on the order of those provided for visiting experts and other short-term specialists.[51]

Consequently, no final decisions could be made. Alexander searched desperately for a solution. He contacted John A. Calhoun on Robert Murphy's staff at POLAD. Calhoun was flabbergasted. "Alexander is of the opinion," he related to his chief, Donald R. Heath, "and I agree with him, that such a decision in effect will mean no reorientation exchanges this academic year from the United States." Calhoun assumed that Murphy was informed on the matter by now. "If you and the Ambassador are in agreement, I think that the importance of getting this program under way should be stressed to General Clay. I am convinced that little can be done this year without American assistance, and the amount required would be only a drop in the bucket. To put off part of this program another year retards the implementation of an integral part of our policy for Germany."[52]

By August, 1947, time had drawn perilously short if the Chicago proposal was to materialize in the fall semester. Alexander decided to fly to Washington. Meanwhile, officials at the Pentagon were placed in the embarrassing position of having to stall Robert Hutchins. Lieutenant Colonel Ray Laux at the CAD gamely relayed a letter from OMGUS: "We are very anxious to take advantage of this very generous offer of the University of Chicago." He also confirmed Alexander's arrival in Washington on August 10 to discuss the matter with a representative from Chicago.[53] However, the meeting merely confirmed that Alexander had been unable to move Clay. He returned to Berlin empty-handed. Robert Hutchins' reactions are not recorded.

Undaunted, Robert Murphy forwarded a confidential message to Secretary of State Marshall, informing him of the impasse and pointing out that Military Government had already accorded commissary privileges to sizable official groups of Americans. "It is evident," Murphy stated, "that Chicago's proposal offers advantages to Military Government and is precisely the type of exchange envisaged by SWNCC 269/8. All expenses would be met by the University of Chicago, and no outlay of government funds would be required, while at the same time the proposal would make available to our reorientation program top-flight men from the American academic world." Although disappointed by Clay's decision, Murphy was anxious to avoid an open breach between two branches of the government. "The foregoing is for the Department's confidential information," he stated, "and not for distribution outside the Department."[54]

Ambassador Murphy was not the only party desiring confidentiality. Alexander feared that his efforts to mobilize support from POLAD would become known to Clay, causing a further deterioration in their relationship.

In relaying Alexander's communications to his colleagues at POLAD, Calhoun commented that "Alexander was hopeful of our support on this matter, but concerned that it might appear to General Clay that he had sought to bring external pressure to bear."[55]

In fact the flareup over Robert Hutchins' project was symptomatic of rising tensions between Alexander and Clay. Soon after, the crisis over Bavarian school reform erupted. There was widespread talk at OMGUS about dismissing Hundhammer then and there. Thus it came as no surprise when Martin Mayes, the acting E&RA chief in Bavaria, received a phone call from Alexander announcing Hundhammer's removal. Only the Land director could order a dismissal, but, when Mayes contacted General Muller, the Land director in Bavaria, the latter was perplexed. He had just returned from a meeting with Clay and knew of no final decision. Muller telephoned Clay only to learn that the education minister's removal was under discussion but that no final decision had been made. Alexander compounded the problem by revealing to the press the fact that Military Government was considering Hundhammer's dismissal.[56] The misunderstanding contributed to the deteriorating relations between Clay and Alexander.

Reverberations from the cancellation of the Chicago project in 1947 continued. Following protracted discussions with officials from the War and State departments and with Hutchins' representatives, Clay finally extended logistical support for the eight faculty members from three months to four. That would allow just enough time for the visiting professors to complete one semester. Their replacements could then continue the program, on a rotating basis, for the intended three years.[57] The first group of distinguished faculty arrived at Frankfurt University in April, 1948, on the hundredth anniversary of the Revolution of 1848. Robert Hutchins accompanied them and undertook an inspection of the German higher educational system. In May, during well-attended ceremonies inaugurating the Chicago-at-Frankfurt program, he offered the opinion that America's educational system was "a poor example for Germany to follow." The statement received widespread attention, especially in Bavaria. But Dean William Russell of Columbia Teachers College observed in a speech to his trustees and to the public that German education in political science, democratic government, and the theory of checks and balances was deficient. "It is unfortunately a fact," he remarked, "that this idea has never taken root among the Germans, as apparently the theory had eluded some American visitors recently in Germany," and he included an unnamed "American university president" in that category.[58]

Shortcomings also surfaced in American efforts to institute the exchange of cultural and educational materials. E&RA's earliest experiences in Germany indicated that severe shortages of reading materials were inevitable.

The lessons learned in Aachen developed on a grand scale in the U.S. Zone. The problem was born of deliberate Nazi isolationist policies, the political perversion of all conceivable literary materials, and, of course, postwar shortages affecting the publishing industry. Outside relief was impossible for a long time because the Germans lacked foreign-currency exchange. To compound the problem, the Germans were voracious readers, consuming four times as much reading matter as average American readers. Thus, the official adoption of SWNCC Directive 269/10, permitting the exchange of cultural and educational materials, in the spring of 1947 was a hopeful step in redressing a chronic problem for E&RA and ICD.

In the meantime, the E&RA staffs had done what they could with limited means. After their harrowing experiences in publishing SHAEF emergency textbooks in 1945, the education staff knew precisely the problems Germans would face in producing their own books. Official Washington had some notion of the problem, too. In late 1945, War and State department officials contemplated an attractive offer by Norbert Manes, a German-Jewish refugee in Lisbon, to publish new works, but they turned it down because of the Germans' inability to pay and because they felt German publishers should rebuild by meeting domestic demands. Taylor knew better; he reported that the few surviving German publishers had neither resources nor paper, and Consul James Wilkinson in Munich heartily agreed. In 1946, E&RA had erected nine "Curriculum and Textbook Centers" stocked with books, reference materials, office supplies, and— not least—an atmosphere conducive to writing. Later these became known as "Education Learning Centers," and their holdings were more comprehensive. Nevertheless, the bottleneck persisted. German authors were turning out valuable manuscripts, but the presses, lacking paper, were not publishing them. SWNCC 269/10 promised eventually to alleviate some of the problem by providing books and periodicals from America, but, like the exchange of experts and personnel, this program encountered start-up problems in 1947 because resources for collection and distribution were still lacking. During a staff meeting on October 8, 1947, E&RA received word that it would not get even the 3,000 tons of paper it had received the year before, despite the fact that its declared minimum was 12,000 tons. At that moment, a young woman from *Newsweek* appeared in their offices seeking information about the relative availability of Soviet and American literary works. Someone politely provided the information, and they returned to their tasks. The significance of her visit was not yet apparent.[59]

As early as May, 1947, articles had appeared in the American press describing the renascent German news media and mentioning, parenthetically, the paper shortage. Simultaneously, Henry Kellermann of ADO, who was attempting to gauge the new reorientation programs, received a visit in Washington from Werner Friedmann, a licensee for the *Süddeutsche Zeitung*. Friedmann applauded the concept of reorientation, but he asked why the Americans were damaging their own programs by withholding paper for books and periodicals. Kellermann replied that paper had no high priority in Military Government, and he suggested that Friedmann, as a participant in one of the first exchanges to America, might mention the problem in American publishing circles. Friedmann acted on this friendly advice.[60]

On October 3, 1947, the *New York Times* carried an article headlined "Soviet Papers Flood U.S. Zone." The source, Morris Ernst, of the American Civil Liberties Union, claimed that the Soviets were winning the propaganda battle because of newsprint shortages. A month later *Newsweek* followed suit, accusing the United States of starving its zone of textbooks. The Soviets and French were publishing millions of volumes. In the U.S. Zone, the article asserted, a Bavarian nun with one book was making hand-printed copies for her forty-five pupils. Results were not long in coming. On November 13, at another meeting of the Berlin E&RA staff, the minutes record that "General Clay's inquiry deals with the printing of textbooks in view of a recent article in *Newsweek*, criticizing the number of textbooks published in the U.S. Zone." E&RA prepared its reply. On December 5, 1947, the *Times* announced that Military Government was allocating $4,000,000 for paper, the bulk of which would go to textbooks. The Cold War was brewing, in which words, not bullets, would be the ammunition, and minds, not bodies, the target. The turnaround provided other practical lessons for the E&RA staff, which they were to use with good effect in 1948.[61]

Doldrums

Despite the promise of relief for the paper shortage, America's reorientation program in the winter of 1947/48 seemed moribund. The effects of denazification were still evident, especially in centers of higher learning. The Bavarian education authorities had embarked on a course of ever stiffening resistance to Alexander's reform demands. The visiting-experts program had proved to be a mixed success at best and in any case had brought only a few dozen individuals to the entire zone in 1947. Morale in all the E&RA staffs was shaky. Finally, the cultural-exchange program appeared to have met with nearly insuperable obstacles on both sides of the Atlantic, and, despite fond hopes, little progress was discernible. R. T. Alexander seemed unable to maintain an effective working relationship with Clay. It was also at this time that Henry Kellermann, of the State Department's ADO, openly expressed the fear that America was about to lose all support from the German intellectuals. There were few signs of hope in the spring of 1948 as the fourth year of the Occupation began.

It seemed improbable that an improvement in E&RA's fortunes might occur in the realm of higher education, where resistance to change was especially evident. On the elementary-secondary level, Alexander and his staff, plus several of the E&RA branch chiefs, sought desperately for a victory by securing passage of a comprehensive school bill in at least one Land in 1948. When none was forthcoming, some education officers pinned their hopes on significant changes in higher education. Yet, Military Government's relations with the universities remained at best uneasy. Despite the early reopenings of the universities and the energetic start made by E. Y. Hartshorne in forming university planning committees (UPCs) at Marburg and elsewhere, the surviving faculties were reluctant to establish new constitutions reflecting American higher-educational practices. In May, 1946, Hartshorne concluded that the UPCs were ignoring his call for draft constitutions, and he informed Minister President Geiler of Greater Hesse that "the time has come for them to perform their last act, which will be the presentation of a plan, namely, a constitution for the restoration of normal conditions."[62] Soon after this, Hartshorne received orders to report to Munich to oversee denazification operations in Bavaria, where he met his untimely death.

It was the British who had taken the lead in organizing an association of university rectors in September, 1945, but Hartshorne had been quick to follow their example with his Marburg *Hochschulgespräche*, or university conference, in June, 1946. By autumn, the university rectors in the U.S. Zone received permission to organize a conference substantially along the lines of the rectors' conference in the British Zone, and in November, 1946, they converged on Heidelberg for their first regularly constituted rectors' conference, where they discussed policy and structural changes proposed by the recent Mission Report. In this and subsequent meetings they also debated ways to modernize curriculum offerings, considered the problem of altering the social composition of student bodies to make them less exclusively middle class, and explored other ways of producing a more democratic climate in the universities. However, they refused to commit themselves to any major structural changes. No university was willing to incorporate a *Kuratorium* (board of trustees). None was willing to dilute the considerable powers of the senior faculty or to allow the existence of an independent, permanently constituted administration on the American model. Instead, they preferred to retain annually elected officers from among their own numbers, i.e., the senior faculty.[63]

Unlike the Bavarian education minister, the university rectors and other high university officials managed to avoid an open confrontation with American educational authorities on structural changes. Leaders like

Walter Hallstein of Frankfurt and Georg Hohmann of Munich enjoyed a friendlier relationship with American education officers than Alois Hundhammer did. Nonetheless, something approaching a confrontation loomed in January, 1947. Following General Clay's January 10 directive to all education ministers to submit school-reform proposals, Fritz Karsen, E&RA's chief of higher education, wrote to R. T. Alexander to propose the founding of a zone-wide commission on higher education with "the objective of assisting in the democratization of the universities." Karsen had decided, during the course of many meetings with university administration and professorial staff, that the Germans had made it evident that they were "hardly able to get rid of the fetters of cloister-like traditions." His plan was to place a broad spectrum of Germans on the commission—representatives from the trade unions, trade and industry, churches, cultural groups, and local governments. He also wished to include a leading American expert on higher education. The commission would survey the major facets of a university—its goals, services, and functions—and then submit its recommendations to Clay. Karsen was not certain what would result from this approach, and he warned Alexander not to expect blanket acceptance of the reforms proposed by Military Government or, on the contrary, a rigid resolve to maintain present university structures intact. The advantage of this approach, Karsen maintained, was that the German people would realize that "the public is called upon to have their say on the commission." Public pressure might force changes despite opposition from traditionalists among the professional ranks. He predicted that his commission approach would "be of inestimable value for Military Government to have shown its confidence in a very democratic method for reforming education." The timing of Karsen's scheme was not propitious. To assume that Military Government would bear the costs of conducting surveys, supporting a commission, and hiring American experts amidst widespread cutbacks in personnel and severe budgetary strains was not realistic.[64]

Nevertheless, the urge to achieve structural change at the universities was irresistible for some Military Government personnel. Nils J. Van Steenberg had succeeded E. Y. Hartshorne as chief of higher education in Bavaria, and in this capacity he attended a series of rectors' meetings at Heidelberg in April, 1947, followed immediately by a conference of the Länderrat on university education. He was dismayed that the American proposal for a board of trustees "was vigorously and emotionally rejected. The permanent office of a president was likewise dismissed without any consideration." Van Steenberg reported to Karsen that the rectors opposed any structural changes whatsoever. "The bellwether of the reaction was Professor Jaspers," he added, "and his speech was a defiance at Military Government to interfere in any way whatsoever with the ancient methods even by suggestion. I deem his speech impertinent." He then urged Karsen and Alexander to undertake discussions "at the highest echelons of Military Government and [reach] a clear-cut decision . . . on whether or not coercion is to be used to liberalize the universities." On this score Van Steenberg himself had no doubts: "some positive action [must] be taken by means similar to that of the T.W.X. of 10 January 1947 on the lower schools."[65]

Fritz Karsen was also displeased with resistance to university reform, but he was convinced that Van Steenberg's solution was too risky, especially considering the widening school-reform contest in Bavaria. He therefore sidestepped the suggestion to approach Clay and to Van Steenberg expressed the lame hope that, by meeting frequently with the rectors, "we may finally succeed in winning them over."[66] In the spring of 1947 the tendency was to irritate the university communities as little as possible. Thus, E&RA leadership was prepared to wink at the 10 percent ceiling on former party members among student bodies, and it finally abandoned the rule that autumn. It was also inclined to react skeptically to rumors of continuing National Socialist influence within some faculties. Karl Lowenstein had played a prominent role in initiating the denazification drive in Munich, especially in the law faculty. He continued to correspond with Taylor and Bergman about individual cases even after his return to Amherst in 1946. Thus, in May, 1947, he complained that the Munich law faculty was succumbing to renazification, and Bergman forwarded his letter to the appropriate university officer. However, J. Glenn Gray, who had taken over responsibility for Munich University from Isidore Barnett, reacted angrily. "I think he is a meddler," Gray informed Bergman. "The Law School is at present quite clean."[67] Gray refused to take further action, recognizing that the time for yet another purge was at an end.

Bergman, also, submitted a lengthy report to Alexander on the condition of the Bavarian universities in June, 1947, and he, too, urged caution. He pointed out that *anyone* who had remained in the universities after the seizure of power had "bent a knee to the Nazi regime." Some had done it more than others, and the dividing line on guilt was exceedingly difficult to draw. Though the recent purge had been drastic, Bergman revealed that there was still pressure within Military Government in Bavaria to shut the universities down completely. "Even though the measures which have been taken fall considerably short of the ultimate in stringency," he informed Alexander, "they came, as it was, perilously near to accomplishing this result." Renewed talk of drastic measures worried him greatly. The universities were the prestigious center of the educational system, and closing them "would have hindered far more than helped the general mission of Military Government." Denazification had undoubtedly been necessary. Bergman's objection was that it had been carried out on the basis of rigid categories and formulas: "In a considerable number of cases," he reported, "it was necessary to effect dismissals of persons who were not otherwise incriminated or objectionable except that they were *technically* illegally employed." Perhaps a *Fragebogen* had not been immediately available or some other piece of documentation was missing or incomplete. Such things counted little with the denazification teams, who were themselves under considerable pressure. Particularly unfortunate was the abrupt manner in which the process had been executed. Some faculty learned of their dismissal by reading about it in the newspaper. Because of the doctrinaire approach, some innocents had fallen into the net, so that the moral effect of the dismissals "was patently so false that it left a most unfortunate impression upon the minds of those who knew such persons, their reputations, and their activities." While the large majority of the removals had been appropriate, public attention had fastened unerringly on the ones in which injustices had been committed. The students, too, were irate, because the dismissals had taken effect when final examinations were scarcely a week away. What Bergman feared now was that "Military Government should be the object of deep resentment on the part of many, a resentment which in many cases may result in a more or less permanent distrust and passive resistance . . . to its policies and its mission."[68]

There was mounting evidence to corroborate Bergman's fears. In April, 1948, a major dispute erupted in Hesse when Education Minister Erwin Stein decided to name Dr. Hermann Brill, a leading Social Democrat, to the Frankfurt law faculty. The law faculty and Rector Walter Hallstein were angered by this incursion on their exclusive right to appoint senior faculty. Presumably the logical forum in which to air the grievance was the next rectors' conference, scheduled for May 20 at Schönberg, near Göttingen. This "Affair Brill" embarrassed the German academics greatly because it might serve as a textbook example of how an independent body, namely a board of trustees composed of public officials, scholars, and neutral parties, could solve a dispute without public scandal. E&RA officials had advocated such a board; German academics had rejected it as an unwanted American import that would doom the independence of the academic community. Since the rectors' conference would include high E&RA officials like Vaughn DeLong and Fritz Karsen, plus a distinguished visitor from America, Robert Hutchins, its German organizers saw to it that the regular agenda for the May 20 meeting would carry no mention of the dispute. Instead the aggrieved parties arranged a separate meeting at Schönberg. Stein and Hallstein then debated in the presence of the other rectors. No clear-cut winner emerged, but the forum expressed "hope that the . . . absolutely indispensable relationship of trust between the [Education] Ministry and the University will soon be restored."[69] Normally the rectors' conference distributed minutes of the meetings to the British and American participants as well as to the Germans, but in this instance the permanent secretary, Dr. Freytag, distributed to the rectors alone a separate set of minutes (*Sonderprotokoll*) concerning the Brill incident, "since," he admitted to a participant, "the standard proceedings will also be available to the foreigners, and it is not desirable that they should receive information on this conflict."[70] By May, 1948, the Americans had their hands full with the growing crisis in Berlin, so that, in retrospect, it is clear that the German educational authorities' anxieties were unwarranted.

The secretiveness at Schönberg was not an isolated event. Six months later the German educational leadership convened at Ravensburg, in the French Zone, under the direction of Education Minister Albert Sauer of Württemberg-Hohenzollern. His conference had no legislative powers, but it adopted twelve policy statements, including a proposal to form a standing bureau at Frankfurt to coordinate trizonal meetings of the education ministers. Another proposal was to create a charitable "emergency organization for German scholarship." The business of the meeting thus seemed hardly exceptionable. True, the French education authorities were somewhat concerned that the standing bureau in Frankfurt might evolve into a centralized educational bureaucracy like that of the Hitler days. However, the only sinister aspect of the meeting was that it took place behind closed doors and that afterwards the participants issued no communiqué. Consul General Wilkinson also took note of the Germans' secretiveness:

> Although Württemberg-Baden education officials, especially Culture Minister Bäuerle, at least ostensibly cooperate fully with E&CR, they have carefully avoided mentioning these conferences, of which Ravensburg is not the first, and have never invited MG to send observers. They have also displayed considerable reluctance to discuss them afterwards. To date, despite repeated requests, it has not been possible to secure either the official minutes of the Ravensburg Conference or informal notes on it from a W-B participant. Although the French source stated that another meeting was to take place in Stuttgart on 1 December to plan the Hamburg meeting of the larger group, E&CR has not only not been informed but has received evasive replies when the question was raised.[71]

What made the episode even more remarkable was the fact that the Americans and British were undisturbed by any of the resolutions agreed upon at the conference. "No matters of political aspect were discussed," an intelligence report stated. "Neither were matters of educational principles considered. . . . School reform was specifically not touched upon."[72] Thus, the Germans' secretiveness at Ravensburg occasioned bemused head-scratching among the Americans. In reality, it simply reflected the accumulated anxieties and uncertainties the German educational authorities had acquired earlier in the Occupation.

Another reason for the spiritual malaise at the universities was the continuing crushing poverty. All Germans shared the miseries of malnutrition, substandard housing, and general impoverishment—which, paradoxically, had finally produced a classless society. In a certain sense the Allies had sentenced all citizens to four years of hard labor on quarter rations in a prison camp called Germany. That fate simply reflected what the rest of Europe had suffered during the war, but few Germans were detached enough to recognize the parallels with the past. Bitterness was especially keen because the innocent suffered in full measure with the guilty. The students' plight, then, was scarcely unique, although they perhaps bore more hardships than other groups, except for the hapless refugees and the countless war orphans. All university towns were terribly overcrowded after the war, whether damaged or not. Consequently, student populations had to make do with deplorable living conditions. At Erlangen, which had escaped the war unscathed, the students huddled under any structure they could find, including lumber sheds and—since livestock had largely disappeared—cattle barns and pigsties.[73] In 1948 the CIC was collecting evidence about a student at Würzburg University suspected of distributing neo-Nazi propaganda. For his address, they entered the notation that the suspect was living in a hovel he had constructed against the back wall of a totally bombed-out building. They did this not to elicit sympathy for the student but to indicate an inconvenience that might hinder speedy investigation.[74] In fact, all residents of ruined university towns, like Munich or Darmstadt, had to step carefully. Even as late as 1949 an American lecturer, John Draper, noted in his concluding report that two students had just suffered serious injury from falling debris.[75] University authorities categorically refused to issue residence permits to any student living within fifty kilometers of the city; the little space available was too sorely needed by those who could not commute. Many students spent a sizable portion of their waking hours riding on overcrowded, bone-jarring public conveyances.

In November, 1946, the Pax Romana, a Swiss-based charitable organization, toured the universities of the U.S. Zone and offered their impressions to Military Government. They found the students' lot "extremely precarious, often positively disastrous, universities destroyed, scattered over different localities, overcrowded, often without libraries, laboratories, reading rooms, etc., insufficiently heated, no textbooks, or even copy books." The professors seemed uniformly old, and there were precious few of them. "Food," they reported, "in almost all the universities is quite insufficient, and, in certain cases [there is] real famine." Disease, they noted, especially tuberculosis, was "spreading to a terrifying extent." The Pax Romana wanted to begin relief operations immediately, but obtaining the necessary permits from each zonal authority required time, especially in the American Zone.[76] Organized relief efforts had begun as early as the spring of 1946 with the formation of CRALOG, which was able to alleviate some of the worst suffering. Along with the CARE program and the reopening of international mail deliveries at about same time, it seemed plausible that with time the drastic dietary deficiencies of the immediate postwar period would gradually be overcome. However, data collected on university students in Greater Hesse in July, 1947, indicated that the students' daily ration was still hovering around 1,500 calories per person. "This figure," the report added, "gives a false picture, since the normal consumer does not succeed in drawing all his food rations, and . . . the rations which are available are notably lacking in necessary food values."[77]

A year later the situation had not changed. On June 16 and 17, 1948, students massed at all of the Bavarian universities to protest their meager rations, which still did not exceed 1,550 calories per day. Carrying signs such as "Even a Dog Needs 1,700 Calories" they marched to Military Government headquarters and to German food authorities to peacefully protest their exclusion from school feeding programs. What had set off the demonstrations was the termination of the supplemental ration of 350 calories per day the students had received during the preceding winter months. Morale had risen with the expansion of the school feeding program to include universities in late 1947, but a situation report added that it was "unfortunate that the prospects for its continuation do not appear bright." The report was correct, as the demonstrations of mid-1948 proved. The students could not have known it, but they were protesting in the last month of the food crisis. By July, 1948, daily rations rose to 1,980 calories, and currency reform encouraged farmers to release their bumper harvests.[78]

By the end of 1947 there were signs that SWNCC 269/10 was beginning to have some local impact. Reports indicated that U.S. and international relief organizations had completed some projects. Typical examples included two barracks constructed for students in the ruins of Würzburg by the Swiss Red Cross at a cost of $20,000. The Würzburg University library received "a large number of books from the Smithsonian Institution in Washington, D.C."[79] As the relief agencies became more experienced, and as distribution improved, the volume of aid swelled. Public appeals for assistance from prominent American educators like Dean William Russell of Columbia, President H. L. Donovan of the University of Kentucky, and Laurence Duggan of the Institute of International Education helped generate support for aid to German educational communities. As Donovan noted: "Germany had made her contribution to American education in the nineteenth century. Would it not be a desirable thing for us in the middle of the twentieth century to make our contribution to the German educators in their hour of great need?"[80] The gathering response in the second half of 1948 and in 1949—the last year of the military phase of the Occupation—indicated that many Americans agreed with President Donovan's appeal. For example, John Park, editor of the Raleigh, North Carolina *Times*, launched a book drive that collected over a million volumes.

Yet, to many contemporary observers, the reorientation program in the U.S. Zone seemed in 1947 on the brink of disintegration. Progress toward comprehensive school reform was stalled in each of the Länder. The new aid and exchange programs were experiencing growing pains and could have little effect in the near future. The intellectuals and academics stood aloof, and physical want continued unabated. E&RA leadership was in disarray and exercised less influence with the Military Governor than at any time since beginning of the Occupation. E&RA had been discredited during the denazification drive of 1946, and the effects were still palpable a year later. Yet, in the midst of the gloom, sweeping changes in American policy were occurring that would prove the doldrums of 1947 to be only temporary.

The broad economic and social policies associated with reconstruction came into general acceptance in 1947, encouraged by the opening salvos of the Cold War. As early as 1945 Byron Price had reported on the need to adopt a reconstructionist approach. In September, 1946, Secretary of State Byrnes's Stuttgart speech held promise of redemption for Germany. Then in March, 1947, George F. Kennan floated his "Mr. X" article on Soviet containment in *Foreign Affairs* and obtained a powerful response. Reconstruction for all of Europe, including Germany, loomed following Secretary of State Marshall's Harvard address in June, 1947. Within a month the State, War, and Navy departments approved a new directive for Germany—JCS 1779—to replace the superannuated JCS 1067. The latter had instructed Military Government "to take no steps to strengthen the German economy," and paid scant attention to education. The new directive demonstrated a marked change in priorities: the Military Governor must now consider it "his fundamental task to help lay the economic and educational basis of a sound German democracy." Later paragraphs were more explicit, holding that "the reeducation of the German people is an integral part of policies intended to help develop a democratic form of government and to restore a stable and peaceful economy." The directive gave some explicit advice to General Clay: "In recognition of the fact that evil consequences to all free men flow from the suppression and corruption of truth and that education is a primary means of creating a democratic and peaceful Germany, you will continue to encourage and assist in the development of education methods, instructions, programs, and materials designed to further the creation of democratic attitudes and practices through education." Earlier, Military Government had honored JCS 1067 more in the breach than in the promise. Now JCS 1779 allowed much greater latitude for positive programs of renascence. It returned American occupation policy to the reconstructionist viewpoint espoused by the State Department, and it recognized the intimate connection among programs of cultural, economic, and social recovery. Reorientation, at the end of 1947, was not as close to the abyss as comtemporary observers supposed.[81]

Already in April, 1947, a task force of six officials from the U.S. Bureau of the Budget arrived in Germany to advise General Clay on organizational improvements for the U.S. armed forces there and secondarily to observe the OMGUS bureaucratic structure as well. This high-powered task force was headed first by Leonard W. Hoelscher and then by James L. Sundquist. After six weeks of examining the problem, they made some highly technical but orthodox recommendations for streamlining the U.S. armed forces and their command system. However, their recommendations with respect to OMGUS structure took everyone by surprise. In effect, the Bureau of the Budget task force was informing Clay that his biggest problem was a glaring weakness in the OMGUS programs of reorientation: the education staff was too small and it lacked stature compared to other functions, such as economics and finance. Moreover, Clay's present advisory staff on policy was spotty and needed broadening. "This requires a new position of adviser on education and cultural affairs," Hoelscher wrote to Clay on May 10. The task force also decided that the entire OMGUS reorientation structure needed reordering: "Those functions aimed at the reorientation of the German culture should be grouped together and given divisional status in the OMGUS organization." In this, the Bureau of the Budget was concurring with the recommendations made by John Hilldring and William Benton in February, 1946, by the Mission Report in October, 1946, and by Robert McRae of the CAD's Reorientation Branch in January, 1947. The question was whether General Clay would accept such advice. Hoelscher observed in his May 10 memorandum to Clay that to date "the organization and activities of OMGUS place heavy emphasis on economic and financial matters. These are important, and in the short run vital. But they must be supplemented by a carefully considered program to stimulate the development of a democratic culture."[82]

By late May the members of the task force were encouraged enough by the effect of their arguments on Clay and OMGUS headquarters that Hoelscher could report back to Donald C. Stone, his chief at the Bureau of the Budget in Washington, that the time for recruiting the long-sought celebrated American educationist for reorientation seemed imminent. James Sundquist also urged the Military Governor to accept an upgrading of the position to that of cultural adviser. He was fearful that unless Clay made an unequivocal commitment on the subject, Daniel Noce, at the CAD in Washington, would simply choose a replacement E&RA branch chief. Sundquist let it be known to Clay that Stone, at the Bureau, would work actively to fill the cultural-adviser slot. Sundquist was only a junior official at the Bureau at the time, but Clay was impressed with his leadership of the task force and with the preliminary reorganization plans for OMGUS and the armed forces in Germany. While the general had as yet made no definite commitment on the subject of a cultural adviser, he was more impressed by the Bureau's recommendations than anyone at that moment knew.[83]

Donald C. Stone, an influential figure in the Bureau, was keeping a close watch on developments as his agency's task force went about its work in Germany. He was delighted with Hoelscher's and Sundquist's views on reorientation and decided to send them a detailed memo outlining his own opinions on the subject, which were similar to theirs. "I did not discuss this problem with you or Larry Hoelscher before you went over," he related to Sundquist, "but it is one to which I have given considerable thought since the initial planning stages by the U.S. Group CC." Stone perceived the current problems of the Germans as engendered by an "absence of adequate moral leadership." The Americans, by imposing unconditional surrender upon their foe, had also become "custodians of the German people and their destiny." In helping them to return to the respected family of nations, the United States would have to go beyond the mere provision of "economic, fiscal, and political programs, as important as all of those approaches are."

Stone stated openly that the success of the reorientation concept depended on the ability of the Americans to influence certain German elites: "In studying the record of history, I have always been struck by the manner in which a leader or a few leaders possessed of a dynamic idea and devoted to high purposes can transform political, social, and other aspects of a whole community or country." To be sure, Germany's recent history had demonstrated the ability of an evil elite to lead an entire nation over the abyss. "We thus see that regenerating forces for good can be kindled as readily as for evil if someone will strike the match." Convinced that there is a "moral law stamped into this universe," Stone urged the American occupation forces to find a new leadership in Germany, one committed to a moral and spiritual reawakening.

> Without such an awakening which changes the lives of people, we cannot expect a new spirit of understanding, brotherhood, humility, tolerance, and honesty necessary for a stabilized society. So far we have done this in what appears to me to be a half-hearted manner, and we have failed to capitalize on many aspects of the plight of the Germans that leave them particularly susceptible to moral encouragement. . . . It is because of the importance of progress in Germany along this front that I have felt ever since the planning phases of the

Occupation that an outstanding person in charge of educational, religious, and cultural affairs should be placed at a point in the organizational structure of the U.S. operations in Germany where he will not have to battle for small matters. In the light of the administrative arrangements which General Clay is instituting, I believe, as your report suggests, that a logical and constructive solution is now available.

Stone felt that the adviser slot had to be filled and that there should be a rationalization of education and information-control functions under one full-fledged division in OMGUS. The adviser would coordinate these functions, which hitherto had been carried out separately and often without adequate coordination. "In short, he would help the Commander-in-Chief provide the leadership in this field which the world as well as U.S. citizens expect from the United States as a great democracy." Stone's lengthy memorandum ended with a strong appeal for Military Government to appoint a cultural adviser: "Such persons exist, but they are tough to get," Stone warned. "They would need a good support staff, with specialists in psychology, education, information, anthropology, religion, and administration." The moment for such action was, by June, 1947, long overdue: "All persons and groups that I know of who are interested in the German problem have regretted what they consider the low estate of the education and religious branches."[84]

Stone circulated his ideas at the Bureau of the Budget and the CAD and its Reorientation Branch. More important, James Sundquist used it in his discussions with Clay in Berlin. Sundquist's job was no easy one. All parties knew that the Bureau's task force was investigating ways to reduce OMGUS operations to a minimum. Clay had informed Sundquist repeatedly that the carpetbaggers who had infested the South after the Civil War were still remembered in his native Georgia and that he would not preside over a bureaucracy in Germany that would leave similar bitter memories. Moreover, at the very moment Sundquist and his team had arrived in Berlin that spring, Clay had announced his intention of eliminating such functions as education and religious affairs entirely. In this Clay was strongly supported by his special advisor, J. Anthony Panuch, a lawyer and one of Clay's closest confidants. State Department officers like Henry Kellermann were fearful that Panuch's viewpoint would prevail.[85]

Sundquist was prepared to endorse drastic reductions, but he requested permission from Clay to at least investigate E&RA operations before any final decisions were made. In June, 1947, he traveled to Greater Hesse to observe the work of E&RA operations there and came away so impressed with the spirit of cooperation between Germans and Americans that he was more determined than ever to rescue the reorientation programs. The fact that Erwin Stein's education ministry had begged him to continue the Americans' work made a powerful impression. It was also at this time that Sundquist showed Clay Donald C. Stone's forceful memorandum. Within weeks the magic worked. By August Sundquist could report to his chief at the Bureau in Washington: "Your memorandum to me on the cultural-affairs program has been well received here. General Clay seems to have been deeply impressed by it, and although we will probably never know just what persuaded him to make the decision, we can probably feel it would not have been taken without the influence of our study and your memorandum." By early September, 1947, Sundquist was reassured enough to inform Hoelscher that, despite widespread cutbacks in OMGUS in such functions as public health and public safety and in technical functions, such as control of airports, highways, and police, the current round of reductions would not affect education and reorientation. The reductions he had made in the other areas were sufficient to enable him to give the education staffs a sense of security for the first time since 1945 and to allow them to "make long-term constructive plans instead of anticipating manpower cuts and arbitrary abandonment of programs." Sundquist further confided to Hoelscher that the Bureau of the Budget had saved reorientation in the American zone. "It can undoubtedly take credit for getting Dr. [Herman B] Wells appointed to this position [as cultural adviser] rather than to the job of Education and Religious Affairs Branch Chief, for which he was originally slated; and it may turn out to be our most important single accomplishment."

Thus, with help from an unlikely source—namely, the Budget analysts charged with reducing OMGUS operations—the education staff acquired permission to obtain a new leader with direct access to General Clay. Moreover, the scale of their operations was no longer endangered by the periodic reductions that had repeatedly hamstrung reorientation programs in the past.[86]

Cold War U.

Amidst the interminable discussions and proposals for university reform during the Occupation, a constantly recurring phenomenon was the desire of one group or another to establish a new university or else to reconstitute an old one along new "democratic" lines. A number of schemes evolved on the subject between 1945 and 1948, but they all foundered on lack of resources.

In early summer, 1945, Dr. Robert Havemann was appointed caretaker of the Kaiser Wilhelm Gesellschaft (KWG), prewar Germany's leading research institution. Then a shudder went through Military Government when intelligence officers learned that Havemann had quietly organized a meeting of German atomic scientists in Berlin. The activity was quickly suppressed. Thereafter, reactions to the KWG were cool. Captain Samuel Shulits, at E&RA in Berlin, informed POLAD of a formal German request in August to revive the multifaceted KWG. Far from agreeing, the POLAD staff proposed that it be closed and thought it "very wise to impound all its archives in the American Sector of Berlin for a thorough examination." In May, 1946, the Americans supported ACA Directive 25 which prohibited scientific research of a war-making capability.[87]

Yet, the idea of a research university lingered on. In February, 1947, John Taylor supported the creation of a research university to Land education ministers: "We have fostered with special interest the plan of the research university in Berlin. We hope that rich institution will extend from there and will fertilize scientific life in all Germany. It is a pleasant duty to thank all in the three States [Länder] who supported so warmly this plan and arranged the means for its development."[88] Taylor's praise was perhaps extravagant. The education ministers were lukewarm at best, and the resultant Institute for Advanced Studies in Berlin limped along half-starved for the remainder of the Occupation and was quite incapable of fertilizing any scientific community. It was lucky to survive at all.

Another experimental university failed in April, 1947. Following the war, Munich was inundated by refugees and displaced persons (DPs). Because of the severe overcrowding at all German universities and because of their own insecure status, the DPs had little prospect of being admitted, and some would-be faculty and students decided to form what was called variously the UNRRA University, International University, or, more accurately, the DP University. There was no support, to put it mildly, from the Bavarian Ministry of Education, and the consensus within Military Government was that such a university would serve only the needs of refugees, who were unlikely to retain a separate identity for long. Despite public displays of their work at the Deutsches Museum, plus emotional appeals from faculty and students of the UNRRA University, Clay ordered its dissolution in April, 1947. He also ordered the German universities to absorb its students and faculty. After much grumbling and prodding, the established universities complied.[89]

The idea of an international university was too attractive to die easily. In Bremen, Harold Crabill proposed that such an institution be funded by the Bremen Merchants Guild, international philanthropic organizations, and Military Government. A quarter of the students and faculty were to be non-German, and the project's sponsors emphasized that it would have a cosmopolitan atmosphere. Its specialties were to include the social sciences, international, commercial, and maritime law, and the natural sciences. Despite its international and humanitarian outlook, the I.U. ran afoul of internal bickering within Military Government and a lack of financial support. The Bremen Senate approved the project on October 4, 1947, but Crabill and Fritz Karsen immediately clashed over its purpose. Karsen felt that international flavor was a poor substitute for orthodox curriculum offerings. Crabill complained angrily to Alexander about Karsen's stuffy conservatism, but Alexander also was unenthusiastic. In any case, funding proved to be an insuperable obstacle, and the I.U. at Bremen lay dormant for the rest of the Occupation.[90] New university projects did not fare well in 1947.

Another difficult winter passed. Then, in the spring of 1948, a seemingly trivial event occurred in Berlin. On April 16 three students were expelled from the University of Berlin because of "publication activity which acts counter to the good manners and dignity of a student." The three who were expelled—Otto Hess, Joachim Schwarz, and Otto Stolz—had entered Berlin University under provisions for anti-Nazi and Nazi-persecuted students. Hess was half-Jewish, the Nazis had branded Stolz a political undesirable, and Schwarz had been linked to Professor Kurt Huber, Hans and Sophie Scholl, and the White Rose resistance movement of students against Hitler at the University of Munich. All three expellees had been active writers in Berlin. Two were editors of a student publication, *Colloquium*, and Stolz, a prominent SPD member, had also published actively. All three were hostile to the Soviet Zone's communist SED Party and had criticized it for taking control of the zone's centers of higher learning, including Berlin University. The three were lucky in a sense because, while the expulsion terminated their chances for a higher education in Berlin, they had escaped imprisonment and punishment by Soviet occupation authorities, a fate that had befallen other students in the preceding three years. However, their educational future in Berlin was bleak. They could move to Bavaria, where no less than 700 Berlin students had already taken up their studies. Another problem was that enrollments at Berlin University had sagged from a prewar total of 12,000 to barely 6,000 in 1948. With an urban population of about three million, Berlin offered bleak prospects in higher education during the Occupation.[91]

In the Western sectors of the city educational resources were limited. The British had revived the polytechnic institute. In the American Sector the anemic Institute for Scientific Research was struggling to survive. Moreover, the attitude of American Military Government toward the students and toward Berlin University was one of deep suspicion. Troubles with the university had begun early. In August, 1945, the Allied Kommandatura Education Committee in Berlin had discussed the fate of the famed university, erected in 1810 by Wilhelm von Humboldt. The Americans, British, and French proposed to form a subcommittee to administer Berlin University's affairs. At first the Soviets were noncommittal.[92] Then, on September 6, the ranking Soviet representative, Colonel Pjartley, announced that Berlin University came under exclusive Soviet governance. Their justification was that it was an institution of the province of Brandenburg rather than a city university. Berlin University, Colonel Pjartley announced, was no longer an issue for four-power discussion.[93] E&RA's Samuel Shulits protested loudly, as did the British and French, but to no avail. On January 29, 1946, Berlin University reopened under exclusive Soviet control. E&RA officers conferred with Robert Murphy's POLAD staff. Ten elements of Berlin University were scattered through the American Sector, plus the polytechnic institute in the British Sector, they stated. The education staff recommended "that the units in the American Sector should not be turned over to the University, especially since school space is so critically needed in our Sector." POLAD agreed: "Since there is no quadripartite agreement, this matter will have to be conducted on a Sector basis."[94]

Frictions surfaced sporadically at the AKEC. The Soviets complained in early 1947 that the Americans' refusal to grant residence permits and ration cards to new students was making it impossible for them to attend the university from the American Sector. The Americans retorted that only SED students were being admitted to the university. There was much adverse publicity when the NKVD (Soviet secret police) initiated a series of student arrests. The Soviets reiterated charges of American noncooperation, citing the four-power agreements that guaranteed students free access to instruction, including permission to reside in Berlin.[95] Finally, at the end of December, 1947, E&RA Branch requested a legal opinion from the Civil Administration Branch (CAB). CAB's advice was that none of the four-power documents guaranteed a student his choice of sectors: "Legally, the position may be fought, with a certain amount of sophistry it is true, but with the maintenance of a technicality." However, Louis Glaser, chief of CAB, held strong personal views on the matter. "The University of Berlin has degenerated into nothing more or less than a hotbed of Communist indoctrination," he replied to Alexander.

> More than that, it is definitely anti-United States. Its lecturers sardonically instruct their students in the false, greedy capitalist manipulations of the United States, and the entire University is a breeding ground of hatred of the United States and of U.S. Military Government. In juxtaposition, it must be considered that there are several hundred students of the University of Berlin in the U.S. Sector at present, and with the benevolent policy of supplying them residence and ration permits in the U.S. Sector there would probably be several hundred more.

But Glaser rejected support for more students from Berlin University.

Let us by all means save what residence space we have in the U.S. Sector for people who may not be for us, but are not at least waging a battle against us. In fact, I think the United States should go farther and protest against supplying thousands of dollars worth of food to feed Soviet Zone embryo-Communist leaders who wish to fatten themselves in Berlin on American rations while they learn to hate America.

The Cold War was in full swing in Berlin.[96]

A few months later the three students were expelled, and a series of events followed that took Louis Glaser and almost everyone else by surprise. Normally, dismissals would have been preceded by a disciplinary-committee review. Such a committee would have included student participation, a traditional right of Berlin students. The university's disciplinary code still preserved that right, but Stolz, Hess, and Schwarz received no such review. As a result of the omission, the student representative to the inactive disciplinary committee resigned in protest, and the Student Council called an extraordinary session for April 20. In an effort to forestall repercussions, the chairman of the Soviet Zone *Zentralverwaltung für Volksbildung* (Ministry of Education), Professor Rompe, decided to act decisively. He announced that the disciplinary committee had declared itself incompetent to rule on the matter. He also warned the chairman of the Student Council that, if the students undertook an "injudicious action," his administration would see to it that "appropriate measures [would] be taken." Undaunted, the Student Council lodged a strong protest against the expulsions. The students called for organized protests, and on Friday, April 23, massive student demonstrations took place in the American and British sectors.[97] By this time a new note sounded in the protests. The students were calling for a transfer of the university's administration from Soviet control to the Berlin Magistrat. The Western press began to take an interest, and student governments in the three Western zones began to file petitions against the dismissals. In Berlin, however, attention had passed far beyond the original issue. The student demonstrators were now demanding a new university in the three Western sectors, free of Soviet or SED control.

By this time Rompe and the *Zentralverwaltung* were looking for ways to defuse the incident. To appease the students' anger, they called for another session of the Student Council on May 3. Rompe was barely able to defeat a strike vote, but his own resolution condemning a second university suffered overwhelming defeat. At the same time, the university's faculty senate voted, with Rompe's approval, to appoint a new disciplinary committee, which would proceed to review the three students' cases. The education ministry and university officials were still hopeful that by defusing the original incident they would derail any attempt to form a new university. A senior medical professor offered to intercede for Schwarz and Stolz at the *Zentralverwaltung* and assured them of reinstatement if they confessed that their press attacks had been unjustified. The two students refused.[98] By then their individual fates had become peripheral to the main issue anyway.

On the day following the mass demonstrations, several student leaders and a young American journalist, Kendall Foss, called on Cultural Adviser Herman Wells at his home to discuss the possibility of founding a new university. "The students," Wells recalled, "said they were being stifled by the heavy dose of communist dogma which they had to absorb at Humboldt." Soon Wells realized that they were not merely playing with an idea. The students were serious. "They proposed the idea most enthusiastically," he said, "and I promised to speak to Clay about the project directly."[99]

Herman Wells had every reason to assume that the Military Governor would not be enthusiastic. Previous university projects had failed uniformly because of poverty and general lack of support. To approach Clay now about founding a university, instantaneously and in a city where international tensions were running high, seemed almost pointless. "I was somewhat skeptical about the feasibility of the whole enterprise and told them it would be a very difficult project to initiate, but I would take it to Clay." For his part, Clay was facing disruptions of Western military traffic, which threatened to widen into a full-scale blockade of Berlin. The students could scarcely have chosen a less propitious moment. Nevertheless, Wells placed the proposal before Clay at the first opportunity. "I was actually somewhat surprised that Clay gave the project enthusiastic support and waved aside the difficulties," he recalled. "In fact, he insisted that we attempt to get the institution open by the fall quarter."[100] Educational policy had entered the international political arena again, and what had once been impossible now became imperative.

Wells appointed Kendall Foss as his special assistant and with Clay's assent formed a committee with Sector Chief Frank Howley and university officer Howard W. Johnston to undertake a feasibility study. By April 28, only five days after the demonstrations, Wells reported back to Clay. It would be possible to open a university by autumn, but Wells had some words of caution: "The new university should be a German university developed by German leadership," he warned. American support was of course indispensable, because no amount of enthusiasm could replace a sound financial underpinning. Wells recommended as the next step the creation of "a small staff of three or four men who can give their full time to the project as aides and liaison officers with a German committee and the British." Wells's immediate shopping list included dollar funds, emergency purchasing procedures, and, in view of an imminent blockade, transportation priority for scientific equipment unavailable in Berlin. Not least, the ambitious undertaking would require "full cooperation from all divisions of OMGUS."[101]

The venture entailed undoubted risks, which Wells did not try to minimize. The Soviets were certain to protest, and Berlin University would be only too ready to exploit any weaknesses in the project. "We must recognize that the competitive factors are such that whatever we do must be done well," he maintained. "This is a difficult project. It would not be attempted in the States under ideal conditions in less than two years' time." But there were certain bright spots in the otherwise gloomy picture. Other committee members pointed out that the student population at Berlin University was still less than half its prewar level: "The needs of the Berlin population are certainly not being met in point of capacity," they observed. There were still several university buildings available in the Western sectors, plus enough furniture and equipment to meet the modest needs of the faculties of social science, education, and public administration. Medicine and the natural sciences would open later. The committee voted its approval, and Clay's enthusiasm had not diminished in the least. He asked Kendall Foss to keep him informed on progress.[102]

With support from the highest quarters of Military Government, planning proceeded at top speed. On May 4 a regular committee formed under the chairmanship of Foss, who took a temporary leave of absence from journalism. Howard W. Johnston represented E&RA, Berlin Sector. Legal, Finance, Civil Administration, and Information Control divisions all sent key personnel to help devise American strategy for helping the Germans. Fritz Karsen observed the initial committee meetings in his capacity as chief of higher education for E&CR, OMGUS, although Foss was the officially designated education representative. It was a high-powered committee, designed to provide answers to complex questions with a minimum of delay.[103]

Fritz Karsen was dubious about the enterprise. Following the opening discussions, he called on Sir Robert Birley on May 5 to gauge British opinion. Karsen found that Sir Robert had misgivings about the project and reported him as saying: "We have to be clear about the political consequences of such an undertaking, which may be grave." The Americans had an obligation to provide financial and even physical security to any German associated with the undertaking. In fact, Birley "considered the matter so important that the British people should be consulted." Karsen replied that such a time-consuming procedure would let the Germans down. However, he, too, was far from feeling confident about the students' cause. In a memorandum to Alexander on May 11, he confided to the E&CR chief his fear that the entire enterprise might be only a flash in the pan.[104] With an East-West confrontation looming, the new university would only complicate matters. "The creation of a new university could only be achieved with our help," he stated. "It would be considered by the Soviets as a severe attack by the U.S." Besides, the protest demonstrations had been an ephemeral, noisy event, perhaps unrepresentative of majority student opinion. "If only 100 students and some professors had started an exodus in protest against totalitarian oppression, such action would have been much more effective than any protest meeting," he claimed. To date only three students had been dismissed, and now the Berlin University administration seemed to be making extraordinary efforts to conciliate them. The Americans would face enormous problems in trying to recruit a competent faculty, and Birley's conversation had not been reassuring. "The U.S. will stand alone with that initiative," he claimed. "I have the impression that the British are not prepared to support our venture." True, there were legitimate reasons to support the undertaking, but, on balance, Karsen, as E&CR's higher-education chief, had concluded that a second university would not succeed: "Much though I wish and have wished all along, together with you, Dr. Alexander, that a Free University should be founded in Berlin, it is my considered opinion that this is a very dangerous moment to start it and that the unjustified dismissal of three students is not sufficient justification for doing it now."[105]

As a witness to failed university projects in the past, Karsen was only being realistic. On May 11, the same day that he wrote to Alexander, the Berlin City Council empowered its Magistrat to establish a "free" university, but the decision did not represent a clear-cut victory for the protesting students. The May 11 resolution was ambiguous: it could be interpreted to mean simply freeing Berlin University from SED control rather than establishing a new university. However, the SPD-sponsored resolution was closer to the notion of a new university than its ambiguous wording implied. Few believed that the SED would voluntarily relinquish control of Berlin University. Nevertheless, while the resolution gave heart to supporters, its ambiguity reinforced the anxieties of skeptics like Karsen.[106] By mid-May two poles of opinion had begun to form in Military Government over the students' proposal.

Kendall Foss, who had chaired the special committee since its formation on May 4, also weighed the pros and cons with his colleagues, and they declared their support to a man. The members deemed it politically and morally worthwhile. Herman Wells conducted further conversations with the British, who were "showing considerably more interest than they did even a month ago." British education authorities in Berlin were reported to have "received rather urgent inquiries from their zone and to be recanvassing the possibility of action in a field where they had previously felt themselves stopped." Foss added that "there are also small signs of awakening French interest." The committee reaffirmed the principle of allowing maximum German initiative in the enterprise, and Foss assured

Clay that U.S. support "could be supplied without placing unusual or unbearable demands on the regular apparatus of Military Government."[107]

Within a few days of the special committee's report, Clay received a sharply differing opinion. Alexander and his deputy assistant, Sterling Brown, had analyzed the special committee's memorandum and found it "inadequately documented . . . vague and indefinite, leaving far too many questions entirely in the air." There was no assurance that the proposed institution could compete with Berlin University for the ablest faculty. Worse, it was Alexander's opinion that "there has been no strong and determined demand on the part of the Germans that such an institution be established." The timing of the venture was, they concluded, "politically unwise."[108] Fritz Karsen's imprint was clearly in evidence too. He had undertaken a twelve-day fact-finding trip through the U.S. Zone and had made an appeal for the project to the zone's financial committee, or *Stiftungsrat*. However, that body had concluded that "the finances of the Länder would not be able to assume this responsibility." Discouraged, Karsen then queried faculty and students at the other universities, and they gave him "the impression that there was no enthusiasm, to say the least, for such a foundation."[109]

Professor Alexander had reasons of his own for opposing the new university. By May, 1948, there was considerable speculation that control of education would revert entirely to the Germans in the impending fiscal year—an idea that he condemned emphatically. As he said to William Russell, "It will be a tragic mistake to turn back to the Germans complete direction of their schools and cultural development at this time."[110] He remained pessimistic about the prospects for a genuinely free university and relayed his misgivings to Clay: "Open-minded and truly democratic professors, as required for a new university, are almost completely lacking." In sum, Alexander concluded that "this is a very dangerous moment for such a venture, and the unjust dismissal of three students does not present sufficient justification for taking such a step."[111]

Tension had also arisen among Military Government officials from the moment that Kendall Foss had formed his special committee. Under normal circumstances and following orthodox bureaucratic procedure, Herman Wells should have appointed Fritz Karsen, his leading expert in higher education at E&CR, OMGUS, to head the special committee charged with aiding the Germans in the creation of a new university. Karsen was an ex-Berliner and, since becoming a naturalized American citizen, had spent two years with Military Government in Berlin. However, the founding of a second university under the current hectic conditions required faith plus a large dose of idealism—traits that were conspicuously absent when Karsen had vigorously opposed Harold Crabill's idea of creating an international university in Bremen. Wells chose Kendall Foss, an unknown, to chair the special committee, much to Karsen's annoyance. At an early date, as the special committee was being organized, Foss and Karsen discussed its future composition. Karsen was not pleased, and he reported to Alexander that "I pointed out immediately that our Branch was apparently not represented on that preparatory committee." Foss replied that, as a special assistant to Wells, he fulfilled that function. Nevertheless, when Foss said that he hoped Karsen would continue to contribute his expertise to the project, Karsen informed the youthful Foss that he had just obtained orders from his superiors at E&CR Division (Alexander and the E&CR liaison officer, Colonel Emil Lenzner) not to have anything further to do with the special committee. "Mr. Foss became greatly excited," Karsen related to Alexander, "[He] said that he did not believe me, that I lied, whereupon I interrupted the conversation immediately."[112] Later Foss apologized, but he and Karsen continued to differ over the feasibility of a new university.

Alexander, also, felt upstaged. He had been concerned with the improvement of Berlin higher education ever since 1945. As one briefing report indicated, German dissatisfaction over the Soviet's unilateral actions in Berlin was not new:

> In 1945 many outstanding professors organized under the leadership of Professor Eduard Spranger and appealed to the American Military Government for help in reopening Berlin University in the American Sector in Dahlem rather than in their former building on Unter den Linden in the Soviet Sector. The Americans refused to help because assistance in such an undertaking at that time could have been considered unjustified unilateral action.[113]

Instead, it was the Soviets who had taken the initiative, despite Western protests. Quietly, Alexander and his staff had at that time begun to study the possibilities of a new institution outside the Soviet Sector. As he related to Clay: "This office has favored the founding of a university in the U.S. Sector of Berlin for more than two years. At first no tensions existed, and a slowly growing university would have met little furious political opposition." Now the only basis on which he could justify such an undertaking was that "the Germans—students and citizenship—in Berlin demand it and demonstrate that students from the Western Sectors are no longer admitted to the University of Berlin and can no longer remain there."[114]

By early June the momentum for a new university began to make Alexander's fears and qualifications irrelevant. Seven prominent political and academic leaders, including Ernst Reuter and Edwin Redslob, called on sixty distinguished citizens to convene on June 19 and lay the groundwork for a new university, to be called the Free University (FU). Simultaneously, Professor Carl J. Friedrich, who was assisting Robert Murphy, wrote to

Clay concerning the project. Friedrich was disturbed by Alexander's resistance, and after conversations with Wells he decided to offer his own assessment. As he saw the situation now, Alexander's evaluation was simply "out of date." Wilhelm Kaisen in Bremen had recently announced wholehearted support for the FU. Widespread appeals for financial and material assistance were meeting with increasing success. Whereas Alexander's report had called for more careful study of the situation, Friedrich disagreed, calling it "an academic viewpoint which overlooks the importance of timing . . . ; the memorandum fails to point out just what such study would produce in the way of further information or insight." Friedrich had seen lists of prospective faculty prepared by Edwin Redslob. It was "impressive," he assured Clay. The Germans connected with the project were showing tremendous resolve: "It is my feeling that there could not be a more determined demand on the part of Germans for the establishment of such an institution than the strong and explicit statements on the part of the governmental authorities involved. . . . There is also vigorous and insistent interest of the students." The final decision now lay with Clay, but Friedrich advised that "the support of Military Government should be generous and not hampered by an inquiry at every point as to whether the Germans had done all they could."[115]

Clay needed no prodding. The day on which the committee of Germans began planning the FU was also the day for converting to the new currency. The solid Deutschmark (DM) was about to replace the worthless Reichsmark (RM) at the ratio of 1:10 for all private citizens. Any Reichsmark accounts still being held by Military Government after June 19 would simply be canceled. Without revealing the fact, Clay, on the advice of Walter Heller in the Financial Adviser's Office, had removed RM 20 million from surplus funds in the Military Government Reorientation Account and deposited it with a German trustee. Thus, on June 19 the FU had a nest egg of DM 2 million, although none of the members of the hardworking planning committee was as yet aware of that fact.[116] At that moment they were meeting in a clubhouse in Wannsee. Foss described the proceedings: "There were no allied nationals present, no allied statements read, no allied promises made. It was a purely German display of initiative and—in Saturday's tumultuous atmosphere of currency reform, closing frontiers, and Russian threats—courage."[117]

The German committee drafted a manifesto and a university constitution and mapped out mechanical procedures needed to call the Free University into existence. One member, Frau Professor Else Knake, delayed the issuing of the manifesto until July 24 because she thought the committee should first secure two things: the approval of the commanders of the three Western sectors and the services of a famed academic leader as rector. By July 23, patience with Knake's caution snapped, and the committee issued the appeal without her assent and without the father figure she felt was necessary.[118] The three sector chiefs cheered the manifesto immediately. Clay replied to Ernst Reuter: "I shall watch its growth with keen interest, and I shall be glad to help in any way possible. The objective it seeks deserves the sympathetic consideration of all who believe in academic freedom."[119]

From the first, the Germans who formed the new university were unlike any founding committee in German history. They included students, politicians, journalists, and businessmen and, significantly, a minority of academic leaders. Their manifesto of July 23 was signed not only by distinguished leaders like Reuter and Redslob but also by one of the original protesters, Otto Hess, and another student, Hans Ringmann. It was indicative of the conditions under which the Berliners were living at the time that Military Government received an anonymous tip that four of the ten signers of the manifesto were living in dire poverty. The informant urged Military Government to provide them with food and some modest financial support, since the four in question were too proud ever to ask for assistance.[120] The FU was beginning on a shoestring.

Within days the German founders established an office in a house in Dahlem that the OMGUS Finance Division had just evacuated. "Student volunteers began dragging bits of furniture from every part of the city with which to equip the offices," Foss recorded. "Firms, individuals, and German municipal offices started making gifts. Prospective professors and instructors began making inquiries."[121] It was, in fact, becoming a people's university, and there was almost a carnival atmosphere when hundreds of curious onlookers converged on Dahlem. Finally, on September 22, the founders solved the problem of securing legal recognition by appealing to the Magistrat for "administrative approval" to operate as a "corporation under public law." This approach avoided any legislative decision, which would surely have drawn a Soviet veto. Of 5,000 students who applied for admission, the new institution had room for only 2,200. The distinguished historian Friedrich Meinecke agreed to transfer from Berlin University to become the new rector, despite his advanced years. While Meinecke's transfer was being effected, Edwin Redslob accepted an interim rectorship with the expectation that he would later become Meinecke's deputy. The majority of the faculty who answered the call came from the Soviet Zone rather than from the West, where politically unencumbered faculty were still in sharp demand.[122]

A gratifying aspect of the whole enterprise was the FU's democratic constitution, which included a board of trustees and prominent student participation in governance. Robert Murphy reported enthusiastically to Secretary of State Marshall: "The Free University is among the most democratically organized higher institutions in Europe, and certain of its principles may well serve as a guide to other universities in Germany. Of particular interest is the fact that it incorporates a concept heretofore generally rejected by German academicians, namely, student membership in the Senate (governing body) of the institution."[123] The innovation was fair and just, for students had provided the initiative for the Free University in the first place.

Murphy also requested the State Department to "familiarize interested university and educational associations and organizations in the United States with the history of this development, particularly with a view to arousing interest and support for the . . . university in America's academic circles."[124] General Clay's original donation of DM 2 million had been a powerful tonic, but it would last only through the first year. Profits from American-controlled publications in Germany were also expected to help but would never suffice alone. Additional aid would have to come from the growing exchange programs, as Murphy had said, plus Military Government support. In the meantime, public and private groups funneled aid into the fledgling university. In the autumn of 1948 OMGUS provided several buildings and opened its 100,000 volume library to students. A million volumes were in storage at Marburg, but because of the blockade they would have to remain there until some future date. Meanwhile, an energetic library committee scoured the city, seeking access to private collections and to official and semiofficial libraries. By opening day the students had the use of 350,000 books—a tremendous feat.[125]

The ceaseless search for books sometimes produced surprises. In mid-October a truck rolled up to an FU building and the driver unloaded 600 valuable medical books, only to disappear before the university authorities could thank him or learn the name of the benefactor. Soon gratitude turned to suspicion: was the FU the recipient of stolen books? University authorities impounded them while Howard W. Johnston requested an investigation by Military Government. It was a wise precaution. Public Safety Branch reported back: "Our investigation has revealed, among other facts, that these books are Polish property. It has further been determined that these books were definitely in the possession of Soviet military authorities in Berlin for an extended period of time after the German capitulation."[126] The Cold War had entered the unlikely arena of academic philanthropy.

Shortly before his departure from Berlin in November, Kendall Foss submitted a final report to Clay on the new university. He referred to it as a newborn infant: "somewhat scrawny . . . it will need careful feeding, but it is alive and it plainly means to stay alive."[127] The spirit of the enterprise profoundly affected those who had participated. "This summer has been something of a cosmic symphony here," Foss observed to Wells. "The birth of the university is just one part of a mighty movement, underscored by the constant drone of the planes and the periodic publication of angry international notes."[128]

The founding of the Free University was the watershed that divided reeducation from reorientation in America's educational programs in Germany. It was a project initiated by the Germans that from first to last exhibited admirable democratic features. Yet the word democracy was seldom employed. The Americans' role was limited to supplying additional resources, cooperation, and abundant good will. It was completely clear that the prime actors were Germans: first the students, then the professional and political circles, and, finally, the West Berliners as a whole.

The founding of the FU underlined the increasing alienation of R. T. Alexander from the new trends in educational policy. In June, 1948, when the call for a new university went out, he issued a lengthy complaint to Dean Russell about the current situation. With "Trizonia" complete and a national constitution in the offing, Alexander was uncertain about the future role of American educational efforts in Germany. "I do not know what provision the German constitution will contain with reference to the field of education," he told Russell,

> but I have very great anxiety that the Germans will be granted their *Kulturhoheit.* . . . The great mass of Germans has learned nothing from the war as yet, and, the more readily they acquire economic security, the more certain they are to take the same pattern as before. It is ridiculous to think that in three years' time we can make over the thinking of a nation that is so badly infected with arrogant nationalism as Germany was. If you have a chance to see President Truman again, I hope you will make this clear to him, because I think it will be too late to do anything about it by the time we have a Republican president.[129]

The events in Berlin that summer were as perplexing to Alexander as the American presidential race was unpredictable. Clay's compromise agreement with Ehard on Bavarian school reform clearly signaled the end of overt attempts to restructure the German schools. Alexander's lack of belief in the Berliners' ability to found and staff a second university with a democratic stamp was completely confounded by events. He departed from Military Government in September, 1948.

The Flowering of Exchange

The success of the Free University was in many ways a victory for Herman Wells's reorientation approach to the programs in Germany. Wells had paid greater attention to the cultural-exchange and aid programs, which had come into existence after 1946 but had been stymied by lack of funds and by organizational difficulties. In the half-year that he served as Cultural Adviser to General Clay, Wells moved far in clearing away those obstacles and paving the way for the blossoming of American reorientation programs in later years. His influence carried directly into the last year of Military Government and into the HICOG era of the early 1950s. Moreover, his chosen successor, Alonzo Grace, continued most of the programs his predecessor had initiated.

Herman B Wells had long been considered a likely candidate to head the education program. In 1945 his name appeared frequently on State Department recruiting lists. He possessed considerable banking experience and had used his fund-raising skills to good effect in elevating Indiana University to the status of a nationally respected institution. During the war he served the State Department as Deputy Director of Liberated Areas. A State Department memorandum at that time rated him as an "excellent personality and an effective worker."[130] However, Wells, like Frank Graham, Edmund Day, and other educational leaders, had already performed lengthy war service, and his board of trustees at Indiana was anxious for his immediate return. It was a familiar story in 1945.

However, when the second search began in January, 1947, for a successor to John Taylor, recruiting difficulties were exacerbated by widespread knowledge of E&RA's shortcomings. Robert McRae's warning that the E&RA's low status would hamper recruiting proved accurate. Clay approached Wells again, and, when Taylor returned to the United States he urged Wells to take the difficult assignment. At about the same time, the Bureau of the Budget task force in Germany and Donald C. Stone in Washington launched their appeal for a cultural adviser, with Wells as the likeliest candidate. Wells flew to Germany in July, 1947, to meet Clay and to observe E&RA operations. Clay was impressed and asked Wells to take the position. But Indiana's trustees first had to agree. Clay immediately contacted the CAD, asking that Secretary of War Patterson write directly to the Indiana board. "Do your best on this one," he pleaded, "as I am impressed with Wells as the man for the job."[131] Clay also appealed directly to Judge Ora Wildermuth, chairman of the Indiana board, and to Indiana Governor Ralph E. Gates. Education was vital to the success of the Occupation, he asserted, indicating that Wells would be fighting communism as well.[132] Significantly, Clay named Wells as Cultural Adviser rather than E&RA chief. The Indiana trustees gave their assent.

Herman Wells saw that his first need was to confer with Washington officials. Donald C. Stone of the Bureau of the Budget discussed future plans with him and forwarded the fruits of their discussion to James Sundquist, Clay's new control officer at OMGUS. They agreed that America needed to approach reorientation from "a broader basis rather than identifying it segmentally, as is done now with the terms 'educational, religious, and information control.' " Future efforts should be "concerned with mobilizing many approaches and techniques in the field of human relationships, which need to be woven into all of our occupation efforts in order that the greatest impact from the standpoint of democratic ideology and stimulation will be brought to bear on the German people." Hitherto, American efforts had tended to be doctrinaire; in the future, the Occupation authorities should "eliminate as far as possible the checking and reviewing approach to German activity." The main thrust should instead be to find "sound leadership and democratic movements in all phases of German life" and to give them "maximum encouragement and material support." Thus, the conclusions Wells and Stone now arrived at were very similar to the ones the policy-planners had come to back in 1942. Implicit in their conclusions was a repudiation of the confrontations presently raging over school reform throughout the U.S. Zone. Wells also found a receptive audience among State Department officials. Kellermann had prepared a summary of the organizational weaknesses that had surfaced in the current exchange program, embodied in SWNCC 269/8: poor coordination among State, Army, and Military Government, excessive dependence on private donations, and lack of effective ways to stimulate donors and to implement exchanges. If the program was to work, Clay must be willing to request appropriations from Congress as part of the Military Government budget.[133]

In his earliest discussions with Clay, Herman Wells had found him reluctant to place much confidence in an exchange program, especially for students. Wells, who had great faith in its possibilities, queried Clay more closely on the matter. "His first reaction," Wells recalled, "was that the students would be received with hostility on the American campus. I told him I thought otherwise, and he finally agreed and told me if I could get the money appropriated he would support the project."[134] Wells was a great fund-raiser (his board of trustees had granted him leave of absence only on condition that he first secure a multimillion-dollar bond issue). From the first he set to work to galvanize private resources, which could be used as a lever for more public funds. With Clay no longer hostile to the project, the raising of the necessary resources seemed less formidable. Wells explored the idea while he was in Washington, found warm support at the American Council on Education, and proposed a future meeting of American university officials in Washington. "This we were able to do," Wells stated, "with the help of a couple of hundred American organizations interested in resuming relations with Germany. Representatives of these organizations were called together at my request by the American Council on Education, and we were able to get the exchange launched successfully."[135] The meeting took place in February, 1948. By then Wells was already in Berlin.

Information control, the fine and performing arts, and many other functions were also his responsibility, but Wells considered the educational
program his immediate functional problem, arriving as he did in the midst
of the Bavarian school-reform crisis. As he stated later: "I devoted most
of my time to education because Clay recruited me particularly to try to
bring some order out of the chaos which he then thought was present in
the organization of the education branch."[136] Wells found that the rumors
of disarray were true. "There was considerable dissension in the branch,"
he recalled. "There was a difference of opinion on the part of the people
in the education division as to what our policies should be, and the administrative structure seemed to be having difficulty functioning."[137]

Wells worked energetically to rectify the organizational deficiencies that
had hampered E&RA's operations for so long. In March, 1948, it achieved
division status, and for the first time a Cultural Exchange Branch took its
place alongside Education Branch. The new administrative unit was re-
named Education and Cultural Relations Division, indicating the shift in
priorities. The changes were much needed. Evidence from memoranda
and staff meetings held during the last months of the old E&RA Branch
pointed to continuing and embarrassing confusion in the exchange program. Students were clearing all the logistical hurdles to enter Brown,
Smith, and other premier institutions in the fall semester, 1947, only to
be halted when the necessary documentation failed to arrive on time.[138]
In December, Alexander complained to his recently retired deputy, Levi
Gresh, about administrative uncertainties and the powerlessness of E&RA
to create order.

> It is quite apparent that we cannot handle the matter here since we
> have no control over the funds and no direct contact with the insti-
> tutions concerned, and can have no contacts except through Wash-
> ington. Our offices are willing to assist in any way we can within
> reason. The SOP [Standard Operating Procedure] on the exchange
> limits our activities to selection and approval and rendering whatever
> assistance we can to the person in question to the port of embarkation,
> which doesn't mean very much, since most any German knows how
> to get on a train and ride to the point of departure.[139]

Within weeks Wells began to sort out the muddled program. Following
his discussions with Washington officials, he developed a structure that
would go into effect in the course of 1948. In January, in Berlin, he
convened a meeting of the education officers who would administer the
exchange program and outlined to them the major features of his plan.
Besides the governmental unit, which would be centered in the CAD's
Reorientation Branch, there would be support from State Department
subgroups; these would aid in so-called "backstopping" functions, in-

cluding security clearances and general policy direction. Wells's major innovation was the creation of a nongovernmental board, made up of distinguished volunteers and supporting staff; this group would organize a series of panels whose members possessed expertise in the areas of basic Military Government functions, such as legal and manpower problems, civil affairs, information control, and the like. Each panel would include civilian experts competent to judge the qualifications of candidates being considered for the exchange program. Wells expected to rely in part on the experience and support of other private foundations in the same fields, such as the Rockefeller and Guggenheim foundations. With new-found cooperation from Military Government, Wells expected to streamline the cultural-exchange program on both sides of the Atlantic.[140]

In April field branches for cultural exchange began to function in each Land. Until then, Germans desiring to travel abroad had had to apply for a Temporary Travel Document and a Military Exit Permit. At that stage such requests passed through successive bureaucratic layers—Public Safety, CIC, and finally the Combined Travel Board—and the process normally took nine months. Beginning in June, 1948, Germans who had received acceptances could submit their letters of sponsorship directly to the Cultural Exchange Branch, which then forwarded them to the Travel Board. "This has reduced the time for granting an Exit Permit to an average of ten days," Charles Winning estimated.[141]

In July, 1948, Wells also created an Interdivisional Reorientation Committee (IRC), which coordinated the exchange requests and aims of all of the participating divisions of Military Government; by autumn this nongovernmental agency had also come to life across the Atlantic. In September the American Council on Education created an Advisory Committee on Cultural and Educational Relations with help from the Rockefeller Foundation; a few months later it assumed a new title: Commission on the Occupied Areas (COA). Wells was by now back in the United States, where, despite his duties at Indiana University, he assumed the chairmanship of the COA. Harold E. Snyder, of the American Council on Education, became its director. The COA proved to be a useful agency, and the experience it accumulated in the complex workings of cultural-exchange programs benefited its successor agencies in later years.[142]

The results of Wells's pioneering work were almost immediately gratifying. Whereas in 1947 the government was able to effect only 81 exchanges between Germany and the United States, in 1948 the number rose to 354. These figures were later dwarfed by the huge increases that accompanied the maturing of the exchange program after the establishment of the High Commission, but Wells had shown intelligence and skill in clearing away the worst obstacles and in instilling confidence, not only in Clay but in official and private circles in the United States, that such a program was feasible. The number of German students and officials who arrived in the final years of Military Government, while not large, included many key individuals in the German educational system, persons whose influence far exceeded their small numbers. For example, Rector Walter Hallstein of Frankfurt University resided at Georgetown University as a law "student" in 1949.[143] Ernst Reuter, West Berlin's mayor and a central figure in founding the Free University, came to the United States in March, 1949, under the auspices of the State Department, to appeal for help for his infant university. His trip was eminently successful, as aid from Columbia University, Swarthmore College, the Rockefeller Foundation, and the Ford Foundation readily proved.[144] Even Alois Hundhammer, R. T. Alexander's old nemesis, participated in the exchange. Alonzo Grace, who had also found Hundhammmer difficult, was not amused at the irony involved: "I suppose you know that somebody in an idle moment saw to it that the Kultusminister of Bavaria spent nine days in the United States," he grumbled to his successor in Germany, John Riedl. "I do not think it was entirely lost; on the other hand, I do not see how anything very profound can come out of these tours."[145]

To be sure, there were still many problems and deficiencies to be remedied in the exchange program; but, unlike the formal educational programs and extensive structural proposals that American education authorities had long urged on their German opposites—to so little effect—the cultural-exchange program was a success. It had the most difficult birth of any reorientation program of the Occupation, but it outlived all other elements in the educational arsenal and continued to exert profound, if unmeasured, influence a generation later. In 1949 Henry Kellermann, who helped organize State Department participation in the exchanges, was asked by the department's budget director, Irving Schwarz, how many Germans they should support in a given year. When Kellermann suggested 2,000, Schwarz replied that they had to make up for lost time. They should budget for 3,500 exchanges instead.[146]

The paradox of America's educational program in Occupied Germany was that it reached organizational maturity at the moment it became irrelevant. The immediate beneficiary of Wells's vigorous new programs and fund-raising success was Alonzo Grace, formerly Commissioner of Education in Connecticut. Grace also laid special emphasis on the cultural-exchange program, and it was during his tenure as director of E&CR that the gathering tide of aid and exchange programs swept through the German educational system. However, the growth of the other branches of E&CR, such as education, religious affairs, and group activities, kept pace, so that E&CR, which before had often been called the "unwanted stepchild of Military Government,"[147] became, instead, one of its largest divisions.

What were all the elementary, secondary, vocational, adult, and other education specialists to accomplish by way of changing the German educational system? The answer was that they continued the "advice and assistance" formula, which Taylor and others had proposed at the outset but which had been eclipsed by the uproar over the school-reform debate. Their chief contributions were made in fields like elementary and special education, guidance and counseling, teacher training, educational testing, curriculum development, and the like. Experimental education, often of a high order, continued beyond 1949 into the HICOG era. Participants contended that the work they accomplished then proved more influential, by far, than the structural debates conducted in the days of Military Government. The combination of private foundation and public assistance, which came into existance in 1948, broadened into a torrent in the years to come. Examples include a Harvard-at-Heidelberg program, which matched the efforts of the University of Chicago at Frankfurt. Munich University organized the first Amerika Institut under the direction of Professor Heinz F. Peters of Reed College, a German refugee who garnered support from Alois Hundhammer. The Rockefeller, Ford, and Carnegie foundations and numerous other trusts, foundations, and philanthropic organizations gave funds either on a sustained basis or as seed money for research institutes, experimental-education institutions, libraries, and other projects too numerous to mention. The so-called McCloy Funds, named after U.S. High Commissioner John J. McCloy (but started by Clay), performed similar functions through U.S. government assistance. McCloy funds plus matching support from Greater Hesse made possible the creation of a highly successful experimental elementary-secondary school, the famed Schuldorf Bergstrasse near Jugenheim. At its high point the American cultural assistance budget exceeded $60 million in one year. Private funding was at least as large. The results of these massive aid and exchange programs are still undetermined, but they have been enduring, as the continuing cultural ties between the two nations suggest. The respect won by German social-science institutions owes a continuing debt to the spadework of visiting experts like Sigmund Neumann and to the support that reestablished the institutes for social-science research. The Volkswagen Foundation took Ford, Rockefeller, and other foundations as its models in the 1950s. The subject of aid and exchange programs belongs more properly to the HICOG era, but their antecedents were clearly visible in the second half of Military Government operations, when Herman Wells, State Department officials, and other influential persons concerned with German reorientation programs made their presence felt in the dark days of 1947.

Decontrol of Education

In the last year of OMGUS operations, Alonzo Grace proved adept at attracting publicity by organizing a large-scale education conference at Berchtesgaden in the autumn of 1948. Even Clay put in an appearance. In his remarks Clay emphasized the virtues of the exchange program rather than structural changes in German school systems, and he voiced his commitment to maintaining a large and active E&CR Division until the last day of Military Government operations.[148] Grace issued intricate manifestos and outlines of the work being performed by an education staff of Military Government that was at least three times what it had been in 1947. In summarizing his program of basic educational policies, he repeatedly underscored the German people's initiative and responsibility for their own educational system. "The true reform of the German people will come from within. It will be spiritual and moral. The types of school organization, or structure, for example, are of less importance to the future of Germany and the world than what is taught, how it is taught, and by whom it is taught." Under point three of his address Grace maintained: "It will not be the purpose of Military Government to superimpose an American system of education on the German people." Point eight stated, even more unequivocally, "No army of occupation has or possibly ever will successfully superimpose an educational and cultural pattern on a conquered people. Military Government will be regarded as military government, irrespective of the high motives of those who would 'reeducate or reorient' a defeated, conquered, occupied Germany."[149] Given the stellar role of the Germans in reconstructing their own educational system, the question remained: What was the role of the American educational effort in Germany to be?

Grace outlined four activities for his enlarged staff:

1. To bring into cooperation with the German people the voluntary nongovernmental organizations that are able to contribute toward the attainment of the common goals.
2. To encourage an effective German program by UNESCO.
3. To identify and encourage known democratic elements in the German population.
4. To support the development or restablishment of institutions and organizations in Germany which will contribute toward the accomplishment of the purposes of this mission.[150]

These goals did not appear exceptionable and seemed to accord well with the notion that the Germans would carry the main burden, with assistance from the Americans. The idea was not new. The State Department's first policy draft in 1944 had offered the same view. However, the conclusion Grace drew from his statements did not appear to be consistent: "The more rapid the material reconstruction and economic recovery, the more difficult becomes the problem of intellectual, moral, and spiritual redemption. The United States will have failed in Germany if materialism is allowed to supersede moral values. A concurrent program of educational and cultural reconstruction on a long-term basis is required."[151]

It was possible to interpret Grace's final statement to mean that the Germans would, with the return of prosperity, be disinclined to engage in further innovations. However, it seemed also to imply that material well-being is a corrupting influence. But prosperity was precisely what General Clay and other officials of Military Government had seen as indispensable to the growth of democracy in Germany, in education and in all other spheres. Grace also made another statement, at the end of 1948, in which he repeated the idea that a long-term program of educational and cultural reconstruction would be necessary; this implied that the Americans' educational activities would continue for years to come. As he wrote in the *American Scholar*: "I would say that the mission in the future will be much more difficult than most of our leaders visualize. We should stay a long time—perhaps twenty years."[152]

Following the 1948 Berchtesgaden Conference, plans went forward for a transfer of authority from Military Government to the State Department. This transfer, which had been deferred in each preceding year, seemed more certain of accomplishment now that "Trizonia," a common currency, and the success of the Berlin airlift has been established. By April, 1949, State Department officials were circulating drafts of their Occupation Statute, which delineated the powers of the future West German government and the controls the Allied High Commission would retain. The Occupation Statute would take effect in the autumn of 1949 at the same time as the new West German constitution or Basic Law began to function. Therefore, there was great consternation when the E&CR staff learned that the State Department's High Commission would not maintain control of German education. According to the draft document, the best the educational program could hope for was a "minimum" staff to continue to advise and assist the Germans with their educational system. That reduced function was a logical deduction from the program Grace had offered at the Berchtesgaden Conference in 1948. The call for redemption of the German people was more appropriate to 1945 than to the final year of Military Government operations. Moreover, Grace's repeated assertions that the Germans must carry the initiative implied a correspondingly reduced role for the American education staff. Yet, Grace was dismayed, and he complained immediately to Herman Wells and George Zook at the COA. He remarked that he had spoken to the French and British education staffs about the sudden development and reported that they were all pessimistic about the future. "We have a very definite feeling," he stated, "that the words 'minimum staff' mean exactly that and that we will be reduced within the year to almost a token staff. This job cannot be done successfully without the present staff and the additions we have requested."[153]

Grace had contacted the COA with the request that they study the Occupation Statute, "but more especially to create an opinion in the United States favorable to the long-term plan and policy which we have developed here." He had come to the conclusion that a diminished program would have no chance of success: "If we have merely an adviser to the High Commissioner and an exchange program of diminished proportions, we will have lost everything that we had planned."[154] Wells and Zook were unsettled by Grace's pessimistic predictions and paid a call on Henry Kellermann at the State Department's ADO for a discussion. They were unsure how to proceed in trying to change the Occupation Statute to restore control of education. Kellerman was sympathetic and recommended that they address a letter on the subject directly to the Secretary of State, Dean Acheson, explaining the problem, imparting Grace's views, and requesting that, in light of the growing awareness among the American public of the importance of education, the State Department should retain explicit controls over education.[155] Without further ado, Wells and Zook, with help from Kellermann, composed their letter to Secretary of State Acheson.

In their joint statement they pointed out to Acheson that, because "the U.S. educational staff in Germany has from the beginning been relatively very much smaller than that of either France or Great Britain, we feel that any major reduction in our education and cultural relations program in Germany will seriously retard the process of reorientation." Their letter was not as strong as Grace might have wished it to be. They did not call for the full retention of current controls: "While we do not advocate the direct supervision of German education over a long period of time, we do feel that the responsibility to 'observe, advise, and assist,' as agreed upon by the four powers in London a year ago, must be maintained for some time to come. It is hard to see how this could be done without maintaining a well-qualified professional staff of approximately the present size." Wells and Zook reminded Acheson that there had been a dramatic increase in interest and aid by American institutions in the preceding year and that these institutions were certain to be apprehensive if the educational programs were scaled down so abruptly. "We therefore trust that you will use your influence to bring about a reconsideration of the Occupation Statute. If that is not possible, we urge that your Department interpret the Statute as broadly as possible in order to permit the maintenance of an adequate program of education and cultural relations."[156]

On behalf of the COA, Wells also contacted Robert Murphy, who was now in Washington, serving as Acting Director of German-Austrian Affairs at the State Department, and asked him "to assist us in interpreting the implications of the new Occupation Statute for the educational program in Germany."[157] Henry Kellermann was also busy circulating among the agencies concerned with reorientation a memorandum that expressed concern about the authority the Americans would retain. Lieutenant Colonel G. P. Lynch, the acting chief at Reorientation Branch of CAD, replied in mid-May with an opinion from CAD's Legal Section: "It is, of course, unofficial," Lynch commented, "but it will give you an idea of the thinking within Civil Affairs Division." The Legal Section had noted that the Occupation Statute included a clause that would permit "the occupation authorities . . . to resume, in whole or in part, the exercise of full authority if they consider that to do so is essential to security or to preserve democratic government in Germany." Furthermore, the three occupying powers were to exercise uniform powers, as determined by the Allied High Commission. Since the occupying powers necessarily had to interpret the Occupation Statute, the CAD's Legal Section believed that "if a least two of the three occupying powers agree as a matter of policy that continuation of an education program is desirable, and also agree on the scope of the program and the size and character of the minimum staff necessary for such programs, they might properly establish this program by directive of the Allied High Commission." Justification for continuing such functions could be based on the need to insure that the Germans gained "official understanding of and 'respect' for the education provisions of the Land constitutions and the provisions of those constitutions and the Federal Constitution concerning basic rights." Furthermore, if the three powers agreed, they could deem the field of education to be "essential to security or to preserve democratic government in Germany."[158]

This intricate stratagem, which could be used to interpret the Occupation Statute rather than to attempt an actual change in its wording, became the ploy the State Department cultural officials used in their efforts to save education controls in Germany. It was too elaborate to work in practice, and, in any case, there was never any unanimity of opinion among the three members of the High Commission on what should constitute a minimum staff or what degree of educational supervision should continue. The British had already allowed control of education in their zone to revert to the Germans in the spring of 1947; they were therefore hardly inclined to interpret the Occupation Statute in such a way as to increase their education staff's authority to a greater degree than was now the case. Moreover, within the State Department many officers who had been concerned with reorientation programs in the Occupation—William Benton, James Riddleberger, and Henry Leverich, among others—had long been apprehensive about the boldness with which some American education authorities had proposed that the Germans take as models the comprehensive school and other particulars of the American system. There was a growing feeling that the end of Military Government was also the logical time to end formal education controls. Therefore, Grace's attempt to retain controls and a sizable staff did not succeed. Wells and the private educational organizations might support him, although with greater caution; Henry Kellermann might offer sympathetic advice, and the Legal Section at CAD could offer intricate interpretations requiring a tripartite consensus. The end result was that the Occupation Statute of April 8 remained unchanged, and the legal interpretation that might have altered it became a dead letter.[159]

For a time Grace did not know whether the tactic would succeed or fail, but by the summer of 1949 all evidence indicated that there would be no unanimity of opinion on the part of the three Western powers on cultural policy and no desire on the part of the German education ministries to slacken their resistance. If anything, the stance of educational leaders like Alois Hundhammer was more adamant than ever, now that Military Government control was nearly at an end. Henry Kellermann was in Paris in June, 1949, for discussions with French authorities about coordinating cultural policy in Germany. He was also engaged in conferences with UNESCO officials about their participation in reorientation programs. However, he reported to a colleague in Washington that there were unmistakable signs of distress among the education officers at OMGUS: "Hardly a day goes by on which a visitor from Germany does not knock on my door, primarily to ventilate his grievances about the present and his concern about the future state of reorientation activities in Germany. To judge from all these contacts, there is a disturbing amount of evidence pointing to a progressive demoralization of the personnel in Germany." He was afraid that, in the absence of concrete assurances that the educational program would remain at its current scale of operations, "we will lose our best talents in the field."[160] Shortly after the changeover from Military Government to the High Commission in September, a reorganization took place in which Education and Religious Affairs was downgraded to a branch in the new Public Affairs Division of HICOG. Alonzo Grace resigned promptly and departed for the United States. Kellermann's assessment was entirely accurate.

Grace's pessimism soon proved unwarranted. State Department officials had by no means abandoned the fight to retain an ambitious reorientation program under the High Commission. Nevertheless, there were some uneasy moments during the last months of Military Government operations. In March, 1949, General George Hays, Clay's successor as Military Governor, circulated a memorandum—probably at Clay's suggestion—to all E&RA chiefs complaining that "we are scattering our efforts and our available funds at present over a rather broad field, with very little knowledge of the concrete results obtained from any project." His criticism was apt, as State Department officials knowledgeable about cultural-assistance programs well knew. But after the creation of the Free University in 1948, Clay was already convinced of the worth of the programs and needed no further urging. Later, in his memoirs, Clay expressed pride that education and cultural affairs was the one sector of Military Government that he maintained at full strength in the final period of operations. His opinion concerning reorientation as a Military Government function had undergone dramatic change since 1945.[161]

In the autumn of 1949 a second "education mission," entirely composed of State Department officials, arrived in Germany to examine cultural programs and needs for the future. Taking inspiration from the precedent set by Herman Wells and the interdivisional reorientation committee under OMGUS, the new commission decided to reorganize cultural assistance around a unified division, covering every facet of reorientation operations. The new Public Affairs Division would be streamlined. A powerful director would preside over it, and reorientation funds would form an integral part of the entire occupation budget maintained by the Army. The proposals of the second "mission" received ready approval in Washington, and the new Public Affairs Division at HICOG brought to fruition the plans and expectations for a large-scale, multifaceted reorientation program based on the "advise and assist" formula first proposed at the State Department at the outset of the Occupation.[162]

The programs of cultural assistance in the era of the High Commission proved to be the apex of the reorientation effort and were to produce incalculable results in the generation to come. They were also fully integrated with other major policies of political and economic reconstruction espoused by the High Commissioner, thus fulfilling the prophecy made in 1944 by David Harris's Interdivisional Committee on Germany: "The German reaction to the whole body of measures taken by the victors will be the major influence in determining future German attitudes, and [this committee] believes that on that German reaction will depend the success or failure of any attempt at scholastic reform."[163]

Conclusion

In September, 1979, a conference of German scholars and educators met with interested colleagues from three of the four former occupying nations in Bielefeld, West Germany, to evaluate the impact of education reform in the Occupation.[1] One result of their meeting was that the Germans and Americans who discussed developments in the American Zone still could not produce any definitive answers on the "success" or "failure" of the American educational programs. In certain respects the facts spoke for themselves. Attempts to create comprehensive schools, to alter university governance, and to impose other changes in educational structures had met with stormy rebuff. On the other hand, the participants recognized that American influence on German education had not ceased in 1949 with the termination of Military Government. On the contrary, it grew with time as the reorientation programs matured. However, while it was easy to see where failures had occurred, the successes could not be captured easily in statements of unequivocal, quantifiable facts. Nevertheless, the influence was real.

Many years earlier—in 1952—Karl Bungardt, a member of the executive committee of the Federal Association of Teachers, had written in the *Allgemeine Lehrerzeitung* that ACA Directive 54 represented the best ideas produced by German education-reform efforts and was still admirable even if it had made a detour through America in order to return to Germany.[2] After the shrill debates of the Occupation had subsided, many German schoolteachers became convinced that the American proposals merited close attention after all and that adoption of any part of ACA Directive 54 did not mean the Americanization of German education, as Alois Hundhammer had skillfully led the public to believe. For those versed in previous debates on education reform, the extensive discussions of the 1960s

312

and 1970s in the Federal Republic covered familiar ground. Even so, these debates on the purpose of education in an advanced industrial society cannot with any assurance be linked to the influence of the American education programs or, more specifically, to the reorientation programs. Similarly, the impact of American popular culture on the Federal Republic had obviously been enormous, yet its connection with American reorientation programs of the 1940s and 1950s is also elusive.

If the Americans achieved little discernible progress in direct attempts to alter the structure of the German educational system, Britain and France fared no differently. Of all the Western occupying powers, the French proved most willing to impose their own plans and ideals rigorously and in elaborate detail. They set in place, in their modest zone, proportionately the largest educational bureaucracy and in some ways the most ambitious programs. Their staff people were often of the highest caliber. Their Occupation authorities were willing to send their nation's most highly respected scholars and intellectuals to Germany, and they instituted a cultural-exchange program in advance of the United States. Their educational efforts in Germany reached such a level that they and their German beneficiaries spoke only half in jest about a *mission civilisatrice*. Yet, this French missionary impulse shared the same fate as its American counterpart: the elaborate programs of formal education reform disappeared in the early years of the High Commission. Nevertheless, the French continued to play a vital if more localized role in ending Germany's cultural isolation and in damping the fires of strident nationalism—on both sides of the Rhine.

Initially, the British programs displayed marked similarities to the American ones, which is scarcely surprising if one remembers that the two nations began to formulate educational policy jointly in the Anglo-American German Country Unit of 1944. But the British, like the French, established a proportionately larger educational bureaucracy in their zone than the Americans did, and they accomplished this much sooner. Perhaps it was easier to recruit education personnel in drab postwar Britain than it was in the United States, where living standards were incomparably higher. From the start, Britain's Education Branch achieved greater autonomy within its military government than America's E&RA did. Moreover, it adopted almost immediately a more pragmatic attitude as to what was possible and what was not. However, despite these more modest expectations, the fact remained that university officers were available in such numbers that the British could afford to place one and sometimes two in each university. The United States did not achieve even one officer per university until late 1948. Britain's university officers interpreted directives from higher authority loosely, most notably with respect to that greatest of occupation headaches, denazification. Geoffrey C. Bird, the university officer at Göttingen, saw his assignment as primarily one of becoming acquainted with university personnel and students. On that basis he could examine attitudes and discuss higher-education policy informally and without appearing to be coercive.[3] In other words, the British upheld their vaunted tradition of muddling through. As a result there were no wholesale purges of the German universities in the British Zone—nothing, at least, to compare to events in the American Zone. American university officers were usually so busy with bureaucratic routine that they had no time to establish personal contact with anyone in a university except, perhaps, the rector. Thus, the students were virtually an unknown quantity for many American university officers.[4]

Perhaps the most striking contrast between British and American policy came in January, 1947, when the British announced that they would return control of education to the Germans at the very time that General Clay issued his ill-fated January 10, 1947, directive ordering school reform. This is not to say that the British attempted no structural changes in their zone's education system. However, when they did so, they claimed to be acting in an advisory role, which accorded well with Anglo-American thinking in 1944 and 1945. They recognized more fully the economic dislocations that stood in the way of desirable democratic features, such as free tuition and textbooks. British efforts to create a school structure more flexible than the rigid two-track system fell short of the American comprehensive-school plan. Even so, their efforts sparked an aroused opposition from German education groups, both public and private. After all, the "Friends of German School Reform" were headquartered not in the American Zone but in Münster, in the British Zone. Then, too, British attempts to deemphasize the central importance of Latin and the classical curriculum in preparing youngsters for the university collided with the views of traditionalists like Josef Schnippenköter. The difference was that the British education authorities retreated before German intransigence more gracefully than their American counterparts.

The only zone in which significant structural changes were produced was, of course, the Soviet Zone. The eight-year comprehensive elementary schools that emerged there laid the foundation for the education system of the German Democratic Republic. To be sure, the authority wielded by the Soviet Military Administration and by its ideological ally, the SED, was far more decisive than anything seen in the Western zones. The East Germans' centralized education bureaucracy, the *Zentralverwaltung für Volksbildung*, counted time as one of its allies, since, in the end, the education system would have to conform to the party's interpretation of Marxism-Leninism. A strategy of delay and passive resistance by traditionalists would have counted for little in the Eastern zone. There was no expectation of waiting until the occupying forces had left. There was also no point in speaking of traditions. The principle of the dictatorship of the proletariat applied fully as much to education as it did to any other realm of social development. Since there was nothing approaching a multiparty system in the Soviet Zone, the Soviet and SED authorities did not have to reckon with reactionary education officials possessing independent political power. Needless to say, Alois Hundhammer would not have remained in office five minutes as an education minister in the Eastern zone. Thus, because of unique circumstances, the Soviet zone was exceptional in being able to institute major structural changes in German education.

When it comes to considering shortcomings in the American education program, it is unrealistic to think that the U.S. Occupation authorities, had they but found the correct formula, could have made sweeping changes. The fate of the French and British undertakings is evidence enough that large staffs, ambitious programs, competent personnel, and a favored bureaucratic status for education staffs were not by themselves sufficient to make a difference. Some American education authorities emerged from their experience with a feeling that, if only they had provided an alternative educational system in the summer of 1945, all would have been different. Instead of reopening that autumn with the old pre-1933 system and allowing it to function for two years before changes were demanded, Military Government should have delayed the reopening until it could implement a comprehensive program like the one called for in ACA Directive 54.[5] However, such a scenario presupposed unanimity of opinion within American policy-planning agencies and within the original E&RA staff. That consensus simply did not exist in 1945. On the contrary, if there was unanimity of opinion, it was that German initiatives and German traditions must predominate, albeit under American supervision.

In view of the obvious difficulties the education staff had in its relations with Military Government, the question arises whether an alternative bureaucratic institution to a military government might have been feasible. Obviously, the State Department appeared to many contemporaries to be that alternative. However, the State Department's reluctance to accept operational responsibility for a massive undertaking like the German Occupation was well known. In the aftermath of war, with an occupation at hand, a military government is simply a fact of life. Consequently, any educational enterprise must reckon with a military bureaucracy as its host authority.

Given that situation, what can be learned from the OMGUS experience? Certainly the shortcomings need not be repeated wholesale. The education staff available in 1945 was too small to carry out its heavy responsibilities. The British experience of maintaining a larger, though by no means large, staff and then reducing it later appears to have worked better. However, the assembling of an adequate staff at the right time requires the existence of a reserve of experienced and talented educational leaders who can offer their specialized skills as part of a pool of civil-affairs experts. This talent was available during World War II, but there were serious shortcomings in utilizing it. The senior education administrators received low-grade commissions, which meant that their status in the military establishment was negligible, and they were held in reserve for two or three years before being sent on the mission for which they had volunteered. All civil-affairs experts suffered from low morale as a result.

From the start it was obvious to informed observers that the status of E&RA within Military Government was too low for a function that official doctrine held to be vital to the success of the Occupation. The inability of the education staff to achieve division status until 1948 was a confirmation of the tendency of Military Government leadership to underestimate the importance and the complexity of education reform. Lucius Clay experienced repeated embarrassments in connection with the education program—embarrassments that might have been avoided. Perhaps part of the problem lay in the fact that education was distinctly a civil-affairs function, and civil affairs did not enjoy a long tradition in the American military establishment. Education directives were repeatedly confounded by other policies. Denazification is the most obvious example of this, although currency reform in 1948 also proved to be a serious obstacle to educational innovation. Clay's January 10, 1947, directive, ordering school reform, contradicted his decision in the autumn of 1946 to return political and social autonomy to the Länder. Clay did not attempt to make significant changes in E&RA's position in 1945 despite the evidence contained in the Knappen Report and the concern voiced by Robert Murphy. Instead, he overreacted to rumors of renazification in 1946 and initiated another purge, despite the advice of E&RA leadership. His decision in March, 1946, to turn down a joint offer by the State and War departments to provide him with a cultural adviser was doubly unfortunate. Lack of such an adviser meant that there were no effective contacts between E&RA and education circles in the United States. The result was that for nine crucial months in 1947 the education staff was led by an acting chief who was temperamentally unsuited to the task. R. T. Alexander had already accomplished much positive work as John Taylor's deputy. It was his misfortune, and ultimately Clay's responsibility, that Alexander came to direct the education effort at the very moment it was drifting into a confrontation with Bavaria's political and educational leadership.

When Clay finally acquired the services of a new leader, the hour was late. Ultimately he had to concede that the education program required greater emphasis. The position Herman Wells accepted was that of cultural adviser after all. By the end of 1947, effective coordination of the education programs was long overdue, and Wells accomplished that. He convinced

Clay that a reorientation program was feasible and that its success depended on American public as well as private resources.

To do this, Wells had to overcome marked resistance on Clay's part. In 1947 Clay assumed that the American people would not be hospitable to German participation in a cultural-affairs program. His reluctance to support the CAD's threefold budget increase for reorientation programs in the spring of 1947 effectively undermined the exchange program for that year. The failure of Robert Hutchins' Chicago Plan in 1947 was simply the most visible evidence of Clay's underestimation of the importance of reorientation programs at that time. There were, of course, logical explanations for his actions. As Military Governor, he was constantly faced with conflicting needs and inevitably had to assign priorities, given the limited resources at his disposal. It was only right that he husband his means to combat the terrible effects of malnutrition. In addition, he faced constant irritations and crises in attempting to make four-power control work. His ultimate decision to take on a cultural adviser produced dividends almost immediately. If he made mistakes, Clay also learned from them.

It was Clay who made the final decision to support the Free University, despite warnings from key education personnel that the project was impossible and politically dangerous. He had the wisdom and the courage to effect a compromise with the Bavarian leadership over school reform once it became apparent that the crisis might expand into a dangerous confrontation between Military Government and a democratically elected political body. His appearance at the Berchtesgaden Education Conference in October, 1948, bespoke a new commitment. Despite a slow start, he came to realize the importance of the cultural-exchange and aid programs associated with reorientation. In the end, he became an advocate of reorientation.

Herman Wells also faced a difficult assignment with Military Government, one that offered every prospect of failure, since America's education programs were in disarray by the time he arrived in Germany. In the face of all this, Wells made a valuable contribution: his energy and competent leadership reversed the gloomy prognosis within a few months. Some of his methods were unorthodox, as when he took an untried young journalist as his special assistant to promote the Free University. He streamlined the education staff's operations in the zone, raised its status and personnel strength to adequate proportions, and went far toward forging the necessary apparatus in Washington and at OMGUS to breathe new life into the exchange programs. His chosen successor, Alonzo Grace, continued his programs and brought much-needed publicity to the education programs, though in the end he succumbed to the temptation to perpetuate his own bureaucracy. Because of his pessimistic interpretation of the evidence, Grace convinced Wells and others of the need to postpone the day when Germans would finally regain control of their own educational system. It was just as well that his attempt failed. Even as early as 1943 State Department policy-makers had observed that it would be a mistake to retain civilian controls once the American military presence was ended. The obvious shift to reorientation made the creation of the Federal Republic the logical moment for the reassertion of the Germans' cultural sovereignty.

The Americans who were extensively involved in education reform in the Occupation were witnesses to a marked change in emphasis in their nation's approach to the delicate assignment. The term "reeducation" did not seem too harsh in 1945, and the basic doctrine, JCS 1067, embodying it has appeared unnecessarily punitive only in retrospect. Policy shifted as time and circumstance dictated. Given American attitudes about education in the mid-1940s, there were bound to be important elements who could not resist the urge to remake a former adversary in their own image and likeness. Such attempts were bound to produce reactionary responses, like those that materialized in Bavaria.

Not even the shift to the subtler reorientation program could guarantee a change in Germany's educational values, although the subsequent history of German and American cultural relations suggests that it played a vital role. As early as 1944 the State Department's Interdivisional Committee on Germany recognized in its first policy statement that education reform would never, by itself, produce any major changes in German society. Reorientation of that society would depend on the sum total of political, social, and economic policies. The promulgation of JCS 1779 in July, 1947, confirmed the validity of that assumption, and reorientation moved from the periphery to the center of the American occupation experience in Germany.

The evolution of education values in the Federal Republic since 1949 has undoubtedly benefited from the education-reform efforts of the Americans, British, and French. The astonishing changes in German society in the period since 1945 have compelled educational innovations that were undreamed of in the Kaiserreich, unattainable in the days of Weimar, ignored by Hitler, and resented during the Occupation. The American experience suggests the naiveté implicit in the assumption that one people can "reeducate" another toward democracy. It also suggests that example and exposure to alternatives are more effective in the long run.

A Note on the Sources

Source materials for this study are extraordinarily abundant, and they are to be found primarily in the U.S. National Archives. The United States has been more liberal than the other three occupying nations in opening its archives on the Occupation to historians. The British have recently begun to grant access to their records. The French resolutely maintain their fifty-year rule. The Soviets have not announced a schedule of public access to documents on the Occupation. Therefore, for the present, the resources in the National Archives and its branches in Washington, D.C., remain the most promising archival collections for historians of the German Occupation.

The following information is intended to aid scholars interested in occupation studies. Naturally, it is biased toward sources on education reform. At least four major record groups are available to the researcher. Many, but by no means all, of the agencies involved in education reform used decimal classifications for their records. The State Department maintained a decimal number 862.42 (Reeducation of Germany), which was then combined with a second set of digits to complete a document's file number. The second cluster represented the date on which a document arrived at the State Department or when it was dated by the sender. Thus, 862.42/5–1445 is a document concerned with German reeducation and dated May 14, 1945. The system is by no means foolproof, since the original document often generated a series of later memoranda, briefings, and related documents, all of which carry the original decimal number. However, it does serve as a rough chronological guide. Other decimal numbers of the State Department for the period of the Occupation include 862.0019 (Control of Germany), covering documents pertaining to overall occupation policy. Before looking at any State Department documents, interested scholars should first consult the published sources of the State Department: *Foreign Relations of the United States*. For a solid study on American cultural-exchange programs that is also a useful guide to the kinds of documents available from the State Department, read Henry Kellermann, *Cultural Relations as an Instrument of U.S. Foreign Policy: The Educational Exchange Program between the United States and Germany, 1945–1954* (Washington, D.C., 1978).

War Department files are also voluminous and reflect the massive manpower and resources at the disposal of the department in wartime. Its numerous collections are often widely separated. Thus, SHAEF G-5 records and the historical documents for the armies and army groups with which they worked are stored in different

repositories. Earl Ziemke's *The U.S. Army in the Occupation of Germany, 1944–1946*
(Washington, D.C., 1975), an excellent study on the evolution of Military Government, has a helpful essay on historical documents covering the early history
of Military Government operations in Occupied Germany. The present work depends in part on material in the files of the War Department's Civil Affairs Division
under the CAD's decimal classification on education: WDSCA 350. Unfortunately,
that designation was not limited to Germany but covered the War Department's
worldwide education programs, with all documents arranged chronologically. As
a result, researchers must examine hundreds of volumes of the WDSCA 350 files
for the years of the Occupation. Finding aids, placed at the beginning of each
volume, allow the reader to bypass countless pages of low-value travel orders,
confirmations, and the like. For General Clay's correspondence with officers of
the War Department and other Washington officials see Jean Edward Smith, ed.,
The Papers of General Lucius D. Clay: Germany 1945–1949, 2 vols. (Bloomington,
Ind., 1974).

The OMGUS documents dwarf even the sizable collections of the State and War
departments. Approximately 10,000 cubic feet of records and several hundred rolls
of microfilm are available in the Washington National Records Center (WNRC)
in Suitland, Maryland, near Washington. At one time the Army hoped to produce
an ambitious multivolume history of Military Government, but the project died
for lack of funds. The documents that survived transshipment to assembly points
in Germany and a roundabout journey to the United States finally reached the
WNRC in the early 1970s. Scholars in meaningful numbers began to use them in
1974, but all who have worked in them agree that they challenge even the most
determined researcher.

Given the enormous quantity of these OMGUS documents, the major stumbling
block in making use of them to date has been the lack of effective finding aids.
In 1951 Army clerks hastily prepared lists of folder titles for each archival box
and then placed them in footlockers in batches of three boxes for shipment to the
United States. However, the titles frequently give only the vaguest hint of the
contents of each folder. A typical reference is 308–1/5, which refers to locker 308,
box 1 (of a possible three), in shipload 5. Currently, the archivists are renumbering
and reboxing all OMGUS documents, but this original numbering system still
remains necessary for locating materials. Researchers must be prepared to encounter a large quantity of irrelevant and historically worthless material. Hermann
Graml, a senior researcher at the Institut für Zeitgeschichte, maintains that only
about 5 percent of the documents are worthwhile. I estimate that figure is, on
average, substantially correct, although some collections are more valuable than
others. Perhaps it was due to the undifferentiated quality of the materials that at
some point during the period when they were being collected, under HICOG
authority, and shipped to the United States hundreds of boxes of them disappeared.
Some estimates run as high as a third of the total that was originally gathered.
Discards are particularly noticeable among records from subordinate offices in the
Land military governments; this lends credence to the theory that early custodians
made value judgements of what was disposable and what was not. As a result, at
least two hundred cubic feet of education documents are missing. Bavarian records

escaped least scathed. Scholars can make good many of the losses by consulting Military Government's numerous monthly, quarterly, and annual reports. The staffs complained, during the Occupation, of having to complete interminable series of reports, but their labors have proved useful after all.

Only rarely did one division of Military Government have sole responsibility for a given policy. Therefore, it is necessary to examine records from several divisions and echelons of Military Government. When it comes to the education staff's activities, for example, a clear understanding of what happened requires research into related organizations, such as Legal, Public Safety, Information Control, and Internal Affairs divisions, among others. Several helpful collections of compact information on the Occupation, which highlight events, are to be found among reports of intelligence-gathering agencies and in the OMGUS historical reports. For example, the Intelligence Branch of ICD in Bavaria regularly published an intelligence digest entitled *Trend*, concerning Bavarian affairs. It is located in the OMGUS documents, 147–1/13 and 142–3/13. To be sure, *Trend* reflects the prejudices of ICD's Intelligence Branch, which at times differed sharply with E&RA on such matters as denazification policy. A broader view of intelligence information for the U.S. Zone is available in Information Control's Intelligence Summaries, which were later retitled as the Information Control Weekly Review. The collection is in 429–1/3. More intelligence summaries are in 234–2/5. A quick guide to published information distributed widely to Military Government personnel is its *Weekly Information Bulletin (WIB)*; a handy subject index to this is located in the *WIB*, no. 160 (May 3, 1949), and the collection is in 414–2/3. Researchers should also consult documents generated by higher echelons of Military Government on important local issues. A valuable high-level source for OMGUS headquarters is the documents issued by the office of the Adjutant General (A.G.). Land directors were also central figures in the operations of Military Government, and their files warrant close examination.

Closely tied to Military Government was Ambassador Robert Murphy's Office of the Political Adviser (POLAD), whose records are arranged in Record Group 84 of the National Archives by decimal classification. Education's file number was 842, and documents under that classification normally accumulated in one archival box for a given year. Thus, for 1945, POLAD education documents appear in box 737; in 1946 it is box 758; for 1947 it is 817, and so on. The POLAD documents are far less numerous than the OMGUS materials, but they are especially important because POLAD acted as liaison between the State Department and Military Government. Robert Murphy's *Diplomat among Warriors* (New York, 1964) also remains useful.

The issue of reeducation has received little detailed attention in the American literature dealing with the Occupation. Perhaps the best general work is John Gimble's *The American Occupation of Germany: Politics and the Military* (Stanford, 1968). See also his more recent *Origins of the Marshall Plan* (Stanford, 1976). However, neither study analyzes cultural or educational issues. The same is true of another major American work on the Occupation, John Montgomery's *Forced To Be Free* (Chicago, 1957). A conference of scholars and high government officials discussed the Occupation from the American perspective at the George C. Marshall

Foundation in 1976, the results of which appeared in Hans A. Schmitt, ed., *U.S. Occupation in Europe after World War II* (Lawrence, Kans., 1978). The discussants omitted the topic of reeducation, as did a follow-up conference on the theme "Americans as Proconsuls" at the Smithsonian Institution in 1977. Its proceedings will appear in print shortly. A reliable but dated study is Harold Zink's *The United States in Germany, 1944–1955* (Princeton, 1957). More recent but uneven is Edward N. Peterson's *The American Occupation of Germany: Retreat to Victory* (Detroit, 1978); as the title suggests, its theme is roughly the same as that of the present work.

A useful collection of studies from the Bielefeld Conference on postwar educational reconstruction is Manfred Heinemann, ed., *Umerziehung und Wiederaufbau: Die Bildungspolitik der Besatzungsmächte in Deutschland und Österreich* (Stuttgart, 1981). A number of recent studies of reeducation in the British and French zones have appeared; among them are Arthur Hearnden, *The British in Germany: Educational Reconstruction after 1945* (London, 1978), Günter Pakschies, *Umerziehung in der Britischen Zone, 1945–1949* (Weinheim, 1979), and Maria Halbritter, *Schulreformpolitik in der Britischen Zone, 1945–1949* (Karlsruhe, 1979). For the French Zone, see Angelika Ruge-Schatz, *Umerziehung und Schulpolitik in der französischen Besatzungszone, 1945–1949* (Frankfurt, 1977). Works on the American Zone are as yet not numerous. The most important is Karl-Ernst Bungenstab's *Umerziehung zur Demokratie? Re-edukation-Politik im Bildungswesen der U.S. Zone, 1945–1949* (Düsseldorf, 1970), but Bungenstab did not have the use of OMGUS or other original documents and therefore does not adequately analyze the operations of American Military Government and other interested agencies. More recent is Jutta-B. Lange-Quassowski's *Neuordnung oder Restauration? Das Demokratiekonzept der amerikanischen Besatzungsmacht und die politische Sozialisation der Westdeutschen: Wirtschaftsordnung–Schulstruktur–Politische Bildung* (Opladen, 1979). Lange-Quassowski's work includes useful sections on American and German conceptions of democracy, and she examines in detail their impact on specialized areas, such as social-studies curricula and textbooks. However, her work virtually omits reference to the abundant OMGUS source materials that have been available since the mid-1970s.

Notes

Introduction

1. U.S. Department of State, *Foreign Relations of the United States*, Diplomatic Papers, The Conference of Berlin (The Potsdam Conference), 1945 (Washington, 1960), doc. 343, vol. 1, p. 483.

2. Marshall Knappen, *And Call It Peace* (Chicago, 1947), p. 3.

3. Thomas Alexander and Beryl Parker, *The New Education in the German Republic* (New York, 1929), pp. 368–72.

Chapter One. Planning for Reeducation

1. John L. Gaddis, *The United States and the Origins of the Cold War, 1941–1947* (New York, 1972), chap. 4; see also Paul Y. Hammond, "Directives for the Occupation of Germany: The Washington Controversy," in Harold Stein, ed., *American Civil-Military Decisions* (Birmingham, Ala., 1963).

2. Gaddis, p. 100.

3. Ibid., p. 103.

4. Earl Ziemke, *The U.S. Army in the Occupation of Germany, 1944–1946* (Washington, D.C., 1975), pp. 14–17.

5. Marshall Knappen, *And Call It Peace* (Chicago, 1947), pp. 56–57.

6. Gaddis, pp. 105–7.

7. Ziemke, p. 86.

8. Henry Morgenthau, *Germany Is Our Problem* (New York, 1945), p. 153; see also Karl-Ernst Bungenstab, *Umerziehung zur Demokratie? Re-edukation-Politik im Bildungswesen der U.S. Zone, 1945–1949* (Düsseldorf, 1970), p. 27.

9. U.S. Department of State, Bureau of Educational and Cultural Affairs, History Files (CU/H), minutes, meeting of the General Advisory Committee on Postwar Programs (GAC), 19 June 1942, pp. 23–25. All documents in the State Department's Bureau of Educational and Cultural Affairs History Files are hereafter cited as CU/H.

10. Ibid., p. 27.

11. CU/H, minutes, meeting of the GAC, 23 February 1943, p. 23.

12. Ibid., pp. 24–25.

13. Ibid., p. 26.

14. Ibid., pp. 27–28.

15. Ibid., p. 29.

16. CU/H, minutes, meeting of the GAC, 9–10 June 1943, pp. 21–22.

17. Ibid., p. 24.

18. Ibid., pp. 25–26.

19. Gaddis, pp. 97–99.

20. See Richard Brickner, *Is Germany Curable?* (New York, 1943); Kurt Lewin, "The Special Case of Germany," *Public Opinion Quarterly* 7 (1943): 555–64. See also Bungenstab, *Umerziehung zur Demokratie?*, pp. 21–24, for general discussion.

21. U.S. National Archives, Record Group 59, U.S. Department of State, Decimal File 862.42 (Reeducation of Germany), file 862.42/8-945, "Program for the Reconstruction of the Schools and the Educational System in Germany." All documents in the State Department's Reeducation-of-Germany decimal files are hereafter cited as 862.42, with file classification.

22. 862.42/2-145, memo, Foreign Nationalities Branch, OSS to director, OSS, 18 January 1945, with report no. B-304, "Five German Writers Discuss What To Do with Germany," attached to memo, Leon Fuller to Archibald MacLeish, 1 February 1945.

23. Interview with Dr. John W. Taylor, 10 September 1977; see also Dorothy Thompson, "Germany Must Be Salvaged," *American Mercury* 56 (1943): 657.

24. Gaddis, pp. 116–18.

25. See Knappen, pp. 43–46.

26. Ibid.; see also Ziemke, p. 21.

27. U.S. National Archives, Record Group 331, Records of the Allied Operational and Occupational Headquarters, World War II, "Handbook for Military Government in Germany Prior to Defeat and Surrender," July 1944 (never issued).

28. U.S. Department of State, *Foreign Relations of the United States*, Diplomatic Papers, 1944, vol. 1, General, p. 337; hereafter cited as *FR*, EAC Papers. See also Knappen, p. 59.

29. *FR*, EAC Papers, p. 350; 862.52/2-145, memo, Fuller to MacLeish, 1 February 1945, referring to reappearance of Interdivisional Committee paper.

30. SHAEF, *Handbook on Germany Prior to Defeat or Surrender*, December 1944; copy in possession of author.

31. Harry Coles and Albert K. Weinberg, *Civil Affairs: Soldiers Become Governors* (Washington, D.C., 1964), pp. 400–404.

32. Interview with John W. Taylor, 23 September 1979.

33. Knappen, pp. 45, 68.

34. 862.42/1-1545, letter, John Hilldring to James Dunn, 7 April 1944.

35. 862.42/1-1545, draft directive for Interdivisional Committee on Germany, "Germany: Pre- and Post-Surrender Policy with Respect to Schools," attached to memo, Howe to MacLeish, 15 January 1945.

36. Ibid.

37. Gaddis, p. 113.

38. 862.42/1-1545, memo, Howe to MacLeish, 15 January 1945.

39. 862.42/2-745, memo, MacLeish to Hovde, 7 February 1945.

40. 862.42/2-1845, memo for Archibald MacLeish, 16 February 1945.

41. 862.42/3-2745, Hovde to MacLeish, 27 March 1945.

42. 862.42/5-1445, summary, meeting, "Reeducation of Germany," 14 May 1945; see also attached Appendix A, "Views of the CAD," War Department (Howe's initial statement).

43. Ibid.; see also attached Appendix B, "Views of SHAEF" (Taylor's preliminary statement).

44. Ibid., attached draft, "Statement of Long-Range Policy on German Reeducation," by Anderson, Bowles, and Fuller; revisions approved by the Advisory Committee.

45. Ibid., p. 2 of summary. See also 862.42/6-145, letter, Niebuhr to MacLeish, 1 June 1945, and *FR*, Conference of Berlin (Potsdam Conference), 1945 (Washington, D.C., 1960), vol. 1, p. 487, for Davis's letter to Truman (hereafter cited as *FR*, Potsdam Conference).

46. 862.42/7-1145, memo, Hovde to MacLeish, 11 July 1945.

47. 862.42/5-1445, summary, meeting, 14 May 1945, Appendix A.

48. CU/H, memo, Henry Leverich to Donald Stone, 21 January 1946.

49. U.S. National Archives, Record Group 260, Office of Military Government (U.S.) for Germany (OMGUS), Adjutant General's Correspondence Files, 1944–1945, box 16, staff study, "Educational Policy Review," 14 May 1945.

50. Ibid.

51. *FR*, Potsdam Conference, 1:482–87.

52. Ibid., pp. 500–503.

53. Ibid., 2:780–83.

54. U.S. Department of State, *Germany, 1947–1949, The Story in Documents* (Washington, D.C., 1950), p. 49.

Chapter Two. First Operations in Germany

1. U.S. Department of State, *Germany, 1947–1949. The Story in Documents* (Washington, D.C., 1950), p. 49.

2. U.S. National Archives, Record Group 260, Office of Military Government (U.S.) for Germany (OMGUS), 308-1/5, memo, "Preliminary Report on Education," 24 February 1945. All Military Government documents are hereafter cited as OMGUS, with file classification. See also SHAEF *Handbook for Military Government in Germany Prior to Defeat or Surrender* (London, December, 1944), par. 814, "Closing of Educational Institutions" (hereafter citied as SHAEF *Handbook*).

3. OMGUS, 308-1/5, memo, 24 February 1945.

4. Ibid.

5. Marshall Knappen, *And Call It Peace* (Chicago, 1947), pp. 64–66; OMGUS, Adjutant General's General Correspondence Files (A.G. Files), 1944–45, box 16, E&RA staff meeting, 14 May 1945; interviews with John W. Taylor, 10 September and 23 September 1979.

6. This statement was inserted, for instance, in a German schoolbook edited by R. Heuer, *Deutsches Lesebuch III (3. und 4. Schuljahr)* (Breslau, 1928), one of the texts reprinted by SHAEF in 1945; copy in author's possession.

7. OMGUS, 308-1/5, "General Report . . . Third Army, 16 to 31 May Inclusive," by Oscar Reinmuth, 1 June 1945, hereafter cited as Reinmuth report.

8. OMGUS, 308-1/5, "Report on Mission," Dumont Kenny to IA&C, 12 June 1945, plus summary on school reopening, 4 June 1945.

9. Reinmuth report.

10. Ibid.

11. Ibid.; statement by Taylor, interview of 23 September 1979.

12. Reinmuth report.

13. Ibid.

14. U.S. National Archives, Record Group 84, Office of the United States Political Adviser (POLAD) for Germany, File 842 (Education), box 737, "Report on Munich-Stuttgart Mission by M. M. Knappen," 26 May 1945. All documents in the Political Adviser's 842 (Education) files are hereafter cited as POLAD.

15. Ibid., with attached letter from Robert Murphy to Lucius Clay, 30 May 1945.

16. Ibid.

17. OMGUS, 307-2/5, E&RA minutes, 4 September 1945.

18. Earl Ziemke, *The U.S. Army in the Occupation of Germany, 1944–1946* (Washington, D.C., 1975), pp. 164–66; Knappen, pp. 75–78.

19. Knappen, pp. 74, 80–81; Harold Zink, *The United States in Germany, 1944–1955* (Princeton, 1957), pp. 194–97.

20. Interviews with Dr. Martin Mayes, 28 December 1979, and with Mr. Vaughn R. DeLong, 7 June 1977; OMGUS, 49-2/10, personnel roster for E&RA, OMGB, education officers, summer, 1946.

21. Taylor interview, 10 September 1977; Knappen, p. 174.

22. OMGUS, 307-2/5, E&RA minutes, 2 August 1945.

23. Ziemke, p. 383; interview with Martin Mayes, 28 December 1979; interview with Colonel William R. Swarm, 10 December 1979. Swarm served as a civil-affairs expert in Military Government. He stated that CAD kept voluminous files of U.S. press reports about the Occupation and dispatched them promptly to Military Government field personnel.

24. *New York Times*, 23 September 1945; see also Lutz Niethammer, *Entnazi-fizierung in Bayern: Säuberung und Rehabilitierung unter amerikanischer Besatzung* (Frankfurt a.M., 1972), pp. 229–40.

25. Ziemke, p. 387; Niethammer, pp. 240–48.

26. OMGUS, 76-3/10, historical report for Third Army, section XV on education, report from Detachment G1H2.

27. Ibid., report from Detachment H6D3.

28. Ibid., report from Detachment I14D3.

29. Ibid., report from Detachment H6D3.

30. Ibid.

31. Reinmuth report, p. 4.

32. OMGUS, 76-3/10, reports from Detachments I6D3, I5A3, and I3H3.

33. *SHAEF Handbook*, pars. 818–22.

34. Knappen, pp. 124–26.

35. OMGUS, 28-1/12, memo, Theodor Heuss to Military Government Headquarters in Stuttgart, 6 October 1945.

36. OMGUS, 76-3/10, reports from Detachments I1F3 and I1F2.

37. OMGUS, 28-1/12, Heuss memo, 6 October 1945.

38. OMGUS, 28-1/12, memo, Theodor Bäuerle to OMGWB, 19 November 1945.

39. OMGUS, 307-2/5, E&RA minutes, 10 December 1945, p. 2; Taylor interview, 10 September 1977.

40. POLAD, box 737, Directive for the Reopening of Secondary Schools, 27 September 1945.

41. OMGUS, 307-2/5, E&RA minutes, 10 September 1945. See also John Backer, *Priming the German Economy: American Occupational Policies, 1945–1948* (Durham, N.C., 1971), pp. 31-46.

42. POLAD, box 737, memo, John J. Muccio to Robert Murphy, 10 July 1945.

43. OMGUS, 307-2/5, E&RA minutes, 4 and 21 September 1945.

44. Karl Jaspers, "The Rededication of German Scholarship," trans. Mary Anne Zuckerkandl, *American Scholar* 15 (1946):180–88.

45. OMGUS, A.G. Files, 1945–46, box 82, Field Intelligence Study no. 41, "Liberal Universities of Baden: Heidelberg," 30 November 1945, p. 28.

46. Edward Y. Hartshorne, "Reopening German Universities," *Weekly Information Bulletin* (published by Military Government), no. 43, 27 May 1946, p. 7, in OMGUS, 414-2/3.

47. POLAD, box 737, "Directive for the Reopening of the Universities . . . ," 21 November 1945.

48. Hartshorne, "Reopening. . . ," *WIB*, no. 43, 27 May 1946, p. 5; OMGUS 302-1/5, E&RA Annual History, 1945–46, Greater Hesse, p. 26 (hereafter cited as E&RA, OMGGH History, 1946); POLAD, box 737, "Directive for the Reopening of the Universities . . . ," 21 November 1945.

49. Hartshorne, "Reopening. . . ," *WIB*, no. 43, 27 May 1946, p. 6.

50. POLAD, box 737, 21 November 1945 directive, "Implementing Instructions," p. 1; OMGUS, 307-2/5, E&RA minutes, 21 September 1945.

51. POLAD, box 737, 21 November 1945 directive, "Implementing Instructions," p. 3.

52. Ibid., p. 4.

53. Ibid., p. 5.

54. OMGUS, 302-1/5, E&RA, OMGGH History, 1945–46, p. 41.

55. Interview with Dr. Edwin S. Costrell, 6 June 1978.

56. OMGUS, 302-1/5, E&RA, OMGGH History, 1945–46, pp. 48–49.

57. OMGUS, 307-2/5, E&RA minutes, 3 August 1945.

58. OMGUS, 307-2/5, E&RA minutes, 15 August 1945.

59. OMGUS, 302-1/5, E&RA, OMGGH History, 1945–46, p. 26.

60. OMGUS, A.G. Files, 1945–46, box 82, Field Intelligence Study no. 41, 30 November 1945, pp. 1–6.

61. OMGUS, 307-2/5, E&RA minutes, 6 September 1945; 308-1/5, report from G-5 headquarters, Berlin District, 4 August 1945, p. 1.

62. POLAD, box 737, report, "Present Status of Heidelberg University," 19 October 1945.

63. OMGUS, 302-1/5, E&RA, OMGGH History, 1945–46, p. 27.

64. Ibid.

65. OMGUS, 307-2/5, E&RA minutes, 10 December 1945, p. 3; Knappen, pp. 130–33.

66. OMGUS, 28-1/12, memo, Württemberg-Baden Kultusministerium's Denazification Committee to Land Military Government in Stuttgart, "Forced Membership in the HJ and NSDAP of the Students of Teacher Training Colleges," 27 December 1945. See also "Temporary Employment of Discretionary Adverse Recommendation Cases," in OMGUS, 28-1/12, 16 May 1946.

67. OMGUS, 302-1/5, E&RA, OMGGH History, 1945–46, pp. 30–31.

68. British Education Branch report, "Conference of Rectors of German *Hochschulen* in the British Zone at Göttingen, 26–27 September," stored in the archives of the Westdeutschen Rektorenkonferenz (West German Rectors' Conference, or WRK) in Bad Godesberg, West Germany. See also Heidelberg's request to the Land Military Government in Mannheim for a similar rectors' conference, in WRK, memo, 9 September 1945.

69. OMGUS, 302-1/5, E&RA, OMGGH History, 1945–46, Annex H, report II.

70. Ibid., p.35.

71. Ibid., pp. 39, 49.

72. OMGUS, 307-2/5, E&RA minutes, 10 December 1945, p. 3.

73. Ibid., p. 6.

74. Ibid., p. 3.

75. Ibid., p. 6.

76. Ibid., p. 1; OMGUS, 307-2/5, E&RA minutes, 3 December 1945. At first a ceiling of about one-third of the E&RA officers was envisaged for return to civilian status, but Taylor assured Clay that E&RA Branch needed only a small number of officers with military rank (Taylor interview, 10 September 1977).

77. 862.42/10-645, telegram, Kefauver to Benton and Anderson, 6 October 1945; memo, Bryn Hovde to Benton, 9 October 1945; memo, Raymond L. Zwemer to Benton, 15 October 1945; telegram from Benton to Kefauver under Byrnes's signature, 19 October 1945.

78. OMGUS, 307-2/5, E&RA minutes, 8 January 1945.

79. OMGUS, 307-2/5, E&RA minutes, 10 December 1945, p. 1.

80. Ibid. (Taylor expected to double his staff through December and January. The freeze on recruitment became obvious only in February, 1946.)

81. Ibid., p. 3.

Chapter Three. A Second Purge

1. U.S. National Archives, Record Group 260, Office of Military Government (U.S.) for Germany (OMGUS), 304-1/5, memo, Knappen to PH&W, 12 February 1946. All Military Government documents are hereafter cited as OMGUS, with file classification.

2. Ibid.

3. OMGUS, 308-2/5, report, "Population and Housing Data on Marburg," December 1945.

4. OMGUS, 308-2/5, report, "Effect of U.S. Troops on Marburg Student Mentality," n.d. [December 1945], p. 2.

5. OMGUS, 308-2/5, report, "Unfavorable Effect of the Occupation on Marburg University Faculty," by E. Y. Hartshorne, n.d. [January 1946], pp. 1–2.

6. OMGUS, 308-2/5, note by John W. Taylor, dated 6 February 1946, written on a route slip with memo, "Relief of Occupation Pressure in University Town, Marburg," 29 January 1946.

7. OMGUS, 308-2/5, memo, Brigadier General F. C. Meade to Chief of Staff, "Relief of Occupation Pressure in University Town, Marburg," 27 February 1946.

8. Photograph of a watercolor by a student artist, R. von Krämer (University of Munich Archives).

9. OMGUS, 308-2/5, report, "Unfavorable Effect of the Occupation on Marburg University Faculty," by E. Y. Hartshorne, n.d. [January 1946], pp. 1–2.

10. OMGUS, 49-3/10, memo, Sten Flygt to Clifton C. Winn, 14 February 1949.

11. Marshall Knappen, *And Call It Peace* (Chicago, 1947), pp. 191–93.

12. OMGUS, 307-2/5, E&RA minutes, 28 February 1946 and 18 March 1946.

13. OMGUS, 307-2/5, E&RA minutes, 2 April 1946.

14. Ibid.

15. U.S. National Archives, Record Group 59, U.S. Department of State, Decimal File 862.42 (Reeducation of Germany), file 862.4/1-2346, letter, Hilldring to Benton, 23 January 1946. All documents in the State Department's Reeducation-of-Germany decimal files are hereafter cited as 862.42, with file classification.

16. 862.42/1-2346, letter, Benton to Hilldring, 8 February 1946.

17. U.S. National Archives, Record Group 165, Civil Affairs Division (CAD), War Department, File WDSCA 350 (Education), letter, Hilldring to Clay, 21 February 1946. All CAD education documents are hereafter cited as WDSCA 350.

18. WDSCA 350, letter, Clay to Hilldring, 6 March 1946.

19. 862.42/7-1045, letter, MacLeish to McCloy, 10 July 1945; OMGUS, Adjutant General's General Correspondence Files (A.G. Files), 1944–45, box 16, E&RA staff meeting, 14 May 1945.

20. WDSCA 350, letter, Clay to Hilldring, 6 March 1946.

21. Ibid.

22. WDSCA 350, letter, George Schulgen to Assistant Secretary of War, 20 March 1946.

23. Irving Wolfson, "The AMG Mess in Germany," *New Republic* 114 (6 March 1946):312.

24. WDSCA 350, memo, Rubin to McCloy, "Utilization of German Universities in the American Zone," 8 September 1945; memo, Hilldring to McCloy, "Procurement of American Teaching Personnel for Work in Germany," 19 September 1946.

25. *New York Times*, 13 March 1946, p. 10; cf. Sidney B. Fay, "Our Responsibility for German Universities," *Forum* 105 (January 1946):396–402.

26. Daniell's story broke first. See *New York Times*, 22 and 26 April 1946.

27. Long's article focused specifically on Munich University; see *New York Times*, 23 April 1946.

28. Drew Middleton's article was buried in the back pages; see *New York Times*, 31 March, sec. VI, p. 10.

29. OMGUS, 306-2/5, telecon, 30 April 1946.

30. OMGUS, 306-2/5, telecon, 10 May 1946.

31. Ibid.

32. Ibid.

33. Earl Ziemke, *The U.S. Army in the Occupation of Germany, 1944–1946* (Washington, D.C., 1975), pp. 400–401.

34. Ibid., pp. 430–32, 439–40. See also Lutz Niethammer, *Entnazifizierung in Bayern: Säuberung und Rehabilitierung unter amerikanischer Besatzung* (Frankfurt a.M., 1972), pp. 272–79, 296–98.

35. OMGUS, 49-2/10, memo, Munich University Screening Committee to E&RA, 15 January 1946.

36. OMGUS, 49-1/10, Report on Education and Religious Affairs, 28 June 1946.

37. OMGUS, 49-2/10, letter, Alfred G. Pundt to Rudolf Pfeiffer, 23 January 1946.

38. OMGUS, 87-3/10, report, Editorial Unit of Intelligence Branch, ICD to Chief of Section, "University of Munich," 9 May 1946; hereafter cited as May 1946 Report.

39. OMGUS, 49-2/10, report, Karl Lowenstein to Legal Division, OMGUS, "The Law School of Munich University and Related Matters," 23 April 1946.

40. OMGUS, 87-3/10, report, Erich Ortenau, "Report to the Director of Intelligence, OMGUS," n.d. [July, 1946].

41. OMGUS, 87-3/10, report, 9 May 1946, p. 9.

42. OMGUS, 49-2/10, letter, Nils Van Steenberg to Frank Banta, E&RA, OMGUS, 6 September 1946.

43. OMGUS, 110-1/10, report, Agent Heinrich Kaltenegger to Lieutenant Peter Harnden, Intelligence Branch, ICD, 3 May 1946.

44. OMGUS, 110-1/10, unsigned report, sent to Chief of Political Affairs Section, ICD, 8 August 1946.

45. OMGUS, 49-2/10, report, E. Y. Hartshorne to Walter Bergman for Lieutenant Colonel Reese, 22 August 1946.

46. OMGUS, 87-3/10, report, Peter Vacca to Director of Intelligence, OMGUS, 19 September 1946.

47. OMGUS, 73-3/10, Military Government photocopy of a letter from N.S. Dozentenführer Dr. Koeppen of the University of Leipzig to Professor Graf von Gleispach in Berlin, 3 June 1935.

48. OMGUS, 73-3/10. These files contain numerous statements, reports, an autobiographical account by the person charged, plus other evidence, including a dismissal notice by the SS, effective as of 28 February 1944. Further evidence is available in the Berlin Documents Center, including the subject's party membership and political as well as professional assessments of his work, dated 30 September 1942, 30 November 1942, and 23 December 1943.

49. OMGUS, 73-3/10, investigative report, Case No. 1656, Special Branch, Munich, 9 August 1946; the files include several Special Branch denunciation reports, including one taken by Agent Metzger on 8 August 1945; see also memo, Captain George J. Bonfield to Commanding Officer, Detachment E201 for Special Branch, 22 August 1945. These files also contain numerous reports and evidence on the subject as well as an autobiographical statement.

50. OMGUS, 49-1/10, numerous reports, statements, prewar correspondence, gun permit from the Gestapo, and other incriminating evidence. The Berlin Documents Center possesses further information, including several decorations, conferred by Hitler himself, such as the Goethe Medaille, awarded 19 April 1939, and the Goldene Treudienst Ehrenzeichen, awarded 13 November 1939.

51. Interview with Dr. Edwin S. Costrell, 6 June 1978.

52. OMGUS, 307-2/5, E&RA minutes, 25 May 1946.

53. OMGUS, 301-3/5, memo, General C. L. Adcock, "Removal of Militarists from German Universities," with accompanying memo by John Taylor to E&RA, Bavaria, "Student Dismissals," 2 July 1946.

54. OMGUS, A.G. Files, 1945–46, box 46, memo, Clay to Director of Internal Affairs and Communications Division, 25 June 1946.

55. OMGUS, A.G. Files, 1945–46, box 46, memo, Taylor to IA&C for DMG [Clay], 19 July 1946.

56. OMGUS, 49-1/10, E&RA, Bavaria, Annual Report, 14 July 1947, p. 1; hereafter cited as 14 July 1947 Report.

57. OMGUS, A.G. Files, 1945–46, box 46, telecon, ICD to Eggleston for Taylor, 17 July 1946.

58. Ibid.

59. OMGUS, A.G. Files, 1945–46, box 46, memo, Taylor to IA&C for Clay, 19 July 1946.

60. Ibid.

61. OMGUS, A.G. Files, 1945–46, box 46, letter, Dorn to Gailey, 24 July 1946.

62. Ibid.

63. OMGUS, A.G. Files, 1945–46, box 46, memo, Gailey to Assistant DMG Adcock, 24 July 1946, together with approval slip by Clay's Office of the Chief of Staff.

64. OMGUS, 87-3/10, report, Peter Harnden, Intelligence Branch, ICD, "Investigation of University of Munich Faculty," 30 September 1946.

65. OMGUS, 49-1/10, directive, Lieutenant Colonel G. H. Garde to Land directors, "Removal of Important German Officials," 21 September 1946.

66. OMGUS, 19-2/8, "Memorandum No. 7 to Field Agents," 10 October 1946.

67. Ibid., pp. 3–4.

68. OMGUS, 19-2/8, memo, Vaughn R. DeLong to Land Director for Hesse, "Policy Relative to Denazification of University Personnel," n.d. [autumn, 1946].

69. OMGUS, 19-2/8, memo, Colonel James Howe to Chief, Policy Enforcement Branch, OMGUS, "Denazification of the Technische Hochschule, Darmstadt," 29 October 1946.

70. Interview with Vaughn R. DeLong, 7 June 1978.

71. OMGUS, 28-2/5, E&RA, Bavaria Historical Report, 1946, Higher Education Section, pp. 123–24.

72. OMGUS, 49-2/10, memo, I. A. Barnett to Minister President, Bavaria, "Teaching Staff of the University of Munich," 12 November 1946.

73. Interview with Dr. Edwin S. Costrell, 6 June 1978; interview with Dr. Martin Mayes, 17 August 1977.

74. Archives of the Westdeutschen Rektoren Konferenz (WRK), Bad Godesberg, letter, R. Sallet to rector of Frankfurt University, 10 September 1946.

75. OMGUS, 49-2/10, E&RA personnel roster; interview with Edwin S. Costrell, 6 June 1978; interview with Martin Mayes, 8 June 1978.

76. OMGUS, 49-1/10, E&RA, Bavaria, report, 14 July 1946, p. 2; for denazification reports and statistics see OMGUS 166-1/3, 304-1/5, and 306-1/5.

77. OMGUS, 49-1/10, memo, Muller to Minister President, Bavaria, 2 October 1946.

78. OMGUS, 28-2/2, memo, Fritz Karsen, E&RA, OMGUS, to E&RA, OMG Württemberg-Baden, 19 January 1947.

79. OMGUS, 301-3/5, memo, R. T. Alexander to E&RA branches, "Former Members of the NASDAP in the Universities," n.d.; OMGUS, 304-1/5, memo, Harry Wann, OMGH, to E&RA, OMGUS, "Inaccurate Reporting of Party Membership by Students," 4 August 1947; OMGUS, 301-3/5, memo, L. D. Gresh to Director, E&RA, Greater Hesse, 13 September 1947.

80. OMGUS, 49-1/10, E&RA, Bavaria, report, 14 July 1947, p. 13.

81. OMGUS, 306-1/5, memo, Rector Josef Martin to Military Government, 23 November 1946.

82. OMGUS, 19-2/8, memo, Gordon Browning to Marvin Boyle, "Würzburg University," 31 August 1946.

83. OMGUS, 19-2/8, memo, Adcock to OMG Bavaria, "Follow-up Report by Lt. Col. Browning on De-nazification of Würzburg University," 16 September 1946.

84. OMGUS, 306-1/5, memo, Charles M. Emerick to Chief, Policy Enforcement Branch, OMGUS, "Denazification of Würzburg University," 7 December 1946.

85. OMGUS, 49-1/10, E&RA, Bavaria, report, 14 July 1947, p. 13; interview with Dr. Edwin S. Costrell, 6 June 1978.

86. OMGUS, 49-1/10, E&RA, Bavaria, report, 14 July 1947, p. 2; E&RA, Bavaria, Historical Report, 1946, Higher Education Section, pp. 123–26 (this report disclosed E&RA's troubles in trying to recruit new instructors).

87. OMGUS, 306-1/5, memo, Charles Emerick to Policy Enforcement Branch, OMGUS, "Denazification of Würzburg University," tab IVC, with a list of the medical-personnel dismissals that took place in October, 1946.

88. OMGUS, 49-1/10, E&RA, Bavaria, report, 14 July 1947, p. 2.

89. OMGUS, 49-2/10, letter, R. Pfeiffer, P. Maas, and E. J. Wellesz to E&RA, Bavaria, 16 December 1946.

90. 862.42/2-2647, minutes of a meeting on the denazification of German educational institutions, 24 February 1947; memo, Henry Kellermann to Hans Speier, 26 February 1947.

91. 862.42/4-1647, American Consul General, Munich, to Secretary of State, "American Press Charges against Bavarian Educational Official," 16 April 1947.

92. Ibid.

93. OMGUS, 49-2/10, investigative report, case no. 1755, by Agent Hans Loesler, 30 September 1946.

94. OMGUS, 304-1/5, memo, Taylor to IA&C Division, OMGUS, "Report on Denazification of Universities in U.S. Zone. . . ," 22 January 1947.

95. Ibid.

96. OMGUS, 19-2/8, memo, Gordon Browning to Marvin Boyle, "Würzburg University," 31 August 1946.

97. 862.42/4-2147, memo, R. J. Sontag to B. C. O'Sullivan, 21 April 1947.

98. OMGUS, 87-3/10, memo, to Chief of Research and Analysis Branch, ICD, Bavaria, 25 June 1947.

99. 862.42/11-2847, memo, Henry Kellermann to Thomas Goldstein, 28 November 1947.

100. 862.42/11-2847, memo, Thomas Goldstein to Henry Kellermann, 1 December 1947.

101. See, especially, Lutz Niethammer, *Entnazifizierung*, pp. 505–37.

102. OMGUS, 306-2/5, telecon, George Geyer to John Taylor, 10 June 1946.

103. Statement by George Geyer, interview, 18 October 1979; 862.42/4-2646, letter, Carr to Kenneth Holland, 26 April 1946.

Chapter 4. *Kulturkampf* in Bavaria

1. U.S. National Archives, Record Group 84, Office of the Political Adviser (POLAD) for Germany, File 842 (Education), box 758, letter, Buhrman to Murphy, 25 March 1946. All documents in the Political Adviser's 842 (Education) files are hereafter cited as POLAD.

2. Ibid.

3. U.S. National Archives, Record Group 260, Office of Military Government (U.S.) for Germany (OMGUS), 307-2/5, E&RA minutes, 10 December 1945. All Military Government documents are hereafter cited as OMGUS, with file classification.

4. Ibid.

5. OMGUS, 308-1/5, letter, O. P. Echols to Clay, 17 April 1946.

6. OMGUS, 308-1/5, memo, Taylor to IA&C Division for Clay, 29 April 1946, returned by IA&C to Taylor.

7. Ibid.

8. U.S. National Archives, Record Group 59, U.S. Department of State, Decimal File 862.42 (Reeducation of Germany), file 862.42/5-646, letter, William G. Carr to David Harris, 6 May 1946. All documents in the State Department's Reeducation-of-Germany decimal files are hereafter cited as 862.42, with file classification.

9. OMGUS, 308-1/5, memo, Taylor to IA&C Division for Clay, 7 May 1946.

10. 862.42/5-46, letter, Carr to Harris, 6 May 1946.

11. U.S. National Archives, Record Group 165, Civil Affairs Division, U.S. Department of War, File WDSCA 350 (Education), memo prepared for the Secretary of War, 19 August 1946. All CAD education documents are hereafter cited as WDSCA 350.

12. Ibid.; 862.42/5-1446, memo, Speier to Anderson, 14 May 1946; 862.42/5-646, letter, Carr to Harris, 6 May 1946.

13. WDSCA 350, memo for the Secretary of War, 19 August 1946; U.S. Department of State, Bureau of Educational and Cultural Affairs, History Files (CU/

H), copy of telephone conversation, Echols to McRae, 22 August 1946. All documents in the State Department's Bureau of Educational and Cultural Affairs History Files are hereafter cited as CU/H.

14. OMGUS, 49-2/10, Report of the U.S. Education Mission to Germany, p. 14.

15. Ibid., p. 16.

16. Ibid.

17. Ibid., p. 19.

18. Ibid., p. 12.

19. State Department, *Occupation of Germany: Policy and Progress, 1945–1946* (Washington, D.C., 1947), pp. 219–20.

20. OMGUS, 49-2/10, copy of Benton's letter of transmittal attached to Mission Report.

21. 862.42/11-1246, letter and accompanying report, Spalding to Benton, 12 November 1946.

22. 862.42/11-1246, letter, Charles M. Hulten to Spalding, 12 December 1946.

23. 862.42/10-1546, letter, Benton to Bell, 28 October 1946.

24. 862.42/10-1546, memo, Leverich to Benton, 21 October 1946.

25. *New York Times*, 24 October 1946, p. 26.

26. OMGUS, 307-2/5, memo, Sumner Sewell, IA&C, OMGUS, to Chief of Staff, OMGUS, with attached cable by Clay, 4 October 1946.

27. OMGUS, 307-2/5, action sheet, Manpower Board, OMGUS to IA&C, OMGUS, 16 October 1946.

28. 862.42/11-1346, memo, Anderson to Leverich, including his "Report on Trip to Germany, Fall, 1946," p. 12, 1 November 1946.

29. OMGUS, 308-1/5, minutes of a conference between E&RA, OMGUS, and Reorientation Branch, WARCAD, 16 January 1947.

30. OMGUS, 308-1/5, letter, McRae to Clay, n.d. [late January 1947].

31. Ibid.

32. Quoted in Lewis Coser, "Germany, 1948: Incidents Taken from the German Press and Letters," *Commonweal* 48 (11 June 1948):208.

33. WDSCA 350, letter, Clay to Hilldring, 6 March 1946.

34. Marshall Knappen, *And Call It Peace* (Chicago, 1947), p. 81.

35. 862.42/11-1846, memo, James Wilkinson to Robert Murphy, 15 October 1946. For Schramm's Hessian scheme, see chapter 5.

36. 862.42/11-1846, dispatch, Robert Murphy, POLAD, to State, with "Proposed School Reform for Bavaria," 18 November 1946.

37. Interview with Vaughn R. DeLong, 7 June 1978. As branch chief for E&RA, Greater Hesse, where the political atmosphere was much less turbulent, DeLong counted himself lucky to be operating there rather than in Bavaria.

38. Interview with Dr. John W. Taylor, 10 September 1977.

39. Staff Study of the Public Affairs Division, High Commission for Germany (HICOG), Communications between the U.S. Office of Education and the State of Bavaria re School Reform, 10 January 1947 to 20 December 1949, compiled by Martin Mayes and Martin Ackerman—hereafter cited as Staff Study (SS); OMGUS, 301-1/5, memo, Civil Administration Division to IA&C for E&RA, n.d.

[February, 1947] with E&RA reply; OMGUS, 301-1/5, memo, Henry Parkman, CAD, OMGUS, to IA&C, 19 February 1947.

40. OMGUS, 301-1/5, speech by Taylor, "American Education Policy: Address to the German Ministries by Dr. John W. Taylor in February, 1947."

41. Ibid.

42. Ibid.

43. Interview with Taylor, 10 September 1977.

44. OMGUS, 304-1/5, memo, Taylor to IA&C Division, OMGUS, 22 January 1947.

45. Sir Robert Birley, "Education in the British Zone of Germany," *International Affairs* 26 (1950):32–33; statement by Mr. Trevor Davies, former education officer, Education Branch, Control Commission (British Element), to Ruhr University Conference on Postwar German Education Reform, held at Bielefeld, 17–20 September 1979.

46. 862.42/4-1147, dispatch, James Wilkinson to State, 11 April 1947.

47. 862.42/5-2147, dispatch, Wilkinson to State, 21 May 1947.

48. POLAD, box 460, directive, G. H. Garde, Adjutant General's Office, OMGUS, to E&RA, OMGB, 14 May 1947. R. T. Alexander sent a nearly identical memo in June; see OMGUS, 303-3/5, memo, Alexander to E&RA, OMGB, 23 June 1947.

49. OMGUS, 308-2/5, E&RA minutes, 27 May 1947.

50. OMGUS, 303-3/5, letter, Alexander to Agnes Snyder, 9 April 1948.

51. OMGUS, 10-3/4, letter, Levi Gresh to Howard Johnston, 30 August 1948.

52. OMGUS, 303-3/5, letters, Alexander to Henry Hill, 19 April 1947, and to Hayes Beall, 27 October 1947. In his letter to President Hill, Alexander wrote: "I feel quite sure that I can be with you in the summer of 1948"—a reference to a proposal that he participate in a series of conferences.

53. OMGUS, 430-3/3, reprint of ACA 54 in memo, "Democratization of Germany," by IA&C Division, OMGUS, November 1947.

54. SS, memo, Al D. Sims, director, IA&C, OMGB, to Ehard for Hundhammer, 25 June 1947.

55. Arthur Hearnden, ed., *The British in Germany* (London, 1978), pp. 46–47.

56. Interview with Taylor, 10 September 1977.

57. *Stenographische Berichte über die Verhandlungen des Bayerischen Landtags* (Munich, 1947), vol. 25, no. 1, 25th session (17 July 1947), pp. 801–12.

58. SS, report, "Analysis and Criticism of Bavarian School Reform Plan of 1 October 1947," by Al D. Sims, 6 October 1947.

59. 862.42/10-247, dispatch, Sam E. Woods to State, 2 October 1947.

60. 862.42/10-2147, dispatch, Woods to State, 21 October 1947.

61. Ibid.

62. 862.42/11-1447, dispatch, Woods to State, 14 November 1947.

63. SS, letter, Lucius Clay to Hans Ehard, 14 November 1947.

64. SS, memo, R. T. Alexander to E&RA Chief, OMGB, plus a copy of Clay's November 14 letter to Ehard.

65. OMGUS, 49-2/10, personnel roster for E&RA, OMGB.

66. Interviews with Colonel William R. Swarm, 24 August 1977 and 29 August 1979; interview with Martin Mayes, 8 June 1978.

67. Interviews with Edwin S. Costrell, 6 and 8 June 1978, and with Martin Mayes, 17 August and 2 September 1977.

68. OMGUS, 308-1/5, report, Mildred English to R. T. Alexander, 23 December 1947 (hereafter cited as English Report). English's report indicated strong tensions between E&RA, OMGUS, and Land Director Van Wagoner. Similar disputes continued into 1948; see OMGUS, 302-2/5, minutes, E&CR Branch Chiefs Meeting in Berlin, 3–4 March 1948.

69. OMGUS, 49-2/10, personnel roster, E&RA, OMGB.

70. Interview with Martin Mayes, 2 September 1977.

71. OMGUS, 308-1/5, English Report.

72. OMGUS, 49-2/10, personnel roster, E&RA, OMGB; 306-2/5, telecon, Taylor to Geyer, 11 June 1946, directing Falk into a position in Württemberg-Baden; English Report; 49-2/10, memo, Louis Miniclier to Deputy Land Director Bolds, 19 April 1948, recommending Falk's promotion.

73. English Report; interview with Martin Mayes, 2 September 1977.

74. English Report.

75. Interview with Edwin S. Costrell, 8 June 1978. Costrell was still unaware, thirty years later, of Falk's religious past.

76. OMGUS, 49-2/10, memo, Miniclier to Bolds, 19 April 1948.

77. OMGUS, 308-1/5, memo, Derthick to Alexander, 5 May 1948.

78. Interview with Martin Mayes, 2 September 1977.

79. English Report.

80. Ibid.

81. OMGUS, 308-1/5, report, L. J. Brueckner to E&RA, OMGUS, 12 February 1948.

82. English Report; OMGUS, 49-1/10, minutes of meeting between E&RA, OMGB, and Bavarian Ministry of Education, 16 December 1947.

83. SS, memo, Falk to IA&C, OMGB, "Non-compliance of Bavarian Government Officials," 23 February 1948.

84. SS, memo, Van Wagoner to Ehard, "Rejection of School Reform Plan for Bavaria," 23 December 1947.

85. SS, letter, Ehard to Van Wagoner, 31 December 1947.

86. SS, radio speech by Minister of Education Hundhammer, 21 January 1948.

87. Staatsarchiv München, document collection no. 60, Philosophische-Theologische Hochschule Freising, letter from rectorate to Ministry of Education, 2 February 1948. All documents from the Staatsarchiv document collection no. 60 are hereafter cited as SM 60.

88. SM 60, petition by Arbeitskreis, "Freunde der Schulreform," Münster, 1 January 1948.

89. SM 60, petition, "Erklärung zur Schulreform," n.d.

90. OMGUS, 141-3/13, School Reform Plan, 31 January 1948, pp. 1–2, 10.

91. SS, memo, "MG Comment on School Reform Question," 29 January 1948; see also OMGUS, 308-1/5, report, L. J. Brueckner to E&RA, OMGUS, 12 February 1948.

92. 862.42/11-1447, dispatch, Woods to State, 14 November 1947; 862.42/1-2248, dispatch, Woods to State, 22 January 1948.

93. OMGUS, 302-2/5, minutes, E&RA Branch Chiefs Meeting, 4–5 February 1948, pp. 17–18.

94. POLAD, box 460, December 1947, Chicago professors' report, "Secondary Education in Germany" (written in October, 1947). Murphy's marginal comment is on page 14.

95. OMGUS, 303-3/5, memo, Alexander to George McKibbon, 25 November 1947.

96. SS, memo, Alexander to E&RA, OMGB, 10 December 1948.

97. SS, memo, Mayes to Director, Internal Affairs Division, OMGB, 24 February 1948.

98. SS, memo, Louis Miniclier to Directors, Legal, Intelligence, and Civil Administration divisions, OMGB, 19 March 1948.

99. SS, memo, John Bradford to Director, E&CR Division, OMGB, 29 March 1948.

100. SS, Paul Moeller, Research Branch, OMGB, to Director, IA&C Division, OMGB, 30 March 1948.

101. SS, letter, Van Wagoner to Ehard, 1 April 1948.

102. SS, report, Charles Falk, "Report on Bavarian School Reform Situation," 26 May 1948.

103. Ibid.; SS, report, Miniclier to Land Director, 26 May 1948.

104. SS, report, Lieutenant Colonel Paul Burns to Civil Administration Division, May 1948.

105. SS, Falk and Miniclier reports, 26 May 1948.

106. OMGUS, 302-2/5, minutes, E&RA Branch Chiefs Meeting in Berlin, 4–5 February 1948, p. 1.

107. OMGUS, 302-2/5, minutes, E&CR Branch Chiefs Meeting in Berlin, 3–4 March 1948, p. 2.

108. Ibid.

109. Interview with Dr. Lawrence G. Derthick, 18 August 1977.

110. Interview with Dr. Charles Winning, 1 August 1978; OMGUS, 306-2/5, telecon, Taylor to Geyer, 11 June 1946.

111. SS, report, Winn to Director, E&CR, OMGB, 15 July 1948.

112. SS, letter, Van Wagoner to Clay, 16 July 1948.

113. SS, cable, Muelder, Acting Director, E&CR, OMGUS, to Land Director,with Clay's approval, 25 July 1948.

114. SS, report, Winn to Director, E&CR, OMGB, 15 July 1948.

115. POLAD, box 460, file W-1948, copy of letter, Faulhaber to Van Wagoner, 19 July 1948.

116. Cited ibid.

117. Ibid.

118. Ibid.

119. Ibid.

120. POLAD, box 460, file W-1948, letter, Van Wagoner to Clay, 28 July 1948.

121. SS, letter, Van Wagoner to Ehard, 4 August 1948.

122. SS, letter, Clay to Ehard, 31 August 1948.

123. POLAD, box 460, file W-1948, memo, Clay to Murphy, 29 August 1948.

124. OMGUS, Adjutant General Files, 1948, decimal no. 007, letter, Clay to Bonner, 5 June 1948.

125. 862.42/10-448, memo, J. D. Beam to Henry Kellermann, 27 September 1948.

126. 862.42/12-3048, dispatch, Woods to State, 30 December 1948.

127. Stenographische Berichte über die Verhandlungen des Ausschusses für kulturpolitische Fragen, Bayerischen Landtag, 22nd session, 4 February 1950 (unpublished stenographic reports in the archival collection of the Bavarian Landtag, Munich).

128. OMGUS, 49-3/10, letter, Lutz Vogel to Van Wagoner, 17 January 1949; letter, Winning to Vogel, 31 January 1949.

129. 862.42/8-1849, dispatch, Woods to State, 18 August 1949.

130. OMGUS, 49-3/10, memo, Winning to Hundhammer, 22 March 1949.

131. 862.4212/2-349, petition, Rudolf von Bennigsen-Foerder, ASTA at Erlangen, to Undersecretary of State C. E. Saltzman, 3 February 1949.

132. 862.4212/2-349, letter, Kellermann to Edgar Hume, Civil Affairs Division, Department of the Army, 12 March 1949.

133. OMGUS, 303-3/5, minutes of Special Committee on Education, Schoenberg/Taunus, 9–10 February 1948, recorded by Heinz Guradze of the RGCO.

134. Archives of the Westdeutschen Rektoren Konferenz (WRK) in Bad Godesberg, letters, Rektor Kroll to Rektor Boehm, 23 and 25 October 1948; letter, Rektor Boehm to Rektor Kroll, 26 October 1948.

135. 862.2/4-247, memo, R. J. Sontag to B. C. O'Sullivan, 24 April 1947.

Chapter Five. Around the Zone

1. Interviews with Vaughn R. DeLong, 7 June 1978 and 3 September 1980.

2. U.S. National Archives, Record Group 260, Office of Military Government (U.S.) for Germany (OMGUS), 303-3/5, unsigned memo, "Lt. Col.Knappen's Trip to the U.S. Zone," 19 December 1946 [sic; the year was in fact 1945]. All Military Government documents are hereafter cited as OMGUS, with file classification.

3. OMGUS, 302-1/5, E&RA Annual Report, OMG Greater Hesse, 1946, p. 4 (hereafter cited as 1946 Annual Report).

4. Ibid., pp. 1–2.

5. Ibid., p. 3.

6. Interview with Vaughn R. DeLong, 3 September 1980.

7. OMGUS, 307-2/5, minutes, E&RA meeting, 10 December 1945, p. 5.

8. OMGUS, 19-3/8, Commemorative Speech by Professor Franz Böhm, n.d. [December, 1945], p. 8.

9. 1946 Annual Report, p. 5.

10. Ibid., p. 6.

11. Cited in Wolf-Arno Kropat, *Hessen in der Stunde Null, 1945–1947* (Wiesbaden, 1979), p. 109.

12. Letter, Geiler to chairman of the CDU in Stadtkreis Frankfurt, 20 February 1946, cited ibid., p. 110.

13. Interview with Vaughn R. DeLong, 2 September 1980.

14. OMGUS, 18-2/8, box 5078, secret memo, unsigned, 12 April 1947, p. 1.

15. 1946 Annual Report, Annex N, "Proposed School Reform in Greater Hesse."

16. Kropat, p. 288.

17. Cited by Kropat, pp. 141–43.

18. U.S. National Archives, Record Group 59, Department of State, Office of Strategic Services (OSS), Office of Institutional Research (OIR), report no. 4237, 3 June 1947, p. 15.

19. OMGUS, 306-2/5, telecon, Taylor to Geyer, 14 May 1946, p. 2.

20. Ibid., p. 1.

21. Ibid.

22. OMGUS, 54-3/6, box 279, telecon, Edward D'Arms to Taylor, 9 December 1946, p. 2.

23. OMGUS, 16-3/8, memo, Harry A. Wann to Erwin Stein, "Investigation of Various School Situations," 19 March 1947.

24. OMGUS, 18-1/8, memo, DeLong to E&RA, OMGUS, "Recommendations for Education Experts—Hesse," 14 September 1946.

25. Interview with Vaughn R. DeLong, 7 June 1978.

26. Survey reprinted in Kropat, pp. 295–97.

27. OMGUS, 16-2/8, minutes, Third Joint Meeting of the Education Division and the Ministry of Education in Land Hesse, Wiesbaden, 20 February 1947.

28. Ibid., pp. 2–3.

29. Ibid., p. 4.

30. Ibid., pp. 5–7.

31. OMGUS, 18-2/8, secret memo, 12 April 1947.

32. Ibid.

33. OMGUS, 17-1/8, letter, Wann to Stein, 1 April 1947.

34. OMGUS, 17-1/8, letter, Wann to E. B. Fred, 12 May 1947.

35. OMGUS, 303-3/5, memo, Stein to Wann, 3 June 1947.

36. OMGUS, 308-2/5, minutes, E&RA, OMGUS, meeting, 20 April 1947.

37. OMGUS, 15-2/8, memo, E&RA staff to Minister of Education, "The New School-Committee Procedures," 12 September 1947, p. 1.

38. Ibid.

39. Ibid., p. 3.

40. Cited in OMGUS, 55-1/6, box 293, report, Wann to Alexander, Report on Proposals of Reform of the School System in Hesse," 30 October 1947.

41. Ibid.

42. OMGUS, 55-1/6, box 292, memo, Alexander to E&RA Branch Chiefs, 23 January 1948 (copy in OMG Bremen E&RA files).

43. OMGUS, 55-1/6, box 293, memo, Wann to Alexander, 30 October 1947 (copy in OMG Bremen E&RA files).

44. OMGUS, 17-1/8, memo, Wann to OMG Hesse E&RA Branch Chiefs, 24 September 1947.

45. OMGUS, 18-1/8, letter, Wann to Charles Hamilton, 19 December 1947; see also OMGUS, 18-1/8, letter, Wann to Frederick Moffitt, 16 December 1947.

46. OMGUS, 303-3/5, letter, Hayes Beall to Alexander, 17 October 1947.

47. Personnel list, Office of the U.S. High Commissioner for Germany, compiled by William R. Wrinkle, 11 March 1953, "Cumulative Record of OMGUS and HICOG Education Advisers, 1946–1953"; copy in author's possession.

48. OMGUS, 303-3/5, letter, Hayes Beall to Alexander, 17 October 1947.

49. Ibid.

50. OMGUS, 303-3/5, letter, Alexander to Beall, 27 October 1947.

51. OMGUS, 17-2/8, minutes, meeting of E&RA Branch Chiefs, Weisbaden, 5–6 November 1947, p. 3.

52. Cited in OMGUS, 437-1/3, memo, James R. Newman to Minister President of Land Hesse, 2 August 1948, p. 110.

53. OMGUS, 303-3/5, memo, DeLong to Alexander, 11 February 1948.

54. OMGUS, 16-3/8, Quarterly Historical Report (QHR), General Education Branch, Hesse, 1 January–31 March 1948.

55. Cited in OMGUS, 15-1/8, report, Office of the Director of Intelligence (ODI), "Why Bavarians Oppose School Reform," July 1948, p. 5.

56. OMGUS, 15-2/8, letter, William L. Wrinkle to Alexander, 1 December 1947.

57. Ibid., p. 3.

58. Ibid., p. 4.

59. Interview with Vaughn R. DeLong, 3 September 1980.

60. Interview with Vaughn R. DeLong, 7 June 1978; OMGUS, 302-2/5, OMGGH, E&RA Annual Report, 1946, pp. 18–19.

61. Annual Report, 1946, pp. 20–21.

62. Ibid., p. 24.

63. OMGUS, 16-2/8, minutes, Third Joint Meeting, Education Division and Ministry of Education, 20 February 1947, p. 4.

64. Ibid., p. 6.

65. Interview with Vaughn R. DeLong, 7 June 1978. DeLong always maintained that it was far easier to reform Hesse's two teacher-training institutions than to try to accomplish the same thing in Bavaria's thirty-five institutions.

66. OMGUS, 16-1/8, Popular History of the E&RA Division (OMGGH), 28 February 1947, p. 4.

67. OMGUS, 16-3/8, Quarterly Historical Report (QHR), General Education Branch, 1 January–31 March 1948, p. 3.

68. OMGUS, 15-2/8, letter, Fair to Flowers, 21 April 1948.

69. U.S. National Archives, Record Group 84, Office of the Political Adviser (POLAD) for Germany, File 842 (Education), box 805, unsigned memo, "Teachers College—Fulda," with attached letter, Stanley Bertke to Robert Murphy, 5 February 1948. All documents in the Political Adviser's 842 (Education) files are hereafter cited as POLAD, with file classification.

70. Ibid.

71. OMGUS, 308-2/5, minutes, E&RA, OMGUS, meeting, 20 June 1947.

72. POLAD, box 805, letter, Alexander to Murphy, 25 March 1948.

73. Ibid.

74. POLAD, box 805, memo, for record, prepared by Murphy, 2 April 1948.

75. OMGUS, 16-3/8, Quarterly Historical Report (QHR), General Education Branch, 1 January–31 March 1948, pp. 2–3.

76. OMGUS, 15-2/8, memo, DeLong to Wann, 25 February 1948.

77. Cited in OMGUS, 437-1/3, memo, "The Six-Year Elementary School," Newman to Minister President, 2 August 1948, p. 111. Newman recounted the course of events leading up to a Military Government order to institute school reform in Greater Hesse. He included the request for data of April 19, 1948.

78. OMGUS, 15-1/8, minutes, Curriculum Committee Meeting, Wiesbaden, 15–16 July 1948, p. 5.

79. Ibid.

80. OMGUS, 15-2/8, letter, DeLong to Wann, 19 July 1948.

81. Ibid.

82. OMGUS, 15-2/8, letter, DeLong to Wann, 24 July 1948. DeLong had informed the other E&RA leaders that disunity within the Hessian education ministry was a prime difficulty. Stein was not, in his opinion, a professional "school man"; he often disagreed with his professional staff and with committees. Politics was also playing too prominent a role in the debates about reforms. Finally, currency reform was slowing progress; DeLong felt that, while Reichsmark budgets had given "extremely valuable assistance" to school reform, the new currency was rapidly impoverishing education budgets. See also OMGUS, 15-1/8, minutes, Curriculum Committee Meeting, Wiesbaden, 15–16 July 1948, p. 8.

83. OMGUS, 15-2/8, letter, DeLong to Wann, 24 July 1948.

84. OMGUS, 15-1/8, minutes, Joint E&RA–Education Ministry Meeting, 26 July 1948, pp. 2–3; hereafter cited as July 26 Meeting.

85. OMGUS, 15-1/8, minutes, Curriculum Committee Meeting, Weisbaden, 25–26 July 1948, p. 8.

86. July 26 Meeting, p. 6.

87. Ibid., p. 7.

88. Ibid., p. 9.

89. Ibid., pp. 16–17.

90. OMGUS, 15-2/8, letter, DeLong to Wann, 31 July 1948.

91. OMGUS, 437-1/3, memo, Newman to Minister President, 2 August 1948.

92. OMGUS, 15-2/8, letter, DeLong to Wann, 7 August 1948.

93. Ibid.

94. Interview with Paul S. Bodenman, 16 March 1981; interview with Martin Mayes, 23 April 1981.

95. OMGUS, 15-1/8, letter, DeLong to Bernice Leary, 4 October 1948.

96. OMGUS, 15-1/8, copy of letter, Stein to Burr Phillips, n.d. [October 1948].

97. OMGUS, 15-1/8, report, Office of the Director of Intelligence (ODI), "Why Bavarians Oppose School Reform," July 1948, p. 1.

98. OMGUS, 15-2/8, transcript, radio broadcast of discussion among DeLong, Stein, and Haupt, "Why School Reform?" n.d. [November or December, 1948].

99. OMGUS, 15-2/8, minutes, Joint E&CR–Education Ministry Meeting, 29 November 1948, p. 8.

100. Ibid., p. 13.

101. Ibid., p. 10.

102. Ibid., p. 17.

103. Ibid., p. 18.

104. Ibid., pp. 17, 22.

105. Ibid., pp. 25, 30.

106. OMGUS, 15-2/8, Information Report no. 389, "Resolution of the CDU Fraction . . . concerning Hesse School Law," George Vadney to Chief, Intelligence Division, OMGGH, 30 November 1948, copy to E&CR, OMGGH.

107. OMGUS, 16-3/8, report, "CDU Membership Meeting," 8 December 1948.

108. OMGUS, 16-3/8, report, "Minister of Culture Dr. Stein Speaks at Meeting of CDU Members," Information Report no. 538—Political, Kassel District Liaison and Security Office, OMGGH, to Chief, Intelligence Division, OMGGH, 15 December 1948, pp. 3–4.

109. Ibid., p. 6.

110. OMGUS, 15-1/8, minutes, German-American Meetings on School Organization, 17, 21, and 27 December 1948.

111. OMGUS, 58-2/6, box 303, memo, Hessian Kultusminister to E&CR Division, "Fifth School Year," 3 February 1949.

112. U.S. National Archives, Record Group 59, Department of State, File 862.42 (Reeducation of Germany), 862.42/3-1849, report of POLAD, Frankfurt to State Department, "Public Education in Land Hesse," 18 March 1949. All documents in the State Department's Reeducation-of-Germany decimal files are hereafter cited as 862.42, with classification.

113. OMGUS, 15-1/8, letter, DeLong to Robert Ebel, 7 December 1948.

114. OMGUS, 15-2/8, letter, DeLong to Fred Hechinger, 23 December 1948.

115. Kropat, pp. 293–94 (see n. 11, above).

116. Kenneth Bateman, "Innovation in German Schools," Educational *Leadership* 25 (March 1968):541–51; Paul S. Bodenman, "The Educational System of the Federal Republic of Germany" (Washington, D.C.: U.S. Office of Education, 1975), pp. 9–10.

117. OMGUS, 53-1/6, box 269, weekly casum (report), "Education and Religion," prepared by Harold Crabill, 30 November 1945, p. 3.

118. Earl F. Ziemke, *The U.S. Army in the Occupation of Germany, 1944–1946* (Washington, D.C., 1975), p. 270.

119. OMGUS, 55-3/6, box 285, E&RA, OMG, Bremen, Annual Report, 1946/47, p. 5 (hereafter cited as Bremen E&RA Annual Report, 1946/47); OMGUS, 53-1/6, box 269, weekly casum (report), "Education and Religion," 30 November 1945.

120. OMGUS, 53-3/6, box 272, "Report on a Conference with Senator Paulmann," 1 October 1945.

121. Bremen E&RA Annual Report, 1946/47, p. 10.

122. Lucius D. Clay, *Decision in Germany* (New York, 1950), p. 92; OMGUS, 54-2/6, box 279, E&RA monthly report, "History, Education," n.d. [November or December 1945], p. 3.

123. OMGUS, 53-1/6, box 269, weekly casum, "Education and Religion," 30 November 1945.

124. OMGUS, 53-1/6, box 272, "Report . . . Paulmann," 1 October 1945.

125. OMGUS, 54-2/6, box 279, report, "History . . . ," n.d. [November–December 1945], p. 2.

126. Bremen E&RA Annual Report, 1946/47, p. 64; OMGUS, 430-3/3, E&RA, OMGUS Report, 1947, p. 64.

127. OMGUS, 302-2/5, minutes, E&CR Branch Chiefs meeting, 3–4 March, 1948, p. 1. The discussion revealed that, although all E&CR organizations were shorthanded, Bremen and Berlin were hardest hit.

128. OMGUS, 56-2/6, box 287, report, "Conference of 14 January 1947 between . . . E&RA and Bremen Board of Education . . . ," 14 January 1947.

129. OMGUS, 56-2/6, box 287, report, "Conference of 20 January 1947 . . . ," 20 January 1947.

130. OMGUS, 303-3/5, memo, "Aims and Proposals of Bremen School Reform," Alexander to E&RA, Bremen, 30 May 1947, with attached memo, "Comments . . . ," by E&RA, OMGUS, personnel.

131. Bremen E&RA Annual Report, 1946/47, p. 2.

132. Ibid., p. 22.

133. OMGUS, 55-1/6, box 283, report, "August–October 1947," p. 1.

134. Ibid., pp. 2–3; OMGUS, 54-2/6, box 278, report, "Denominational Schools in Bremen," n.d. [August, 1947].

135. OMGUS, 55-1/6, box 282, minutes, "Conference . . . , 18 August 1947 . . . ," p. 1.

136. Ibid., pp. 2–4; OMGUS, 55-1/6, box 283, report, "August–October 1947," p. 3.

137. OMGUS, 17-2/8, minutes, meeting of E&RA Branch Chiefs in Wiesbaden, 5–6 November 1947, pp. 2–3.

138. OMGUS, 56-2/6, box 292, memo, Crabill to Dunn, "Supervision of German Education . . . ," 24 January 1948.

139. OMGUS, 56-1/6, box 291, memo, Thomas Dunn to Christian Paulmann, 3 February 1948.

140. OMGUS, 56-1/6, box 291, memo, Christian Paulmann to Crabill, 5 February 1948.

141. Robert Birley, "Education in the British Zone of Germany," *International Affairs* 26 (1950):32–34; Arthur Hearnden, ed., *The British in Germany: Education Reconstruction after 1945* (London, 1978), pp. 21–29.

142. Hearnden, pp. 16–21; Birley, p. 36. Birley's suggestion of a commission to study reforms allowed Schnippenköter, by accepting the idea, to delay making any decision for at least five years.

143. Hearnden, pp. 30–36.

144. Birley, pp. 34–35.

145. OMGUS, 56-2/6, box 292, memo, Crabill to Director, OMG, Bremen, 24 January 1948, p. 4.

146. OMGUS, 57-1/6, box 295, unsigned memo, "School Reform," prepared for a Länderrat report, 2 March 1948.

147. OMGUS, 57-1/6, box 295, minutes, E&CR Curriculum Meeting, Munich, 21 May 1948, p. 3.

148. OMGUS, 57-1/6, box 295, minutes, E&CR Curriculum Meeting, Bremen, 17–18 June 1948, p. 7.

149. OMGUS, 57-2/6, box 296, translation of a memo, Senator for Legislation and the Constitution to Senator Paulmann, 6 February 1948; copy in Crabill's files.

150. OMGUS, 57-2/6, box 296, carrier sheet and memo, Crabill to Legal Division, OMG, Bremen, 13 February 1948, with attached reply, R. W. Johnson to Education Division, 13 February 1948.

151. OMGUS, 58-2/6, box 304, memo, "School Legislation," Crabill to Muelder and Riedl, E&CR, OMGUS, 11 March 1949.

152. OMGUS, 57-2/6, box 296, memo, Thomas Dunn to President [Kaisen] of Senate, Bremen, 15 May 1948.

153. OMGUS, 56-1/6, box 291, minutes, "Schulleiterkonferenz," 2 September 1948.

154. OMGUS, 57-2/6, box 296, memo, Crabill to Dunn, 4 September 1948.

155. OMGUS, 56-1/6, box 291, memo, Dunn to Paulmann, 7 July 1948.

156. OMGUS, 56-3/6, box 293, letter, Crabill to Volker Hoffmeyer, 4 August 1948.

157. OMGUS, 56-3/6, box 293, memo, "Dismissal of Teachers in Bremerhaven," Crabill to Dunn, 3 September 1948.

158. OMGUS, 56-3/6, box 293, memo, Johann Lohmann to OMG, Bremen, "Resolutions of Bremen High School Parents Meeting," 4 October 1948.

159. OMGUS, 56-3/6, box 294, report, "Scrutiny and Violations," by Frederick Mellinger, n.d. [October 1948].

160. OMGUS, 57-1/6, box 295, report, "Elementary-Secondary Conference at Wiesbaden," 18–19 November 1948, p. 8.

161. OMGUS, 58-2/6, box 304, memo, Crabill to Charles Jeffs, 23 February 1949.

162. OMGUS, 58-3/6, box 306, memo, Crabill to Jeffs, 11 January 1949.

163. OMGUS, 58-2/6, box 304, memo, Crabill to Norman Metal, Bremen OMG legal adviser, 21 February 1949, p. 3.

164. OMGUS, 58-2/6, box 304, memo, Crabill to Jeffs, 23 February 1949.

165. Ibid.

166. OMGUS, 58-2/6, box 304, memo, Crabill to Muelder and Riedl, "School Legislation," 11 March 1949.

167. George F. Kennan, *Memoirs, 1925–1950* (Boston, 1967), p. 438.

168. See chapter 6.

169. 862.42/4-1949, Bremen School Law, enclosure to dispatch no. 177, 19 April 1949, p. 7.

170. Ibid.

171. Ziemke, pp. 307–8 (see n. 118, above).

172. Interview with Colonel William R. Swarm, 29 August 1979.

173. Richard G. Banks, "The Development of Education in Württemberg-Baden under United States Military Government" (M.A. thesis, University of Virginia,

1949), p. 109; hereafter cited as Banks thesis. Banks served for three years in a leading capacity in the Land. His thesis was based on official reports from OMGWB and on personal notes.

174. Ibid., p. 78.

175. Ibid., p. 81.

176. OMGUS, 306-2/5, telecon, 14 May 1946, p. 1. See also Banks thesis, pp. 83–84.

177. Banks thesis, p. 114.

178. Ibid., p. 128; OMGUS, 308-3/5, box 93, memo, R. T. Alexander, "Teacher Education in Germany: American Zone," 16 February 1946.

179. Banks thesis, p. 128, footnote.

180. Ibid., p. 129.

181. Ibid., p. 160.

182. Ibid., p. 161, Banks's complaint was a common one. Recruiters for E&RA at the Pentagon experienced difficulty in attracting able personnel. See OMGUS, 306-2/5, telecon, 10 June 1946; 54-2/6, box 279, telecon, 23 December 1946, p. 6.

183. Banks thesis, p. 161.

184. OMGUS, 307-2/5, E&RA minutes, 10 December 1945.

185. Banks thesis, pp. 154, 196.

186. Interview with Paul S. Bodenman, 16 March 1981; Banks thesis, pp. 180–82.

187. Banks thesis, p. 184.

188. Ibid., p. 186. OMGUS, 85-1/12, box 26, memo, Bäuerle to E&RA Division, "School Reorganization," 30 March 1947. Bäuerle pointedly reminded the Americans of the Land's village-school tradition.

189. OMGUS, 252-1/5, *News of Germany* 2, no. 109 (27 March 1947):1 (a publication of Information Control Division). Simpfendörfer returned to his post as a school director but later served as an education minister in the 1950s.

190. Banks thesis, p. 189.

191. OMGUS, 85-2/12, box 26, topical report, "Summer 1947, Schools Branch," p. 3.

192. 862.42/3-1148, Weekly Intelligence Report no. 4, 28 January 1948, issued by OMG Württemberg-Baden, enclosure to dispatch no. 76, 11 March 1948, from the American Consulate, Stuttgart; hereafter cited as OMGWB Weekly Intelligence Report, with file classification.

193. OMGUS, 303-3/5, translation of a speech made by Minister Bäuerle, Education Ministers' Conference in Stuttgart, 19–20 February 1948, p. 2.

194. OMGWB Weekly Intelligence Report no. 4, 29 January 1948, p. 5.

195. OMGWB Weekly Intelligence Report no. 44, 29 October 1947, p. 12.

196. OMGWB Weekly Intelligence Report no. 4, 29 January 1948, p. 7.

197. Ibid., p. 8.

198. Ibid.

199. OMGUS, 87-2/12, memo, Payne Templeton to Christian Caselmann, 27 January 1948.

200. OMGUS, 87-2/12, memo, Richard G. Banks to Theodor Bäuerle, 14 February 1948.

201. OMGUS, 57-2/6, box 295, memo, R. T. Alexander to chiefs of E&RA, "Interpretation of Control Council Directive No. 54 . . . ," 1 December 1947.

202. OMGUS, 87-2/12, memo, Banks to Bäuerle, 14 February 1948.

203. OMGUS, 85-1/12, memo, Steiner to Bäuerle, 26 April 1948.

204. OMGUS, 56-3/12, minutes, curriculum meeting held in Bremen, 17–18 June 1948, pp. 10–11.

205. OMGUS, 85-1/12, memo, Theodor Bäuerle to John Steiner, 5 July 1948.

206. OMGUS, 58-1/6, box 304, minutes, E&CR directors' meeting held in Stuttgart, 17–18 August 1948, p. 10.

207. 862.42/11-148, dispatch no. 455, 1 November 1948, American Consulate, Stuttgart, to State, p. 3. This dispatch was prepared by James Wilkinson, who earlier had reported on education progress in Munich.

208. OMGUS, 85-1/12, box 26, unsigned memo, "Status of School Legislation," 1 November 1948, p. 1.

209. OMGWB Weekly Intelligence Report no. 42, 20 October 1948, cited in 862.42/11-148, dispatch no. 455, p. 2.

210. OMGUS, 85-1/12, box 26, unsigned memo, "Status of School Legislation," 1 November 1948, p. 2.

211. Ibid.

212. OMGUS, 308-3/5, box 93, memo, "Teacher Training Institutions," 19 December 1947. See also Banks thesis, p. 221; OMGUS, 430-3/3, report, "Progress of Education, 1946–1947," pp. 61–64; OMGUS, 85-1/12, unsigned memo, E&RA to Bäuerle, n.d. [October 1947], in which the E&RA staff desired "the placing of all teacher training on the university level."

213. 862.42/11-148, dispatch no. 455, 1 November 1948, p. 3.

214. OMGWB Weekly Intelligence Report no. 43, 27 October 1948, attached to dispatch no. 462, 5 November 1948, American Consulate, Stuttgart, to State, copy in POLAD, box 805; OMGUS, 85-1/12, box 26, memo, Bäuerle to E&RA, "School Reorganization," 30 March 1947, p. 2. Bäuerle had consistently reminded his American colleagues of the need "to coordinate the organization of the Württemberg-Baden school system . . . with the programs of the other Länder of the U.S. Zone of Occupation and, whenever possible, of all the occupied zones."

215. The French organized summer programs for hundreds of young people in several different locations of their zone. They made a point of matching German students with an equal number of French students, plus half again as many foreigners. They also widely advertised their programs in the other zones. See OMGUS, 56-1/6, letter, French Consul A. Schober to Thomas Dunn, Bremen, 25 May 1948, with attached prospectus of French summer programs.

216. OMGWB Weekly Intelligence Report no. 43, 27 October 1948.

217. Ibid.

218. 862.42/1-2448, dispatch no. 8, 24 January 1948, American Consulate, Baden-Baden, to State, p. 2. Dorothy Barker, a consular official, prepared this lengthy memorandum on French educational programs.

219. Helen Liddell, "Education in Occupied Germany: A Field Study," *International Affairs* 23 (1947):40–44; Percy Bidwell, "Reeducation in Germany: Emphasis on Culture in the French Zone," *Foreign Affairs* 27 (October 1948):78–85.

220. OMGWB Weekly Intelligence Report no. 43, 27 October 1948, p. 3.

221. 862.42/12-1748, dispatch no. 146, 17 December 1948, American Consulate, Baden-Baden, to State. Dorothy Barker detected a significant stiffening of German resistance to the French educational authorities by the end of 1948.

222. OMGWB Weekly Intelligence Report no. 48, 1 December 1948, cited in 862.42/12-1348, dispatch no. 506, 13 December 1948, American Consulate, Stuttgart, to State.

223. Banks thesis, p. 254. Liddell noted a similar discrepancy between the attempts of French education officers to maintain friendly contacts with the Germans and the attitudes adopted by other divisions of French Military Government; see Liddell, "Education . . . ," *International Affairs* 23 (1947):42–43.

224. OMGUS, 58-2/6, box 304, minutes, E&CR Directors meeting, Stuttgart, 17–18 August 1948, p.10.

225. 862.42/11-148, dispatch no. 455, 1 November 1948, American Consulate, Stuttgart, to State, pp. 3–4.

226. OMGUS, 308-1/5, memo, unsigned report, "Education and Religious Affairs," 4 August 1945, pp. 1–2.

227. Ibid., p. 2; OMGBS, "Four Year Report, 1945–1949, Education," p. 102; hereafter cited as "Four Year Report"; copy in author's possession.

228. Ibid., pp. 3–4. See also Ziemke, *The U.S. Army in the Occupation of Germany*, pp. 297–305, for the delays in placing American occupation personnel in Berlin in the summer of 1945; and John J. Maginnis, *Military Government Journal: Normandy to Berlin* (Amherst, Mass., 1971), pp. 258–59ff., which gives a vivid idea of the general conditions and of the difficulties involved in setting up the Kommandatura machinery.

229. POLAD, box 805, memo, J. C. Thompson to E&CR, OMGUS, 12 July 1948, p. 1.

230. Ibid., pp. 2–3.

231. See chapter 6.

232. POLAD, box 805, Thompson memo of 12 July 1948, p. 3; OMGBS, "Four Year Report," p. 102.

233. POLAD, box 805, Thompson memo, p. 3.

234. Intelligence Summary prepared by Information Control Division, OMGUS, and identified as Information Control Intelligence Summary (ICIS) no. 61, 28 September 1946, p. 5, found in 862.42/9-2846; hereafter cited as ICIS Report.

235. Ibid., p. 6; OMGUS, 430-3/3, E&RA, OMGUS, Annual Report, p. 13. Though it is anonymous, this report was almost certainly prepared under the direction of R. T. Alexander.

236. ICIS Report; OMGUS, 302-2/5, minutes, Branch Chiefs meeting, Stuttgart, 2–3 October 1947, pp. 15–21. This meeting was marked by the rare appearance of a Soviet representative, Mr. I. Artuchin, who described Soviet control of education in detail. Artuchin stressed that the education reforms accomplished

in the Soviet Zone were German-inspired: "We do not disseminate the system of Soviet education in our policy," he told Alexander and the other chiefs.

237. OMGUS, 16-1/4, minutes of AKEC meeting, 24 June 1946, p. 2.

238. OMGUS, 16-1/4, minutes of AKEC meeting, 1 July 1946, p. 1.

239. POLAD, box 805, Thompson memo, p. 3.

240. Cited in OMGUS, 16-1/4, draft letter to Nestriepke, proposed by Colonel Sudakov, n.d. [early 1947].

241. Ibid., p. 4; OMGBS, "Four Year Report," p. 101.

242. POLAD, box 805, Thompson memo, p. 4.

243. OMGUS, 16-1/4, minutes of AKEC meeting, 15 December 1947, p. 13.

244. Ibid., pp. 13–14; OMGUS, 308-2/5, box 91, report, "School Reform—Kommandatura," by John R. Sala, 10 January 1948, p. 1; hereafter cited as Sala Report.

245. 862.42/1-1448, telegram, Murphy to Secretary of State, 14 January 1948, with reference to Spellman telegram to POLAD.

246. Sala Report, p. 4.

247. OMGUS, 16-1/4, minutes of AKEC meeting, 21 December 1947, pp. 14–15.

248. OMGUS, 17-2/8, minutes, meeting of E&RA Branch Chiefs, Wiesbaden, 5–6 November 1947, p. 4.

249. OMGUS, 16-1/4, minutes of AKEC meeting, 21 December 1947, p. 16.

250. POLAD, box 805, Thompson memo, p. 5.

251. 862.42/7-148, dispatch no. 1016, POLAD to State, 1 July 1948, "School Law for Greater Berlin," par. 25; hereafter cited as Berlin School Law.

252. OMGUS, 16-1/4, minutes, AKEC meeting, 28 May 1948, pp. 6–7.

253. OMGUS, 56-3/5, box 295, minutes, curriculum meeting, Munich, 21 May 1948, p. 2, statement by Dr. Harry Wyman.

254. Berlin School Law, par. 3.

255. POLAD, box 805, Thompson memo, p. 4.

256. OMGUS, 17-2/8, minutes, meeting of E&RA Branch Chiefs, Wiesbaden, 5–6 November 1947, p. 4.

257. OMGBS, "Four Year Report," p. 102; POLAD, box 805, Thompson memo, p. 4.

258. OMGUS, 10-3/4, memo, John R. Sala to Deputy Commandant, OMGBS, 23 March 1948.

259. OMGUS, 16-1/4, minutes of AKEC meeting, 31 October 1946, p. 2.

260. OMGUS, 16-1/4, minutes of AKEC meeting, 20 October 1947.

261. OMGUS, 302-3/5, minutes, meeting of E&CR Division Directors, Berlin, 3–4 March 1948, p. 13; 10-3/4, memo, John R. Sala to Deputy Commandant, OMGBS, 20 April 1948.

262. POLAD, box 805, Thompson memo, p. 5.

263. OMGUS, 16-1/4, Sala Report, p. 2.

264. OMGUS, 16-1/4, memo, E&CR Branch to Deputy Director, OMGBS, "Violation of AKB Agreements," 13 September 1948.

265. OMGBS, "Four Year Report," p. 105.

266. U.S. Department of State, *Germany, 1947–1949: The Story in Documents* (Washington, D.C., 1950), p. 49.

Chapter Six. From Reeducation to Reorientation

1. U.S. National Archives, Record Group 59, U.S. Department of State, Decimal File 862.42 (Reeducation of Germany), file 862.42/2-1845, draft statement by Archibald MacLeish, "German Education under Military Government," 18 February 1945. All documents in the State Department's Reeducation-of-Germany decimal files are hereafter cited as 862.42.

2. 862.42/5-1445, Draft Statement of Long-Range Policy on German Re-education, 14 May 1945.

3. 862.42/8-945, memo, Julius Lips, chairman, Council for a Democratic Germany, to James W. Riddleberger at the State Department, 9 August 1945.

4. 862.42/4-546, memo, Eugene Anderson to Hans Speier, Henry Leverich, John Hilldring, 5 April 1946.

5. Ibid.

6. 862.42/4-946, memo, Anderson to Leverich and Speier, 9 April 1946.

7. Ibid.

8. State Department, *Occupation of Germany: Policy and Progress, 1945–1946* (Washington, D.C., 1947), p. 220.

9. U.S. National Archives, Record Group 260, Office of Military Government (U.S.) for Germany (OMGUS), Adjutant General's General Correspondence Files (A. G. Files), 1945–1946, box 82, SWNCC Directive 269/8, 24 October 1946. All Military Government documents are hereafter cited as OMGUS, with file classification.

10. 862.42/11-1346, memo on his trip to Germany, Eugene Anderson to Henry Leverich et al. at the ADO, 1 November 1946.

11. Ibid.

12. Ibid.

13. 862.42/11-1346, cited in second memo, Anderson to Leverich, 13 November 1946.

14. Ibid., p. 2.

15. OMGUS, 18-1/8, memo, Vaughn R. DeLong to John Taylor, 14 September 1946.

16. OMGUS, 306-2/5, telecon, Taylor to Edward F. D'Arms, 9 November 1946.

17. OMGUS, 308-1/5, minutes of meeting of E&RA, OMGUS, with Reorientation Branch, CAD, 16 January 1947.

18. Ibid.

19. Jean Edward Smith, ed., *The Papers of General Lucius D. Clay: Germany, 1945–1949* (Bloomington, Ind., 1974), vol. 1, p. 309, Clay to Daniel Noce, 31 January 1947; hereafter cited as Clay Papers.

20. OMGUS, 49-3/10, memo, Walter G. Bergman to Chief, E&RA, OMGUS, 16 June 1947.

21. Ibid.

22. OMGUS, 49-3/10, memo, Walter Hepner to Walter Bergman, 12 May 1947.

23. OMGUS, 17-1/8, Wann to Fred, 12 May 1947; 15-1/8, copy of letter, Stein to Phillips, n.d. [October, 1948]; Richard G. Banks, "The Development of Education in Württemberg-Baden under U.S. Military Government" (M.A. thesis, University of Virginia, 1949), pp. 162–66.

24. OMGUS, 49-3/10, memo, Bergman to E&RA, OMGUS, 16 June 1947.

25. Henry J. Kellermann, *Cultural Relations as an Instrument of U.S. Foreign Policy: The Educational Exchange Program between the United States and Germany, 1945–1954* (Washington, D.C., 1978), p. 44.

26. U.S. National Archives, Record Group 165, Civil Affairs Division (CAD), War Department, file WDSCA 350 (Education), letter, Marvin Pittman to General Daniel Noce, 16 June 1947. All CAD education documents are hereafter cited as WDSCA 350.

27. OMGUS, 303-2/5, education report from E&CR, OMGWB, July, 1949; 301-2/5, memo, Milton Muelder to James E. King, 20 June 1949, plus answering memo, J. F. Golay to Muelder, 22 June 1949.

28. OMGUS, 49-3/10, memo, Louis Miniclier to Clarence Bolds, Deputy Land Director, OMGB, 31 March 1948.

29. OMGUS, 295-2/5, comment on Mission Report, L. D. Clay to O. P. Echols, 20 September 1946.

30. Clay Papers, vol. 1, p. 309, 31 January 1947.

31. Kellermann, *Cultural Relations as an Instrument of U.S. Foreign Policy*, p. 63.

32. Ibid.

33. OMGUS, 308-1/5, minutes, meeting of E&RA, OMGUS, with Reorientation Branch, CAD, 16 January 1947.

34. OMGUS, 308-1/5, report, Robert McRae to Clay, January 1947.

35. WDSCA 350, letter, Edgar Fisher, Institute of International Education (IIE), to Secretary of War Patterson, 10 June 1947.

36. OMGUS, 303-3/5, letter, R. T. Alexander to Student Volunteer Movement, 27 March 1947.

37. WDSCA 350, letter, Donald Watt, Experiment in International Living, to Daniel Noce, 3 February 1947.

38. OMGUS, 303-3/5, letter, R. T. Alexander to Edward D'Arms, 24 March 1947; OMGUS, 303-3/5, letter, R. T. Alexander to Henry H. Hill, president of Peabody Teachers College, 19 April 1947.

39. WDSCA 350, letter, Edgar Fisher to Secretary of War Patterson, 10 June 1947.

40. WDSCA 350, letter, General G. E. Eberle to Edgar Fisher, 30 June 1947.

41. Laurence Duggan, "Are We Serious about German Reeducation?" *News Bulletin* [of the IIE] 22 (May, 1947):3–4.

42. OMGUS, 141-3/13, Historical Report, E&RA, OMGB, p. 169.

43. OMGUS, A.G. Files, 1945–1946, box 28, letter, Clay to Roger Williamson, 11 May 1946.

44. OMGUS, 303-3/5, letter, R. T. Alexander to Philip M. Hayden, 22 April 1947.

45. WDSCA 350, letter, President Robert Hutchins to Robert McRae, 23 June 1947.

46. Ibid.

47. WDSCA 350, letter, Colonel R. H. Chard to Robert Hutchins, 9 July 1947.

48. OMGUS, 303-3/5, memo, R. H. Chard, to R. T. Alexander, 10 July 1947.

49. U.S. National Archives, Record Group 84, Office of the United States Political Adviser (POLAD) for Germany, File 842 (Education), box 817, memo, minutes, Thomas B. Stauffer to Robert Murphy, 16 July 1947. All documents in the Political Adviser's 842 (Education) files are hereafter cited as POLAD.

50. Ibid.

51. Ibid.

52. POLAD, box 817, memo, J. A. Calhoun to D. R. Heath, 21 July 1947.

53. WDSCA 350, letter, Ray J. Laux to Robert Hutchins, 6 August 1947.

54. POLAD, box 817, dispatch, "Exchange Program between the United States and Germany under SWNCC Directive 269/8," Murphy to Secretary of State Marshall, 20 August 1948.

55. POLAD, box 817, memo, J. A. Calhoun to D. R. Heath, 21 July 1947.

56. Interview with Martin Mayes, 29 August 1979; also see Edward A. Morrow, "Bavarians Ignore U.S. Policy," *New York Times*, November 28, p. 5. Until Alexander's revelations to Morrow, the public was unaware that Hundhammer's dismissal was being considered.

57. OMGUS, 49-1/10, E&CR minutes, 3–4 March 1948, p. 4.

58. OMGUS, 15-2/8, address, Dean Russell to trustees of Columbia Teachers College, 1 June 1948, pp. 5–6.

59. 862.42/9-2645, copy of letter, Norman Manes to Herman Baruch, 31 July 1945, with attached reply from Anderson to American Mission, Lisbon, 14 March 1946; 862.42/2-1947, dispatch, Wilkinson to State, 19 February 1947; OMGUS, 306-2/5, telecon, Taylor to Geyer, 13 May 1946; OMGUS, 308-2/5, E&RA minutes, 8 October 1947.

60. Clara Meng, "Slow Progress," *Commonweal* 47 (9 May 1947): 95; interview with Henry Kellermann, 2 September 1980.

61. *New York Times*, 3 October 1947, p. 11; *New York Times*, 5 December 1947, p. 8; *Newsweek*, 3 November 1947, p. 84; OMGUS, 308-2/5, E&RA minutes, 13 November 1947.

62. OMGUS, 49-3/10, memo, E. Y. Hartshorne to Minister President Geiler of Greater Hesse, 24 May 1946.

63. OMGUS, 303-3/5, proceedings of rectors' conference, Heidelberg, 25–27 November 1946.

64. OMGUS, 307-1/5, memo, Fritz Karsen to R. T. Alexander, 30 January 1947.

65. OMGUS, 308-2/5, memo, Nils J. Van Steenberg to Fritz Karsen, 2 May 1947.

66. OMGUS, 308-2/5, letter, Karsen to Van Steenberg, 14 May 1947.

67. OMGUS, 49-2/10, letter, Karl Lowenstein to Walter Bergman, 26 May 1947, with attached action sheet from J. Glenn Gray to Clifton C. Winn.

68. OMGUS, 49-1/10, topical report, Bergman, E&RA, OMGB, to Chief, E&RA, OMGUS, 11 June 1947.

69. Archives of the Westdeutschen Rektorenkonferenz (WRK) in Bad Godesberg, minutes of the Sonderausschuss der Hochschultagung, Schönberg, 20 May 1948, p. 10. Materials from the files of the Westdeutschen Rektorenkonferenz are hereafter cited as WRK.

70. WRK, Secretary Freytag of the Nordwestdeutschen Hochschultag to Rektor Raiser, Göttingen University, 9 June 1948.

71. 862.42/12-1348, dispatch, James Wilkinson, American consul in Stuttgart, to State, 13 December 1948, with attached intelligence report.

72. Ibid.

73. OMGUS, 301-3/5, "Memorial of the Social Position of the Students at Erlangen University," by students of the *Studentenwerk*, n.d.

74. OMGUS, 87-3/10, agent's report, "Nationalistic Propaganda in the University of Würzburg," 31 May 1949.

75. OMGUS, 49-3/10, report by John W. Draper, visiting lecturer at Munich University, 1 August 1949.

76. OMGUS, 301-3/5, Summary Report, Pax Romana, n.d. [January, 1947].

77. OMGUS, 307-1/5, report, "Data on the Situation of Students . . . in Hesse," July 1947.

78. OMGUS, 141-3/13, Quarterly Historical Report, October–December 1947, for E&RA, OMGB, p. 166; 70-1/10, memo, Erich Isenstead to Director of Intelligence Division, OMGB, "Student Demonstrations in Bavaria," 18 June 1948.

79. OMGUS, 141-3/13, Quarterly Historical Report, October–December 1947, p. 165.

80. H. L. Donovan, "Observations on German Universities in the American Zone," *Peabody Journal of Education* 26 (September 1948):70–75.

81. U.S. Department of State, *Germany 1947–1949: The Story in Documents* (Washington, D.C., 1950), pp. 34, 40–41.

82. U.S. National Archives, Record Group 51, Files of the Bureau of the Budget, Sub-Record Group 5, Files of the Bureau's International Activities Branch, Decimal File 39.18, box 28, memo, Leonard Hoelscher to General Clay, 10 May 1947. All Bureau of the Budget files concerning the task force in Germany are hereafter cited as BoB, with file classification.

83. Letter, James L. Sundquist to Leonard W. Hoelscher, 19 May 1947; copy in author's possession.

84. BoB, Decimal File 39.18, box 28, confidential memo, Donald C. Stone to James L. Sundquist, 10 June 1947.

85. Interview with Henry Kellermann, 4 September 1980; letters, James L. Sundquist to James F. Tent, 15 October and 2 November 1981.

86. Interview with James L. Sundquist, 11 December 1981; letters, James L. Sundquist to Donald C. Stone, 25 August 1947, and James L. Sundquist to Leonard W. Hoelscher, 5 September 1947; copies in author's possession.

87. POLAD, box 737, memo, F. J. Mann to D. R. Heath, 19 October 1945; John J. Maginnis, *Military Government Journal: Normandy to Berlin* (Amherst,

Mass., 1971), p. 315; OMGUS, 11-2/4, memo, "Kaiser Wilhelm Gesellschaft," Samuel Brown to Paul Shafer, 4 August 1947.

88. OMGUS, 301-2/5, speech by John W. Taylor to German ministers of education in Munich, 19 February 1947.

89. OMGUS, 301-2/5, petition to Military Government for an "UNRRA University," including a letter from Ihor Suchowerskyj, student-government chairman, 28 April 1947; directive from Clay to IA&C, OMGB, for C. C. Winn, ordering that German universities accept DPs as students.

90. OMGUS, 55-3/6, letter, Harold Crabill to R. T. Alexander, 22 December 1947.

91. OMGUS, 266-3/5, report on Berlin University, n.d. [18 or 19 April 1948].

92. OMGUS, 16-1/4, minutes of Education Committee of Allied Kommandatura (AKEC), 20 August 1945.

93. OMGUS, 16-1/4, AKEC Minutes, 6 September 1945.

94. POLAD, box 758, memo, John J. Muccio to Robert Murphy, 14 February 1946.

95. OMGUS, 16-1/4, AKEC Minutes, 6 January 1947, pp. 8–10.

96. OMGUS, 10-3/4, memo, Louis Glaser, Civil Affairs Branch, OMGBS, to Chief, E&RA, OMGUS, 19 January 1948.

97. 862.4212/5-445, airgram, W. M. Chase, chargé d'affaires, to State, 4 May 1948.

98. 862.4212/5-1348, report, Richard Sterling, Political Adviser's Office, to State, 13 May 1948.

99. Letter from Herman B. Wells to James F. Tent, 28 December 1977; in author's possession.

100. Ibid.

101. OMGUS, A.G. Files, 1948, box 128, memo, Wells to Clay, 28 April 1948.

102. Ibid.

103. OMGUS, A.G. Files, 1948, box 128, memo, command directive by General George Hays, with signature of A.G.'s Colonel G. H. Garde, to all divisions of OMGUS establishing a special Committee on the Establishment of a German University in the U.S. Sector of Berlin, 4 May 1948.

104. OMGUS, 301-2/5, memo, "Preparing for a German University in Berlin," Karsen to Alexander, 6 May 1948.

105. 301-2/5, memo, "New University in Berlin," Karsen to Alexander, 11 May 1948.

106. 862.4212/5-1348, R. W. Sterling to State, 13 May 1948.

107. OMGUS, A.G. Files, 1948, box 128, memo, Kendall Foss to Military Governor, 21 May 1948.

108. OMGUS, A.G. Files, 1948, box 128, R. T. Alexander and Sterling W. Brown to Clay, 29 May 1948; hereafter cited as May 29 Report.

109. OMGUS, 301-2/5, memo, Karsen to Alexander, 26 May 1948.

110. OMGUS, 303-3/5, letter, R. T. Alexander to William F. Russell, 10 June 1947.

111. May 29 Report.

112. OMGUS, 301-2/5, memo, Karsen to Alexander, 7 May 1948.

113. OMGUS, 11-2/4, background report, J. C. Thompson, E&CR Branch, OMGBS, to Tripartite Kommandatura, 6 August 1948.

114. May 29 Report.

115. OMGUS, A.G. Files, 1948, box 128, memo, Carl J. Friedrich to Clay, 19 June 1948.

116. OMGUS, A.G. Files, 1948, box 128, cited in memo, Foss to Clay, 21 May 1948.

117. OMGUS, A.G. Files, 1948, box 128, memo, Kendall Foss to Clay, 21 June 1948.

118. OMGUS, A.G. Files, 1948, box 128, memo, Kendall Foss to Clay, 4 November 1948.

119. OMGUS, A.G. Files, 1948, box 128, letter, Clay to Ernst Reuter, 30 August 1948.

120. OMGUS, 10-2/4, anonymous letter in German from two students to Howard W. Johnston, 6 August 1948.

121. OMGUS, A.G. Files, box 128, memo, Foss to Clay, 4 November 1948.

122. Ibid.

123. 862.4212/11-2048, dispatch, Robert Murphy to State, 20 November 1948.

124. Ibid.

125. OMGUS, 10-2/4, memo, Johnston to Henry Dunlap, OMGUS librarian, 8 September 1948.

126. OMGUS, 10-2/4, memo, Johnston to Intelligence Office, OMGBS, 25 October 1948; Donald A. Gaiduk to Johnston, 17 November 1948.

127. OMGUS, A.G. Files, box 128, memo, Foss to Clay, 4 November 1948.

128. Letter, Foss to Wells, 23 October 1948; copy in author's possession.

129. OMGUS, 303-3/5, letter, R. T. Alexander to William F. Russell, 10 June 1948.

130. 862.42/7-945, memo, "Director of German Re-education Program," MacLeish to Thomson, 9 July 1945.

131. Telegram, Clay to Noce at CAD for Secretary of War Patterson, 7 August 1947, cited in Clay Papers, vol. 1, p. 394 (see n. 19, above).

132. Telegram, Clay to Noce, 11 September 1947, including contents of letters to be sent to Judge Wildermuth and Governor Gates; cited in Clay Papers, vol. 1, pp. 424–25.

133. Kellermann, pp. 31–32 (see n. 25, above); WDSCA 350, memo, Stone to Sundquist, 15 November 1947.

134. Letter, Wells to Tent, 12 December 1977; in author's possession.

135. Ibid.

136. Ibid. See also Kellermann, p. 31.

137. Letter, Wells to Tent, 12 December 1977, in author's possession.

138. OMGUS, 308-2/5, E&RA minutes, 27 August 1947.

139. OMGUS, 304-1/5, letter, R. T. Alexander to Levi D. Gresh, 31 December 1947.

140. OMGUS, 308-2/5, E&RA minutes, 26 January 1948; see also Kellermann, p.63.

141. OMGUS, 49-1/10, memo, Charles Winning, E&CR, OMGB, to Director, Intelligence Division for Report Control Branch, 17 August 1948.

142. Kellermann, pp. 66–67.

143. OMGUS, 301-3/5, memo, Colonel Leon Irvin, Reorientation Branch, CAD, to Eric Clarke, 24 February 1949. Hallstein had been a prisoner of war in the United States and had worked with T. V. Smith and others in the so-called "idea factory" at Fort Kearney, Rhode Island, for developing seminars for discussions on democracy among German POWs.

144. 862.4212/3-849, airgram, James Riddleberger to Henry Kellermann, 9 March 1949; see also 862.4212/11-749, letter, Franz Neumann to Henry Kellermann, 7 November 1949, indicating support from Columbia University for the Free University.

145. OMGUS, 303-2/5, letter, Alonzo Grace to John O. Riedl, 30 June 1950.

146. Interview with Henry Kellermann, 6 September 1980.

147. Interview with Professor Harold Hurwitz, 23 August 1978.

148. Kellermann, p. 35. See also Lucius Clay, *Decision in Germany* (New York, 1950), p. 303.

149. Alonzo Grace, *Basic Elements of Education Reconstruction in Germany* (Frankfurt a.M.: E&CR Division, OMGUS, 1948).

150. Ibid.

151. Ibid.

152. Alonzo G. Grace, "Islands of Democratic Ferment in Germany," *American Scholar* 18 (Fall 1949):350.

153. 862.42/5-249, cited in letter, Herman Wells and George Zook to Secretary of State Acheson, 29 April 1949.

154. Ibid.

155. Interview with Henry Kellermann, 6 September 1980.

156. 862.42/4-2949, letter, Wells and Zook to Acheson, 29 April 1949.

157. 862.42/5-249, letter, Herman Wells to Robert Murphy, 2 May 1949.

158. 862.42/5-1049, letter, Colonel G. P. Lynch to Henry Kellermann, 10 May 1949, with attached memo, "Education Programs in Germany under the Occupation Statute."

159. Harold Zink, *The United States in Germany, 1945–1955* (Princeton, 1957), pp. 195, 207. Zink was a veteran of Military Government and chief historian for HICOG. His account depicts Grace as an "empire builder," a view shared by Charles Winning, as I learned when I interviewed Winning on 1 August 1978. On the other hand, Martin Mayes felt that Grace was a skilled administrator who succeeded in maintaining interest in and support for educational programs in the last year of Military Government (interview with Mayes, 29 August 1979). See also Kellermann, pp. 76–80, for his account of the maneuvering at the State Department to retain a control function.

160. 862.42/6-1549, letter, Henry Kellermann to Colonel Henry C. Byroade, 15 June 1949.

161. Bureau of Educational and Cultural Affairs, U.S. Department of State History Files (CU/H), memo, Hays to E&CR directors, 23 March 1949; interview

with Henry Kellermann, 4 September 1980; Lucius Clay, *Decision in Germany* (New York, 1950), p. 303.
162. Kellermann, pp. 80–83.
163. 862.42/1-1545, draft, "Pre- and Post-Surrender Policy . . . ," 19 July 1944, attached to memo, Howe to MacLeish, 15 January 1945.

Conclusion

1. Manfred Heinemann, Ed., *Umerziehung und Wiederaufbau: Die Bildungspolitik der Besatzungsmächte in Deutschland und Österreich* (Stuttgart, 1981).
2. Cited in Henry Kellermann, *Cultural Relations as an Instrument of U.S. Foreign Policy: The Educational Exchange Program between the United States and Germany, 1945–1954* (Washington, D.C., 1978), p. 51.
3. Interview with Geoffrey C. Bird, 18 September 1979.
4. Interview with Dr. Edwin S. Costrell, 6 June 1978.
5. Edwin S. Costrell, "Reforming the German People: German Reeducation and the American Occupation, 1945–1949" (Ph.D. diss., Clark University, 1949), pp. 291–93. See also OMGUS, 56-2/6, box 292, memo, Harold Crabill to Thomas Dunn, 12 May 1948.

Index

357